THE SEVERAL LIVES OF
JOSEPH
CONRAD

John Stape, Research Fellow at St Mary's University College, Strawberry Hill, London, has taught in universities in Canada, France, and the Far East. He has edited *Notes on Life and Letters* and *A Personal Record* for The Cambridge Edition of Joseph Conrad and has co-edited Volumes 7 and 9 of *The Collected Letters of Joseph Conrad*. The editor of *The Cambridge Companion to Joseph Conrad*, he is Contributing Editor of *The Conradian: The Journal of the Joseph Conrad Society* (UK). He has also written on E. M. Forster, Virginia Woolf, Thomas Hardy, William Golding, and Angus Wilson.

THE SEVERAL LIVES OF
JOSEPH CONRAD

JOHN STAPE

arrow books

First published in Great Britain in 2007 by William Heinemann

Arrow Books
Random House, 20 Vauxhall Bridge Road,
London SW1V 2SA

www.rbooks.co.uk

Addresses for companies within The Random House Group Limited can be found
at: www.randomhouse.co.uk/offices.htm

The Random House Group Limited Reg. No. 954009

A CIP catalogue record for this book
is available from the British Library

ISBN 9780099478676

The Random House Group Limited supports The Forest Stewardship
Council (FSC), the leading international forest certification organisation. All our
titles that are printed on Greenpeace approved FSC certified paper carry the
FSC logo. Our paper procurement policy can be found at:
www.rbooks.co.uk/environment

Typeset by SX Composing DTP, Rayleigh, Essex
Printed and bound in Great Britain by
CPI Bookmarque, Croydon, CR0 4TD

For Raymond,
in memory

It is when we try to grapple with another man's intimate need that we perceive how incomprehensible, wavering, and misty are the beings that share with us the sight of the stars and the warmth of the sun. It is as if loneliness were a hard and absolute condition of existence; the envelope of flesh and blood on which our eyes are fixed melts before the outstretched hand and there remains only the capricious, unconsolable, and elusive spirit that no eye can follow, no hand can grasp.

Lord Jim
(1899–1900)

Contents

Preface

A biography by necessity includes elements of fiction. The proportion of fact to it is partly a matter of what documents have happened to survive, the temper of the time (both the subject's time and the writer's), and the biographer's life-experience and temperament. Fictions abounded about Józef Teodor Konrad Korzeniowski, the man who became 'Joseph Conrad', during his lifetime, and only in the 1950s, as Jocelyn Baines laboured over the first scholarly biography of the writer, did the systematic sifting of fact from fancy properly begin. Conrad applied his formidable fictional talents to aspects of his own life in his published reminiscences, *The Mirror of the Sea* (1906) and *A Personal Record* (1908–09; 1912), as well as in his letters, and he told a few howlers to friends. A degree of scepticism about these is axiomatic, and any biographer attempting to recount the facts of Conrad's life faces a task that involves much filtering and weighing. Yet we desire, it seems, a certain element of romance to cling to the life of an artist who has enriched and deepened our own perspectives, shaped our attitudes, and, famously, in Conrad's case, taught us 'how to see', the ambitious aim he set himself in his artistic manifesto, the Preface to *The Nigger of the 'Narcissus'* (1897). And Conrad did have an extraordinary life, with considerable elements of 'romance' and the 'exotic', variously recreated when he sat down to his desk, arguably a highly adventurous act in its own way.

Those who knew Conrad have, at times, been no more reliable about him than he was himself. His wife and two sons produced recollections of varying interest and accuracy. His sometime friend and collaborator Ford Madox Ford, in writing about him, comes at times close to contributing to the list of his own fiction. Richard Curle and Jean Aubry, friends to the writer in his later years, were keen to protect and to maintain a shrine they had worshipped at. And the fallibility of memory, the passage of time, and what might be called the 'Chinese whispers' factor have encouraged outright fictions to parade as fact. Recalling a man whom she knew when she was a little girl, Muriel Dobree wrote to a friend, 'His father came of a very old, highly connected Polish family and Joseph Conrad was really a Polish Count, altho' he never took the title. Both his father and mother died in Siberia and he himself was outlawed and was brought up by an aunt in France, – a princess.' (Conrad, of a gentry background, was not a 'count'; his father died in Cracow and his mother in the Ukraine; he was never 'outlawed'; and although he indeed lived in France as an adolescent, he had no blood relations there, and certainly knew no princesses.) A reviewer of A Personal Record believed that Conrad studied at Cracow University, was offered a career in the Austrian Navy, and had run off to Turkey to fight in the Russo-Turkish War of 1877–78. (All untrue.) And Richard Curle could barefacedly assert that 'as a boy he had been ceremoniously introduced to the Emperor Francis Joseph in private audience at the Hofburg in Vienna'. (One would think that emperors, even drowsy ones, to recall Yeats's famous phrase, have much more to do with their time than to receive schoolboys happening to pass through their capitals.)

Debunking myths can be a pleasant occupation, but it is only part of the biographer's task. Not creating any oneself is the least that decency owes to its subject, which, our self-conscious age tells us, is always, partly appropriated. Still, to think up 'mistresses' for Conrad when none existed, as has notably been done with Jane Anderson or has been suggested in the case of Miss Hallowes, Conrad's secretary, is to play by a different set of rules. Attempting to restrict oneself to the record is harder, and perhaps less fashionable.

Many facts about Conrad's life have yielded to painstaking scholarly enquiry, and even the finest of scholars of biographical inclination have made slips or fudged emphases. Baines's 1960 biography is the foundation upon which all later biographers have built, and to which they have added, as letters and documents have come to light and as once closed archives have opened. Zdzisław Najder's Joseph Conrad: A Chronicle (1983), the labour of two decades of archival delving, benefited from the patient work, generously shared, of the pre-eminent enquirer into the facts of Conrad's life, the late Dutch scholar Hans van Marle. Najder added, magisterially, to the record of Conrad's life. The late Frederick R. Karl's 1,000-page *Joseph Conrad: The Three Lives* (1979) emphasises Conrad's career and assays a Freudian reading, following tracks opened by Bernard C. Meyers, a practising psychiatrist whose *Joseph Conrad: A Psychoanalytical Biography* appeared in 1967.

Anyone who writes about Conrad's life can only be aware of an immense debt to the labours of others, stretching over scholarly and critical generations. And anyone bold enough to do so must confront absences of various kinds. Very little is known about the crucial decade 1880–90, for instance. And one can regret that several of the people Conrad knew, although still alive when serious scholarly interest in his work began in the 1940s, were never contacted. Miss Hallowes lived until 1950. Eric Pinker, his literary agent from 1922 to 1924, lived until 1973, and Pinker's sister Œnone until 1979. But it oftimes proves easier to track down the dead than the living. As a fourth-generation Conrad biographer (*post* Aubry and Curle, Baines, Karl and Najder), I have done much tracking of that sort, but by chance was able to spend a hot June afternoon in 2006 with Mrs Nina Hayward, then eighty-nine, a niece of Jessie Conrad, who lived with her in the 1920s, and who, as she charmingly wrote to me, is 'the last woman alive to have been kissed by Joseph Conrad' (a bedtime peck at Oswalds, the Conrads' home from 1919 to 1924, where her mother and she occasionally visited).

Unlike my predecessors, I have been fortunate in having the whole of Conrad's correspondence available to me; the several archives that have opened since the 1980s (not least of which figure the Censuses of England and Wales from 1841 to 1901); and access to the World Wide Web, not even in existence when the third-generation biographers were collecting material for their lives of Conrad. That there remained new facts to be ferreted out and more original work to be done than I first anticipated have been only two of several surprises and pleasures.

Brevity has been an aim here, particularly as biographies of late have tended to bloat, stuffed with undigested facts or marred by distorting 'angles'. Those interested in literary criticism have a huge body of work to turn to. John Batchelor's *The Life of Joseph Conrad* (1994) usefully updates Baines as a critical biography, not an angle pursued here. The present book is thus deliberately constrained, addressing not the work *and* the life, but, rather, as its title suggests, the *lives*, in the hope of offering a portrait of a man who was so unremittingly private. A review of Conrad's *Some Reminiscences* (1912) was rightly titled: 'An Elusive Personality', and one of his acquaintances refers to him as 'Conrad the elusive, Conrad the recluse'. And so he remains despite the varied evidence about his life that has come to light since 1924, when he died. And it might be appropriate to recall that Conrad became 'a bit short' with callers who addressed him 'As an author' or 'Being an author', replying 'Yes, I am an author but I am also a human being. Pray don't forget that!' Not forgetting that has been a conscious intention in the pages that follow. The speculative urge has, I hope, been decently reined in, and laying one's cards on the table, even if they are not always the hand one might have wished for, a deliberate policy.

Conrad spoke of himself as having three lives – as Pole, as seaman, and as writer – but that is to neglect unduly other, more intimate, sides of him, other 'lives', as husband, father, and friend, roles that undoubtedly enriched and variously influenced his fiction. This biography attempts to offer perspectives on these lives to the extent that documents and the witness of observers allow them to be glimpsed. And Conrad's self-definition as a *homo duplex* has also been extended to *homo multiplex*, which better suits his life-experience and, early in the twenty-first century, is perhaps truer to our understanding of him.

Writing a book of this kind is, of necessity, a collaborative effort, involving the patient, sometimes highly determined, labours of scholars, friends, and scholar-friends, known personally and not. Numerous debts, specific and general, have been incurred, and thanking everyone to whom any measure of thanks is due would run to far too many pages. Limiting myself to a baker's dozen of names, as I had originally hoped, has proved impossible, and beginning, in chronological order, I am grateful to the late Bruce Harkness, Andrzej

Busza, and the late Hans van Marle, genial influences present at the opening of my own Conradian life. The Conrad scholarly community is an extraordinarily generous one, and it is a genial task to thank, in particular, Dr Keith Carabine, Dr Laurence Davies, Owen Knowles, Dr Gene M. Moore, Professor Zdzisław Najder, and Dr Allan H. Simmons, who have, without stint, made available specialist knowledge and offered inspiration, advice, and hospitality.

I am especially grateful to my agent, David Miller of Rogers, Coleridge, & White, Ltd, for wise counsel, practical advice, and numerous courtesies beyond the call of duty; his scholarly work on Conrad has fuelled and stimulated mine. I am likewise hugely indebted to Ravi Mirchandani, latterly of William Heinemann, not only for commissioning this book but also for his helpful advice and painstaking editorial input; to Susan Sandon as well as Jason Arthur and Alban Miles for shepherding it to publication; and to Sonny Mehta and Dan Frank of Alfred A. Knopf in the United States, to Maya Mavjee and Tim Rostron of Doubleday, Canada, to Nikolaus Hansen and Tim Jung of Marebuch verlag in Hamburg, to Andreu Jaume of Editorial Lumen in Barcelona, and to Emile Brugman and Denise Larsen of Uitgeverij Atlas, Amsterdam.

The Joseph Conrad Society (UK) and the Tokyo-Kyoto Conrad Group have liberally and sometimes unknowingly encouraged the work that appears here. The former has also generously funded, through the Juliet and Mac McLauchlan Bequest, some of my genealogical research, particularly that on Jessie Conrad's family. Special thanks are also due to the Conrad Center, the Institute for Bibliography and Editing of Kent State University, and its director, Professor S. W. Reid.

For assistance with specific queries and general help, I am grateful to Anne Arnold-Fontaine, London; Mrs P. M. Barnes, Howick, South Africa; Sister Mary Bernard, St Bernard's Convent, Slough; Professor Joseph V. O'Brien, John Jay College of Criminal Justice, New York; Dr Stephen Donovan, Uppsala Universitet; Linda Briscoe Meyers, Photography Department, Harry Ransom Research Center, University of Texas at Austin; Mrs Nompumalelo Mfazi, Cemetery Clerk, East London City Council, South Africa; Dr John G. Peters, University of North Texas; Mme Véronique Pauly, Université de

Versailles; Dr Steven Rothman, Philadelphia; Dr James Sexton, Camosun College, Victoria; Yasuko Shidara, Tokyo; and Graham K. C. Smith, Honorary Secretary to the Association of Old Worcesters.

Captain Alston Kennerley generously shared his forthcoming work on Conrad's periods of residence at the London Sailors' Home and his previously unknown stay at the Dreadnought Sailors' Hospital, and Dr Susan Jones likewise shared with me her forthcoming work on the painter Alice S. Kinkead. Dr Richard Niland, Oxford, helpfully obtained copies of Borys Conrad's and Robin Douglas's records for their time in the HMS *Worcester* at the Marine Society, London. I am indebted to Molly O'Hagan Hardy, of the Harry Ransom Humanities Research Center, for inviting me to discuss Conrad's life with the Modernism Interest Group, an occasion that provided me with the title of this book; to Andrzej Busza, who usefully commented upon the pronunciation of Polish names and words in the Guide to Pronunciation; and to Dr Katherine Baxter, who thoughtfully allowed me to read her unpublished essay on Conrad's literary London. R. A. Gekoski, Bookseller, and Peter Grogan most graciously facilitated access to unpublished letters held in a private collection.

Mrs Nina Hayward and Mrs Gill Woods have kindly shared with me their memories and knowledge of Jessie Conrad's family, extending courtesy and hospitality to a stranger interested in their family's history. Professor Robert Hampson provided logistical support and genial company on an excursion to seek out tombstones in the Surrey village of Shere to pin down dates for the Nash Sex family tree. I am grateful to Professor Ulrich Menzefricke of the Rotman School of Management, University of Toronto, for helping sort out for me the money equivalences between Conrad's day and ours, and to Donald J. Shewan for drawing the maps. I am also grateful to friends who have encouraged and supported me throughout the course of my work, in particular Karen Erickson, Dr Gail Fraser, Robert J. Grant, Nourdine Majdoubi, and Dr Gregory A. O'Neill.

I owe thanks to the curators and librarians of the Berg Collection, the New York Public Library, Astor, Lenox, and Tilden Foundations; the George Arents Library for Special Collections at Syracuse University; the Firestone Library, Princeton University; the Huguenot Library, London (librarian Ms Z. E. Hughes); the Hugh Walpole

Papers, Keswick Museum and Art Gallery; the Lilly Library, Indiana University; and the Beinecke Rare Book and Manuscript Library, Yale University; the Shere Museum (curator Ms Elizabeth Rich). I am also indebted to the Bibliothèque Nationale de France, Paris; the British Library and British Newspaper Library, London; the John P. Robarts Library, the University of Toronto; and the Walter C. Koerner Library, the University of British Columbia Library, Vancouver. I have also drawn upon the resources of the Family Record Centre and Guildhall Library, London, and the National Maritime Museum, Greenwich.

I owe particular thanks to the Harry Ransom Humanities Research Center at the University of Texas at Austin, for an Andrew W. Mellon Fellowship in its 2005–06 award year, and to the Lilly Library, Indiana University, for an Everett Helm Visiting Fellowship taken up in 2007.

List of illustrations

Ford Madox Ford (1915), photograph by E. O. Hoppe. © Bettmann/ Corbis.

Edward Garnett in the Friends' Ambulance Unit, 1917. Mortimer Rare Book Room, Smith College Library, Northhampton, Massachusetts.

Borys Conrad (1922). Photography Department, Harry Ransom Humanities Research Center, University of Texas at Austin.

John and Borys Conrad during the Great War. Courtesy of Mrs Nina Hayward.

John Conrad as a boy. Photography Department, Harry Ransom Humanities Research Center, University of Texas at Austin.

John Conrad with his sons Richard and Peter with their dog, Nero. Courtesy of Mrs Nina Hayward.

Joseph Conrad, Jane Anderson, Jessie and Joseph Conrad. Reproduced from Zdisław Najder, *Joseph Conrad: A Chronicle* (1983).

Jessie, Joseph and John Conrad at Capel House (September 1913)

Jessie Conrad (mid-1920s). Photography Department, Harry Ransom Humanities Research Center, University of Texas at Austin.

Lilian M. Hallowes, Conrad's secretary, in the New Forest, 1930s? Collection: Charlotte and Peter Hallowes. Courtesy of David Miller.

Conrad in Corsica with J. B. Pinker (left) and an unknown person, February 1921. Beinecke Manuscript and Rare Book Library, Yale University (Image ID No. 1009410).

Conrad seated in a deckchair aboard the *Tuscania*, arriving in New York, 1 May 1923. © Bettmann/Corbis.

Conrad's funeral cortège, Canterbury Cemetery, 8 August 1924. Berg Collection, New York Public Library, Astor, Lenox, and Tilden Foundations. (Left to right: undertaker, John and Borys Conrad, their uncles Albert and Walter George, R. B. Cunninghame Graham, Jean Aubry, Richard Curle, Count Edward Raczynski, the Polish Ambassador's representative.)

Conrad at Oswalds, June or July 1924. The Joseph Conrad Society (UK).

List of maps

A note about place-names

The map of the world, particularly that of Eastern Europe, has been reconfigured several times since Conrad's birth in 1857, and national boundaries and the names of cities and towns have changed, sometimes more than once. For the sake of clarity, the following principles govern the use of place-names in the text:

(1) English or Anglicised forms are used for well-known locales; hence, for instance, Cracow rather than Kraków and, obviously, Singapore rather than Singapura.

(2) Official names of the relevant period are used; thus, Lemberg rather than L'viv (Ukrainian) or Lvóv (Polish) to refer to the city in the Austro-Hungarian Empire of Conrad's lifetime now in Ukraine (in his time 'the Ukraine').

(3) Present-day place-names are not provided when the name in question has been thought likely to be familiar to the reader; thus, Marienbad, Constantinople, and Bombay are not glossed as Mariánské Lázně, Istanbul, and Mumbai. Similarly, alternative names have not been provided where the reader should encounter no difficulties (for example, the Samarang of Conrad's time, now Semarang).

A note about money

Conrad's income, debts, and expenditure are detailed from his letters and other contemporary sources. During his lifetime, there was little inflation. Since his death in 1924, however, two factors must be taken into account in order to understand the changing relative value of money: considerable inflation and an overall increase in wealth in the United Kingdom.

Anyone interested in pound sterling equivalents in terms of today's values needs to make calculations for each year of Conrad's life in England (1878 to 1924). For each of these years, the equivalent figure in 2005 terms, the most recent year available, can be obtained by consulting the Economic History Services website (www.eh.net), which is supported by the Economic History Association and affiliated organisations. (The calculator itself is hosted at www.measuringworth.com). This website gives annual values for the following five economic indicators: (1) the retail price index, (2) GDP deflator, (3) average earnings, (4) per capita GDP, and (5) GDP. The first two indicators can be used to adjust for inflation; the second two can be used to account for the increase in wealth.

Consider, for instance, the equivalent value in 2005 of 1 pound sterling in 1910. In terms of price inflation alone, using the retail price index, £1 in 1910 was worth approximately £68 in 2005; using the GDP deflator £1 was worth about £89. This establishes a roughly seventy-five-fold decrease in the value of money due to inflation. But even adjusting for inflation, average income increased dramatically over the period 1910–2005. It is thus also useful to adjust the relative value of £1 for this increase in wealth. Using average earnings, £1 in 1910 was worth £360.50 in 2005; using per capita GDP, £1 was worth

£426.97. This establishes an approximate 400-fold increase in relative value. For example, then, the £2,700 that Conrad owed to his agent, J. B. Pinker, in 1910 may be placed into perspective in terms of the 2005 value of the pound as follows: in terms of price inflation alone the equivalent figure would be about seventy-five times as much – approximately £240,000. Expressing this debt in relation to average income yields a figure 400 times higher, or approximately £973,000.

The 2005 figures quoted in this work, in round brackets following figures given by Conrad or by other sources, use the average earnings index as the most effective indicator of relative value. Sums have been rounded off.

Important earnings, debts, and other figures are usually given a 2005 equivalent. To do so in every case where a figure is cited might unduly interrupt the flow of the narrative. The information provided here should allow a rough computation of current value; accessing the website mentioned above will permit an exact one.

'Pole-Catholic and Gentleman'
(1857–1878)

'Balzac got married in Berdichev. I must write that in my notebook.
Balzac got married in Berdichev.' In Chekhov's *Three Sisters*,
Chebutykin, memorably described by Randall Jarrell as that 'one-
character Theatre of the Absurd', happens upon this fact while
reading a newspaper. Some hundred miles south-west of Kiev in the
western Ukraine, Berdichev was a strikingly unexpected and
unfashionable venue for the wedding ceremony, in 1850, of the father
of the French realist novel. It was arguably an even more unlikely
place for the birth on Thursday, 3 December 1857, of a great English
novelist: Józef Teodor Konrad Korzeniowski, coat of arms Nałęcz,
later to become 'Joseph Conrad'. As he himself acknowledged when
preparing his reminiscences for publication, the town was an
impossible starting point: 'Could I begin with the sacramental words,
"I was born on such a date in such a place?" The remoteness of the
locality would have robbed the statement of all interest.'

In the mid-nineteenth century, Berdichev's population was around
50,000. Passing through it in 1847, on his way to the estate at
Wierzchownia of his beloved Countess Hanska (whom he married
three years later), Balzac observed, with a novelist's eye, that its
houses, tiny and 'as clean as pigsties', were 'all dancing the polka'. His
impressions may have been coloured by an unfortunate incident while
he was there: a small crowd of a couple of dozen Jews had gathered to
inspect his gold watch-chain, and he beat them off with his walking-
stick.

Polish from the sixteenth century, Berdichev fell to Russia, along with other substantial pickings from the Polish Commonwealth, in the Third Partition of Poland in 1795. It enjoyed an ethnic and linguistic diversity of a kind usual in Eastern Europe's trading centres. A mainly Jewish community (around 80 per cent), the town boasted a strong Hassidic tradition, its cantors famed throughout the Ukraine by the mid-nineteenth century. The rest of the population was made up of the *szlachta*, the Polish gentry class,* which was Roman Catholic and Polish-speaking, and 'Ruthenians', as Ukrainians were then known, who were largely Orthodox, Russian-speaking, and mainly peasants. These communities, each largely self-enclosed, rubbed elbows for trade and services, but they spoke their own languages, maintained independent cultural identities, and followed different, and sometimes antagonistic, religious traditions.

By the time of Conrad's birth, some sixty years after Russia had hived off this territory, ethnic Poles formed a minority in the region. Like many a minority, they clung jealously to their past, to their language and traditions, and some, like Conrad's father, dreamt that, despite its actual ethnic composition, the territory would again some day make up part of a reconstituted and independent Poland. Conrad's parents on both sides were ethnic Poles (not Ruthenians), whose ancestors had lived in the region for two centuries. To clarify matters of considerable complexity: although Conrad is almost always referred to as 'Polish', at the time this was an ethno-linguistic and cultural, not a political, identity. Although he did live for part of his childhood and youth on the territory of the present-day nation-state of Poland, he was born and spent most of his early years and some of his adolescence in what today is Ukraine and was, until 1919, part of the Russian Empire. Until he adopted British nationality and petitioned for release from Russian nationality, he was a subject of the Tsar and had lived in the Austro-Hungarian and in the Russian

---

* Conrad's self-characterisation as 'a Polish nobleman, cased in British tar' is, in British terms, somewhat misleading. The *szlachta*, a relatively numerous class, comprising as much as 10 per cent of the population of pre-Partition Poland, was roughly equivalent to having the title 'esquire' in England or *don* in Spain, and did not necessarily imply holding land. No distinctions were made between the gentry and nobility, and the class saw itself as egalitarian. By Conrad's time, it embraced both the quite well-to-do and the relatively indigent.

Empires, but not in 'Poland', which at the time, having no political existence, was absent from the map of Europe.

Conrad's birth in a predominantly Jewish town was to give rise to a rumour that he himself was Jewish, one he vigorously denied but with no hint of racial prejudice: 'Had I been an Israelite I would never have denied being a member of a race occupying such a unique place in the religious history of mankind.' The town, in any event, played only a small role in his life, since his parents left it when he was an infant; on the other hand, it explains a sense of marginality that is often given expression in his writings and formed part of his psychology. A degree of mystery long persisted about the precise location of his birth, partly owing to his own misleading statements. His baptismal certificate indicates not his birthplace but the location of his baptism, or rather two baptisms, the first in a private ceremony performed in Zhitomir, a nearby town, by a priest of the Carmelite order belonging to Berdichev's monastery, and the second in Berdichev's parish church. The two baptisms suggest that there were fears for his life. When completing his British naturalisation papers, Conrad gave Zhitomir as his birthplace, and biographers later variously proposed Ivankivci and Terechowa, respectively south-east and south of Berdichev (see Map 1).

Conrad's forebears, not distinguished, were solidly respectable – 'land' rather than 'trade' – and on his mother's side included provincial officials. Towards the end of the eighteenth century, his paternal great-grandfather, Stanisław Korzeniowski, married Helena Choińska, who bore him six children, the first some time before 1793, the last in 1809. The paternal surname means 'someone from Korzeniów or Korzeniew'. A number of places are so named, and the precise one is irrecoverable at this distance in time. The maternal side of Conrad's family has not been traced much further back. We know that his maternal great-grandfather, Stanisław Bobrowski, fathered four children between 1790 and 1796, the year he died, a year after the Third Partition of Poland and three years after Louis XVI's execution at the guillotine.

Both of these events were to have an impact upon Conrad's life, although they occurred well before it began. Poland's prolonged political agonies – by the eighteenth century, discounting Turkey as

3

only nominally European, she was the Sick Man of Europe, 'a laughing-stock to foreigners who believe in efficient government and progress' – culminated in the Partitions of 1772, 1793, and 1795. Its lands ripe for the plucking, the country was easily divided up by her territorially ambitious neighbours, Austria, Prussia, and Russia, disappearing as an independent nation-state from 1795 until 1919 when the Treaty of Versailles restored her independence.

The Partitions of Poland involved geo-political rivalries and alliances of a complexity that makes hopeless any potted summary of them; in short, their effect was to make Poland a ghostly presence in Europe, her peoples under foreign rule and varyingly subject to assimilation by the powers that had divided the nation-state. The Tsar pursued a policy of intense Russification, with the result that Russian domination was virulently opposed in the territories that she had taken. Insurrections against Russian rule occurred in 1830 and 1863 when, rising up against the Russian yoke, Poles futilely attempted to re-found the Polish nation-state although facing vastly superior and better organised forces as well as entrenched interests. The political situation was further complicated by ideological upheavals in France, which foreshadowed and then finally effected the end of totalitarian rule out of which rose Napoleon and his new vision of his nation and Europe. Conrad's writings display considerable interest in the political and social convulsions of the French Revolution and the Napoleonic period, both of which had substantially affected 'Poland' (an ideal or 'nation' in the French sense – that is an ethno-cultural grouping). Like many members of his class, he was both Francophone and Francophile from early childhood, and in writing about Poland he insisted upon her Western European character, particularly her French affinities and connections, in order to offset any association with what he contemptuously referred to 'Slavo-Tartar Byzantine barbarism' (that is, Russia).

Conrad's maternal great-uncle Mikołaj Bobrowski (1792–1864), vividly recreated in A Personal Record, was a believer in the grande illusion that Napoleon dangled before the Poles. In return for their support, they would, in due course, be rewarded, with the restoration of their country's independence. Napoleon's promise to patriot-dreamers when he was in need of canon fodder was both a cynical and a successful ploy. In the Battle of Somosierra (1808) during the Peninsular War to subjugate Spain, Spanish troops defended their country by proceeding to kill or wound two-thirds of the Polish Cavalry sent against them, and in an effort to restore slavery on Haiti, Napoleon sent a contingent of Poles to fight against the rebellious slave-leader Toussaint L'Ouverture. (Those who did not die fighting or succumb to malaria – a mere 600 of the 6,000 men who took part survived – mostly married and remained on the island.) Polish commitment to the Emperor proved unwavering, and contingents of Poles not only eventually accompanied Napoleon to Elba but also gathered round him for the Hundred Days.

Very much an idealist, Mikołaj Bobrowski joined Napoleon's *Grande Armée* in 1808 at the age of sixteen. He worked his way up from sub-lieutenant to captain, his military career ending in the fateful year of 1814, the year of Bonaparte's defeat and exile to Elba. He served loyally and with courage, receiving the title *chevalier* in the Légion d'honneur, and thus automatically receiving Poland's highest military award, the Order Virtuti Militari. He saw action under the command of Marshal Marmont, duc de Raguse, and in the decisive Battle of Leipzig (1813) gained glory, being the last man over the bridge crossing the River Elster before it was destroyed.

Bobrowski, who remained blindly loyal to the Emperor of the French throughout his life, may be a source for the Napoleon enthusiast Ferraud in Conrad's short story 'The Duel'. Bobrowski's youthful idealism even survived the 1812 Retreat from Moscow during which, in the dark and cold forests, hungry and fearing for his life, he at one point ate a life-restoring meal of Lithuanian dog. The incident was immortalised by his grand-nephew a century later:

The dog barked . . . He dashed out and died. His head, I understand, was severed at one blow from his body. I understand also that, later on, within the gloomy solitudes of the snow-laden woods, when, in a sheltering hollow, a fire had been lit by the party, the condition of the quarry was discovered to be distinctly unsatisfactory. It was not thin – on the contrary, it seemed unhealthily obese; its skin showed bare patches of an unpleasant character. However, they had not killed that dog for the sake of the pelt. He was large . . . He was eaten . . . The rest is silence.

Eating mangy dog, in Conrad's treatment of the incident, becomes a metaphor for dismembered Poland's experience under foreign domination. Swallowing their humiliation and pride, and already living with a sense of defeat, Poles enthusiastically threw in their lot with Napoleon, joining him in a force some 100,000 strong. His view of their future was, however, vaguely formulated, and although he considered the Partitions 'unfair' he unhesitatingly blamed the country's aristocracy for her demise and also expected Poles ultimately to fend for themselves. He committed himself to nothing concrete, but cynically fomented Polish hopes. For their part, the Poles willingly closed their eyes to the fact that their regained freedom would be purchased at the cost of that of others.

Another Napoleonic family connection is less direct. Conrad's paternal grandfather, Teodor Korzeniowski as a young man served as a lieutenant in the army of the Grand Duchy of Warsaw, in effect a Napoleonic puppet state, participating in the indecisive Battle of Raszyn (1809) against Austria. The Duchy provided concrete evidence of the Emperor's good intentions towards the Poles, but the nationalist dream faded as the *Grande Armée* reeled and then collapsed, leaving unfinished business for later generations. Until the end of the First World War, Polish independence remained a dream, and suffering, defeat, and martyrdom were integral to Poles' national self-image. But though 'crucified' and tormented, faithful daughter of the Roman Catholic Church and martyr amongst nations to nineteenth-century nationalists, Poland would in time not only redeem herself but by doing so save all Europe.* A cult of nobility,

* Under repressive conditions, an ardent patriotism of quasi-religious character developed and became integral to early- and mid-nineteenth century Polish cultural identity. Shortly after Conrad's birth, a group of priests calling themselves the 'Catholic Clergy of the Kingdom of Poland' proclaimed Roman Catholicism the country's national religion. Identifying itself with the 'suffering' nation, the 'suffering' church became a political force, although with little support from the Vatican, which did not actively oppose Tsarist control. (In Polish territory under Russian rule the content of sermons was overseen, patriotic hymns were banned, and the Church headed by a member of the Orthodox clergy.)

fidelity, and loyalty, of decidedly nostalgic character, took hold of the Polish collective conscious. 'Polish Messianism', the idea that Poland's sufferings would redeem her, partly a product of late Romanticism, was to colour the nation's sense of herself for nearly a century. Theorised and celebrated by the great poet of Polish patriotism, Adam Mickiewicz, it was to bloom luxuriantly after the failed November 1830 Insurrection in Russian Poland.

Teodor Korzeniowski left the Polish army and sold his lands to live on his wife's estate in 1820, the same year that his son Apollo was born, but his family's well-being was to be sacrificed to the nationalist cause: for supporting the Insurrection, his property was confiscated. The loss involved him with the Bobrowskis. A land-owning couple, Józef Bobrowski and Teofila Biberstejn-Pilchowska, between 1827 and 1840 had eight children. Apollo Korzeniowski fell in love with the oldest girl, Ewa Bobrowska, born in 1832. Conrad observes that Józef Bobrowski disapproved of his parents' relationship, which began around 1847. But the love-match survived both Bobrowski's hostility and a lengthy engagement, the wedding eventually taking place at Oratów (the Bobrowski family estate) on 4 May 1856.

Bobrowski's opposition to Apollo Korzeniowski was, in part, simply economic. The Korzeniowskis' prospects were uncertain, and he seems simply to have wanted to hold out for a bigger and better (that is, better off) catch for his daughter, the dream of many a doting father. With the Korzeniowski lands now in other hands, from the age of eleven Apollo Korzeniowski's inheritance consisted mainly of a sense of life's instability, and the realisation that he would have to rely on his wits to make his way in the world. After completing secondary school in the market town of Zhitomir, Volyhnia District's provincial capital, he went to St Petersburg where he studied law, languages, and literature from 1840 to 1846 without, however, completing a degree. The latter subjects provided the basis for his brief life's work.

Bobrowski may also have objected to elements in his prospective son-in-law's personality, which, according to one observer, possessed elements of sarcasm, stubbornness, and impracticality. It has had both its contemporary and posthumous detractors and apologists. Beauty lies in the eye of the beholder, and the only hard evidence that matters is that Ewa Bobrowska was sufficiently charmed. She remained so during the long years between love more or less at first sight and her eventual trip to the altar. Surviving photographs of Korzeniowski in early middle age suggest that the beauty she discerned was of the inner kind. Extravagantly bearded, with unruly shoulder-length hair, short of stature and slight of build, he confronts the camera with almost disconcerting austerity and self-assurance. Earnestness, that quintessentially nineteenth-century virtue, is deeply engraved upon his brow. He appears as if only partly tamed and, whether seated or in mid-stride, ready to spring from the enforced pose. A later photograph in which he sports a trimmed black beard and tightly clipped moustache suggests a fundamental sternness.

The dirge he addressed to a Poland divided up among three great Powers, written to celebrate his only child's birth, reveals more about the man than any surviving photograph:

> Baby son, tell yourself
> You are without land, without love,
> without country, without people,
> while *Poland – your Mother* is in her grave.
> For your only *Mother* is dead – and yet
> She is your faith, your palm of martyrdom.
>   Hushaby, my baby son!
> Baby son, without . . .
> Without Her . . .
> Without Her . . .
> And no salvation without Her!

This combination of mawkish religious sentiment and intense, high-flown patriotism is not unfamiliar in bad verse. Korzeniowski was also drawing on the late Polish Romantic tradition: affected, exalted, and detached from terrestrial realities, its poetry, as one critic has remarked, was written with a 'peacock-quill dipped in sky'.

Whatever the histrionic elements of this effusion, there is also genuine feeling: Korzeniowski, a man typical of his time, was deeply religious and fervently patriotic, defining elements of Polishness strongly forged under several pressures (and still vital today). Dated 23

November 1857, the Old Style date of Conrad's birth, the poem titled 'To My Son, born in the 85th year of Muscovite Oppression, A Song for his Christening Day' is only nominally addressed to his child. Borrowing from traditional Polish *kolęda* (Christmas carols), this elegy on the nation reveals both the complexion and complexities of Korzeniowski's character. Even the moment of fatherhood is politicised: options are being foreclosed, boundaries drawn, and only two alternatives offered – stiffening one's backbone for the eventual fray against the foreign oppressors or decamping altogether.

Conrad chose the latter course, leaving martyrdom and the entombed 'Mother' behind. He did so in the company of the some 3 million Poles who made their way to more hospitable social and economic climes elsewhere in Europe and in North America between 1870 and the outbreak of the First World War. And it is perhaps no accident that the plot of *Almayer's Folly* (1895), his first novel, involves a daughter's rejection of her tyrannical father's dreams for her, and her making her own life in a foreign land. In *The Secret Agent* (1907), a father-figure of unstable finances, connected to clandestine revolutionary activities, is responsible for blowing his 'son' up.

Instability characterised the early years of the Korzeniowskis' married life, as Apollo Korzeniowski cast about for means to support his wife and child. The couple spent their first year together in the small town of Łuczyniec in the District of Podolia, where Korzeniowski managed an estate. On receiving his wife's dowry, he leased a small farm. And then, with Ewa Korzeniowska in the final stages of her pregnancy, they moved again, this time to Terechowa, where her widowed mother and her sister-in-law Emilia Korzeniowska both lived.

In 1859, poor harvests brought the experiment with farming to an end, and the Korzeniowskis moved again, this time to Zhitomir where Apollo Korzeniowski invested in a publishing house and worked on his writing. The move may have been motivated by his desire to become involved in clandestine political activities. His ideological commitments were already well established. In the mid-1850s, he was writing journalistic poetry of social and topical concern about the Ruthenian (Ukrainian) peasantry. (A rough English equivalent might be Tennyson's 'The Charge of the Light Brigade'.) Over subsequent years, in addition to journalism and poetry, Korzeniowski produced translations of Shakespeare's *Comedy of Errors* and Dickens's *Hard Times*, the poetry of Alfred de Vigny, all but one of Victor Hugo's plays and several of his novels. (Few of these translations were published, and the manuscripts have been lost.) The list testifies to fashionable nineteenth-century tastes, but it is interesting that Korzeniowski's translations drew from the two cultures his son was later to adopt.

Aware of Korzeniowski's involvement in the dissident cause, the suspicious Russian authorities closed down the publishing house in Zhitomir, a town where Polish-language culture – a theatre, concerts, bookshops, publishing houses, and several schools – flourished. Korzeniowski's finances again became rickety. In May 1861, he managed to extract permission from the Russian authorities to leave the Ukraine for Warsaw (passports were required for internal travel), where he became involved in literary journalism, again probably a cover for political activity. By this time the police were routinely opening his letters to his wife. Ewa and their three-year-old son remained behind, first in Zhitomir and then in Terechowa. In his pattern of frequent moves and financial instability, Korzeniowski was placing his ideological commitments above his family.

Arriving in Warsaw in early October 1861 just before the city's Russian rulers declared a state of emergency, Ewa Korzeniowska and her not quite four-year-old son had moved from a hotbed into a vigorously stoked fire. Zhitomir had witnessed waves of anti-Tsarist sentiment, culminating in a petition to the Tsar, signed by Korzeniowski (but not by his brother-in-law, Tadeusz Bobrowski), to join the Ukraine to the Congress Kingdom.* Poles owned large tracts of agricultural land and were active in industry, but constituted only about a third of the Ukraine's population. Shot through with nostalgia, Korzeniowski's politics focused on recreating a conservative utopia that had never been.

---

* Congress Poland or the Congress Kingdom of Poland referred unofficially to the puppet kingdom created out of the Duchy of Warsaw at the Congress of Vienna (1815). It effectively lost its semi-independent status altogether after the November Uprising of 1830, although its administrative organisation was sufficiently distinct for the name to remain in use until 1863 when it was wholly amalgamated with Russia.

Warsaw offered several cultural attractions, even if the Korzeniowskis had little opportunity to enjoy them. It was also the focus for virulent opposition to Russification, so vigorously promoted by Tsar Alexander II. Political tensions that had quietly smouldered since the November 1830 Uprising now broke out in force. Korzeniowski's nationalist commitment, already a major aspect of his character, now took the shape of secret meetings in his flat in Nowy Świat, a street of attractive classical-fronted buildings in the centre of Warsaw. But Russian surveillance proved ruthlessly efficient. Arrests began, and several hundred 'suspects' were rounded up. Korzeniowski's knock on the door came at half-past midnight on 20 October 1861, and he was spirited away within minutes. There were presumably tears but no recriminations, for Ewa Korzeniowska shared her husband's politics. Wistful, dignified, and sweet of face, she wore full mourning to lament the nation's sufferings and in protest against the death of five Poles in Warsaw, who, in February, had demonstrated against Russian rule and been killed by the Cossacks. She dressed her son in a mourning-frock; black necklaces, cuff-links of the Polish eagle in a crown of thorns, and jewellery featuring the palm of martyrdom were widely worn at the time as symbols of mourning for the buried nation.

Only a fortnight after being reunited with his wife and child, Korzeniowski was in the Warsaw Citadel, an 'ever-ready machine of destruction . . . an immense dungeon where tsardom buries Polish patriotism'. The legacy of the 1830 Insurrection, this forbidding and vast fortress could accommodate up to 3,000 prisoners. Conrad's first memory, he later claimed in a letter to a Polish correspondent, went back to this time: 'in the courtyard of this Citadel – characteristically for our nation – my childhood memories begin'. This was on a visit to his father whose forced and extremely sudden removal must have been traumatic. Ewa's mother hurried to Warsaw to offer support and help.

In due course, a series of nocturnal interrogations led to formal charges. With the onset of the grim and unrelenting winter, conditions in the Citadel worsened, and Korzeniowski contracted scurvy. He also suffered from rheumatism, not a condition usually experienced by men barely in their forties. According to his wife, he was allowed to work on a translation, never published, of Hugo's *Le*

Roi s'amuse (1832). If accurate, this information is somewhat startling. The play's depiction of a profligate king presumably passed by gaolers otherwise keen to sniff out any potential anti-Tsarist or anti-monarchical sentiment.*

In early May 1862, Korzeniowski's eight-month imprisonment ended in conviction and a sentence of exile to Perm, in the Urals, and to life under permanent police surveillance. He was, technically, innocent of the carelessly laid charges brought against him, having neither fomented patriotic brawls nor written an inflammatory pamphlet. Searches of his apartment turned up nothing incriminating. Ewa, his sympathetic collaborator, was sentenced in her own right for conspiring against the state.

Perm was not quite a death sentence. A distant district capital and industrial centre, it possessed the rudiments of a cultural life, although temperatures could dip to minus 45°C in midwinter. But at the request of the provincial governor, a former schoolmate of Korzeniowski's, the couple and their infant son were, in fact, sent elsewhere. They reached Vologda, about 300 miles east of Moscow, in mid-June 1862. The train journey, 'under the strictest military escort', had been difficult, with officials arbitrarily polite or hostile, but the Korzeniowskis' greatest cause of anxiety had been their son, who in Moscow came down with pneumonia. The boy was bled with leeches and dosed with calomel, a mercury-compound. Vologda, founded in the twelfth century and once a flourishing trade centre, became notorious in the nineteenth century as a place of exile for political prisoners, both Polish and Russian. The populist anarchist Petr Lavrov, author of *Historical Letters* (1870), spent 1867 to 1870 there.

The town's characteristic wooden houses, its baroque and neo-classical centre, and its abundant churches have interested architectural historians, and the young Wassily Kandinsky, on an ethnographic expedition in 1889, was so impressed by its folk art traditions that they altered his painting style. For Korzeniowski, it was a miserably cold, raw-looking swamp, home to a population of around 17,000 souls: 'Vologda is a huge quagmire stretching over three versts,

---

* In an Italy also seething with nationalist turmoil, its adaptation as an opera, *Rigoletto*, was in effect self-censored, Verdi and his librettist cannily demoting the King to a mere duke.

cut up with parallel and intersecting lines of wooden foot-bridges, all rotten and shaky under one's feet . . . A year here has two seasons: white winter and green winter. The white winter lasts nine and a half months, the green winter two and a half.' His views of the inhabitants were no less caustic: 'Take an hour-glass where scrofula runs instead of sand; throw something coloured over it; set it on two abominable tortoises wrapped in filthy rags and let it waddle along; fasten to each wrist a badly baked brick to which five carrots are attached – and there you have a Vologda woman with arms and legs. Horrible things.'

He and his wife joined the community of exiled Poles, remaining aloof from local contacts. A publisher later recalled that Korzeniowski 'held himself very proudly; he met almost no one from the local society', and Tadeusz Bobrowski noted that his brother-in-law added to his sufferings by neglecting the demands of the northern climate and stubbornly insisting upon wearing 'Polish clothing, which was imprudent and undermined his weak health'. A photograph of the time portrays a man deeply withdrawn, darkly morose, and obviously suffering severe depression. His ardent patriotism and comradeship with fellow exiles offered no defence against the arctic conditions that by October had fully returned: 'We are bitterly cold here. For the last couple of days we had plenty of snow. Firewood is as expensive as in Warsaw.'

In the new year of 1863, their situation improved slightly, official-dom allowing them to relocate to Chernighiv, a regional centre 80 miles north-east of Kiev. Its milder climate and both the change and their return to a relatively familiar environment must initially have boosted their morale. Their relief proved cruelly short-lived, however, as larger political events once again impacted upon their lives. On 22 January, an insurrection broke out in Russian Poland. The news that trickled as far as the Ukraine was discouraging and then bad. Korzeniowski felt crushed and humiliated.

Woefully ill prepared, the Uprising had failed spectacularly. The outnumbered Polish forces harried their antagonists for more than a year, but harsh reprisals predictably followed. Lands were confiscated (again), Russification became more severe, insurrectionists were sent into exile, and thousands of Poles fled to Western Europe, including Chopin and Mickiewicz, in the 'Great Emigration'. The Congress

Kingdom was abolished. As the weeks went by, the Korzeniowskis' situation increasingly mirrored the national one. Apollo Korzeniowski's brother Hilary was arrested. In mid-April, Ewa Korzeniowska's youngest brother, Stefan, who though only in his twenties had been a leader of anti-Russian activities, was killed in a trumped-up duel outside Cracow. (It had, in effect, been more of an execution or an assassination, as the short-sighted patriot faced a renowned marksman, going to certain death over a point of honour.) Apollo Korzeniowski's father died a fortnight later. Ewa Korzeniowska's brother Kazimierz was imprisoned. The couple's feelings of helplessness must have mingled with a growing sense of complete collapse.

Ewa Korzeniowska's health, affected by the climate, began to cause serious concern. Notorious for under-nourishing its prisoners, the Tsarist penal system provided barely adequate shelter. And there was also the unremitting psychological pressure. In August, Ewa was granted a three-month 'leave' to seek treatment and visit relatives. She took her son to Nowochwastów, the estate of her brother Tadeusz's in-laws. The reprieve proved temporary, but on Conrad, aged almost six, it made a lasting impact. He claimed to have learned 'not only to speak French, but to read it as well' from 'good, ugly Mlle. Durand', his governess. Her tearful parting words were 'N'oublie pas ton français, mon chéri' (Don't forget your French, my darling). He never did.

The first known composition wholly in his hand, dating from this period, testifies to emerging linguistic abilities. (An earlier note was written with his mother guiding his three-and-half-year-old hand.) It is scrawled on the back of a photograph sent to his maternal grandmother, Teofila Bobrowska, who, after his parents died was to become his guardian: 'To my dear Grandmama, who helped me to send pastries to my poor papa in prison.' It is signed 'Grandson, *Polak-Katolik* [Pole-Catholic], and *szlachcic* [gentleman], Konrad'. The letters are poorly formed, but the self-description, obviously not spontaneous, harbours adult aspirations, with a guiding parental hand providing, even insisting upon, an allegiance to overlapping traditions.

Her request to extend her 'leave' unanswered, Ewa Korzeniowska returned to her husband in the late autumn. Her health continued to decline, perhaps because she lacked the psychological strength for recovery; she also seems to have been suffering from depression. Visiting Chernighiv for the New Year of 1865, somewhat more than a year after he had last seen her, her brother Tadeusz was shocked at her condition. He later recalled that after she returned from Nowochwastów she 'persisted in paying no heed to her steadily deteriorating poor health and despite her mother's insistence . . . refused to undergo treatment'.

Apollo Korzeniowski realised that psychological factors were complicating the situation: 'Despair has been slowly eating like rust into my wife's physical constitution. For a year and a half the poor girl has been blaming the state of her nerves for everything.' This no doubt contributed to her decline, but her self-diagnosis fell far short of the mark: she was wasting from 'consumption' (pulmonary tuberculosis). Either a warmer climate or an operation was needed, but she was already too weak for surgery. The authorities rejected Korzeniowski's request to move to Odessa, a city known for its balmy climate. By mid-March, the disease had entered its terminal phase, and Ewa Korzeniowska's mother and her brother Tadeusz hurried to Chernighiv. Ewa Korzeniowska died six weeks later on 18 April 1865, at the age of thirty-three.

Her husband grieved deeply and uncontrollably, and his already pronounced tendency to melancholy increased. He, too, was now tubercular, and – still financially insecure – he faced bringing up a seven-year-old boy alone. He took refuge in work, and gave his son lessons in mathematics, French, and Polish. They read Polish Romantic poetry aloud together. The grieving widower took refuge in his paternal responsibilities, clasping his son to him. The emotional intensity was claustrophobic: 'I guard him against the influence of the local atmosphere, and the little mite is growing up as though in a cloister,' he wrote to friends. The child, so recently deprived of his mother, was now also being robbed of his childhood. By the following spring even Korzeniowski must have needed a respite, and he sent Conrad to spend the summer with 'Grandmama' at Nowochwastów. His time there is undocumented, but one can easily imagine that the motherless boy and the woman mourning her daughter found comfort and relief in each other's company.

During the next year or so, Conrad himself suffered from various unspecified ailments, apparently complicated by 'nerves' and repeated relapses. In August, his grandmother, Teofila Bobrowska, returned him to his father in Chernighiv. Not long after, she accompanied the boy to Kiev for medical treatment. A brief stay with his Uncle Tadeusz, who had become fond of him, the sole reminder of his much-loved sister, was the first presage of their later relationship.

There was further treatment in Kiev and Zhitomir, and in the summer of 1867 Bobrowski appears to have taken his nephew to Odessa, probably for the boy's health. Some 300 miles south of Kiev, the cosmopolitan Black Sea port offered 'climate', the usual range of seaside holiday diversions, and a desperately needed change of atmosphere. If the visit did indeed take place – its mention comes in a somewhat unreliable account – it would have afforded Conrad his first sight of the sea. But where memory fails, it tends to invent, and in A *Personal Record* Conrad places the moment at Venice's fashionable Lido.

As anxiety over his son's health continued to oppress him, Korzeniowski's loneliness increased. At the end of the year, permission to 'travel abroad for the benefit of his health for three years' came too late. Unable to afford the trip to Madeira or Algiers, the proffered options, he went only as far as Galicia (the southern part of present-day Poland and western Ukraine, including the major cities of Cracow and Lemberg), thus enabling father and son to leave the Russian Empire for the Austro-Hungarian one and a less oppressive political situation.

The move ushered in a period of rootless wandering. In February 1868, Korzeniowski joined Conrad at Nowochwastów. They left after a few weeks, stopping for a couple of months in Lemberg (now L'viv, Ukraine), then experiencing a cultural revival and an industrial boom. Mahler, who was there for the première of his first symphony, deemed it 'a filthy place': 'one couldn't imagine anything dirtier than the Polish Jews'. Korzeniowski also disliked it intensely, resenting its envy of Cracow and its lack of 'Polishness'. Indeed, all Galicia displeased him: 'the Galicians know best everything but their own extreme stupidity . . . They have forgotten what it is to feel – they know not how to speak – they read nothing.' Korzeniowski and his son spent April and May at a friend's estate at Kruhel Wielki, a small 'polka-dancing' town on the outskirts of Przemyśl, and in mid-June, in nearby Topolnica, 'an obscure hole, very beautiful and quite deserted', Korzeniowski began a four-month cure – draughts of mountain air and sheep's whey.

He responded favourably at first, but quickly relapsed. His emotional state was precarious: never quite recovered from his wife's death, he suffered a sense of insecurity that must have been unremitting, and the steady diet of disillusionment and dashed hopes exacted its toll. Returning to Lemberg, Apollo Korzeniowski realised that he was a broken man: 'I am . . . fit for nothing, too tired even to spit on things.' To another friend, he wrote in a similar bitter vein: 'I am nearing my end; it ought to come with the least expense and trouble.' In February 1869, he made the final move in his Galician odyssey, leaving Lemberg for an equally wintry Cracow, where he was to report upon Russia and England for the newly established liberal newspaper *Kraj* (The Nation). He and his son settled into a flat in Poselska Street, No. 6, near the Market Square. His tuberculosis was far advanced, but he was making plans. He placed his son's education in other hands. Conrad took lessons, but no evidence supports his later claims to have attended the prestigious St Anne's Gymnasium. Later he was to deny any knowledge of German, the school's medium of instruction, although his use of the phrase 'six months' extra grinding at German' when he was contemplating going to Pola (now Pula, Croatia) for sea training suggests basic competence.

In middle age, Conrad painted a touching portrait of himself as his father's life drew towards its end: 'I would be permitted to tiptoe into the sick room to say good-night to the figure prone on the bed, which often could not acknowledge my presence but by a slow movement of eyes, put my lips dutifully to the nerveless hand lying on the coverlet, and tiptoe out again. Then I would go to bed, in a room at the end of a corridor, and often, not always, cry myself into a good, sound sleep.'

In early May 1869, Apollo Korzeniowski took to his bed for the last time. Before he did so, his portrait was painted and he destroyed private papers, a holocaust Conrad later described as the act of a 'vanquished man'. Last Rites were administered. He lingered until 3.30 in the afternoon of the 23rd. A death mask was made, and two days later, in the evening, his remains were taken to the nearby Church of St Peter and St Paul for the requiem mass the following day. The funeral procession was, in a sense, hijacked by politics. A crowd of several thousand – university and gymnasium students, members of the trade guilds, ordinary people – accompanied the black-draped coffin and Korzeniowski's eleven-year-old son through the narrow streets of Old Cracow as patriotic songs alternated with hymns.

Korzeniowski's tombstone in Rakowice cemetery reads: 'Apollo Nał ęcz Korzeniowski, victim of Russian oppression. Born 21 February 1820. Died 23 May 1869. To the man who loved his homeland, laboured for her, and died for her – his compatriots.' The absence of the word 'poet' or 'writer' is a surprise, for Korzeniowski's service to his homeland had been by his pen. From one point of view, he had sacrificed both his life and his family to his nationalist vision. As Stefan Buszczyński, his closest friend, put it in his memorial pamphlet: 'The suffering of his motherland was the inexhaustible source of his own suffering.' His son, on the other hand, would later write: 'A man haunted by a fixed idea is insane. He is dangerous even if that idea is an idea of justice; for may he not bring the heavens down pitilessly upon a loved head?' Despite Apollo Korzeniowski's ardent hopes, his stern idealism, and determined efforts, his son would choose another destiny, other dreams, and different compatriots. He was to set about laying ghosts that could, otherwise, have haunted him always.

The next stage of Conrad's life began with another journey, his first outside Eastern Europe. Teofila Bobrowska took her grandson for a water cure, the first of several he would undergo. A hilly region on the edge of the Black Forest, the Kingdom of Württemberg in south-west Germany is peppered with spas and enjoys a temperate climate. Whatever the area's physical benefits, the stay also marked a break from months of emotional stress. On their return to Cracow, Conrad and his grandmother settled in the heart of the city centre at Szpitalna Street, No. 9. When the school year began, and for the next couple of years, Conrad took lessons from Ludwik Georgeon, who ran a small pension for boys in Floriańska Street. Conrad boarded at the pension when his grandmother was travelling, or when she may simply have wanted relief from minding a growing boy. (She must have been at least sixty, and more likely somewhat older, having given birth to the first of her eight children in 1827.)

Few specifics are known of Conrad's education. The Classics, modern languages, geography, the sciences, and mathematics dominated the standard curriculum. At St Anne's, for instance, Latin was emphasised, the boys studying Cæsar, Livy, Sallust, and Ovid (the *Metamorphoses* and *Tristia*). A not particularly reliable account suggests that the boy was adept at story-telling and getting up little dramas. Perhaps unsurprisingly, at a period when 'the dark places of the earth' were yielding up their last secrets to scientific exploration, his interest in geography was considerable. (His great-aunt, Regina Korzeniowska, was an editor of geographical atlases.) He neglected his assigned school-work to spend hours reading about Arctic exploration and the mapping of Africa, drawing maps – and shaping his imagination. The story, recalled in both *A Personal Record* and 'Heart of Darkness', about putting his finger upon a blank spot in central Africa – 'When I grow up, I shall go *there*' – is suspiciously similar to ones told in at least two books about African exploration that Conrad read. For all its boyish ardour, the longing to go far away, to confront the unknown and carve out one's own path often represents a wish to escape past and present troubles.

In the spring of 1870, the tensions that were about to break out into the Franco-Prussian War counselled against a return to Württemberg, and Conrad was taken to Krynica, a resort closer to Cracow in the Carpathian foothills. Famed from the late eighteenth century for its mineral-rich springs, the town's pump-rooms were among the Austro-Hungarian Empire's most fashionable. Conrad's travelling companion was his tutor Adam Pulman, a twenty-four-year-old student enrolled in the widely renowned Faculty of Medicine in Cracow's Jagiellonian University. Their chosen destination, one offering bracing mountain air, opportunities for long walks, and famous waters, suggests a continuing concern over Conrad's health.

He and Pulman returned to Krynica in the spring of 1871 and 1872. Conrad's health and education were being placed on a more secure footing. In the spring of 1873, on doctor's orders, Conrad left Cracow for six weeks in Switzerland and Italy. On this occasion Pulman was charged with discouraging the boy's wish to go to sea. Conrad mythifies this holiday in *A Personal Record*, recalling his first sighting of the Swiss Alps; his encounter with an 'unforgettable Englishman', striving up a mountain, a member of the engineering team beginning work on the St Gothard Tunnel; and the Adriatic at Venice.

Every step on the tour worked to undermine Pulman's mission. Shortly after they boarded the Cracow–Vienna train prospects of discovery beckoned. Hotel life and seeing the sites offered stimulation, and by the time they stood gazing at the peaks of the Bernese Alps, Pulman's mission was doomed. He urged the youth to change his mind and to submit to the wisdom of his elders. Conrad, at fifteen, was confident that he knew what he wanted and declined to do so. Pulman hesitated, then gave in. They continued their travels to Milan and Venice, making their way back to Cracow by August, their return delayed for six weeks by an outbreak of cholera. Little is known about Pulman. He seems to have developed a genuine liking for the youth in his charge, and tried to keep up with Conrad's news for the next decade, although letters went astray. In the end, the rhythms of his own life took over: he married and settled into a medical practice in the Ukraine.

The immediate future held out more schooling, and in September Conrad left for Lemberg and a pension for boys orphaned during the 1863 Insurrection. It was run by Antoni Syroczyński, a cousin of Conrad's uncle Tadeusz. Bobrowski, though at a distance began to act *in loco parentis*, in effect jointly sharing guardianship of the boy with Teofila Bobrowska, his ageing grandmother. Conrad would not have been out of place at 'Uncle' Antoni's. Unhappy childhoods are not rare, but Dickens's experience at the boot-blacking factory arguably pales in comparison with Conrad's early years. It was time, perhaps more than time, for the boy to stretch his wings. His grandmother, his legal guardian since August 1870, was occasionally in ill health, and had decided to move to Warsaw. Syroczyński's pension would provide a new atmosphere and companions. But frustratingly little is known of Conrad's activities, emotional state, and intellectual development during this crucial period. There was a schoolboy crush on a little patriotic girl, 'an uncompromising Puritan of patriotism', but we know no more. Bobrowski's on-going efforts to obtain Austrian nationality for him proved unsuccessful. His uncle's efforts were possibly urged on by Conrad's dream of going to the Habsburg Empire's academy of seamanship at Pola on the Adriatic. While he remained a Russian subject, this could only be wishful thinking.

But why the sea at all? To the adventurous its appeal is archetypal. Conrad had read James Fenimore Cooper's sea novels and Captain Marryat, but many a boyish dream fades before coming to fruition. His tenacity testifies both to youthful rebellion and imagination, and as an orphan, the son of political exiles, he had few obvious prospects. He wished to follow neither his father's path (political protest and self-sacrifice) nor his uncle's (gentlemanly farming), and the sea, which would be a break from everything he had known, including the life of his nation, offered liberation from the past.

Conrad later told his friend Hugh Clifford that during the course of this year he ran away to Trieste to demonstrate the strength of his resolve to go to sea and that Pulman, duly delegated by Conrad's guardians, brought him home. The upshot of this episode (if, indeed, it occurred) was a promise from Bobrowski that he would seriously consider the boy's ambitions were he to do well in his exams. Conrad also seemingly claimed that as a youth he had run off to Constantinople to 'fight with the Turks, then at war with Russia, the hereditary enemy'. This story of ardent patriotism sounds like pure invention, or is a much-garbled version of Conrad's later sighting of Russian troops in Turkey at San Stefano. By contrast, the flight to Trieste, which combines youthful rebelliousness and the dream of going to Pola, seems just plausible.

Whatever occurred in the emotional tug of war between Conrad and his guardian about the lad's desire to go to sea, Bobrowski's practical and cautious nature ensured that his charge was purposefully engaged: 'not that which is easy and attractive must be the object of your studies but that which is useful, although sometimes difficult', he insisted a few months after his brother-in-law's death. Conrad either attended a gymnasium or received lessons at 'Uncle' Antoni's.

By his Easter holiday of 1874, spent with Pulman in the Carpathians, changes were afoot, and plans for Conrad's departure were made. The sea it was to be, and Bobrowski undertook arrangements, making contact with Victor-Jean-Adam Chodźko in Marseilles. Then in his mid-twenties, the Paris-born Chodźko had himself been at sea and had contacts in shipping circles. Bobrowski undertook to cover his nephew's expenses until he became self-supporting. In *A Personal Record*, Conrad recalls Poland's long-standing sympathy for French culture as playing a role in the final decision, but Bobrowski's choice of France was a practical one. In Chodźko he had a connection in Marseilles whom, he believed, he could count on to show Conrad the ropes and provide guidance, and Conrad's good French was yet another argument for France.

By late August, strings had been pulled and letters written, and Conrad and his uncle, in Cracow together, attended to last-minute practicalities and farewell rituals, which included having a photograph taken at Walery Rzewuski's studio. When the great day, 13 October 1874, finally arrived, Conrad's grandmother shed tears, and Bobrowski confessed to an avuncular tug at the heart. The sixteen-year-old boarded the train for the long journey to Marseilles, travelling alone for the first time (that is, if he hadn't run off to Trieste). The train's ultimate destination, as he later put it, was less a specific point on the map than dreamland: 'one September day in the year 1874 I got into the train (Vienna express) as a man gets into a dream – and here is the dream going on still'.

The actual journey was presumably both romantic and liberating. After the first stage via Vienna and Zurich, Conrad dutifully made a brief stop in the Swiss town of Pfaffikon to see a friend of his father's, before continuing to Lyons and Marseilles. Shortly after he arrived, Conrad was welcomed by Jean-Baptiste ('Baptistin') Solari, a friend of Chodźko who was related by marriage to César Delestang, a well-to-do shipowner, who, with his son Jean-Baptiste, ran Delestang et Fils, Négociants et armateurs (wholesalers and shipowners). With offices at 3 rue Arcole, a small street within easy walking distance of Marseilles's Vieux Port, the family firm (established around 1851) had commercial interests stretching as far as the French Antilles.

Conrad later wrote that in Marseilles 'the puppy opened his eyes'. Just how much they took in is another matter: he was dazzled. Notwithstanding his later claims to have felt at home from the outset, the city, with its handsome elm- and plantain-lined boulevards, its vibrant café life, its polyglot population, and combination of sophistication and loucheness, could not but impress him. Speaking his second language, with a career opening before him, and knowing no one offered the youth a chance to reinvent himself, he seized it with enthusiasm. Hypersensitive, self-conscious, and intelligent, he quickly kicked off any traces of provincialism that might have clung to him. We get a rare glimpse of what he may have felt in a chance retrospective comment: 'Since the age of 17 I was no longer a boy . . . A man that takes care of himself is no longer a boy.' Characteristically, there is no self-pity here, and 'taking care of oneself' at a tender age was common enough in the late nineteenth century; there is, however subtly registered, a sense of a loss, a wistfulness for things that might have been, and for once a self so carefully hidden is glimpsed between the lines.

With its setting, climate, and history, Marseilles offered a theatrical backdrop, and the port town invited some understandable late-adolescent posturing. Conrad seems quickly to have adopted adulthood as his own, though in fact he was still young and shedding provincial perspectives and habits. He lodged at 18 rue Sainte, a gently sloping street near the Vieux Port, the famed Cannebière, and the Grand-Théâtre. All three locations were settings in his life there: for employment, for lounging in cafés and enjoying a vibrant night-life, and for high culture. He frequented the opera, his later view that Meyerbeer was 'a great composer' formed by opera-going in this period (which provided allusions in his writings to *Il trovatore*, *Lucia di Lammermoor*, and *Faust*).

Two months after his arrival, and shortly after his seventeenth birthday, Conrad left for the French Antilles, as passenger by special arrangement on the *Mont-Blanc*,* an old and terribly leaky barque belonging to Delestang. Apparently after calling at a storm-tossed Majorca, she headed for the open Atlantic. She sailed through the Florida Channel, passing the Bahamas, then blighted, as he later recalled, with 'stagnation and poverty', reaching Saint-Pierre, 'The

---

* A seaman serves 'in a ship', not 'on a ship', the latter expression referring to a passenger's prerogative. This distinction, which is observed here, has Conrad's sanction: in *The Mirror of the Sea*, he castigates newspaper writers 'who *will* persist in writing about "casting" anchors and going to sea "on" a ship (ough!)'.

Little Paris of the West Indies', on Martinique in early February. She remained in harbour for six weeks.

On the sun-drenched island, with its palm trees, bougainvillaea, rum distilleries, and Jardin des Plantes, Conrad rubbed shoulders with a stunningly handsome pale-coffee-coloured people. The Greek-born American writer Lafcadio Hearn, a visitor in 1889–90, saw the port town – 'the quaintest, queerest, and the prettiest withal, among West Indian cities' – almost entirely in terms of colour: 'Most of the buildings are painted in a clear yellow tone, which contrasts delightfully with the burning blue ribbon of tropical sky above; and no street is absolutely level; nearly all of them climb hills, descend into hollows, curve, twist, describe sudden angles . . . And as you observe the bare backs, bare shoulders, bare legs and arms and feet, you will find that the colors of flesh are even more varied and surprising than the colors of fruit.'

Conrad's voyage gave him his first taste of sea life, with its routines and rituals. He acquired French nautical terms pronounced with a marked Provençal twang; got down the tricks of an ancient trade; and heard and remembered seaman's yarns. Precisely how he spent his time in this 'exotic', smallish port remains unknown. In retrospect, he accounted his land contacts 'short, few, and fleeting', his memories of his time in Caribbean comprising 'bits of strange coasts under the stars, shadows of hills in the sunshine, men's passions in the dusk, gossip half-forgotten, faces grown dim', but this is a later gloss on ten months spent in these ports, at a time 'when everything was so fresh, so surprising, so venturesome, so interesting'. The contrast with wintry Cracow, fixated on its past and preoccupied with its future could hardly be more striking.

Captain Duteil's special charge, 'Le jeune Polonais' would have had ample opportunity to look around. The humidity, the exotic food and flora, the port at the foot of an active volcano were novel experiences. 'Monsieur Georges' – the name (and mask) Conrad apparently adopted – was learning about himself as opportunities to explore things he had only imagined or read about opened up. Jack, or in this context, Jacques Tar ashore stereotypically sinks into sensual amusements – whoring, drinking, yarning, gambling – as a relief from the rigours and routines of sea life. Transplanted French culture existed in Saint-Pierre, which boasted an imposing theatre, and Conrad, 'a reading boy' in the heyday of Daudet and Hugo, Maupassant and Zola, had much to read. And as his work shows, he was always an acute observer of people and places.

The *Mont-Blanc* set sail at the end of March 1875, arriving in Marseilles in late May. Conrad remained ashore for only a month before leaving for Martinique, once again in the *Mont-Blanc* but this time as a fully fledged apprentice, not as a passenger. The ship reached Saint-Pierre on 31 July, five weeks later, and as Mont-Pelée hove into view, Conrad reached a new stage in his maritime career. The Caribbean port town was this time familiar, and like any voyager he would have felt the self-congratulatory rush of owning his experience. Again, almost nothing is known about his two months in port, and only the bare bones of the next few are documented. We have a perfervid recollection of 'a black and youthful Nausicaa' glimpsed by the banks of a stream with her attendants: 'The vivid colours of their draped raiment and the gold of their earrings invested with a barbaric and regal magnificence their figures, stepping out freely in a shower of broken sunshine.' Eroticism is evident, but Conrad records only that he prudently – his word – retreated from the 'hot, fern-clad ravine'. (The memory is worked up in the description of Kurtz's African mistress in 'Heart of Darkness'.)

In late September, the *Mont-Blanc* left for Cap Haïtien via Sankt Thomas, part of the Danish West Indies (now St Thomas in the American Virgin Islands). Having avoided a cyclone that had just passed through the region, the ship docked in Cap Haïtien for the whole of October, departing in early November. She arrived at Le Havre just before Christmas 1875 after a rough voyage in wintry seas. Conrad stayed briefly, and then after a few days in Paris, a city he never much cared for, he returned to Marseilles, virtually without baggage, having somehow lost a trunk that included family mementoes. The loss – unconsciously or not Conrad was jettisoning his past – occasioned a reproach from Bobrowski: 'Do you need a nanny – and am I cast in that role?'

Conrad's first extended stay in Marseilles, a period lasting six months, was crammed with experience: 'And in Marseilles I did begin life,' he later wrote. Details can be pieced together from Bobrowski's

meticulous account of financial outlays. The time was one of wild
oats, self-discovery, and of a thorough apprenticeship in an unsustain-
able *vie douce*. The eighteen-year-old was also gathering material,
consciously or not, for his fiction, including several fictions about his
life. The character of Monsieur George in *The Arrow of Gold*, partly
modelled upon himself or upon an imagined self, is nicknamed 'Young
Ulysses'. Conrad had not yet wandered much, but the tag reveals
aspirations, even greediness, for experience, much as a nickname can
suggest a desire to adopt a new personality, or, at least, a novel
persona.

This period also sees him establishing lifelong habits of overspending, getting into debt, and counting upon others to bail him out.
The telegraph lines between Marseilles and the Ukraine hummed as
Uncle Tadeusz, who also pointedly reminded his feckless nephew that
he lived 30 miles from the nearest railway station, raged about
inconvenience and irresponsibility but unfailingly delivered needed
advances as Conrad, on the razzle, rapidly ran through his allowance.
The Mediterranean atmosphere perhaps conspired against caution.
The opera and theatre afforded entertainment, both serious and light.
Sardou's new play *Férreol* was having a highly successful run. In
February, Carnival revels filled the town – 'disguised humanity
blowing about the streets in the great gusts of the mistral that seemed
to make them dance like dead leaves on an earth where all joy is
watched by death'. The late winter and the spring saw performances
of Offenbach's frothy *La Boulangère des écus* and *La Belle Hélène*,
Meilhac and Halévy's *La Vie parisienne*, and Johann Strauss's
Orientalist opéra-bouffe *La Reine Indigo*.

It has been suggested that Conrad had typical *szlachcic* habits – a
perceived need to entertain and a pressure to maintain appearances,
whatever his actual means – but he was also simply and almost
hopelessly feckless, and the checks on him, loose to start with,
had disappeared. Chodźko as stand-in guardian was a distant
presence, concerned with his own affairs. Solari, if upon the scene,
may, indeed, have encouraged excesses. A stake in clandestine
activities may be another reason for outrunning his income, and
during these months Conrad got to know Toulon, long France's
main naval base, and the country's southernmost tip, the craggy and

highly indented Hyères Peninsula, where smuggling had a long tradition.

His half-year in Marseilles closed with another voyage – his last to the Caribbean and his last for Delestang et Fils. The *Saint-Antoine* left in early July, arriving in Saint-Pierre in mid-August 1876. Moving up the ladder of ranks, Conrad shipped as steward this time. Among the crew was Dominique Cervoni, a Corsican born in Luri, later recalled in the gun-running scenes in *The Mirror of the Sea* and providing material not only for Tom Lingard in the 'Malay Trilogy' but also for the title-character in *Nostromo*, for Dominic in *The Arrow of Gold*, for Peyrol in *The Rover*, and Attilio in *Suspense*.

Conrad glimpsed the Colombian coast and stepped ashore on the 'dreary coast' of Venezuela at Puerto Cabello on the Golfo Triste. From a hill near the port town of La Guayra, he sighted Caracas, 20 miles away. The *Saint-Antoine* remained firmly anchored in Saint-Pierre's harbour, and any trip further west must have been on local mail-steamers and brief enough for Conrad to return in time for the voyage to Marseilles. But what of the motives for one? Possibly he was in on some arms-smuggling for the conservative Catholic faction in the Colombian civil war: if so, this was a chance to make money rather than to idle away time in port.

Five weeks after her landfall at Saint-Pierre, the *Saint-Antoine* docked for a fortnight in the free port of Charlotte Amalie on Sankt-Thomas. Conrad experienced the strong earthquake there on 19 October. According to his retrospective account, he also met the man upon whom he modelled *Victory*'s 'plain Mr Jones' in a small hotel there, his first recorded encounter with a homosexual man. It is unlikely to have unsettled him: at this stage, he had lived in Marseilles for some months, and France with her *Code Napoléon* was already much more sophisticated than is Poland even today about such matters. The homosocial camaraderie of sailor life could also shade into 'situational' homosexuality. Conrad was, moreover, jettisoning other inheritances. His *Polak-Katolik* identity weakened, his *szlachta* one was also undergoing revision. Although on record for detesting class distinctions – 'Class for me is by definition a hateful thing' – his disdain for rank did not prevent him from signing off* two English ships as 'de Korzeniowski', the nobiliary particle setting himself off from his shipmates.

The *Saint-Antoine* then docked for more than a month at Port-au-Prince on Haiti, a major rum and sugar entrepôt, leaving Mirogoâne for Marseilles two days before Christmas 1876, and arriving home in mid-February. The only established fact of this voyage, aside from landfalls and departures, is that Conrad dutifully wrote at least one letter to Tadeusz Bobrowski, to whom he felt 'more in the relation of a son than of a nephew' and who was now his closest family tie. In 1875, when Conrad was in the tropics, his grandmother had died. Little of Teofila Bobrowska's personality can be glimpsed from the scattered references to her or in her few surviving letters. Her son Tadeusz paints a conventional portrait of a deeply religious woman, determined, perhaps even opinionated, and long-suffering. (She stood at the graves of several of her children and grandchildren, and suffered from palsy in the legs, from which she fully recovered after a prolonged illness.) A photograph of her, in deep mourning, whether for the buried 'Motherland' or a relative or friend, displays the stoic and careworn face of one who has endured rather than enjoyed life. Her whereabouts are only at times known. The notebook that contains Conrad's very first stab at *Lord Jim*, which Conrad inherited from her, contains Romantic poems that she had copied out and suggests a woman of conventional culture and sensibility. By her orphaned grandson she had done her duty, picking up the pieces after her daughter and son-in-law had died.

Fictions perhaps inevitably gather round a writer's life, and in the absence of much in the way of facts for the period from February 1877 until the end of the next year or so they have swirled busily round Conrad's. Some of his tracks have been thoroughly covered; other gestures skilfully put one off the scent. *The Arrow of Gold* and *The*

---

* 'To sign off a ship' is a nautical expression meaning formally to give notice of 'leaving', that is, ceasing to be employed in a ship, at the completion of a voyage; it is followed by being 'paid off'. In English ships of Conrad's time, a Certificate of Discharge, signed by the captain and with comments on competence and conduct, would, by law, be issued to a sailor, completing the formalities of signing off. 'Signing on in a ship' was the formal engagement for a voyage at a specified rank and rate of pay, with the sailor's name added to the crew list. A ship's 'articles' laid out the company's responsibilities to its employees.

Mirror of the Sea are the main 'sources' for these myths. Three refuse to die, despite lack of evidence: that Conrad was involved in smuggling or gun-running related to Spain's Third Carlist War; that he was wounded in a duel, and that he had a tortured love affair.

The gun-running episode emerges from mist only to retreat, but perhaps contains a grain, if just that, of truth. In his swashbuckling reminiscence 'The *Tremolino*' in *The Mirror of the Sea* Conrad colourfully dramatises gun-running out of Barcelona. A French critic, who carefully compared Conrad's account to geographic and other facts, judged it, although dramatically compelling, awash in an ocean of '*irrealité*'. Dominique Cervoni, whom Conrad had worked alongside for the Delestangs, is the main 'character' in this vivid memoir. Then in his mid-forties, he served not only as a surrogate father but also as a projection of several things Conrad was not but at times wished to be. A man of action and of Mediterranean temperament, Cervoni is depicted as at ease with himself in a way that the young *szlachcic* turned mariner could only fantasise about.

Chronology, however, weighs heavily against Conrad's involvement in any gun-running for the Carlist pretender to the Spanish throne. The 'Nouvelles d'Espagne' column regularly featured in *Le Petit Marseilles* reports on skirmishes, arms-smuggling, and the movements of the twenty-seven-year-old claimant Don Carlos (the would-be Carlos VII). In the bloody civil war, which had begun in 1872, the Carlists had some success, notably in land-locked Navarre, but Don Carlos's cause was nearly spent by the time Conrad arrived in Marseilles. In February 1874, his rival, Don Alfonso de Borbón y Borbón, acceded to the Spanish throne as Alfonso XII and proceeded to consolidate his hold on power. The Carlist movement's death agonies were prolonged, but on 17 February 1876 it suffered the *coup de grâce*, when its forces were decisively defeated at Estella, their final Basque country stronghold. For much of the period between his arrival in Marseilles in October 1874 and February 1876 Conrad was aboard ship or in Caribbean ports. When he was in the South of France, he was a young foreigner and an inexperienced seaman, and thus, for shady dealings, either an ideal candidate as a non-entity or a person without credentials and to be avoided.

The casual (and tantalising) statement to a friend that he 'stood on

Irun bridge' in 1876 suggests a journey to north-western Spain's Basque country, the only possible window being the six months between his arrival in Le Havre in late December 1875 and his departure from Marseilles in late June 1876. Whether with friends or for Delestang et Fils (the firm was engaged in unspecified shady dealings), a land journey can be discounted if gun-running were at issue. But Cervoni's *balancelle*,* whether or not named the *Tremolino*, was unsuited to such a long trip through the Mediterranean to the Bay of Biscay. Perhaps – a large 'perhaps' – the possible gun-running in Colombia (*if* that occurred) was being reworked to give a tinge of adventure to a period that involved considerable routine work. In the end, unless new documents turn up (highly unlikely given that meticulous archival sleuthing has been done) this is all that can be said.

Of the other two stories told of this time, the duel was a colourful invention by Conrad to paper over a suicide attempt, and the love affair, mainly cobbled out of *The Arrow of Gold* (in its way a pot-boilerish version of *Carmen*, Conrad's favourite opera), is a romantic fantasy. One candidate proposed as the object of Conrad's ardent attentions, Paulina Horvath, a Hungarian who spoke little German, was Don Carlos's mistress. Research has demolished her claims, weak anyway given her linguistic skills and Conrad's (if indeed he had any German), but the myth of a love affair, refusing to die, has more recently been resurrected in the claim that Conrad had a tragic affair with Victor Chodźko's married sister and precipitated her suicide, a speculation, however, lacking any basis in hard evidence as is the claim that she took her own life. So much for the myths.

By July 1877 Conrad had temporarily alienated Delestang and needed a job. A ready tongue seems to have caused the breach, but as in all such stories the truth is unrecoverable. A proposed voyage to India was the immediate issue. Delestang may have behaved imperiously towards his prickly young employee, or may have endured a provocation (or several) that finally proved too much for his Gallic pride. An insult appears to have been hurled, possibly, '*épicier*'

---

* A small Mediterranean boat with a single sail, pointed and raised prow and poop, and either under sail or propelled by oars.

(grocer) or '*marchand*' (shopkeeper). Whatever the exact details, over the following months Conrad was increasingly lacking in self-control and emotionally adrift. From the Ukraine, Bobrowski fretted over whether his nephew was learning English, advancing in his studies, and dutifully avoiding the pursuit of castles in Spain.

Matters came to a head in February and early March 1878 in Monte Carlo, where Conrad gambled away his half-yearly allowance from Bobrowski as well as a recent cash gift from a relative. He returned to Marseilles out of pocket, without prospects, and depressed. Telegrams – despite Bobrowski's warnings – had to go off to the Ukraine: CONRAD BLESSÉ ENVOYEZ ARGENT – ARRIVEZ [CONRAD WOUNDED SEND MONEY – COME]. The dramatic message, swiftly followed by news that its subject was slightly better, caused his uncle to board a train for Marseilles on 8 March. Arriving from Kiev three days later, he found his nephew already out of bed. The wound, he discovered, had been self-inflicted. Conrad had been living beyond his means (and needs), had quarrelled with his employer, and had probably already drawn in any outstanding IOUs held by friends. Unable to erase the past, Bobrowski, ever a man of practical bent, turned to investigating what had just happened and resolving immediate problems.

His investigation revealed Conrad in a '*situation irrégulière*' with regard to employment. Lacking the permit from the Russian consul to make his voyages that was required of all the Tsar's subjects liable to military service, he had flagrantly breached French Merchant Service regulations on the employment of foreign nationals. Broadcasting this fact had prevented another planned voyage to the French Antilles – and had removed his source of income. Bobrowski mentions that while he was in Marseilles to order his nephew's affairs, Conrad had twice been sent for to help bring a ship into port, as does Lord Jim in the novel after being stripped of his certificate. Bobrowski optimistically interpreted this as evidence that his nephew had progressed in his calling enough to find work.

Casual (and probably ill-paid) employment presumably forced Conrad to make economies – on café-going, the opera, the theatre – to survive. He invested in a contraband scheme off the Spanish coast got up by Captain Duteil with whom he had shipped in the *Mont-*

Blanc. The scheme collapsed, or Conrad was swindled; further out of pocket, he was for once reluctant to turn to his indulgent uncle. How wildly he began to struggle is suggested by his plan of travelling to Villefranche to join an American naval vessel docked there. Arthur Rimbaud, penniless in Bremen in 1877, had addressed a similar desperate plea to the American consul: 'Would like to know on which conditions he could conclude an immediate engagement in the American navy.' Conrad borrowed money from Richard Fecht, a German lodging as he did at 18 rue Saintes, and lost the lot at Monte Carlo.

The crackle of 'Monsieur Georges'' burning bridges – with Delestang, the French port authorities, and, presumably, at least some of his acquaintances – was audible as far as the Ukraine. The attempt to kill himself appears an act of self-assertion and a plea for someone to manage his life. Bobrowski's plans for settling his nephew in a profession had foundered, but the older man again picked up the pieces, inducing both himself and his nephew to look towards the future. Conrad's 'irregular' status proved beyond 'regularising', and during an unpleasant and tense fortnight, certainly for Bobrowski, a new plan was concocted. The British Merchant Marine, the world's largest, was also the most cosmopolitan. Always needing sailors, it asked few questions and demanded fewer formalities than the infamously bureaucratic French. Even for him to consider such a move, Conrad's English must have been at least rudimentary, whether learned in formal lessons or otherwise. He is likely to have picked up some English on Sankt Thomas, where the language served as the European population's lingua franca, Danish having made little headway on the very distant possession, where, by the time Conrad landed, there was already talk of selling the island to the United States.

As a surrogate father, Bobrowski had again served his nephew well, even nobly. The contrast with Conrad's introspective and gloomy father, brooding over the past and caught up with his unrealisable political dreams, is strong. However much Bobrowski might by some be seen as a political appeaser of narrowly practical talents (his brother-in-law had thrown in his lot for the cause of independence while Bobrowski was a realist), his equable approach to life's problems helped his deeply troubled nephew. His generosity involved not only money, but also his emotions, and it extended to viewing his feckless charge as 'not a bad boy, only one who is extremely sensitive, conceited, reserved, and in addition excitable'. Unfailingly loyal, Bobrowski, despite many sharply worded complaints, was unstintingly kind. His nephew, who later characterised him as a 'most distinguished man' of 'powerful intelligence and great force of character', paid him an even higher compliment: 'I attribute to his devotion, care, and influence, whatever good qualities I may possess.'

Conrad would only see Bobrowski a handful of times during the remainder of his uncle's life, but the letters from remote, often snowbound Kazimierówka, by turns chiding, affectionate, and chatty, followed him – to the Orient, to India, the Congo. The motto Bobrowski adopted for himself, *Usque ad finem* ('Until the very last'), implying devotion to duty, proved more than an empty boast. As for his nephew, his second fresh start got under way on 24 April 1878, when, as an unofficial apprentice in the British steamer *Mavis*, Conrad left Marseilles's Vieux Port for Constantinople. The dream Conrad had fought for while gazing at the Alps had, in its fashion, come true, and the voyages of 'Young Ulysses' began in earnest.

'Tell me the Sea': Apprentice, Mate, and Master (1878–1890)

Anciens exilés chers
Dîtes-moi la mer.
Rimbaud, 'L'Esprit', 'Comédie de la soif' (1872)

After leaving Marseilles, the *Mavis* called briefly at Valletta's magnificent Grand Harbour, the entrance to Malta, en route for Constantinople. From there she was to pass through the Bosporus to the Black Sea port of Kerch and then sail further into Russian waters, to Yeysk on the Sea of Azov. Conrad's liability for Russian military service suggests that he may have remained in Constantinople as the ship ventured deep into Russian territory. The authorities would have rapidly determined that he did not 'belong to' the ship, being merely a premium apprentice (a man who paid for his training). If he did remain behind, rejoining the *Mavis* three weeks later on her homeward voyage, he would have experienced a riotously cosmopolitan and polyglot city, famed, among other things, for its bazaars, its hammams, and its whirling dervishes, the centre of an old empire tottering on the verge of collapse. This time would also have afforded Conrad's his first exposure to Islamic culture and mores.

The French writer Théophile Gautier, who visited Constantinople in the 1850s, viewed it as almost unreal, an operatic set bathed in Orientalist fantasy:

No line more magnificently chequered undulates between sky and water: the soil rises out of the sea, and the buildings present an amphitheatre, the mosques overtaking that ocean of greenery and multi-coloured houses, softening their bluish cupolas and shooting up white minarets surrounded by balconies, ending in a sharp point in the clear morning sky and giving the city an Oriental and fairy-like shape to which the silvery sheen bathing its misty shapes powerfully contributes.

Conrad's first service in a British vessel and in a steamer came at a time of subsiding international tension, with the Russo-Turkish War recently concluded with the Treaty of San Stefano of 3 March 1878, just two months before his arrival in Constantinople. His later memory 'as we went up the Bosphorus we saw the tents of the Russian army at San Stephano', whatever its misspelling and geographical confusion,* vividly captures the historic moment of the war's end, as Russian troops, idly waiting for the order to return home, were combating not only insalubrious conditions but also rain and the threat of typhoid fever.

In early June, Conrad caught his first glimpse of the land he would adopt as his own, seeing the white cliffs of the Kent coast. The Downs, he later recalled, were 'thick with the memories of my sea life'. On 8 June, the *Mavis* passed Dungeness, and lay in the Strait of Dover off the Cinque Port of Hythe, 'the historic anchorage where as a very young seaman I lay at anchor for the first time'. She then steered north to Lowestoft, arriving at England's most easterly town two days later, and the apprentice seaman set foot on British soil for the first time (assuming that he did not step ashore at Malta, a Crown Colony since the Treaty of Vienna).

Some now characteristic bridge-burning marked his arrival. He had quarrelled with his employer and had to forfeit some of the premium he had paid to sail under the *Mavis*'s Captain Samuel Pipe. He had not yet made a permanent decision about a career, and shortly after arriving in Suffolk, set out for London, where he overspent, once

---

* San Stefano, in Conrad's time a town of elegant summer houses about 15 miles west of the capital (it is now Yeşilköy, the site of Istanbul's Attaturk airport), is not on the Bosporus but faces the Sea of Marmara.

again appealing to his indulgent uncle for help. Bobrowski delivered, although his tone had noticeably stiffened; calculating the sums spent over the past few years, he railed: 'up till now what has it produced – nothing!!!' His postscript, though not hysterical, lacks nothing in force: 'Write what you are going to do.' Striking chords he knew that his uncle enjoyed hearing, Conrad regaled him with plans; joining the French navy was one such, although discipline, working to direction, and kowtowing to his superiors had not hitherto figured among his strong suits.

In the short term, his affairs got on a firmer footing as he signed on in a family-run schooner, *Skimmer of the Sea*, making three return voyages from Lowestoft to Newcastle. During them he learned seamanship and improved his English from 'East Coast chaps each built as though to last for ever, and coloured like a Christmas card'. Of his shore connections we know only of a friendship with the son of a French tailor, a link with the language and culture he had recently left behind, and good relations with the *Skimmer*'s master, Captain William Cook, waggishly nicknamed 'The Great Circumnavigator'. (He had reputedly never been out of sight of land, commanding a collier that made unvarying rounds between Lowestoft and Cardiff. He is a probable model for Captain Hagberd in the story 'To-morrow'.) Conrad received coaching in navigation and seamanship, and had opportunities to improve his linguistic skills, the port boasting a public library on the Marina as well as a free library and reading room at the Sailors' and Fishermen's Home in Commercial Road. The Home, which also offered temporary accommodation, was possibly the first place at which Conrad lodged in England; later, he apparently took lodgings with the French tailor and his family.

With nothing in hand, Conrad signed off the *Skimmer* in late September. Why he did so is unknown, whether from disenchantment with the work or a sense that service in a provincial ship was only a stopgap. Perhaps he longed for the proverbial bright lights. After Marseilles, Lowestoft was provincial and sleepy. In retrospect, he claimed two motivations for his commitment to a life at sea: 'though mainly prompted by curiosity (as well as by a genuine liking for the profession), I was conscientious, passing all the necessary examinations, winning the respect of people (in my modest milieu) who, certainly not out of sheer affection, attested to my being a "good sailor and a trustworthy ship's officer."' Conrad made the three-hour train journey to London, confident of landing a job in the world's most important port. As he emerged from Liverpool Street station, he felt like 'a traveller penetrating into a vast and unexplored wilderness', poignantly recalling that 'No explorer could have been more lonely.'

Whatever the brighter prospects for him in the British Merchant Service – foreign nationals comprised about 15 per cent of crews and were particularly numerous in deep-water ships – it may still have been fortunate that Monte Carlo was far away. Having spotted an advertisement in a newspaper, Conrad had written to James Sutherland, a shipping-agent located near the Tower of London, about obtaining employment as an able-bodied seaman. Shipping regulations prevented direct recruitment, and Sutherland was in the very different business of providing ships with premium apprentices. The rules were bent slightly (perhaps some money passed hands), and Conrad walked out of the office, situated in a 'Dickensian nook of London, that wonder-city', with his first proper berth. Able hands were needed for the work of Empire; he could lay claim to British work experience; and his spoken English, polished in the *Skimmer* and in Lowestoft, must have been at least adequate.

Conrad's time in the *Duke of Sutherland* marks a turning-point. The voyage to Sydney, round the Cape of Good Hope and then across the Indian Ocean and the Pacific, was his longest and most challenging to date, lasting from mid-October 1878 to late January 1879. Conrad crossed the Equator for the first time, an event marked by age-old initiation ceremonies – traditionally raucous – sending up the dangers of the deep as 'pollywogs' become 'shellbacks' under the amused eye of King Neptune and his 'wife'. One recollection of crossing-the-line ceremonies in the *Duke of Sutherland* involved a stunsail-rigged 'bath' (usually filled with unspeakable stuff) for the pollywogs, followed by a rough shave by the ship's barber, and then grog.

Shipboard conditions were new to him. Conrad chafed immediately, finding them less comfortable than in French ships. The new 'shellback' did not get on well with the ship's officers, his attitudes to authority already well established. As the ship passed Kerguelen's Land in the southern Indian Ocean, a wind- and snow-swept island visited by Captain Cook in 1776, Conrad was reading Flaubert's *Salammbô*, set in the burning sands of ancient Carthage. This berth also involved his most extended stay yet in a foreign port – four months in Sydney, from the beginning of the balmy Antipodean autumn to the start of its mild 'winter'.

Docked at Sydney's busy Circular Quay (a marker there now recalls his presence in Australia), the ship provided easy access to the 'The Rocks', then the city's commercial and entertainment district, crowded with markets, hotels, pubs, and, inevitably, brothels. George Street, its principal thoroughfare, featured a handsome Sailors' Home (built in 1864 and still standing) that provided shelter as well as a refuge from solitude and boredom. Conrad apparently remained aboard ship, serving as her unofficial nightwatchman. This deepened his knowledge of human nature's seamier side: he witnessed drunken brawls; watched police patrols apply the law; and overheard the harsh language of rough men, later recollecting the 'night-prowlers, pursued or pursuing, with a stifled shriek followed by a profound silence, or slinking steadily alongside like ghosts'. He got a black eye one night from a thief who, hotly pursued, sought refuge on board. He had happier memories of the area's cheap dining spots at which he acquired familiarity with Chinese fare, a Chinese population having established itself in Australia during the gold rushes of the 1850s and 1860s. 'Sun-kum-on's was not bad,' he later recalled of one Chinese restaurant in The Rocks.

The experience in port provided a whiff of the Far East. Its ships filled the harbour, and its inhabitants, produce, and foodstuffs were features of the burgeoning, raw-edged town. At this time or during his stay in Australia the following year, Conrad became interested in the debates over the 'White Australia' policy and the Colony's ties to Britain. He investigated trading possibilities in the Sunda Islands, east of Java, perhaps briefly glimpsing more adventurous alternatives to life at sea. In the end, his service in the *Duke of Sutherland* represented a more permanent commitment to his chosen profession than had his time in the *Mavis* and the *Skimmer*, and when he returned to London a year after he had left it, he had taken, perhaps not dramatically but with some degree of resolution, another step towards maturity and independence. At twenty-one the 'incorrigible, hopeless Don Quixote', as Adam Pulman had called him, was coming into his own.

During two months ashore in London, when he lodged at the Sailors' Home in Well Street near the Tower for five weeks, Conrad again found employment, signing on for a six-week tour of the Mediterranean as an able-bodied seaman in the steamer *Europa*. The ship called at Genoa and Naples – Conrad's first sight of Italy since his trip with Pulman five years before – and then went on to Patras, on the north-western coast of the Peloponnese (his sole contact with the Greek mainland) and to Palermo on Sicily. She returned to London at the end of January 1880, and Conrad signed off, staying overnight in Well Street. There had again been a flare-up with his employer's representative, and in the space reserved for comment on 'Professional Ability' his Certificate of Discharge reads 'good' – in seaman's terms a damning with faint praise.

Although Conrad contemplated becoming private secretary to a man with money in the railways, he continued to keep his eye on the sea, seeking out a reference from Delestang in order to take the Board of Trade examination for second mate. The testimonial generously stated that he was at sea for 'three years of continuous service', when his time, in fact, amounted to somewhat more than a year. Unconcerned with the document's accuracy, Conrad submitted it when he applied to be examined. He took lessons at a crammer, and on 28 May 1880 sat and passed the exam at Saint Katherine's Dock House. But even as Conrad was securing his professional credentials, maritime trade was undergoing a worldwide convulsion as improved technology reduced the need for manpower. Armed with his second mate's certificate, Conrad set about looking for work, securing a berth as third mate in the *Loch Etive*, a wool-clipper. Just before departing on his first voyage to the Eastern Seas as a junior officer, he would have got wind of the *Jeddah* affair. In early August, news came of the abandonment in rough weather of a ship that had set out from Penang for Jeddah with pilgrims bound for the Hajj at Mecca. The incident, closely reported on, caused comment in the London papers, and was raised in Parliament. An official inquiry held at Aden, where the ship had been safely towed by a passing French vessel that had noted her in distress, found the European crew guilty of dereliction of duty. The subject of port gossip for months, the affair would provide the kernel for the pilgrim-ship episode of Lord Jim.

Bound for Sydney, the Loch Etive left the Port of London in August, and arrived in Australia in late November. A planned month's stay stretched to six weeks, and she did not leave until early January 1881, Conrad experiencing the southerly buster he remembers in Lord Jim, a wind common to the Antipodean summer. He undoubtedly heard of the Cutty Sark incident shortly after arriving in port, providing more material for Lord Jim as well as for his short story 'The Secret Sharer': in early September, Captain James Wallace, who had helped his first mate escape a charge of murdering a fellow crew member, jumped overboard in the Anjer Straits off Java. The incident and Wallace's unknown motives – guilt or fear of repercussions – stimulated Conrad's imagination.

Dereliction of duty hit even closer to home. Some of Captain William Stuart's belongings had disappeared, and the Loch Etive's crew was mustered in the presence of the police. A barmaid from the Circular Quay recognised the man who had given her goods to store, and two men were taken off to gaol, one a Norwegian by the name of Wanabo (a name remembered as Wamibo in The Nigger of the 'Narcissus'). On the ship's homeward voyage she encountered an American whaler throwing her a Christmas gift, a recollection worked up, with a major chronological inaccuracy (Conrad misplaced the year), in the late memoir 'Christmas Day at Sea' (1923).

Conrad signed off the Loch Etive in London in April 1881, and four months later signed on in the Palestine. While in port he was engaged in a speculative venture with his former captain, William Stuart, known in the trade for fast (and hence profitable) voyages; he also cast about for a job, and was perhaps purposefully extending his leave ashore to prepare for his first mate's examination, although he required more experience before he sat it. On arriving, he lodged at the Sailors' Home, but by early May had established himself at 6 Dynevor Road in Stoke Newington, a characterless lower-middle-class area of north London whose main attraction for 'young, single gentlemen' was relatively easy access to the city centre. Charles Booth's famed Inquiry into the Life and Labour of the People in London (1886–1903) notes Dynevor Road and environs as 'An artisan neighbourhood', and describes the street itself thus: '2 & 2½ storied. 6–8 roomed (including two kitchens). lodgers usual. pink.' Conrad's landlord, William Ward, formerly an Entry Officer at the Sailors' Home, was a commercial clerk at the Chelsea Pensioners; his son, fifteen-year-old William, who worked as an assistant storekeeper at the Home, possibly provided the connection with his parents' lodgings. While staying at the Wards', Conrad became friendly with a fellow lodger, thirty-year-old Adolf Krieger, a commercial clerk born in Prussia. Krieger married in early September, and left for other lodgings, but Conrad maintained the contact and the friendship deepened with time. He obviously also got on well with his landlord, to the tune of being able to borrow £3 (£1,400 in 2005 terms) from him by September. As an introduction to English family life, his experience with the Wards was thorough. William and Dolores Ward had four boys and four girls, ranging in age from early childhood to early adulthood. Walter, then four, was the youngest; Elizabeth and Amelia, aged twenty and nineteen, were already earning their livelihoods as 'machinists'. On and off, Conrad used the house as his shore base for the next few years.

Another friendship, already begun in James Sutherland's shipping offices where Conrad was seeking work, gained in importance. He had met Fountaine Hope either after his stint in the *Duke of Sutherland* in which Hope had earlier sailed, or after Conrad's service in the *Europa*. In his mid-twenties and recently married, Hope, the son of a county solicitor, had trained in the famous *Conway* training-ship in Liverpool. Conrad also became friendly with his brother, Linton, later a well-known yacht architect. The friendships suggest much about Conrad's social position in a class-conscious, stratified society in which he lacked the usual attachments of family and school ties. He fell in with men of his profession, but was set apart from them by his education and intellectual and cultural interests. Although eccentricity among seamen is hardly unknown, a taste for Meyerbeer, Bizet, and Flaubert, as much as fluency in French, tend to fall outside the average sailor's range then as now.

One of the few things known of this period is that Conrad wandered the vast city at night. The preface to *The Secret Agent* recalls 'solitary and nocturnal walks all over London in my early days'. His recollections, which threatened, he observes, to overwhelm that novel, testify to vivid experience. But of what exactly? Great cities after dark are alternately threatening and seductive; the bonds of the conventional loosen, and anonymity and solitude can be appealing – or can intensify loneliness. Conrad was, if nothing else, honing his skills of observation. The single documented fact of this summer is a ten-day stay at the Dreadnought Sailors' Hospital in Greenwich, where he recovered from a bout of measles, a disease 'very prevalent' in London during July and still causing 'very numerous' infant deaths in August.

Discharged from the hospital on 11 August, Conrad set about looking for work, but on finding it was unenthusiastic. The old saw that satisfaction fails to stimulate contains a grain of truth: this voyage, which was to end in disaster, was to provide the raw material for the story 'Youth' (1898). Destined for Bangkok, the *Palestine* set out on 21 September 1881, mooring at Gravesend for a week before setting out for Newcastle to ship coals for the Far East. Meeting with heavy gales, she took three weeks to reach the northern port, known to Conrad from his earlier runs in the *Skimmer*.

The slow progress and bad weather proved ill omens. After six weeks in port, the ship finally left Newcastle, fully two months after leaving London. Another month later, after yet more heavy weather and damage to the ship, the crew refused duty, and on Christmas Eve the *Palestine* turned towards Cornwall. Setting in at Falmouth for repairs, she remained in port for eight months. Conrad, who did not leave her, was presumably paid for his loyalty. Duties in port would have been light, and, if 'Youth' can be taken as testimony, he may have made the occasional foray to London to relieve his boredom. He continued to keep in touch with his uncle, to whom he wrote regularly and from whom he received practical advice urging caution and a safe and clear course in life: meeting his responsibilities, keeping out of debt, and steadily advancing in his career.

In September 1882, almost exactly a year after her first attempt, the *Palestine* again set sail for Bangkok. She never reached the Siamese capital, sinking off Sumatra on 14 March 1883, after a laborious six-month voyage. The crew heroically attempted to save the ship after the first whiffs of smoke had been noticed, but by then the coal, stored in the hold for more than a year, was a raging fire. After days of unrelenting effort in the tropical heat and humidity, and in the face of real and grave danger, all had come to naught. 'Do or Die' is the fictional *Judea*'s motto in 'Youth', and the crew, which had certainly 'done' their best, abandoned ship, loyally remaining by her to watch her sink. In open boats, they made for Muntok, the principal port of Bangka Island on the east coast of Sumatra, and a few days later shipped as passengers on the *Sissie* for Singapore, where Conrad signed off the *Palestine* on 3 April.

He had arrived in the Far East as a passenger, was unemployed, and had had a traumatic brush with possible death or injury. He spent a couple of weeks in Singapore, his first stint in what even then was a cosmopolitan city on the make. He looked for work, or turned up his nose at the kind available – inglorious drudgery in country ships (those registered not in London but in a colonial port) – and sailed for England as a passenger. As he did so, he was already planning to see Uncle Tadeusz on the Continent, their first encounter since Marseilles five years previously. Having logged more experience, if not quite the amount demanded by regulations, Conrad was also looking forward to taking his first mate's examination.

On reaching England, he brushed up on seamanship, and in late July arrived in fashionable Marienbad where Bobrowski, a rapidly ageing fifty-three, had gone for a water cure. Meeting his uncle on Austro-Hungarian territory was, in effect, 'going home'. As in an emotionally tinged passage of *Lord Jim* about rendering an account, Conrad would face the only person in his life who was of any strong emotional consequence: 'it is the lonely, without a fireside or an affection they may call their own, those who return not to a dwelling but to the land itself, to meet its disembodied, eternal, and unchangeable spirit – it is those who understand best its severity, its saving power, the grace of its secular right to our fidelity, to our obedience'. In Conrad's case, there was not even a land to return to. But he had travelled widely, entered the profession of his 'youthful fancy', and could report at least modest success in it.

Proud of his 'Admiral', Bobrowski had grown still closer to the young man whom he had raised at a distance, and continued to watch over as surrogate father, mentor, and banker. The event, a true holiday for both, ended with a stay in Teplice, 50 miles north-east of Prague. Making his way back to England via Germany (in Dresden he posted a letter to his uncle), within less than a month Conrad was bound for Madras as second mate in the *Riversdale*. His rapid engagement suggests that he may have found the berth in the clipper before leaving for the Continent. However that might be, the journey to India, by contrast, was laboured: the ship, which left London in mid-September, arrived at Port Elizabeth in South Africa in early December 1883 but remained in port for two months. The stop gave Conrad his first experience of Africa, which he had previously sailed near but not set foot on. The town had few attractions, and he was left with considerable time on his hands, possibly for reading. Leaving Port Elizabeth, the *Riversdale* took a further two months to reach Madras.

Once in port, Conrad again had problems with his superior officer, even more serious than usual and due neither simply to pique nor to a difference in temperament. Captain Lawrence Macdonald, a tetchy Scot whose wife and children shipped with him, fell ill, and Conrad, sent to fetch a doctor, appears to have conveyed the impression that his captain was suffering from alcohol poisoning. This reached, and scorched, the captain's ears. Conrad wrote an apology, which he later regretted and claimed was untrue, and the affair dragged on until later in the year, when an official investigation cleared him.

On the spot, however, the damage proved irreparable. Conrad was dismissed; his Certificate of Discharge issued with 'No Comment' in the space reserved for 'Conduct'; and his pay docked to cover the expense of finding a replacement. Madras was apparently a difficult place to pick up a crew, and that, or his captain's hostility, encouraged Conrad to travel to Bombay to seek a new berth. That destination, rather than the nearer Calcutta, suggests that he had a homeward-bound voyage in view. The Great Indian Peninsula Railway having linked Madras to Bombay during the previous decade, he crossed the subcontinent by train in the gathering heat of April.

At his journey's end, Conrad had a needed stroke of luck, soon landing a position as second mate in the *Narcissus*. Engaged in port duties, he had a place to sleep, was earning a wage, and logging experience for his next examination. He suffered from a liver ailment (possibly jaundice?), but continued to explore the city, recalling it in both *The Nigger of the 'Narcissus'* and *Lord Jim*. The voyage home, begun in early June 1884, ended in Dunkirk in mid-October. On arriving in London, Conrad put up for a few days at the Sailors' Home, his last documented stay there. He had left England more than a year before, and had returned with a rich treasure-trove of experience and impressions that he would exploit in later writing. He also returned with a monkey – a vicious, invariably dirty, and typically smelly creature. This eccentricity suggests a turn of character, perhaps the cocking of a snook at the world at large. Aboard ship the animal must have been a minor nuisance; back in London, Conrad rapidly got rid of it, but only after it had wreaked havoc at Barr, Moering, & Company, shipping agents with offices and a warehouse in the City, in which he had a small interest through Krieger.*

A month after his return, Conrad, with the required period of service at sea behind him, sat and failed the first mate's examination. He resat the exam a fortnight later, on 3 December 1884, his twenty-seventh birthday, and passed. The short interval between the first and second sittings suggests that he had failed on a technicality. In *A Personal Record*, he glosses over being 'plucked' and presents his examinations as experiences that passed off without a hitch. The demands of compression and dramatic impact rather than strict adherence to the facts govern much of that memoir, and Conrad's preference for art's tidiness rather than life's messiness is, arguably, a rational choice. His first mate's 'ticket' in hand, he set about finding a berth, but failed to do so until April 1885. Whilst shipping was subject to cyclical downturns, the length of time he was unemployed seems excessively long. He was still receiving an allowance from Bobrowski and had a

---

* In 1891, the company (apparently a firm from Stuttgart, where it did business under the name Barr, Möhring) had offices in London at 95 Upper Thames Street, EC4, and 35 Camomile Street, EC3 (near Liverpool Street station), both addresses appearing in Conrad's correspondence. An 1895 Postal Directory of London lists it both as a 'Forwarding Agent' at 72 & 73 Fore Street and 18 & 20 Fore Street Avenue and as 'Shipping Agents' at the Fore Street addresses as well as at 35–41 Wapping High Street. (Conrad's working for the firm again raises questions about his denial of any knowledge of German.)

financial stake in Barr, Moering; unlike most of his fellow junior officers, he could afford to be choosy, and his allowance could see him through fallow periods.

The five-month stretch between passing his examination and signing on as second mate in the clipper *Tilkhurst* in Hull is a blank possibly filled by service in the *John P. Best*, a steamer owned by an Antwerp company of that name. In a list of ships Conrad claimed to have served in she figures between the *Narcissus* and the *Tilkhurst*. The ship made a trip out of Antwerp to London and then to the Black Sea and Sardinia, before returning to her home port. In *The Mirror of the Sea*, Conrad noted his familiarity with several river ports, including Antwerp's, but proof goes no farther.

While in Hull, he could not have failed to notice the large numbers of European transmigrants, particularly from northern Europe, making their way through the ports of Hull and Grimsby en route to Liverpool and thence to North America. Although he was famously allergic to the theatre, in the week before he left the city he could have seen the famed actress Madame Modjeska at the Theatre Royal in *As You Like It*, Scribe and Legouvé's *Adrienne Lecouvreur*, or adaptations of Dumas's *La Dame aux camélias* and Schiller's *Mary Stuart*.

In joining the *Tilkhurst* as her second officer, he was shipping below his new rank and thus receiving a lower salary than he ought to have received. If the writing was on the wall about his choice of profession, he either did not see it or brushed off its warning. Technical advances were changing life at sea: newer ships could manage greater tonnage; the number of ships was consequently in decline; and manpower requirements began to fall. Conrad was gradually being squeezed out of a job even before he had properly landed one, entering the labour market during the so-called 'Long Depression' that began in the early 1870s and continued until almost the end of the century.

Sailing from Hull out of the River Humber in late April bound for Singapore, the *Tilkhurst* reached Cardiff to pick up a cargo of coal in mid-May. During some days ashore, Conrad got on friendly terms with a master gold- and silversmith, an émigré Pole, Władysław Spiridion (né Kliszczewski), to whom he had undertaken to pay back a loan on behalf of another Polish seaman, like himself a rarity in the British

Merchant Service. Conrad also befriended Spiridion's English-born son and business partner, Józef.* The connection with both also apparently involved a speculative business venture that never materialised. The friendship endured for a while but was of the kind that never really takes fire, brightening and then dying out rapidly. For a man as much on the move as Conrad was, shore links tended to be deep and enduring or sincere but passing. Conrad certainly could be reserved, even aloof, in his dealings with the world, and his emotional life is often difficult to reconstruct.

The ship continued to Penarth, from where it set sail at the beginning of June, docking at Singapore three and half months later. Conrad reacquainted himself with the town in the month it took to unload and load the ship and then set out for home, with Calcutta her first port of call. A week after she left Singapore, a crew member injured in a drinking spree serious enough to become a police matter, jumped overboard and drowned. The *Tilkhurst* reached Calcutta in early November, remaining there six weeks to load jute. Conrad's first surviving writings in English, a handful of letters to the younger Spiridion, date from this period. They are performances rather than intimate communications, discoursing at length on current politics and continuing a conversation begun in Cardiff.

The *Tilkhurst*'s homeward passage was leisurely, and the ship reached Britain only in mid-June. The ship docked at Dundee, where Conrad briefly lodged at the Sailors' Home before taking the train to London. He made plans for a career in trade with Phil Krieger (apparently the name his friend went by rather than 'Adolf') but, hedging his bets, also sat for his master's examination at the end of July, six weeks after he had arrived in Scotland. He was 'plucked' at his first try (a failure again edited out of his vivid description of his examinations in *A Personal Record*), and succeeded at his second, in early November. On receiving his examiner's congratulations, he walked away content: 'I had vindicated myself from what had been cried upon as a stupid obstinacy or a fantastic caprice.' However

---

* This individual appears in previous Conrad scholarship under the incorrect name 'Spiridion Kliszczewski'. His given name was Józef, and for the sake of convenience he went by Spiridion as his surname. For details, see 'Conrad's circle: A select Who's Who', p. 293 below.

fleeting, the backward glance catches the youth whose dreams have been realised. Captain Korzeniowski (a name almost always cruelly mangled in shipping news) had attained his, and his uncle's, long-planned goal.

During the to-ing and fro-ing between distant ports and at a time when he had few emotional ties, he forged one signally intimate link: in July, he had applied for British nationality. On taking the required oath of allegiance, he affirmed commitment both to a sentiment and an ideal. To Józef Spiridion, an armchair Polish nationalist who neither spoke Polish nor had lived in his father's homeland, Conrad wrote from Singapore: 'When speaking, writing or thinking in English the word Home always means for me the hospitable shores of Great Britain,' and as he later told a friend: 'I am more British than you are. You are only British because you could not help it.'

After Christmas, Conrad signed on as second mate in the *Falconhurst*, making a five-day voyage from London to Penarth, a town that was booming with the Welsh coal trade. An obvious stopgap, his first job after he received his master's ticket established a pattern: for the remainder of his time at sea he was to find berths below his rank. The *Falconhurst* proved a rare exception in one respect: rather than being underpaid, he was extravagantly well paid, receiving a month's wages, £5, for the five-day passage.

The stop in Penarth enabled a New Year's visit to the Spiridions in nearby Cardiff, by which time he had learned from his agent of a position in the *Highland Forest*, a Glasgow-owned ship moored at Amsterdam that required a first mate for a voyage to Java. Fountaine Hope, meeting Conrad at Holborn station on his return from Wales, recalls that his friend was delighted to have landed the berth. When Conrad arrived in Amsterdam, he spent some time in the city centre making arrangements with the Dutch charterers, Hudig & Blokhuyzen, taking refuge from the wintry weather in the luxurious Hotel Krasnapolsky's coffee-room. Responsible for stowage, he oversaw the loading of the *Highland Forest*, and formally signed on in mid-February 1887, a couple of days before the ship set out for Java from the Oostelijike Handelskade (Eastern Trade Quay). As part of his duties, Conrad undertook the training of her four apprentices. For once, he was on good terms with the ship's captain, John McWhir,

Scottish, like the ship's name and register. The *Highland Forest*, however, proved skittish, her cargo loaded strictly by the book but none the less causing her to roll. She encountered heavy seas on her southern passage, and had a near-brush with a submerged ice floe. By the time she arrived in Samarang in central Java in mid-June, a crew member had died. The ship had also wreaked her vengeance on Conrad for the way he had loaded her: he was struck by a falling spar.

At Samarang, he consulted a Dutch doctor, who advised that the injury was serious enough to require hospitalisation and convalescence. The ten or twelve days Conrad spent in the town renewed his contact with Malay culture, this time in its Javanese heartland. On 2 July, the day after he signed off, he left for Singapore as a passenger on the SS *Celestial*. There, he was admitted to the European wing of its General Hospital at Sepoy Lines, on a gentle slope two miles from the city centre. If Jim's experience in *Lord Jim* can be transposed to the novel's author, Conrad spent 'many days stretched on his back, dazed, battered, hopeless, and tormented as if at the bottom of an abyss of unrest'.

On recovering, Conrad left for the Sailors' Home for Officers near the Esplanade, close to the city's commercial centre. As in Amsterdam, he may have visited first-class hotels for the occasional luxury – tiffin, billiards, a peg of gin – but he lacked the means to stay in them. (The oft-repeated claim that he stayed at Raffles Hotel is pure fantasy.) He knocked about town; had dealings with its Master Attendant, a colourful Irishman recalled in *Lord Jim*; and rubbed shoulders with the officers and resident staff at the Sailors' Home. The city's Chinese, Malays, and Tamils formed a colourful backdrop, much like the decorations marking Queen Victoria's Golden Jubilee, celebrated just before his arrival. Distanced by race, class, and language, Conrad nevertheless engaged with the local population imaginatively. He was also educating himself in the region's history, soaking up port gossip and sailor's tales and probably reading history and absorbing local lore. First glimpsed unromantically at Muntok, 'The East' had begun to captivate him. If there was ever a temptation to 'lounge safely through existence', as the omniscient narrator in *Lord Jim* contemptuously puts it, the devil could not have picked a better time than Singapore's unbearably humid 'summer'.

Conrad found work in a country ship. He may have needed ready money, or may have wanted to sate his curiosity about the Celebes and Borneo, for Europeans then the edge of the known world. The Dutch had an established presence beyond Java and Sumatra, but in several places their 'outposts of progress' were tentative and nominal. Officially abolished in the Netherlands' far-flung Empire in 1863, slavery was still practised, and local tyrants held sway as they had for centuries. As in British India, the authorities in Batavia (today's Jakarta) interfered little with the native states, which were run on 'traditional' lines. As Kipling characterised their equivalent in India, they touched 'the Railway and the Telegraph on the one side, and the days of Harun-al-Raschid on the other'. Life and property could be insecure under such 'benevolent' despots, and head-hunting and ritual cannibalism, pace recent revisionists, had not disappeared from the remoter jungles.

On 22 August 1887, Conrad left Singapore in the *Vidar*, a small, Arab-owned ship plying ports on the Celebes and Borneo. The steamer had a chequered history. The Dutch suspected that although officially trading in island produce and coal she had also been a slaver and dealt in contraband. During Conrad's four voyages in her, ports of call included Samarinda, Berau, and Bulungan on Borneo; Pulau Laut (Sea Island) at the island's south-eastern tip; and Donggala on the Celebes. Some of these towns were literally backwaters, located far inland and reached via large, deep rivers.

Conrad picked up a smattering of trade Malay, *pasar Melayu*, a stock of words sufficient to ensure food, shelter, and transportation, supplemented by sea terms. He had an opportunity to observe more closely the social and mental habits of the people, even if much of his contact was with rougher specimens, the seamen with whom he shipped. Hugh Clifford, a civil servant and writer with whom Conrad became friendly after his first novels appeared, was to complain that Conrad 'didn't know anything about Malays'. Conrad too readily conceded that, but his intentions were not anthropological, and his writing suggests that he was profoundly moved by what he saw. As he later put it, a morning came in early 1889 when in rented rooms in Pimlico, he was visited by 'Malays, Arabs and half-castes', who 'in their obscure sun-bathed existence' demanded expression.

*

In Berau, 'something happened'. Conrad met with a Eurasian trader named Karel Olmeijer, the prototype of Almayer of *Almayer's Folly*, a man eking out a livelihood in a setting hostile to his endeavours, dreaming large dreams, and hoping to escape from the heat and tedium of the tropics. Fact and fiction bleed into one another here. The known facts of his life are few – he fathered eleven children, was married to a Eurasian, and died in 1900 – but whether Conrad knew much of his history is doubtful and also unimportant. Their few encounters stimulated meditations upon humankind's common destiny, and as the *Vidar* steamed in and out of Berau, Conrad's profits proved more substantial and enduring than the cargo the ship had gathered.

By early January 1888, when his connection with the ship ended, he returned to Singapore a changed man. At thirty, he had encountered riotously luxuriant landscapes and animal species and human types new to him. He had learned how to adapt, even flourish, in 'exotic' and sometimes challenging situations. The impact of his travels in the Malay Archipelago, wholly out proportion to their extent in time and space, proved deep and permanent. His fiction was assisted by his reading about the region, but this served as an *aide-mémoire* to peoples and sights he had fleetingly seen. His imaginative work returns to no other time of his life with such regularity.

Conrad left the *Vidar* without immediate prospects, shoring up at the Sailors' Home for Officers for a fortnight, and jettisoned plans to return home when chance offered the command of an Australian ship moored in Bangkok. Her captain had died, and the firm, passing over any claims her first mate may have had, wished to replace him with a man holding a master's ticket. The experience of first command forms the core of *The Shadow-Line*, later exaggeratedly characterised by its author as 'exact autobiography'. The offer confirmed, Conrad quickly made his way to the Siamese capital, arriving on the *Melita* in late January. On his arrival, he boarded his first command, the *Otago*, a 367-ton iron-hulled barque built in 1869 and registered in Adelaide. (Owned by a syndicate that included Captain John Snadden, Thomas Elder, and J. L. Simpson, the ship was often employed by Henry Simpson & Son, a firm dealing mainly in coal.) Conrad found some of her crew ill, and called upon the British Legation's physician, William

Willis, *The Shadow-Line*'s 'sympathetic doctor', to treat them for 'Fever, dysentery, and Cholera'.

In addition to seeing to the crew, his time was spent in securing the ship's cargo, dealing with Jucker, & Sigg & Company, a Swiss firm located on the east side of Bangkok's Chao Phraya River. Some time during his stay in port, he was robbed by a Chinese, who, as he later told Bertrand Russell, 'stole all my money one night in Bangkok, but brushed and folded my clothes neatly for me to dress in the morning, before vanishing into the depths of Siam'. Whether the *Otago*'s departure was delayed by the crew's illness, a significant plot element in *The Shadow-Line*, or by the hostility of the tug-owner who had to take ships over the river's treacherously shallow bar into the Bight of Bangkok, Conrad seems to have been concerned about how the delay would be understood by her owners in Adelaide. Thoroughly professional (delays cost the firm money), his concern may also have been self-interested: if he hoped to keep this berth, efficiency and a timely departure would recommend him. Further delayed by bad weather, the ship finally left Bangkok for Singapore on 9 February 1888. She apparently put in at Chantabun on the east coast of the Gulf of Siam, where Conrad claimed that a group of Chinese had 'tried to kill me (and some other people) in the yard of a private house'.

The 'Bangkok Trilogy' of 'Falk' (1903), 'The Secret Sharer' (1912), and *The Shadow-Line* (1917) tempts any writer on Conrad's life to milk fiction for biographical purposes. *The Shadow-Line* tells of a young captain who receives his first command in Singapore, hurries to Bangkok to take it up, deals with a crew laid low by malaria, and confronts calms that threaten his ship's life, the lives of his fellows, and his reason. The three works variously circle round the themes of transgression (dereliction of duty, cannibalism, murder), expiation, initiatory experience, and profound alienation and loneliness. It is tempting to see beyond the similarities of setting to an emotional coherence derived from reality, and then to discover in Conrad's fiction a set of inner problems. The sense of loneliness – a need for 'understanding' and emotional companionship – must indeed have been acute. At thirty, he had no close ties, no fixed abode, and had committed himself to a profession that was inherently unstable in that even a steady berth demanded long absences from 'home'. Apart from

Krieger and Hope, his contacts were with the men with whom he worked and from whom in many fundamental ways he differed. On the other hand, the ideas treated in the fiction are, broadly, universal, and the experience of alienation so quintessentially part of contemporary Western reality that we need to remind ourselves that this was not always so.

Battling unfavourable winds, the *Otago* took three weeks to arrive in Singapore, where she was immediately quarantined and some of her crew were confined to hospital. Conrad hunted out replacements and sailed for Sydney in early March, arriving two months later. The ship encountered light winds at the outset of her voyage followed by heavy gales. Whatever his concerns about keeping his position, Conrad had pleased his employers and in May made a trip from Sydney to Melbourne. At the latter port, although modernisation was being planned, ships were required to anchor in Hobson's Bay where cargoes were unloaded on to lighters for transportation up the Yarra River. Tedious, costly, and time-consuming, double-handling translated into a five-week stay.

The *Otago* arrived back in Sydney to a maritime crisis. Tense negotiations on wages and staffing between the Seamen's Union of Australasia and the steamship owners finally collapsed. As emotions became heated, police were required at the docks, and angry union men attempted to block ships from leaving. Conrad had a rare encounter with the past here: the highly itinerant Wards (some of their children had been born in Gibraltar, others in South Africa) with whom he had boarded in Stoke Newington were entertained aboard 'his' ship. They were all older and wiser, and he could show off his professional success, and even bask in a bit of glory. On 7 August 1888, the *Otago*, bound for Mauritius with a cargo of soap, fertiliser, and tallow, narrowly squeaked out of a port gripped by labour problems and threatened by violence. Conrad's later verdict on unionised seamen was succinct: 'Asses.'

Conrad's confidence in his sailing skills as well as his employer's trust is measured by the course he took to reach Mauritius. He struck northward for the Torres Straits, separating Australia and New Guinea, claimed for Britain by Captain Cook; the route was the more dangerous and then the less taken. Conrad was staking a symbolic claim to maritime traditions by doing so, having to convince his employers of the wisdom of his choice.

The voyage to Port-Louis took nearly two months. The great natural beauty of Mauritius and the cleanliness and culture of its main port town, founded by the French in the early eighteenth century, had impressed Darwin, who, arriving there in the *Beagle* in 1836, had noted its bookshops and opera house. He enthused: 'The whole island, with its sloping border and central mountains, was adorned with an air of perfect elegance: the scenery, if I may use such an expression, appeared to the sight harmonious.' There in the mid-1890s, Mark Twain, who also commented on the city's ethnic diversity, wrote excitedly of the island's famed beauty: 'From one citizen you gather the idea that Mauritius was made first, and then heaven; and that heaven was copied after Mauritius.'

Conrad's seven weeks in port were spent during the end of the island's dry 'winter', with the rains of the hot humid 'summer' setting in. Misunderstanding plagued him from start to finish. The local papers announced the *Otago*'s arrival and departure under Captain 'Korzeniouski', 'Korsoniwski', 'Korsoniowski', and 'Kozenrowski'. As well as going about his duties for his employers and overseeing the loading of the cargo (490,000 kilos of sugar) Conrad, in a departure from habit, made contact with local society. The French families, long established among the Indo-Mauritian and Creole populations, still maintained flourishing businesses under the English administration. He developed 'romantic interests' to the point of hoping to marry, and was, it seems, jilted. The story 'A Smile of Fortune' (1911 serial; 1912 book version), a singularly ironic title given the events on which it is based, is bitter about one of these relationships – that with Alice Shaw, a local shipping agent's seventeen-year-old daughter. The balance of fact and fiction in the story leans towards the latter, but Conrad had another, more serious, interest in Eugénie Renouf, aged either twenty-four or twenty-six, whose family he got to know through her uncle, Captain Gabriel Renouf.

A mid-century traveller's account speaks of the island's French-women as having a 'Creole languor' that agreeably softened a tendency to vivacity: 'Their costume is spotless white, and they walk to the bazaar in the early morning, or promenade at sunset, with uncovered heads – in fact, just as they are dressed indoors, excepting the parasol.' There were social occasions with the Renoufs, and excursions to the Jardin de Pamplemousses, a tropical pleasance. Not long before the *Otago*'s departure, Conrad formally asked for Eugénie's hand from one of her brothers, only to learn that she was already engaged to a French-born cousin, a pharmacist sixteen (or eighteen) years her senior.

Mademoiselle Renouf may have been a heartless coquette – or a canny one, egging on Conrad in a vain attempt to escape an arranged marriage. On the other hand, the flirtation may have been largely one-sided, or Conrad may simply have acted on impulse. Possibly, he thought of settling in Australia or Mauritius with Eugénie Renouf, but as to that the record is blank. He was certainly no catch as a potential husband: he had no permanent position and few resources with which to set up a household. When he sailed from Port-Louis at the end of November, he may (or may not) have left with a broken heart, but he had managed his employers' interests to their advantage (the cargo consisted of typical island products: sugar, molasses, and tea) as well as to his, by turning a profit on dealings in potatoes.

On 5 January 1889, Conrad arrived back in Melbourne, where he continued to work for Henry Simpson & Sons in the growing port town, staying aboard the anchored *Otago* or lodging at the elegant neo-classical Sailors' Home in Spencer Street. In mid-February, his employers directed him to sail for Port Minlacowie, on Yorke Peninsula's western side, to ship a cargo of wheat. The *Otago* remained in the small outport for a month – after Port-Louis and Melbourne the boredom was doubtless oppressive – before making its way to Adelaide. There Conrad suddenly signed off, and on 3 April departed for Europe as a passenger on the *Nürnberg*, a Norddeutscher Lloyd steamship engaged in the passenger trade between Germany and Australia. Designed to carry immigrants to North America but refitted for the German Imperial Mail service to the Far East, the ship returned via the Suez Canal to her home port of Bremen. Conrad seems to have had a glimpse of the port's main business, recalling the horrors of immigrant ships in his story 'Amy Foster' (1903): 'People groaned, children cried, water dripped, the lights went out, the walls of the place creaked, and everything was being shaken so that in one's little box one dared not lift one's head.'

In mid-May, he arrived in England after an absence of two years. Why did he decide to return? He had abandoned good prospects and a secure berth, and had not (for once) quarrelled with his employers, even obtaining a warm testimonial from them the day before he left Adelaide. Transporting sugar, wheat, and potatoes over the high seas perhaps lacked glamour, but at the time 'Joseph C. Korzeniowski', as he signed himself in Port-Louis's shipping register, had expressed no other ambitions.

There is merely the bald fact: he had returned to London with no definite plans and was casting about for work, possibly pitching in at Barr, Moering. Shortly after his arrival, he settled into lodgings in Bessborough Gardens in Pimlico, just to the south of Millbank Prison. When he lived there (the exact house is unknown), the 'Gardens' themselves were delta-shaped, like the famous of *The Secret Agent*, a novel that draws heavily on this period of his life. Booth's survey notes the area's several boarding-houses, and characterises Bessborough Gardens as 'more disreputable' than Bessborough Street, drawing attention to the 'Notorious brothel at corner of Vauxhall Bridge Road' nearby. Already somewhat dilapidated, the mainly working-class area was densely populated.

Whatever his plans when he left Australia, the summer found Conrad at loose ends. The search for employment proved frustrating, part of this spilling over into his first work of fiction, *Almayer's Folly* (1895), which centres on a man dissatisfied with life and aching to escape his circumstances. Conrad's mental escape to the tropics is hardly surprising, although why reverie became transformed into writing remains an intractable mystery. Aside from the trivial 'The Black Mate', written in 1886 for a short-story competition in the magazine *Tit-Bits*, no earlier attempts at writing are known. Later he recalled that one morning he sat down after breakfast had been cleared away and began to write. That version of events is itself unabashedly fictional. Men or women do not in real life impulsively take up the pen; there must, at least, have been prior meditation, some jotting down of ideas, perhaps successful story-telling that received encouragement and suggested talent. As a first novel, *Almayer's Folly* glows with authentic genius, and it is hard, almost impossible, to credit the received version that only letters and business correspondence had flowed from Conrad's pen before he embarked on it. But if he had not been writing, he had certainly long been attentively reading in the Classics, Flaubert, and contemporary French literature. (His general interest in French culture as well as elements of *The Secret Agent* suggest that he perhaps attended the Lyceum's season of French plays that summer, seeing Sarah Bernhardt in Sardou's *La Tosca*, later turned into a libretto for Puccini.)

The other momentous decision – to write in English – has engendered speculation out of proportion to its interest. From a certain perspective the 'choice', to use the very word Conrad objected to, seems natural. English was the language of his everyday reality. He had won his professional credentials in it, and had, in a real sense, struggled to master it. Writing or speaking an acquired language can be liberating, and Conrad went considerably out of his way to scotch the rumour that he had deliberated between French and English: '*had I been under the necessity* of making a choice between the two, and though I knew French fairly well and was familiar with it from infancy, I would have been afraid to attempt expression in a language so perfectly "crystallized" '. If the italics, which are his, perhaps 'protest too much', they had reason to do so by 1919, the year he wrote this. His account silently glides over another possible choice for his creative work: writing in Polish. But even as his writing life began, that language, with which he had had little daily contact for years, was growing remote to him; he would fatally have lacked a sense of audience; and his preferred literary ancestors were French and English. This is to leave aside the practical problems of marketing his writing and managing a career at a distance, for he had shown no inclination to 'return', there being, indeed, nothing to 'return' to.

Conrad's new endeavour flourished. He had drafted as many as three chapters by the end of the year, while still on the lookout for a ship. Not particularly good in an overcrowded market, his employment prospects worsened dramatically in mid-August, when the Dockers' Union began a strike that gained momentum among both unionised and non-unionised labourers. By the end of August, the Port of London was paralysed: some 130,000 men were withholding their labour. Large demonstrations paraded through the streets, and this extraordinary move by the working poor rattled the establishment. By mid-September, shortly after 'The Great Dock Strike' ended victoriously for the dockers, Conrad's hopes for 'a decent livelihood' had forced him to look to the Continent. An arrangement to sail to Mexico and the West Indies for Walford & Company fell through, and he was now using his connections with Barr, Moering to explore possibilities in Belgium. His fluency in French and his experience in Antwerp's *John P. Best* (if he had, in fact, shipped in her) stood in his favour. Just before he left to be interviewed in Brussels, the East End was again gripped by the Ripper case, a murder having been committed with 'Jack's' signature brutality and recalling the previous year's 'Autumn of Terror'.

A sufficient number of strings had been pulled for Conrad to be asked for an interview with the deputy director of the newly founded Société Anonyme Belge pour le Commerce du Haut-Congo (Belgian Limited Company for Trade on the Upper Congo). It took place at the company's headquarters in Brussels, at 9 rue Brederode immediately behind the Royal Palace, where Léopold II, King of the Belgians, an 'Attila in modern dress' as one historian has called him, oversaw his vast business interests, the Congo Free State having been his personal property outright since 1885. With withering irony 'Heart of Darkness' immortalises Conrad's meeting with one of the King's minions. Marlow, in part Conrad's surrogate, meets 'an impression of pale plumpness in a frock-coat. The great man himself. He was five feet six, I should judge, and had his grip on the handle-end of ever so many millions. He shook hands, I fancy, murmured vaguely, was satisfied with my French.'

The 'frock-coat' – forty, square-faced, heavy-set, and balding – was Colonel Albert Thys, already a major player in the Congo's rape. He did indeed deal in 'millions', on his own account as well as at his sovereign's bidding. Among others, he ran the Compagnie du Chemin de Fer du Congo (The Congo Railway Company), the Compagnie du Katanga, and the Banque d'Outremer (The Overseas Bank). In due course, Belgium honoured him for his role in what Conrad characterised as 'the vilest scramble for loot that ever disfigured the history of human conscience and geographical exploration': in 1904 the Congolese town of Sona Qongo was renamed Thysville, and a ship, the SS *Thysville*, was later named after the town. (Rue Général-Thys can still be found in Brussels today.)

Africa was also much in British news at the time. The Welsh-born American journalist and explorer Henry Morton Stanley was engaged in consolidating the Empire's ambitions in East Africa through his expedition to rescue Mehmed Emin Pasha (né Eduard Schnitzer, a German), the Governor of Equatoria in the Egyptian Sudan, who was cut off from Egypt by a revolt led by a Muslim religious zealot known as 'The Mahdi'. Stanley's mission of 1888 and 1889 excited widespread public interest in East Africa, and he made treaties with African leaders on Britain's behalf. By 1889, he had persuaded Emin Pasha to withdraw. As press reports of the expedition filtered in, Conrad's intense childhood interest in geography and the exploration of the continent took a real turn. He was impatient to be gainfully employed, even as he was taking steps towards a new private identity as a man who 'writes', even if he was not yet a 'writer'.

Meanwhile Conrad was making plans to see Bobrowski, now approaching sixty, whom he had last seen in Marienbad in July 1883. In an era of short life expectancy, Bobrowski had passed the average, and an opportunity to see his wandering nephew was to be seized upon. For Conrad, Africa was in the offing, but his eyes now turned towards the Ukraine.

Crisis: Finding a Home
(1890–1895)

Aware that his nephew's search for employment had taken him to Brussels, Bobrowski wrote of a distant relation (Conrad's maternal grandmother's first cousin) who, after exile in France in the wake of the 1863 Polish Uprising, had settled in the city. On his way to the Ukraine, Conrad arrived in the Belgian capital on 5 February, meeting the fifty-five-year-old Aleksandr Poradowski only a few days before he died. He established a sympathy with his widow, Marguerite-Blanche-Marie Gachet de la Fournière, born in Belgium of a family with roots in Lille, the daughter of a distinguished philologist and historian. She had become a novelist and translator from Polish.* Her fiction often focuses on Ukrainian life, rendered with local colour gathered during her period of residence in Lemberg with her husband. (In period style, her 1889 novel *Demoiselle Micia* bears the subtitle *Moeurs galliciennes* [Galician mores]). Ten years older than Conrad, she was a published writer well connected with *La Revue des Deux Mondes*, the distinguished literary and political fortnightly founded in Paris in 1829, and boasting among its contributors Stendhal, George Sand, Delacroix, Victor Hugo, Turgenev, Chekhov, and d'Annunzio.

Conrad remained in Brussels for four days, looking for work. A virtual stranger and busy himself, he could have seen a little more of Poradowska, who, under intense emotional strain, was arranging her

---

* Her cousin, Paul, twenty years her senior, a homeopathic doctor, has, in a sense, won world fame: he was Van Gogh's physician, and the artist's *Portrait of Dr Gachet*, which, in Van Gogh's words to Gauguin, caught 'the heart-broken expression of our time', is a modern icon.

husband's funeral and enmeshed in the legal machinery that follows a death. Dressed in deep mourning, she is in part the source for 'The Intended' (also living in Brussels, although the city is unnamed) in 'Heart of Darkness'.

In Berlin's Friedrichstrasse Bahnhof, Conrad, tired from his overnight rail journey, left one of his bags in a café. It contained the only copy of the first few chapters of *Almayer's Folly*, evidence of his newly evolving identity. Luckily, an attentive railway porter restored the Gladstone bag to him, and he boarded his train for Vienna, hoping to work on the manuscript during his trip. Greeted by a family retainer, Conrad left Kalinówka railway station for an eight-hour sleigh journey, passing through snow-covered fields on the way to his uncle's estate, Kazimierówka. During his two-month stay, as wintry blasts mellowed into spring, he left his novel untouched and wrote only a few letters to Marguerite Poradowska, both a significant and a sympathetic act, given the brevity and circumstances of their acquaintance.

To the local burghers, distant relatives, and neighbours and acquaintances seen for the first time in fifteen years, the English sea captain was something of a phenomenon. Having travelled far geographically and culturally, he was the object of curiosity as well as envy, and apparently responded with some frostiness. A reminiscence of the visit, written nearly half a century later and laced with provincial resentment, describes him as aloof and unsympathetic, indifferent to local and to patriotic issues, as he well might have been, having established himself in the wide world remote from backward and backward-looking Kazimierówka.

Conrad's homeward journey included a stop in Lublin with relatives, the Zagórskis, followed by another visit to relatives in nearby Radom, including the widow of his mother's brother, Kazimierz. He returned to London at the beginning of May, again via Brussels, where he almost certainly called upon Poradowska. But his time in London was brief, word finally coming from the Société du Commerce de la Haut-Congo that he had received a post. Conrad had even enlisted Poradowska in his cause, though her attempted string-pulling (remembered in 'Heart of Darkness') proved unsuccessful. As so often, a last-minute vacancy, rather than dogged persistence, precipitated movement: the company needed to replace Johannes Freiesleben, the Danish captain of their steamship *Floride*, who had been killed by natives in the Congo three months previously. (His name appears as Fresleven in 'Heart of Darkness'.) Conrad hurried back and forth between London and Brussels a few times, briefly saw Poradowska amidst the flurry, and on 10 May 1890 left Brussels for Bordeaux by train, departing for Africa on a three-year contract.

Given the heavy death toll among Europeans – fever and the usual tropical illnesses were rife – the length of his contract approached the fantastical. As the traveller Mary Kingsley put it: 'there is no other region in the world that can match West Africa for the steady kill, kill, kill that its malaria works on the white men who come under its influence'. And beyond malaria-carrying mosquitoes there was the climate. In her view, a man like Conrad with his nervous temperament and history of childhood ailments was ill-suited to survive it: 'a certain make of man has the best chance of surviving the Coast climate – an energetic, spare, nervous but light-hearted creature, capable of enjoying whatever there may be to enjoy, and incapable of dwelling on discomforts or worries'. One wonders how much Conrad knew about conditions in the Congo, or, if he was aware of them, whether he optimistically thought he could brave them unharmed. If the experience of Marlow, the narrator of 'Heart of Darkness', can here be read as Conrad's own, he came down with '"a little fever", or a "little touch of other things" – the playful paw-strokes of the wilderness, the preliminary trifling before the more serious onslaught which came in due course'.

Even as he was preparing to leave Europe, the international 'Brussels Conference relative to the Africa Slave Trade', which concluded in July 1890, was hammering out a statement declaring the Congo's slave trade illegal and making provisions for international co-operation in the area. Whatever Conrad expected on his departure, he was striking out for 'the dark places of the earth full of the habitations of cruelty'. His experience of the depths of rapacity, inhumanity, and cynicism was to alter his views of life for ever, and his contact with the climate permanently damaged his health.

In Bordeaux, a city prospering on the Africa trade, he shipped as a passenger on the *Ville de Maceio*, a steamer of Le Havre's Compagnie des Chargeurs Réunis (United Shipping Company) just beginning to serve western Africa as France's interests in the region expanded. The ship's rain-sodden leave-taking of Old Europe seemed a symbolic harbinger of things to come: 'Dismal day, a not very cheerful departure, some haunting memories, some vague regrets, some still vaguer hopes. One doubts the future.' After Tenerife in the Canaries, her first port of call, she bounced on and off the African mainland, proceeding to Grand Bassam on the Ivory Coast and the trading town of Grand-Popo in Dahomey before arriving in Libreville on the Gulf of Guinea. Making her way further down the Congo Free State's coastline, she then sailed about 60 miles up the Congo River to Boma, the state's administrative centre, docking there in mid-June. During the month-long trip, Conrad could not have misread the auguries. The torrid heat beat down as the ship crawled among the ramshackle ports dedicated to channelling inland goods, particularly ivory and rubber, to European markets hungry for them.

He had again taken *Almayer's Folly* with him, but whether he continued to work on it is unknown. Writing would have been a refuge from the company aboard – economic adventurers and free-wheeling daredevils. Disembarking from the *Ville de Maceio* at Boma, Conrad left the following day for Matadi, around 30 miles further upriver, the first step into what he would memorably call the 'Heart of Darkness'. Before taking that step, he unburdened himself in a long and sentimental letter to Poradowska. His extreme loneliness and sense of alienation are palpable: he kept a diary for the first and only time in his life. In its first, retrospective entry, he records reaching Matadi on 13 June. Here he encountered the first of a series of frustrations, and with respect to his later experience the partial solar eclipse visible there on the 17th seems signally apt. Delayed for a fortnight by the station chief, he had the unexpected compensation of meeting Roger Casement, the human rights activist later knighted and in time hanged for his involvement in the Irish cause, then also employed by a Thys interest, the Compagnie du Chemin de Fer du Congo (the Congo Railway Company).

Conrad and Casement worked together, rounding up labourers to build the railway. Conrad's diary describes Casement as well spoken, 'most intelligent and very sympathetic'. In the circumstances, cultivated company came as a surprise, but intelligent conversation proved a short-lived pleasure as Conrad soon took a 'very friendly' leave of Casement by the end of June, Casement leaving Matadi a few days before Conrad set out overland in a caravan of thirty-one porters. Prosper Harou, another Thys employee who had just returned to the Congo, accompanied him. Their goal, Léopoldville (now Kinshasa), involved a 230-mile trek in challenging conditions. Covering 10–12 miles a day, they were plagued by cold nights and by mosquitoes, despite its being the dry season. Harou, who fell ill, had to be carried for part of the journey. On 1 August, the day before it ended, Conrad recorded in his diary: 'Mosquitos [sic] – Frogs – Beastly. Glad to see the end of this stupid tramp. Feel rather seedy.'

Matters were not to improve. Conrad appears to have had an unpleasant initial encounter with his superior, Camille Delcommune, with whom he left the next day, continuing up the Congo in the *Roi des Belges* (King of the Belgians), a claptrap sternwheeler under the command of a twenty-four-year-old Dane, Ludvig Rasmus Koch. Three other company agents were on board, including one Alphonse Kayaerts (whose name Conrad recalled in the story 'An Outpost of Progress', and may have mutated into Kurtz in 'Heart of Darkness'). The ship's two dozen crew members were probably Bangala, a Bantu people from the river's upper reaches. In 'Heart of Darkness' the native crew are cannibals. Stories about this last taboo were rife, and the missionaries, who reported on it and on slavery, did little to conceal their horror and revulsion.

During the month-long voyage, undertaken to assist the ill-fated *Ville de Bruxelles*, a company sternwheeler that already had a history of troubles,* Conrad kept a log of the river's intricate navigational demands. Dry, factual, and exact, 'The Upriver Book' testifies to professional expertise; it also suggests he had plans to stay on with the

---

* The ship's fraught history suggests the difficulties European boats laboured under in Africa. Built in Belgium, the ship was reconstructed in Léopoldville and launched in July 1888. Inadequate isolation between the boiler and the wooden deck almost caused her to burn shortly after. Repaired, her planking began to rot, and with her caulking loosened she began taking on water; she was thereupon put in slip for two months for further repairs. Relaunched in late June 1890, by 18 July she was grounded and remained immobile for a considerable time.

Société, although he had already written to Bobrowski of his intense dissatisfaction. The diary covers more than half of the thousand-mile trip and then breaks off. Its sudden cessation has been variously interpreted. Was it caused by illness, the decision to leave the company's employ, or by news that he would be otherwise engaged? Perhaps he simply continued writing in another book, now long lost. The manuscript of *Almayer's Folly* had nearly fallen into the river as he was about to leave the Congo, and throughout Conrad's life both his manuscripts and his few family keepsakes had a tendency to disappear.

If not quite as nightmarishly as in 'Heart of Darkness', Conrad himself witnessed and heard of cruelty and barbarism, resulting partly from sheer incompetence and stupidity. The garden decorated by shrunken and dried human heads maintained by Captain Léon Rom of the *Force publique*, the security branch of King Léopold's enterprise, vividly suggests how degenerate some actors on this stage had become. Having suffered from fever on the trip upriver, Conrad was now felled by an attack of dysentery, followed by depression. He now thoroughly regretted his decision to come to Africa; was getting on badly with his employers, particularly with Delcommune; and saw no possibilities for advancement, or, indeed, even of any work that would draw on his professional training.

Captain Koch had, like Conrad, fallen ill, and on 6 September Delcommune temporarily relieved him of his duties, officially appointing Conrad, now in improved health, to the captaincy of the *Roi des Belges* pending Koch's recovery. The ship began her downriver journey shortly after Conrad took command, and his careful attention to navigating the river no doubt paid off, yet by the time the ship arrived at Léopoldville on the 24th, Koch had resumed his duties. Among the passengers on the return trip was a young man who died of dysentery three days before the ship docked on the 29th: Georges-Antoine Klein, the company's agent at Stanley Falls, was buried at Chumbiri, a typical village surrounded by palm forest and banana trees. A traveller's account published earlier in the same year presents it as prosperous and almost idyllic:

Palm trees abound, planted in avenues, and under their friendly shade are the huts of the natives, built in streets and open squares. These palm-forests, combined with graceful banana-trees of different hues, and occasional fan and borassus palms, form a beautiful picture in the strong, tropical sunlight . . . There is a great variety of food in this village – pumpkins, sweet potatoes, egg-fruit, bananas, plantains, palm nuts, palm wine, maize, peanuts, manioc; also many plants used by the natives as vegetables, most of them resembling spinach in flavour. Portions of old canoes turned upside down, and placed at right angles, with a grass roof over them, form seats and are used for native palavers, palm-wine drinking, and general places of assembly.

Dramatically reworked, Klein's death forms the climax of 'Heart of Darkness', with its famed pronouncement on genocide, atrocity, and the depths of human degradation: 'The horror! The horror!' Conrad, a creative magpie, later transmuted observed reality in his creative imagination. Several individuals have been proposed as models for Kurtz, who, an archetype and composite, was assembled from the scattered bits and pieces of things observed, read, and imagined. 'Heart of Darkness', a key work of literary Modernism, is not a documentary account of selected events witnessed by Conrad, and still less a work of social realism. The novella imaginatively recreates a historical moment when Death, accompanied by the Seven Deadly Sins, danced merrily over the length and breadth of Léopold II's Congo Free State. For Conrad, the work was also threnody for what little of his innocence remained to him.

He stayed in Léopoldville only long enough to write a few letters – 'Everything here is repugnant,' he told Poradowska; glimpse preparations for Alexandre Delcommune's exploratory expedition; and make some of his own for an expedition up the River Kassai. As it turned out, the company changed its plans, marking him out for more mundane tasks, less glorious and much in keeping with his previous assignments, such as packing ivory in casks, which he disliked: an 'Idiotic employment', as he calls it in his diary. He was sent by canoe to Bamou, a village 30 miles away and in French territory, 'to select wood and have it cut for the construction of the local station', a job slated to take a few weeks.

His hard-won credentials in the British Merchant Service counted for little, and his frustration was building even as fever and dysentery assailed him, this time more seriously, perhaps even threatening his life. By the end of October he was being carried in a hammock, as Harou had been, and by December he was back in Matadi, recovered but severely weakened both mentally and physically. Somehow he had got out of his three-year contract with the Belgians (the dissatisfaction was entirely mutual), and he was now looking forward to going home to England.

Nothing is known of his return journey, probably on a French steamer via Bordeaux as on his voyage out. By late January 1891 he was in London, apparently not yet settled as he was using Barr, Moering, & Company as his address. His health had improved sufficiently for him to seek out a job, but his experience in the Congo had not furthered his career, nor could he expect a glowing reference from his Belgian employers. In mid-February he cast his hopes on Antwerp, but a planned trip there with Fountaine Hope was first postponed and then cancelled. He next tried his luck in Scotland, perhaps aware of a specific position. If so, this came to naught.

Through Krieger, he was admitted to the German Hospital in Dalston in north London. Emotionally exhausted by the Congo fiasco, Conrad had also been dealt a blow by dysentery and fever, and, while a patient, he complained of stomach troubles and, apparently, rheumatism. Census Day, 5 April 1891, found his presence in the institution duly recorded, but Germanised as 'Johann [*sic*] Conrad', and given the incorrect age of thirty-two, 'Master Mariner', born in 'Poland, Russia'. In the year he was admitted for treatment, male patients vastly outnumbered female ones, and a sixth were designated as of 'Russian' origin. (Poles, not separately listed, presumably made up a significant proportion of the 'Russians'.) Conrad improved gradually, and in April could finally leave.

A claim that he became involved with a woman attached to the hospital and even fathered a son by her has not withstood investigation. Although he may have had unusually strong emotional needs after his brutal experience in Africa, it is doubtful that Conrad was in any condition, physical or psychological, for a love affair. His emotional life seems to have focused, platonically, on 'Tante [Aunt]

Marguerite', a revealing mode of address at once intimate and distancing. Upon recovering from her husband's death, Poradowska did not, in fact, lack admirers, principal among them Charles Buls, a member of Belgium's Chamber of Representatives and Brussels's burgomaster. But the nature of her relationship with Conrad has been the subject of speculation. A romantic entanglement has been concocted mainly out of a few jokey and vaguely misogynistic references to Poradowska in letters from Bobrowski (who seems altogether hostile to her); however, the supposed love affair was probably neither more, nor less, than a bond of affectionate friendship.

Conrad's physician, Dr (Rudolph) Gustav Ludwig recommended a water cure in Switzerland to his patient, but Conrad did not set out immediately. During this year he settled in at 17 Gillingham Street, which he shared with seven other boarders. His rooms, a few minutes' walk from Victoria station, served as his London base for the next six years. According to Booth's survey, the street was then 'Fairly respectable on north side east of Wilton Road: the west of the street notorious for brothels and by the Wilton Road prostitutes: also some drunk.' Writing of his intention to compose a letter one night in late August 1895, Conrad commented on 'the hot, noisy and dissipated night of my neighbourhood'. He had, it seems, exchanged 'darkest Africa' for 'darkest London'.

Still suffering from depression, he probably put aside *Almayer's Folly*, with lethargy and lack of concentration precluding serious work. Continuing frustration at the inability to find a position aggravated his mental condition; his finances were shaky; and he was in a period of drift. He decided to heed his doctor's advice, which Bobrowski supported, and arranged for hydropathic therapy, arriving in Champel-les-Bains on the outskirts of Geneva in mid-May. The choice was unfashionable: Carlsbad, Marienbad, and Davos were the playgrounds of the rich and ailing. He lodged at the Pension-Hôtel La Roseraie on the River Arve, favoured by those of more modest means. Maupassant, in the final stages of syphilis, arrived shortly after Conrad had left, and complained about the treatment he received: 'for a doctor I had the most pretentious and exploitative charlatan I have seen in my whole life . . . You have to commit for a month, and then he does not administer the showers himself, but brutes do. Everything in that mousetrap is got up in order to annoy and brutalise the patient.'

The rigours of the water cure, probably involving both hot and cold water douches as well as a strict diet, temporarily lifted his depression, and Conrad returned to *Almayer's Folly*, probably now reaching its seventh chapter of a final twelve. En route to London, he visited Poradowska in Paris's fashionable Passy, where she maintained an apartment. The flying visit surely casts cold water on speculation about a 'romance'. Had the relationship indeed been a romantic one, nothing prevented a longer stay. Once back home, Conrad looked for employment and was apparently offered a position in a steamer on the River Niger, where British trade interests were entrenched and growing. Given his mental and physical health and his body's response to the tropical climate, his decision to decline was wise, but it also meant falling back on his old friends, Hope and Krieger, to find work. He had earned nothing in the five months since his return from the Congo and called upon both Bobrowski and Krieger for financial help, receiving a loan from the latter.

He may have tried to make ends meet by doing some translating for an Oxford Street agency. Whatever its usefulness in teaching a fledgling writer discipline and craft and honing language and style, this work, often ill paid, could only have been a temporary solution to economic pressures, and Conrad began managing Barr, Moering's warehouse, a job arranged no doubt as a favour. The drudgery of this work was better than the work he had done in the Congo – at least in terms of psychological and physical stress – and he occupied himself by introducing a new system of bookkeeping and reorganising the storage system for the firm's straw plait warehouse, the material apparently used for packing. For a man of his training and intelligence it was frustrating and tedious work that little advanced his professional aspirations. It was simply a means of supplying necessities, another stopgap of which his life had been accumulating too many.

Joining Fountaine Hope for excursions on the Thames Estuary on his yawl, the *Nellie*, Conrad found relief from summer in London. Probably on one of these outings, Conrad, a gifted raconteur, regaled the company with his travails in Africa. The real-life audience ('Heart of Darkness' features a lawyer and an accountant) included Hope's friends Edward Gardner Mears, a meat merchandiser, who, like Conrad and Hope, had served in the *Duke of Sutherland*, and William Brock Keen, a chartered accountant in his mid-thirties.

Conrad's persistence in looking out for more suitable employment finally yielded results. A casual acquaintance of some years, Captain Walter Cope of the *Torrens*, required a first mate. As usual, the rank was below Conrad's qualifications, but the berth in a clipper renowned for her speed would liberate him from Barr, Moering and would at least draw on his professional expertise. It was, in fact, the best offer he had had for some time, and the association, although brief, proved rewarding. A passenger ship on the Plymouth to Adelaide route, the *Torrens* offered a different experience from any ship he had, in sailor parlance, 'belonged to'. He mixed with her passengers and struck up friendships, both passing and enduring. Almost equally novel is that Conrad got on well from the beginning with her no-nonsense captain.

The *Torrens* arrived in Adelaide on the last day of February 1892, a ninety-five-day trip far from her record of sixty-five days, set in 1880. The ship remained in port for a month, with Conrad 'terribly busy' yet afflicted by 'mental torpor'. He also made a professional gaffe, losing one of the ship's anchors during a manœuvre and entailing expense as a diver had to be hired to recover it. And it was here, not in Calcutta, as he misremembers in *A Personal Record*, that he received news that Adam Pulman had died on 30 January 1891: yet another tie to the past, however worn thin, had snapped. On her homeward voyage the *Torrens* called at Cape Town and St Helena, before arriving in London in early September. Either in port or on his way home, Conrad re-read Flaubert's *Madame Bovary*. His choice of reading is significant. *Almayer's Folly* was quietly simmering, and Flaubert's influence on it, not least in the treatment of its hero, a dreamer fatally at odds with himself and his circumstances, is great.

During the seven weeks he spent at home, Conrad claimed to be particularly busy, perhaps involved with the ship's business but also, possibly, on the lookout for a captaincy. (His association with the well-known *Torrens* would have stood him in good stead on the job market.) But again he left for Adelaide from Plymouth on 31 October. He seems to have relaxed into his chief officer's role. The most significant contact during this voyage out was with William Henry Jacques, a twenty-three-year-old with a first in Classics from Trinity College, Cambridge. Like many of the ship's passengers, he was going out 'for health' – in other words, he was a consumptive escaping the English winter. Before the ship passed the Cape of Good Hope, Conrad felt sufficiently friendly towards the young man to show him the manuscript of *Almayer's Folly*. His act was rewarded with precisely the understated encouragement he needed, and for all his retrospective down-pedalling of this event in *A Personal Record*, it was momentous in his artistic development. His self-confidence, keen for a sympathetic response, got the approbation it sought.

When the *Torrens* docked at Adelaide at the end of January 1893, Conrad, who had been ill during the voyage with 'Reminders of Africa', took a week's leave on 'higher ground', to benefit from the 'much cooler climate', the heat having once again affected a constitution weakened in the Congo. In port till mid-March, he was occupied with the ship's affairs. John Galsworthy, who joined her as a passenger to Cape Town, colourfully recalled his first sight of Conrad: 'He was engaged on "the weight of her burden" in other words "stowing cargo" and what with the heat, worry and dirt had the air of a pirate.' Lasting ties were established between the 'pirate' and the well-to-do graduate of Harrow and Oxford, who had recently been admitted to the Bar and was travelling to recover from a broken heart. Conrad also got to know Galsworthy's travelling companion, Edward ('Ted') Sanderson, who, like Jacques, had read Classics at Cambridge. Sanderson was returning home to become a schoolmaster in his clergyman father's school, Elstree, a small establishment combining, in the fashion of the time, sports, muscular Christianity, and an education in the Classics.

These friendships suggest Conrad's ease in associating with persons 'above his station', the attractions of his personality, and the beginning of his integration into middle-class English life by virtue of his impeccable manners, conversational skills, and wide reading. His *szlachta* origins had little purchase in Britain, and, professionally, he was a junior officer *in*, not the captain *of*, a crack ship. At the time, the social distance between men who had attended public schools and the ancient universities and those living in rented quarters near

Victoria station would have been nearly unbridgeable.* But by mid-May, when the *Torrens* docked at Cape Town and Galsworthy disembarked, a connection that led to later intimacy had been established, and Galsworthy would later, despite time and distance (with Conrad in Kent and Galsworthy often in Devon), remain especially close to Conrad, who wrote of him that he was the 'most steadfast, the most dependable, the most sympathetic of friends'.

Conrad himself seems to have had a gift or a knack for deep friendships that endured time, vicissitude, cantankerousness, and too great a readiness to be slighted. It is difficult to reconstruct the precise emotional tone of his attachments, the manly camaraderie of the late-Victorian and early modern periods appearing naïve and impossibly dated to our more knowing time. But in the Oxford and Cambridge of the 1890s, it was commonplace to see male undergrads walking arm in arm in the street, and swimming nude with a friend in the Isis or the Cam would not have raised an eyebrow. The most sensitive portrait of friendship in late-Victorian fiction is that in *Lord Jim*, where Marlow's concern about his 'very young brother', whose keeper he most certainly is, transcends a number of boundaries and arguably reveals its author more than his letters do. That friendship, begun suddenly and by chance, originates in the emotional borderland that Montaigne so touchingly summarises in his essay 'On Friendship': '*Par ce que c'estoit luy; par ce que c'estoit moy*' (Because he was he; because I was I), a 'reason' of the heart, as Pascal put it.

As the *Torrens* inched her way along the African coast, the crew provided entertainment at St Helena, the fun including a sketch called 'Soothing Syrup'. Within a fortnight of Conrad's signing off in London he was again on the move, travelling, via Berlin and Warsaw, to see Bobrowski. In the latter city, he chided some university students on their social-democratic sentiments. The visit at Kazimierówka lasted a month. He fell ill, but the nature of his ailment is unknown, and Bobrowski's health was possibly a cause for concern, for he was dead in less than six months.

---

* In April 1891, the lodgers at 17 Gillingham Street, where Conrad took rooms in September, included an architect's clerk, a printer's compositor, a tobacconist, a New-York-born general labourer, a clerk at an estate agent's, a clerk to a diamond merchant, and an Italian-born waiter.

Back in London, Conrad, as usual, was jobless, the *Torrens* having proved another cul-de-sac. Unless Captain Cope wished to abandon his prestigious berth, there was no opportunity for advancement. Yet Conrad had already established a pattern of overthrowing a secure berth for the unknown; given the condition of the labour market, this could be recklessness, but it derived from a deep-rooted need for change, and Conrad, as his history at Monte Carlo and his later keen interest in lotteries demonstrate, was a gambler. The next job that came his way was a stroke of luck. At the offices of the Shipmasters' Society, Captain Albert Froud, the Society's chairman, remembered that Conrad spoke French, and arrangements were made for him to take a berth as second mate (yet a further step down) in the *Adowa*, an old ship long active in the pilgrim trade in the Far East and with a history of being leaky. On this occasion she had been chartered to carry emigrants from France to Quebec City and Montreal. Conrad signed on in late November. Before the ship departed for Rouen, he caught up with Galsworthy, a sign that their friendship was developing. (Galsworthy claimed that they went to Covent Garden to see *Carmen* together, but there were no London performances between July and November 1893 so the evening at the opera must have occurred later.)

The month Conrad spent at Rouen was in part devoted to *Almayer's Folly*: he recalled writing aboard ship in the cold weather, almost unrelievedly cloudy until early January. A couple of days after the *Adowa* docked, French newspapers reported on anarchist activity in London. The police had discovered one Snyder, an American described as a 'traveller in explosives', in Hampstead in possession of several pounds of nitro-glycerine and dynamite The news caused consternation in the City. On the 9th, there was a dynamite attack on the French Chamber of Deputies, and anarchist activities figured in the news almost daily throughout Conrad's time in France. To Poradowska, he claimed that he himself had been involved in a nasty altercation when trying to collect a parcel from her containing her latest novel, *Le Mariage du fils Grandsire* (1894), at Rouen's railway station. The uncooperative clerk (a model French official), his feathers ruffled, accused Conrad of being a bomb-carrying anarchist, and shouted for help. The tone of Conrad's letter suggests that the story might be a playful invention got up to amuse his correspondent and relieve his boredom. In an earlier letter, although rather more clearly in a spirit of fun, he told Poradowska that he had mugged a man in the street. On the day the *Adowa* left port, the man responsible for the attack on the Chamber of Deputies, Auguste Vaillant, was condemned to death.

Mostly content to remain at home, the French did not join in the waves of European emigrants flooding into North America, and by mid-December the Compagnie Franco-Canadienne was in litigation. Conrad, with time on his hands, could have visited Rouen's cafés or attended the opera: *Carmen*, Meyerbeer's *Le Prophète* and *L'Africaine*, and Gounod's *Faust* were all playing at the Théâtre des Arts. He became friendly with the ship's first mate, William Paramor, remaining in contact with him for some years, and also got on with another shipmate, Richard Cole, whose banjo-playing he recalls in *A Personal Record*. The *Adowa* made her way back to London empty, and it is tempting to view this fiasco as a symbol, for, as it turned out, Conrad's time in her was his last service at sea; hardly, in fact, 'at sea' since he spent most of it moored in port.

Given his employment history and the fact that, although a captain, he had shipped in the *Adowa* as second mate, Conrad must have paused to take stock of his situation. The prospects of a long-distance voyage seemed unappealing – he had applied for some kind of job at Suez (which came to nothing) – and he was again unemployed and back in his poky rooms in Gillingham Street. Looked at directly, most of his successes had been qualified triumphs. The dedication to *The Mirror of Sea*, which recalls 'the first dark days of my parting with the sea', succinctly but powerfully suggests his emotions at this time. Beneath the conventional phrasing are hints of depression, self-doubt, and worry. He was putting behind him for ever what he calls 'my great passion for the sea': 'I call it great because it was great to me. Others may call it a foolish infatuation. Those words have been applied to every love story. But whatever it may be the fact remains that it was something too great for words.' And as at any passion's end, there must have been, both now and later, regrets and nostalgia. Conrad's feelings are typically couched in a rhetoric that dissuades intimacy, but his emotions on leaving something loved, familiar, and hard won evidently lingered.

And the days to come were darker still. In early February 1894, news of Tadeusz Bobrowski's death, at the age of sixty-three, was sent by telegram from the Ukraine. Conrad now lost his last significant tie to the past and to his former homeland, and after his uncle's death he never again returned to the Ukraine. He grieved in solitude. A journey was not apparently on the cards: his finances were stretched, and Bobrowski had left his own affairs in good order. Conrad inherited the equivalent of roughly a year's income. The spiritual legacy Bobrowski left to his nephew was larger, more various, and, ultimately, is difficult to assess from a few handfuls of yellowing documents.

When Conrad called on Poradowska in Brussels in March, this time it was he who was grieving. On this visit they attended the first Belgian production of Wagner's *Tristan und Isolde*, sung in French. He almost certainly went with Poradowska, who was interested in music and later wrote on Chopin. Another significant visit, perhaps likewise recuperative, was to Sanderson at Elstree. Conrad had been before, encountering a boisterous 'English' atmosphere fomented by the twenty-seven-year-old Ted's numerous brothers and sisters almost all in their teens. (Ted was the eldest of the Sandersons' fourteen children.) Ted's friend was introduced to the schoolmasters, and got on particularly well with Ted's mother, Katherine, 'Miss Kitty', attractive, vivacious, and high-spirited, with whom he also shared the manuscript of *Almayer's Folly*, Ted having read it on the *Torrens*. Friendly advice was offered on certain points of English usage, and Conrad began the novel's last chapter during the visit. If, as the opening of *A Personal Record* claims, 'Books may be written in all sorts of places', there remains a certain incongruity in Conrad's drafting a chapter about the disintegration of Almayer's family in the congenial atmosphere of Elstree. At the time he was also establishing a friendship with his Ted's sister Agnes, then about nineteen. Teasing banter played a large role in the friendship, evidence of his further assimilation into middle-class English life, and he and Agnes Sanderson remained in contact until his death.

As technological advances drastically cut the manpower required in ships and as sail gave way to steam during the 1880s and early 1890s,

Conrad was entering the writer's market at a time of upheaval and change. Reforms in Victorian education had created a new mass literacy, and the audience for fiction, both at the market's highbrow and at its gutter ends, had expanded dramatically. In 1891, the Chace Act put an end to the literary piracy in the American market that had so outraged Dickens, establishing an international copyright convention between Britain and the United States. Literary magazines, eager for copy, were sprouting to meet demand, and the literary agent, a new phenomenon, was altering the way business was done. While the changes taking place at sea were to Conrad's disadvantage, he was to profit – in due course handsomely – from those occurring on the London publishing scene.

He sent his first novel to the publisher T. F. Unwin in early July, with a hopeful, if diffident, covering letter. There are two versions of why he chose Unwin: in the one he had passed by the publisher's premises near Paternoster Square and, seeing slim volumes in the display window, thought his own would fit in; in the other, recounted by Ford Hueffer* to Arnold Bennett, he noticed a volume of the Pseudonym Library on sale in Vevey, Switzerland, and was inspired to write. He may have solicited the Sandersons' advice. However that may be, the firm, with a diverse list – travel writing, popular novels, serious works, and the 'exotic' – was to prove an inspired choice. In 1895, the Pseudonym Library, a series of short works established by Unwin and overseen in part by his reader Edward Garnett, boasted Yeats's poems, Louis Becke's collection of South Sea stories *By Palm and Reef*, Mimosa's *Told on the Pagoda: Tales of Burmah*, George Gissing's *Sleeping Fires* – and Joseph Conrad's *Almayer's Folly*.

Conrad proved a nervous 'father' to his novel after he delivered the manuscript. As he waited to hear from Unwin's, his health took a downturn, partly owing to anxieties about placing his book, and he decided to return to Champel for another water cure. Clutching

---

* Born Ford Herman Hueffer, this individual went under the name Ford Madox Hueffer until 1919 when he changed his name to Ford Madox Ford. He is referred to here as Hueffer, the name under which he was published and by which he was known publicly and to his friends until 1919. In the Notes, references to Conrad's letters to him are referenced to 'Ford', the editors of *The Collected Letters* having used that surname to refer to him throughout their edition.

desperately at straws, he suggested to Poradowska that she translate *Almayer's Folly* into French and that it appear under the name 'Kamudi' (Malay for 'rudder'). He left London not knowing the book's fate. By the time he returned to Gillingham Street in early September, he had begun a short story, again set in distant Borneo. Then called 'Two Vagabonds', it was an embryonic version of *An Outcast of the Islands*, his second novel. He had enjoyed reading Maupassant in Switzerland, but was now hunting for a job even as *Almayer's Folly* was making its way through Unwin's. In a fit of anxiety, he wrote to the publisher asking if the manuscript had been received. Unwin himself was abroad at the time, but there had been two positive reports, the first by Wilfred Chesson, who forwarded it with a recommendation, to his colleague Edward Garnett.

Both men, steeped in literature, were well connected in the literary scene. W. H. Chesson wrote reviews and fiction. (Unwin published his novel *Name this Child* in 1894.) Like Chesson, Garnett reviewed for the literary papers, and, in common with many cogs in the publishing machine, nursed diverse and never entirely fulfilled literary ambitions. His wife, Constance, translated Turgenev, Chekhov, Tolstoy, and Dostoevsky, and he kept his heavily spectacled eyes focused on happenings in the world of letters. More sympathetic readers would have been hard to find, and Garnett's immediate response on reading the manuscript was 'Hold on to this'. The firm took this advice, and in early October offered Conrad £20 (about £8,600) for the book's copyright. A few days later the new author called at Unwin's offices at 11 Paternoster Row in the City, near St Paul's, where he met Chesson and Garnett, who complimented him so 'effusively' that he doubted their sincerity. He was then ushered into Unwin's presence.

Conrad later confided to Garnett that his first step into the literary world was 'as inviting as a peep into a brigand's cave and a good deal less reassuring'. He explains no further why he felt so intimidated, but he was again changing identities and, as his occasional search for a berth over the next year or so suggests, was going through a transitional period, during which he was still emotionally attached to the sea, and, not surprisingly, unsure about his prospects as a writer. His father's success had been modest, and Poradowska's writings and translations brought her a certain amount of recognition not only in Paris, but also in Poland. But, as far as we know, Conrad at this stage had no connections in literary London; no friends in England who wrote for a living, either journalism or fiction; and probably had only a vague knowledge of publishing practices. He had read Dickens and Trollope and, aboard ship, had become acquainted with the work of Henry James and Israel Zangwill; he had a pronounced interest in travel writing and memoirs. But, like any reader, he would have gained little insight into how books made their way into print. Brigands or not, publishers and their ways would mainly have been a mystery to him.

A closer relationship between Conrad and Garnett began within a month or so of their introduction, when they met at the handsomely appointed National Liberal Club in Whitehall, under Unwin's auspices. Unwin talked about politics and current 'house' writers, 'John Oliver Hobbes' (Mrs Pearl Craigie) and S. R. Crockett, both then well regarded, if now only brief entries in reference books. Garnett spoke encouragingly, even with ardour, and the new author and the publisher's reader strolled as far as the Strand before parting.

Conrad's other significant acquaintance at about this time was Jessie George, the woman he would later marry. She was then twenty-one years old (thus sixteen years his junior), and was working in the City for the American Writing Machines Company.* According to one of her later accounts, she met her future husband through Fountaine and Ellen Hope; in a subsequent retelling, she met the Hopes only *after* her engagement. According to Ellen Hope, she and her husband had known Jessie when she was a child. And yet another version of the first meeting is George family legend: she fell on an icy road, and Conrad, who happened to be passing by, gallantly put her in a cab and took her home.

The only certain evidence is found in an inscribed copy of *Almayer's Folly* dated 2 April 1895; the gift makes her a close friend of

---

* Conrad's previous biographers have followed him in giving her employment as a typist ('typewriter', as the term then was), but the 1895 *Postal Guide to London* indicates that the company she worked for was a manufacturer of Caligraph typewriters, not a typing agency. Mrs Nina Hayward, who lived with Jessie Conrad in the 1920s, recalled her aunt as 'a two-finger typist', and doubted she had professional training. Her statements are bolstered by the fact that the typescripts that Jessie Conrad typed for her husband display a barely adequate and, more often than not, poor typist at work.

Conrad's by that date. The other known facts are that when Conrad met Jessie George she was living with her large family in Camberwell, south of the Thames, a mainly lower-middle and working-class area, once a village but by the mid-Victorian era part of London's commuter belt as the city, hungry for labour, grew and prospered in the course of the Industrial Revolution. Jessie George's background was solidly working-class on both sides. Her maternal great-grand-father, John Nash Sex was a bricklayer; his son, John James, earned his livelihood as a plasterer. John Nash Sex, the first of the name, was base born in 1792. At the time, it was customary for an illegitimate child to bear both the father's and mother's name, the mother's being dropped when the couple married, but John Nash Sex's parents never did so and the double name continued in use. The Nash Sexs had roots in the Surrey village of Shere, on the edge of the North Downs about 6 miles from Guildford, but drifted to Lambeth in the great population migration into London and its outlying villages that took place in the nineteenth century. A painter and glazier, Thomas George, Jessie George's paternal grandfather, born about 1806, fathered eight children. His father, Richard (born around 1775) had been a baker. Family legend has it that the family is of Huguenot descent, tracing its origins to the French Protestants who arrived in England in several waves after the revocation of the Edict of Nantes in 1685. The name was possibly originally 'Georges' before under-going Anglicisation, although the surname also appears without the terminal 's' in Huguenot records.

One of nine children, Jessie George was helping out her widowed mother when she and Conrad met, her father, Alfred Henry George, a publisher's warehouseman, having died suddenly, aged forty-seven, about two years previously. Having returned home on the night of 18 February 1892, after singing at a private party (his fine tenor voice supplemented his income) he was discovered dead on the first floor of his house by his wife, Jane. A slightly built man, he was physically unsuited to his job, which had ruined his health. The official cause of death was 'acute pulmonary congestion and syncope', the latter a failure of the heart to supply oxygen to the brain (commonly the result of lowered blood pressure). Placing stress on his lungs may well have aggravated a latent condition. As to the family he left behind, it is known that Jessie George had received some education – the 1881 Census, taken when she was eight, lists her as attending school – and the George family clung to 'respectability', her sister Florence teaching piano and her brother Alfred working as a wine merchant's assistant to make ends meet. Contrary to many claims, including that of Henry James to Lady Ottoline Morrell, Jessie Conrad was not a Roman Catholic, nor were her parents, who married in Lambeth's parish church. (Several of her siblings did turn to Rome, and one of her brothers studied for the priesthood, but her mother converted only on her deathbed.)

As Conrad's circle widened, 'Two Vagabonds' grew from a short story into a novel. This sustained period of creativity tends to suggest a degree of emotional stability. Even as Conrad announced to friends the 'big news' that he had a first novel coming out, he still continued to search for a job at sea. The new author had made at least one further call at Paternoster Row, for by the new year of 1895 he was on sufficiently friendly terms with Garnett to invite him to dine at a restaurant in Wilton Street, followed by conversation in his nearby flat. The transition from seaman to writer, although undramatic, was firmly under way, the exact moment when the one life ended and the other began impossible to pinpoint.

The publisher's reader and the firm's new author got on well, sharing several intellectual interests and mutually enjoying the mentor–protégé relationship they quickly fell into. Conrad's 'foreignness' proved a draw. Constance Garnett had travelled to Russia to improve her command of the language and when her husband and Conrad met she was putting the finishing touches to her translation of Turgenev's *On the Eve* and starting work on *Fathers and Sons*. Both Garnetts were interested in things 'Slavic', Constance, in an unconventional marriage, taking her interest so far as to be in love with Sergei Stepniak, a prominent revolutionary and writer. Conrad would eventually rebel against his friend's tendency to pigeonhole him as a Slav, insisting upon a Western European cultural identity. He once told Garnett that he was so Russianised that 'you don't know the truth when you see it – unless it smells of cabbage-soup when it at once secures your profoundest respect'. Despite his and his wife's 'leftist' leanings (Constance was active in the Fabian Society and, before her marriage, had worked as a librarian at 'The People's Palace' in Whitechapel), Garnett had impeccable establishment credentials: his father was a translator and essayist and Assistant Keeper of Books at the British Museum and his grandfather a distinguished philologist. Having lost Bobrowski, Conrad had found a 'Father in Letters', even though the surrogate father was a decade younger than he was. Confident of his tastes and knowledgeable about the publishing business, Garnett was an ideal mentor, supportive rather than flattering, and his astute critical skills led to his discovery of several new talents. To call him, as Ford Madox Ford did, 'the literary dictator of London' is wholly to misread his manner of recognising and teasing out potential: instead, he acted as a subtle influence, making judicious suggestions, weighing carefully, and setting but not imposing standards.

The friendship developed rapidly, and its business aspects proved advantageous to Conrad. Authorship now involved him in writing a preface to his first novel, possibly solicited by Garnett but in any case by Unwin's. (The piece was eventually dropped, and remained unpublished until 1920.) There was also proof-reading, a new task, involving not only correcting misprints but also, in a more 'gentlemanly' age of publishing, rewriting, sometimes extensive. Conrad now seems to have devoted himself seriously to composition. When Garnett visited his 'snug bachelor quarters' in Gillingham Street in January 1895, he was shown the manuscript of 'Two Vagabonds', which by February had already reached its tenth chapter – an astonishing contrast to the snail-like progress of *Almayer's Folly*. Bobrowski's legacy was giving Conrad both time and the sense of a breathing space.

Nevertheless, Conrad experienced a bout of depression and cancelled plans for a proposed trip to Newfoundland, possibly on some speculation involving his inheritance. Instead he visited Brussels in early March, staying at the Hôtel Royal Nord (not at Poradowska's home). Although literary topics had long been part of their extensive correspondence, he could now meet Poradowska as a fellow author, with one book in proof and another in progress. He continued to discuss with her the possibility of her translating *Almayer's Folly* into

French. Having sold the novel's copyright to Unwin, he retained only the book's translation rights. The arrangement proved to have greater sentimental than economic value: the first translation, into Danish, did not appear until 1916, the first French translation three years after that, and a Polish translation only in 1923. Progress on 'Two Vagabonds' continued.

Almayer's Folly was published on 29 April 1895, an unpropitious moment. The attention of literary London was focused upon Oscar Wilde, who soon after losing his libel case against the Marquess of Queensberry, was arrested, charged with gross indecency with other male persons, and on the 26th of the month was in the dock at the Old Bailey. His name was stricken from the playbill of his new comedy, *The Importance of Being Earnest*.

Almayer's Folly was well and – for a first novel by a wholly unknown writer – widely reviewed. For all his personal abrasiveness, Unwin pushed his authors, to their advantage and, of course, to his. In an unsigned notice in the *Saturday Review*, extracted by Unwin's for an advertisement in *The Times*, H. G. Wells described the story as 'powerful' and declared boldly that the novel would 'certainly secure Mr. Conrad a high place among contemporary story-tellers'. Wells's adjective 'powerful' was recurrent: the *Academy*'s reviewer found that 'The book leaves an impression of grasp and power'; the *Scotsman*'s commented that the story was 'powerfully imagined'; and the *Bookman*'s judged Conrad a 'powerful' painter of setting, if a somewhat less successful one with regard to character. The narrative's laboured development and the exotic locale – Kipling's name was inevitably invoked – were criticised, but Henry Norman's review in the *Daily Chronicle* (anonymous like the vast majority at the time) alone ought to have offered all the encouragement a fledgling author might want: 'Mr. Conrad may go on, and with confidence: he will find his public, and he deserves his place.' Sniffing out the reviewer's identity, or hearing it on the literary grapevine, Conrad sent Norman a letter of thanks.

Almayer's Folly appeared in the United States a few days after it came out in England. It was published by Macmillan of New York in a print run of no more than 650 copies. The processes involved in placing it are undocumented, but Unwin's was probably responsible for arrangements. This modest beginning in America was not a harbinger of things to come: in due course, but only after a decade and more, this market became extremely important financially to Conrad, as it did to other British writers of the period. In America, as in England, Conrad's early work appeared under several imprints. Serialisation, as much a force in publishing as it had been for the great Victorian novelists, was in Conrad's case often subject to separate negotiations, a work either appearing through a publisher's house journal (or *de facto* house journal) or hawked to the highest bidder. Only Conrad's first two novels did not appear as serials, a mode of publication that could impact significantly on a work's evolution, as famously occurred with *Lord Jim*, the novel evolving and expanding even as it was appearing in *Blackwood's* monthly issues.

The new author ought to have been pleased by the reviews of *Almayer's Folly*, but public recognition that he had made the right choice of a new career came too late to stave off a bout of depression so severe that he decided to go to Champel to rid himself of it. He arrived in early May via Neuchâtel, apparently not stopping in Paris en route to see Poradowska. Again putting up at La Roseraie, he soon befriended the Briquels, a well-to-do French family from Lunéville, near Nancy, with whom he discussed his literary tastes and ambitions. Paul, then eighteen, had literary interests, and even sought out possible epigraphs for the evolving 'Two Vagabonds'. Conrad's closer friendship with twenty-year-old Émilie developed rapidly, and hydropathic sessions were punctuated by excursions into town. Conrad displayed his nautical skills on Lake Geneva; they chatted at breakfast and dinner in English and French; and played croquet, dominoes, and billiards. She sang and played the violin and piano for him, Conrad turning the pages as she made her way through period favourites. The planned three weeks at Champel became a month's stay, and the Briquels seemed to have been charmed by their new novelist friend, from whom Mademoiselle Émilie had received a dedicated copy of *Almayer's Folly*.

Conrad promised to see Poradowska on his way home, but if he did, his stay was short: leaving Champel on the 30th, he was in London by 4 June. On his return, he called on the Sandersons, perhaps a refuge from financial worries; considerable losses on an investment precipitated his return. The fiasco, known only from Émilie Briquel's diary and echoed in the words 'many worries' in a letter to Poradowska, cannot be fleshed out. Any blow to Conrad's pocket was serious: he had drawn his last regular salary in the *Adowa* a year and a half before, and his earning powers as a writer were untried.

He seems now to have flirted with Émilie Briquel, who initially was taken with him, the affection passing almost as rapidly as it had begun. The little of her diary in print suggests that she was a fairly typical product of her class and time. She possessed the usual parlour accomplishments; was taking English lessons; was well brought up; and had an eye for the conventions. She comes across as impressionable and perhaps slightly empty-headed. Older gentlemen with impeccable manners, a cultivated air, and engaged in intellectual and artistic pursuits have never lacked an audience, perhaps not large but sufficient, among a certain class of well-bred woman.

Should Conrad have truly felt inclined to marry her, what were the impediments? The family liked him. Some excursions with Émilie had been with *maman* as chaperon; Paul, the future poet, and he had discussed literature. His finances, however, would not bear much scrutiny, and whatever the charms of the gentleman from London with a published novel to his name, this may have proved a stumbling-block. The provincial family may, on the other hand, already have fixed upon a suitable local boy. Conrad mentioned a possible visit to Lunéville in the autumn, but he seems to have got cold feet about the connection. Émilie's diary repeatedly indicates that she thought of him as a 'friend'. Perhaps both gave off mixed signals. Whatever the real nature of the relationship, it soon petered out, and in early 1896, Émilie Briquel married a twenty-nine-year-old doctor, Edmond Lalitte.

Conrad makes no mention of Briquel in his letters from Switzerland to Poradowska, but the degree of his closeness to his 'Aunt' is as uncertain as events in Geneva. Because they no longer exist, it has been assumed that Poradowska 'destroyed' his letters to her from June 1895 to 1900. Any correspondence relating to an emotional disappointment is, however, unlikely to have extended much beyond early 1896, when Conrad married. Why, then, should Poradowska 'destroy' his letters up to 1900? If there were hurt and anger, perhaps they broke off writing for five years. But – and this seems the likeliest of the various alternatives – these letters may simply have disappeared as Poradowska moved back and forth between Paris and Brussels (to say nothing of Marseilles, where she occasionally wintered), or have been lost after her death. Conrad's letters to Bobrowski, an invaluable witness to his early adulthood, were burnt when Kazimierówka went up in flames in the First World War, and his letters to his friend Perceval Gibbon were destroyed during the Nazi occupation of the Channel Islands.

Another presumed affair of the heart, or flirtation, dates roughly to this time. Conrad had maintained friendly relations with Arthur Burroughs, an apprentice in the *Tilkhurst*, now a captain, and visited his home at 3 Alfred Terrace in Camberwell. In the mid-1890s, the twenty-five-year-old sailor was living with his widowed mother Louisa, then in her early fifties. Conrad, who struck up a friendship with her, also supposedly showed interest in a family friend, a seventeen-year-old named Ida Knight. Meanwhile, Louisa Burroughs's sister, Annette, became attracted to the sailor-writer. Jealous ructions broke out, and Conrad quit the scene.

Amidst these emotional ups and downs is an obvious desire for attachment and grounding. Although in his mid-thirties, Conrad's romantic history seems nearly to have been a blank. By his own account, there was a schoolboy crush in Lemberg; there just may have been a romantic flutter in Marseilles (not, however, with Victor Chodźko's married sister); there were the Alice Shaw and Eugénie Renouf fiascos in Mauritius; an affair at the German Hospital seems improbable; and he had met Jessie George, with whom at this stage he enjoyed – if the Briquel episode is anything to go by – a friendship, not a romantic involvement. On the whole, his preference seems to have inclined towards younger women. But all this is inference and guesswork. The meaning of the idyll in Champel is hard to read; the story about Ida Knight sounds like mere gossip.

To his friends, Conrad was 'the single gentleman'. Krieger had three children; Hope had four. In his late twenties, Ted Sanderson was unmarried, quite usual for someone of his class. (He was to wed in 1898.) Galsworthy, who had gone on his Pacific travels to recover from an unhappy love affair, lived a tortured romantic life, being in love with his first cousin's wife, Ada Pearson. Garnett, not yet a true intimate, was married and had a three-year-old boy, David, the future novelist. In 1895, Conrad's entanglements finally augured, like Shakespeare's Benedict, the prospect of 'Conrad the married man'.

At the time when romance, or something resembling it, entered Conrad's life story, his imagination was deeply engaged with a character locked in an unhappy marriage to a drab wife whom he believes to be beneath him. In escaping her, he becomes entangled with a *femme fatale* in the remotest Bornean jungles, a black widow spider who lures him to his death. Peter Willems's uncontrollable erotic impulses lead him to debauchery, oblivion, and extinction. If that sacred – and much sentimentalised – cow of the Victorian middle class, 'the family', comes off badly, disintegrating in *Almayer's Folly*, in *An Outcast* the conjugal state is one of shared psychosis. The novel also deals with dishonesty, betrayal, and a benevolent father figure's abandonment and rejection of a wayward adoptive son. Conrad's personal preoccupations are much in evidence.

As 'Two Vagabonds' advanced, Conrad took a break for a fortnight's sailing with Hope in the Channel and the North Sea. He was also caught up in business partly for or with Hope, who had investments and financial commitments in South Africa, where he had worked. After his holiday, Conrad shuttled between Paris and London several times to attend to these. It is uncertain what exactly he was up to, and we do not know if he took time off to see Poradowska. He signed a contract with Unwin for his second novel, now well advanced, and was in all probability planning a third. That work, *The Sisters* (an alternate title was *Thérèse*) proved a false start, and Conrad wisely abandoned it on Garnett's advice but not before it had taken up time and energy. Ford Madox Ford's summary of what the novel was to have been is illuminating:

Stephen was to have met, fallen in love with and married the elder sister. The younger sister, failing in the religious vocation that her uncle the priest desired her to have was to come to Paris and to stay with the young couple in Stephen's pavilion, the tyrannous character of her aunt being such that she could not live with the orange merchant and his wife. The elder sister proving almost equally domineering Stephen was to fall before the gentler charm of the younger. And the story was to end with the slaying of both the resulting child and the mother by the fanatic priest.

Adding the requisite pound of salt to what Ford has to say on almost all matters relating to Conrad, this unpromising melodramatic material, even if we know only the partial truth about it, suggests why Conrad eventually abandoned the work.

After returning the proofs of *An Outcast*, Conrad continued to look for employment in shipping, but he had been away from the sea for some time; job opportunities had, if anything, worsened; and he was already shuffling off his identity as a seaman. The following extremely important months of his life are poorly documented. In mid-December, he was planning a trip to Paris over Christmas to see Poradowska; if this did come off, he was back in town by the end of the year, sending conventional New Year's greetings to Émilie Briquel, who, married in early February 1896, had already engaged her heart elsewhere.

4

Husband and Writer
(1896–1898)

Conrad proposed to Jessie George on a January morning in 1896 on the steps of the National Gallery, perhaps an appropriate location for a novelist then writing about a painter. Lunch followed her acceptance, and the engaged couple then went their separate ways, apparently both somewhat shaken. Jessie's confused version of the event (all we have to go by) claims that the proposal occurred after Conrad had spent a month in Champel, a trip that is supported by no other evidence and probably in fact was his Christmas trip to Paris. According to Jessie, the proposal was unexpected; Conrad insisted that the wedding take place quickly, revealed that he was in poor health with little time to live, and said that there could be no children. It is difficult to take much of this as a record of fact, but Conrad may have proposed awkwardly and become emotionally muddled.

The Briquel episode suggests confidence in the motions of court-liness, and Conrad's impeccable manners are a constant thread in observations about him. At this crucial moment, however, some gauche fumbling would perhaps be unsurprising. Given his tendency to self-protectiveness, his reasons for wanting to marry at all are unknown. He may – the usual reason – have been in love; he may have felt social pressures to do so, for then as now most people marry; he may have been lonely. He had no family ties and had formed only a few close connections with men (Hope and Krieger, notably), not, with the exceptions of Galsworthy and Sanderson, his intellectual or cultural equals. (Garnett, to whom he was growing closer, was still no more than an acquaintance.) Having been orphaned at a young age, Conrad may also have needed mothering, not a wholly unusual need in hypersensitive men, who can thus relax into a state of dreamy unconcern in which the world's pressures can be escaped – at least for brief periods. He already had well-established patterns of dependence, and may have sensed Jessie George's motherly impulses. He could not have been unaware of her experience as sometime surrogate mother to her siblings. The second girl of a large family, maternal duties would have devolved on her as a matter of course, even more so after her father's death as Jane George faced bringing up several young children alone. Jessie Conrad's confession late in her life, 'I am very *motherly*', can be taken largely at face value. This aspect of the Conrads' married life grew as time passed – after visiting the Conrads in 1913, Lady Ottoline Morrell pronounced Jessie Conrad a 'reposeful mattress' – but its seeds may have been present early, even in their courtship.

The Mauritius episode offers a precedent for the choice of a younger, non-intellectual wife; the Briquel one confirms a taste for a younger woman. Being the older, more educated partner allows one to remain 'in charge'. But the question 'Why Jessie George?' so frequently asked in writing about Conrad's life is, like many, unanswerable. Perhaps Conrad's 'eligibility' ought to be the real question: from the George family's perspective he was 'a foreigner', not gainfully employed, and had a long history of bad health and nervous problems, some of which he revealed to his prospective spouse.

Conrad went to Grangemouth, Scotland, with Jessie George and Fountaine Hope in mid-February, accompanied by Jessie's twenty-five-year-old sister Ethel as chaperon, to inspect a ship he was thinking of buying. The plan, which hints that Conrad and his wife might go to sea in some kind of business venture, fell through, and soon a prolonged honeymoon in Brittany, perhaps a prelude to a longer period in France, was being prepared. Probably chosen for reasons of economy, the destination also offered proximity to the sea.

An Outcast of the Islands, dedicated to Ted Sanderson, no doubt in recognition of the encouragement Conrad had received from the entire family at Elstree, came out in early March 1896. The publication of a second novel represented a commitment to writing, signalling more clearly than *Almayer's Folly* the transition from a seaman who 'writes' to a professional who earns his living by doing so. Conrad was carving out new territory: in the growing body of 'exotic' and Orientalist fiction, the distant Malay world had remained *terra incognita*, and the novel found immediate critical recognition. This time even the word 'genius' was used, and the reviews were of a kind that should have encouraged any writer. There were predictions of bright hopes – 'we shall be surprised if Mr. Conrad does not make a name for himself in the near future' – comparisons with Kipling (again), and the word 'power' recurred. There were also strictures. The influential editor T. P. O'Connor, writing for the *Weekly Sun* (a paper he founded), mixed praise with blame: 'If it be possible to, at the same time, pare down his redundancies, avoid over-emphasis, and retain all the vigour, glow, and poetry of his writing, Mr. Conrad may do far greater things than anything he has yet done.' However gladdened by these compliments, Conrad wisely did not close his eyes to the less flattering comments: 'there is plenty of criticism also. They find it too long, too much description, – and so on. Upon the whole I am satisfied.' And well he might have been, but his current rate of progress was troubling, and he became aware that he had taken a wrong turn. According to his version of events, he abandoned *The Sisters* about this time, 'scared off it thinking it out ahead, one winter evening, alone in my lodgings'.

His other major decision was already taken. He married Jessie George at the St George Hanover Square Registry Office, on Tuesday, 24 March 1896, a day Conrad remembered as 'sunny'. Hope, Krieger, and Jessie's mother, Jane George, acted as witnesses. The choice of a civil ceremony suggests how far Conrad had travelled from his 'Pole-Catholic' inheritance: not only had he taken up a new nationality, he had jettisoned the religion that had come with his birth. His change of status was celebrated modestly, with lunch at 'a little café in Victoria' (that is, close to Gillingham Street) followed by a celebratory and farewell call on the George family in Camberwell, and dinner at Overton's near Victoria. Seen off by Jessie's mother at Victoria station, the newlyweds spent the first full day of their married life in trains and aboard boats travelling, via Southampton, to Saint-

Malo. After an appalling crossing, the Conrads made their way to Lannion, a quiet town nestled in the Léguer Valley between the Côte de Granit Rose and the Côte des Bruyères. A hotel served as a temporary halting-place while they sought out accommodation.

For Conrad, the move to France was a return to familiar things: the French language and the sea. The regional specialities (lobster, scallops, and other seafood) would have tempted his refined palate, even if they lacked the richness of the food he had grown used to in Marseilles. For Jessie, all this would have been entirely unfamiliar, and it was a period of adjustment for them both as the realities of a shared existence took hold. An only child and an orphan, Conrad had to learn to share by dint of circumstance: he had lived in tight quarters aboard ship and in spartan and close ones in various Sailors' Homes, but sharing his life in this intimate way required adjustments.

Soon after the Conrads arrived, Jessie fell ill. The event unsettled Conrad, whose description of the event to the motherly Katherine Sanderson is curious: 'I am glad to say your first letter to me as a married man and done for has not miscarried. I had it one day after dispatching to you my dismal note with the news of Jessie's indisposition . . . I would not go through such [*sic*] three days again for a diamond mine!' Horribly scared, he had to offer 'proofs' of his 'nursing qualifications'. He seems to have had an attack of panic, little justified by his wife's simply feeling 'somewhat unwell for three days', as he related to Garnett. He indicates the nature of this illness no more precisely, and one wonders if Conrad was suffering belated second thoughts while caring for a sick woman he was just getting to know, or if she had had a miscarriage (a word used, though in a different sense, in his letter). If indeed his wife miscarried, this might account for the hasty, somewhat fumbling proposal and the long honeymoon abroad.

The small house the Conrads rented on Île-Grande (despite its name not, in fact, an island) was 'all kitchen downstairs and all bedroom upstairs', and spacious compared to Conrad's Gillingham Street lodgings. For his south-London-born wife, whose first trip abroad it doubtless was, the whole experience must have had the character of an adventure. The house is situated at the corner of the rue du Port (now rue Joseph-Conrad), its windows looking westwards.

The newlyweds moved in on 9 April. Conrad felt enthusiastic about the setting: 'The coast is rocky, sandy, wild and full of mournful expressiveness. But the land at the back of the wide stretches of the sea enclosed by the barren archipelago, is green and smiling and sunny – often even when the sea and the islets are under the shadow of the passing clouds.' The fine days did not last, and Jessie Conrad recalled cold, windy nights well into May and June.

In his work Conrad returned to the sun-drenched Malay Archipelago. He had written about a dozen pages of a new novel, *The Rescuer* (later *The Rescue*), before arriving at Île-Grande, where he intended to focus on his writing. There were few distractions; the couple went on excursions along the coast in a hired boat, when the weather permitted. Jessie Conrad probably had little, if any, French, the local variety in any case offering challenges even to a native speaker, and Breton was still widely spoken. Although an object of mild curiosity, *les Anglais* would have been rather isolated from the community and thrown much upon their own company. Jessie, who had just left a large family, felt lonely, and when she had worked her way through the books she had brought with her and typed up her husband's manuscripts, she filled her hours by writing letters home.

After settling in, Conrad began working, but things soon began to go off. He sent a batch of the new project to Garnett, who had now assumed an active mentoring role: 'Is the thing tolerable? Is the thing readable? Is the damned thing altogether insupportable?' Are these genuine doubts, or a kind of inverted boastfulness? Writing for a living tends to require some degree of emotional stability, and at this point Conrad fell ill, apparently seriously. The return of the depression that had sent him to Champel the previous year offers one explanation, while his time in Africa manifested itself in bouts of ill health for the rest of his life. But physical illness can have complicating and immediate psychogenic factors, especially for someone so prone to depression. His body seems simply to have rebelled.

His new wife had a shock as Conrad drifted into a feverish coma accompanied by chills, and as his condition worsened she left the cottage to seek help from their landlady, Mme Coadou-Brinter. When they returned, Conrad's eyes were glittering with fever, and he failed to recognise her as he raved in his native language. One can imagine the young woman, attempting to make herself understood, upset, worried, alone. Conrad, for his part, recalls the moment in his short story 'Amy Foster': the provincial Amy is alarmed by her husband's utter foreignness, when in a fever he resorts to his native Polish to beg for a drop of water. Conrad recovered and returned to his desk, but something had happened. The crisis repeated itself, with the alternating rhythms of illness and writing dominating so much of his life from this point forward.

Over the following six weeks another shift occurred. So far as we know, Conrad wrote *Almayer's Folly* and *An Outcast of the Islands* without a sideways glance, however lengthy the gestation of the first. He had abandoned *The Sisters*, losing time and energy, and danger signs now began to appear with *The Rescuer*. At first he warded them off with a new work, 'The Idiots'. Set in the Brittany countryside in which he and his wife were then immersed, the short story attempts a Poradowska-like exploration of peasant mores in a tragic tale of a woman constrained to provide sex – and a brood of mentally defective children – to a brutal husband. She eventually escapes from her hell by stabbing him and then killing herself. In all likelihood the bleakest story ever written during a honeymoon, it has, as one biographer has ventured, provided 'great fun for all Conrad's future psychoanalytical critics'. Whatever critical 'fun' there is to be had from the story, it can also be read as a bitter meditation on enforced creativity. In it, however, and more happily, Conrad was returning to his engagement with Maupassant and Flaubert, his contact with the French language renewing his long-standing interest in their writing as it served as a model and goal for his own.

Part of the story's bleakness may reflect his increasingly dramatic problems with *The Rescuer*. Like Susan Bacadou, the hapless heroine of 'The Idiots', he felt forced to produce against the grain. Depression struck again, but Conrad pressed on, sending the first part of the new novel to Garnett, who responded excitedly: 'Just a line to say *you have never done better than in the part of 'The Rescuer'* which you sent me. At last you have got to the real sea. Bravo! . . . I will send you some notes on various passages, notes of *encore* & still *encore*. I think the public will be hit & brought down as well as the critics. Go on! Go on!'

Garnett's sense of the literary market was deep but not unerring, and Conrad did 'go on' for a while, with 'the real sea' emerging soon and quite differently in *The Nigger of the 'Narcissus'*. A flattering request for a short story from the prestigious *Cornhill Magazine* (founded in 1860), which had in its time published Trollope, George Eliot, and Tennyson, could only have encouraged him. But the story on his desk, focusing on rape within marriage and idiot children, would scarcely suit its conservative middle-class audience. The market for short stories was large, and payments high: the *Cornhill* offered a guinea per 450 words.* 'The Idiots' had got itself written, but would probably prove hard to place, and for all Garnett's enthusiasm, *The Rescuer* was foundering. Conrad confessed to an inability to concentrate coupled with inertia, symptoms typical of depression: 'It is as if something in my head had given way to let in a cold grey mist.'

Still avoiding *The Rescuer*, which had already become an albatross dangling about his neck, Conrad once again turned his hand to something new: 'A Victim of Progress', the first 'loot', as Conrad later called it, from his time in Africa. Its original title – the story later became 'An Outpost of Progress' – hints at a slightly different plot from that of its final version, which concentrates, in the manner of Flaubert's posthumously published *Bouvard et Pécuchet* (1881), on an odd couple, a bureaucrat and a soldier, adrift culturally and morally in the (unnamed) Congo Free State. Shortly after completing it, Conrad, in an astonishing burst of creativity, quickly wrote 'The Lagoon', a story set in Borneo that revolves around betrayal and death. Its 'magazine' length suggests deliberate shaping for a market, something he would attempt with varying success as his career began to flourish. The *Cornhill* took it immediately; more professional recognition came with the news that Tauchnitz of the Leipzig, which published and distributed books in English on the Continent, was negotiating to include *An Outcast* in its 'British Authors Collection'.

Conrad began *The Nigger of the 'Narcissus'*, his first major sea story, during this summer of 1896, its seeds possibly sown by Garnett

---

* To place this in perspective: 'The Lagoon', a 5,500-word story fetched £10 (£4,250 in 2005 terms), while Unwin had bought the 65,000-word *Almayer's Folly* for £20.

who had been so encouraging about the presentation of the sea in *The Rescuer*. The novel marks a major artistic breakthrough. The congenial setting drew on his intimate knowledge of ships, and the novel was more daringly experimental and original in structure than anything Conrad had yet written. Whatever its political status (as a celebration of Empire, or criticism of it), it dealt with deeply personal material. 'A respectable shrine for the memory of men with whom I have, through many hard years lived and worked', it marked Conrad's final farewell to his sea life, transmuting its reality into the subject matter for his fiction. The immediate motivation for writing yet another short story (as *The Nigger* was originally conceived) in the midst of a longer work may in part lie in a financial crisis. Conrad's investments, placed with Hope in South Africa, had largely evaporated in a failed mining venture.* The poorly documented circumstances allow little more than the bare statement. The loss did not seem to upset his mood for work, but did perhaps make the need more urgent.

There was some discussion, in the end not serious, of the couple's removing to the Basque country for a while, but in early September the Conrads departed for home, via Saint-Malo and Southampton. With Conrad's career developing, and with Garnett acting as his unofficial agent, being on the English literary scene looked a wise move. Conrad apparently wished to live just outside its centre, opting for Stanford-le-Hope, a small town of some thousand inhabitants about 30 miles and an hour and a half by rail from Liverpool Street Station. Ford Hueffer characterised Stanford, set on Essex's mudflats a few miles from the Thames Estuary, as 'rather lugubrious'. Having enjoyed the tranquillity of Île-Grande and wishing to be near water, the Conrads' main reason for choosing Stanford was the presence of Fountaine and Ellen Hope, then living with their children at The Bungalow in Fairview Avenue, from where Hope commuted to the City. Conrad found his new lodgings a 'Damned jerry-built rabbit

---

* In late 1895, Conrad had invested in Rorke's Roodepoort, Ltd, a gold-mining venture established by Fountaine Hope's former brother-in-law, John Rorke, who died in November of that year. (Hope's sister had died in 1886.) It is unclear whether Conrad had invested in another company, or whether Rorke's liquidation had taken so long that he had only just become aware of the full extent of his losses.

hutch'. Close to the railway station and not far from a brewery (see Map 6), the newly built semi-detached house in Victoria Street (now Victoria Road) was poky and 'suburban'. It was also damp and draughty, with warped woodwork, a badly hung door, and a temperamental fireplace. But once settled in Conrad continued to work on *The Nigger* almost within sight of the Thames, while Jessie, in addition to her duties as a typist (whether professionally trained or not), began looking for a new, more suitable home.

With the new novel progressing, Conrad made plans to place it. More confident of his market value than when he had sold *Almayer's Folly*, he proposed higher terms to Unwin, who had a notoriously 'difficult and mischievous temperament'. The publisher refused, and Conrad, with Garnett's discreet guidance, began to look elsewhere. In referring to Unwin, Conrad in his communications with Garnett had already taken to referring to the publisher ironically as 'The Patron', short for 'The Enlightened Patron of Letters', and he now felt confident enough to realise that his interests might be better served elsewhere. Smith, Elder, the *Cornhill*'s publishers, seemed a likely alternative given their expression of interest in his work, but in the end the distinguished and long-established house proved unenthusiastic. The publishers of Darwin and *The Dictionary of National Biography* had a diverse list, but the fiction they had been publishing had, over time, tended to the conventional, and *The Nigger*, with its complex narrative method and impressionistic effects, was, in a sense, an experiment.

More promising was the interest expressed by Sidney S. Pawling of Heinemann's, a newish house (established in 1890) and aggressively eager for new voices. It had already built an impressive list, the practical Pawling – also reputedly the fastest bowler in England – providing an anchor for the visionary 'Willie' Heinemann. By the end of the decade, they were publishing Stephen Crane, H. G. Wells, and Rudyard Kipling in addition to Conrad. Through Pawling, too, lay the route to W. E. Henley, whose *New Review*, published through – and partly owned by – Heinemann, was open to the unconventional. Wells's *The Time Machine* had appeared in Henley's magazine the *National Observer* (1894), and a nod from Wells, who had reviewed both *Almayer's Folly* and *The Outcast* favourably, may have helped conquer Henley. If Conrad indeed began *The Nigger* as early as June, it is improbable that he had a specific venue in mind, only retrospectively seeing that the *New Review* might entertain work so challenging to the general reader. (Henley's editorial policy ensured that the magazine was already in a wobbly financial state, and it collapsed with the December 1897 issue that contained the last instalment of *The Nigger*.)

As Conrad settled into married life in 'the wilds of Essex', as he jokingly referred to Stanford-le-Hope, he apparently contemplated going to Lublin to see Karol and Aniela Zagórski. Or perhaps he merely fantasised about going away; for he could ill afford to interrupt his work, which was then going well: 'I have been writing, writing endlessly.' The alternative was Christmas in Wales, and the Conrads set out on 21 December 1896 to spend the holiday with the Spiridions in Cardiff, the advancing *Nigger of the 'Narcissus'* in their luggage. The original plan for a fortnight's stay was cut short. Recalling the old Roman adage about guests and fish seems appropriate: for Conrad the visit just skirted disaster. Jessie, on the other hand, enjoyed herself, becoming friendly with the children, and was 'always recalling the good time we had last Christmas'. Ever the patriotic fanatic, Spiridion had rounded on Conrad at Christmas Eve dinner for not writing in Polish. Patriotism, that 'last refuge of a scoundrel', as Dr Johnson called it, seems in Spiridion's case to have had a compensatory and showily exaggerated character. Józef Retinger, Conrad's other Polish friend in England (for a period of five or six years after 1912), remembered how Spiridion 'clung jealously to his country, sending his children to Poland to be married, and . . . faithful all his life to his Polonism'. Spiridion's attack on Conrad is passing strange. He was born in Hampshire of an English mother, probably of Scottish descent; his wife, Marie, hailed from St Fagan's, Glamorgan; his three children, born in Cardiff, bore English names: Alfred, Hubert, and Clement. Spiridion spoke no Polish, and, like his late father (the elder Spiridion had died in 1891), had not hesitated to adapt when financial convenience was at stake, doing business as 'Spiridion & Son' and thus avoiding Kliszczewski, a wholly 'unpronounceable' and impossible to spell surname.

If Conrad retorted that he would lose his audience by writing in

Polish,* he was not only correct but also realistic. The first translation of his work into Polish, indeed into any language – *An Outcast of the Islands* appeared in January 1897 – was miserably butchered in the attempt to domesticate it for its audience. The novel's Dutchmen were, oddly, turned into Germans; its nautical terms systematically cut; and its Malay words and phrases effaced. On a personal level, Conrad had not only 'moved on', but, like any artist, he was also taking a stand for the freedom of the imagination, asserting by his reply that he had the right to discuss the topics of his choice in the language of his choosing. The facts for once speak for themselves. Out of contact with Polish affairs, having left Cracow some twenty years before at the age of sixteen, he was living his daily life in English, the language of his professional achievement as a seaman. He had in his work thus far drawn upon his experience in the Malay world, in Africa, and at sea. His 'exotic' subjects were of doubtful interest to a late nineteenth-century Polish audience, Poland being of even less interest to a late nineteenth-century English one. Conrad's work, like his life after adolescence, was cosmopolitan in setting and language. The call to nationalism fell upon deaf ears, which were hardly, as some sentimental versions have it, scorched. Spiridion's strictures were as irrelevant to Conrad's circumstances as those of the Polish novelist and feminist Eliza Orzeszkowa, who virulently attacked him on the same grounds in *Kraj* in 1898: 'My gorge rises when I read about him.' Her passion matches her complete ignorance of her subject: she lashed the 'traitor' for writing 'popular and very lucrative novels in English' at a time when he was barely managing to keep a roof over his head, cadging loans from friends, and seeing his work printed in runs of a couple of thousand copies.

The visit to Cardiff, despite this unpleasant episode, proved a salutary break. Back in Stanford-le-Hope, Conrad re-entered his 'torture

* Our knowledge of this incident comes from an account published in Poland in 1932 by Witold Chwalewik (1900–85), a scholar best known for his controversial 1956 monograph *Polska w 'Hamlecie'* [Poland in *Hamlet*], which appropriated *Hamlet* for Polish history and culture and claimed that Shakespeare borrowed from Polish sources. Not a direct witness to the Christmas fiasco, he must have heard of it from either Spiridion himself or his children.

chamber', as he called his study, to make the final creative push with *The Nigger* over the next fortnight, although it came at the cost of nightmares and neuralgia. Revision and polishing awaited. He was fully aware that he had been venturing into new territory, but hardly took a break before he began another story, 'Karain: A Memory'. A return to a Malay setting, the longish story also further develops the narrative experimentation of *The Nigger*. Centred on a guilty passion for a woman, the betrayal of a friendship, murder, the fear of haunting, and themes of cultural relativism and conflict, 'Karain' (much influenced by Prosper Merimée's story 'Tamango') offers several interests. It took two months to complete, interrupted by a move in mid-March 1897 into more spacious quarters as the Conrads finally exchanged the 'rabbit hutch' for Ivy Walls Farm, a fifteenth-century cross-wing farmhouse of lath and plaster in Billet Lane just outside Stanford. The rent was £28 a year.

However bogus the legend that Queen Elizabeth once slept in it, the house had a long history. Considerably more congenial than the semi-detached villa in Victoria Street, it was still shared. A farm labourer and his wife lived in the west wing, the Conrads in the ivy-covered east one. Protected from the winds off Mucking Flats by a windbreak of elm and lime trees, its second floor offered a view of the Thames. Conrad's habits changed little: he remained aloof from village life, an artist of reclusive disposition and sometimes eccentric habit living alongside simpler, labouring and farming folk; he went yachting with Hope, who encouraged his turn to writing; and he discussed books with his friend's well-read wife, Ellen. Jessie Conrad, who became pregnant not long after the move, busied herself in the orchard and garden. Gregarious and good-natured, she occasionally found her isolation burdensome and grew into her new role as help-meet slowly. She sometimes invited one of her younger sisters to stay 'to help', but the real motivation for these invitations was to provide her with company.

Garnett continued in his supportive role, offering an expert mixture of encouragement and judicious criticism, and 'Karain' made its way, via Unwin, whom Conrad was, in effect, using as an agent, to David Meldrum, a reader at Blackwood's London office and himself a novelist. For Conrad, its acceptance proved the beginning of grander things. A highly respected publishing house with a well distributed magazine, the firm, run by William Blackwood since 1879, was one of the names in British publishing, its founder, the first William Blackwood, having brought out Sir Walter Scott and Thomas de Quincey. Although a man of highly conservative tastes and views, Blackwood, raised up in the trade, knew how to nurture literary talent. Through his firm Conrad was to consolidate his place as an original and major writer. Conrad's meeting with Henry James a couple of months earlier had also marked his rise. Having sent 'The Master' a dedicated copy of *An Outcast* in February 1897, he received by way of return a copy of *The Spoils of Poynton*. Unfailingly polite, the patrician New Englander was extending recognition to a fellow labourer working in a nearby field. Conrad's personal connections in the literary world were growing as the 'cave of brigands' became more familiar. James lunched him at his club, the Reform, in late February 1897. If ever lunch were a rite of passage, this was, with James ceremoniously presiding over Conrad's acceptance into the tribe.

As recognition came in by one door, troubles entered by another. Never one for scrimping, Conrad sought out loans from Spiridion and Krieger, as he embarked upon 'The Return', a lengthy short story in the Jamesian manner and treating an unhappy marriage. It took several months to write, and when no serial buyer could be found, first appeared in Unwin's new collection of Conrad's stories, *Tales of Unrest*. To the writer's frustration, it thus represented 'wasted' time, payment for serialisation making up an essential part of his income. More promisingly, Heinemann was negotiating for *The Rescuer* in August, as Conrad wrote his artistic credo, the Preface to *The Nigger of the 'Narcissus'* memorably stating his programme 'to make you hear, to make you feel – and above all, to make you see'.

Further evidence that his career was on the boil was a request from Pawling to lunch with Stephen Crane, whose *Red Badge of Courage* had recently appeared in Heinemann's 'Pioneer Series of Modern Fiction'. The young American had expressed an interest in meeting Conrad after reading an instalment of *The Nigger* in the *New Review*. The event came off in mid-October, shortly before Crane's twenty-sixth birthday and as his novel (a damp squib in the United States) was enjoying a runaway success in England. Pawling apparently sensed that the two writers would get on, and after the athletic cricketer left them, they walked for hours, dining at Monico's on Piccadilly Circus where, amidst the din of 'hundreds of waiters and the clatter of tons of crockery', they discussed Balzac.

It was a case of friendship at first sight. A common interest in exploring literary impressionism and a shared sense of artistic calling were only part of the mutual attraction. Both outsiders, they formed a community *à deux*. Crane, the youngest of fourteen children of a Methodist minister, had repudiated his country's often simplistic morality to explore life's rougher and darker edges. (The novelist Hamlin Garland, an early friend, characterised him as 'an alley cat', deplored Crane's habits, and hinted at drug addiction.) When Conrad and Crane met, Crane was living in Sussex with Cora Howarth Stewart, who went by the name 'Mrs Crane', a 'marriage' ceremony having been performed in the presence of H. G. Wells and a couple of other witnesses indifferent to legal forms. A once and future brothel-keeper, Cora was intelligent, resourceful, and deeply in love with Crane, whom she kept afloat emotionally.

Intense and deep, Conrad's friendship with 'Stevie' marked a departure. Barriers of nation and age were crossed, and Conrad was reaching out, emerging from the carefully constructed carapace that surrounded his emotional centre, which Crane touched to the quick. (The relationship presages his later need for a circle of young male admirers – a role filled by Richard Curle, Perceval Gibbon, and Hugh Walpole.) Crane's visit to Ivy Walls Farm not long after the two men met cemented the friendship.

Another friendship that came to Conrad through his writing began the same week that Crane came to Stanford-le-Hope, when Conrad went to town to dine with Robert Bontine Cunninghame Graham, an aristocratic socialist and established writer, just back from Morocco. Graham had written a letter of appreciation for 'An Outpost of Progress'; one letter led to another, and the curiosity of each had been piqued. Admitting to being 'interested in the man', Conrad also thought Graham might be useful: 'the chiel' – Scots for 'fellow' – 'writes to the papers, you know'. However cynical this may sound in prospect, friendship, as it were, struck again. *The Nigger*, with its hostility to the unionisation of seamen, can hardly have appealed to Graham, but the two bonded: 'He is a most interesting man not at all bigoted in his socialistico-republican ideas which I treated to his face with a philosophical contempt. We got on very well . . . I like him – and I verily believe he likes me.'

At this point, there was a falling out with an old friend, when Krieger became insistent about money long owed to him. 'The Return' had failed with the likely magazines, and *The Rescuer*, again taken up, was progressing haltingly. Conrad's finances were shaky, and Heinemann and F. N. Doubleday, an American publisher later to make a major impact but then relatively new to the business, were subsidising him at the rate of £10 a month to keep him writing. Jessie, now entering the final stages of pregnancy, had neuralgia, and Conrad succumbed to anxiety, taking refuge in reading Crane's and Turgenev's short stories, the latter translated by Constance Garnett, and Robert Louis Stevenson's *Ballads*, a Christmas gift from Cunninghame Graham. On Boxing Day 1897, he lamented to Ted Sanderson: 'The future is as mysterious as ever and every added happiness is another terror added to life. Sometimes I think I am following an ignis fatuus that shall inevitably lead me to destruction: sometimes I try not to think at all. And all the time I am trying to write.'

He was doing so as reviews of *The Nigger*, published in book form by Heinemann on 30 November 1897 and dedicated to Edward Garnett, poured in, and were of the kind to puff up their recipient. Conrad's bold, even startling, originality went neither unnoticed nor unpraised; the *Spectator* in its Christmas Day issue unhesitatingly acclaimed him (for the second time) 'a writer of genius'. The private letters of congratulations were unstintingly complimentary. Constance Garnett, relating Conrad's style to Turgenev's, enthused: 'On board the Narcissus I have a delightful feeling – not unmixed with awe – of being in a new world.' The essayist E. V. Lucas, a friend of Garnett, wrote: 'that such a slight episode can be made as enthralling & memorable as you have made it, is to me miraculous'. Chesson, who had helped to bring Conrad into the literary world, observed: 'there is a beautiful anatomy, dexterously [sic] contrived, under all this display of imagination. "The Nigger" is not an episode of the sea; it is a final expression of the pathology of Fear.' The book signalled Conrad's arrival as a writer. The sea had a more immediate appeal to a late-Victorian audience than the jungles of Borneo, and the novel broached highly topical subjects – maritime labour disputes, Socialism, and Empire – at a time when the London Dockers' strike and agitations for the unionisation of seamen were recent memories.

Tales of Unrest could ride on *The Nigger*'s coat-tails. Conrad at first feared that the books might interfere with one another, and he convinced the enthusiastic Unwin to delay publication of the story collection until April 1898. A 50-guinea prize from the prestigious *Academy* for the collection vividly represented recognition from his peers. (Garnett had connections with the journal and must have worked for Conrad behind the scenes.) It also gave notice that Conrad's literary apprenticeship had been served. The man and woman in the street, an audience less discriminating and not one to which his talents were naturally suited, still needed to be conquered. For all the critical praise for *The Nigger* and Pawling's intentions to 'bang' the book with booksellers, popular success proved elusive: 'My books! . . . They appear, are praised and drop into the past like a stone into water,' Conrad lamented. The pattern would dog each of his books for a decade, as the critics and intellectual elite gathered to admire, and the wider reading public continued to spend their money on Marie Corelli and Hall Caine, respectively, a writer of 'mystical' and philosophical bent interested in the occult – 'a woman of deplorable talent . . . accepted as a genius by a public to whose commonplace sentimentalities and prejudices she gave a glamorous setting', and 'The Bard of Manxland' and best-paid writer of his day, famous for his moral fervour and local colour.

As Jessie's confinement approached, the Conrads' home in Stanford-le-Hope was alive with expectation. One of her sisters was visiting, but returned home just before the event. Alfred Borys Leo Conrad, 'an infant of male persuasion', in Conrad's words, arrived at midday on Saturday, 15 January 1898. Conrad appears to have celebrated the occasion with a bout of insomnia that engendered a creative spurt. Unable, or too nervous, to sleep, he began 'Youth' the same evening, writing in pencil by the light of a solitary candle in 'a little two-penny pocket book'. In this version of events, he completed the story the next day. Anther less colourful version of its beginnings dates its writing five months later; and yet another version, by Conrad himself, dates it as 'exactly a month younger than Borys', thus pushing it into mid-February.

Do these details matter? For once, yes – and in several ways. The story gives birth to Marlow, with Conrad finding an involved narrator so congenial that this teller of tales would also be used as the narrator of 'Heart of Darkness', *Lord Jim*, and *Chance*. Psychologically, 'Youth' – a fictional version of the *Palestine*'s disastrous voyage and end – returns to Conrad's younger days to take a final farewell of innocence. Its central incident, the explosion and sinking of a ship, marks a turning-point in Marlow's life, and as a way of responding to fatherhood (*if* it is, indeed, that) 'Youth' is a remarkable and problematic psychological document, dealing with destruction, rebirth, and discovery. There are elements of a projected self in Marlow, but whether he expresses anxieties about Conrad's social and cultural identity is less certain.

Fatherhood was a real shock and, at first, seems to have been somewhat uncongenial. The arrival of Borys – for so the boy was called, Jessie choosing 'Alfred' to honour his Anglo-Saxon side – disrupted his parents' established routines and further strained the Conrads' finances. Jessie's fourteen-year-old sister 'Dolly' (Alice Dora) took up residence to help with the newborn and to improve her own health with some months in the country. The 'magnificent' boy's crying filled the house. Conrad informed Aniela Zagórska in Lublin that mother and child were well, the latter with his 'dark hair, enormous eyes', looking 'like a monkey', a more flattering description than that accompanying a photograph he sent to Cora Crane: 'doesn't he look like a little pig?' Conrad celebrated the ninth day of his son's life with a 'nervous disturbance' that brought on fatigue and an attack of gout. He was in a state of panic, and the warning to Cora Crane that a 'strong iron cage' might be needed to tame the baby's ferocity on a planned call is a joke with bite.

The Rescuer clung mercilessly, Conrad somehow producing words, if dispiritedly and even against the grain. A comment to Cunninghame Graham, made during a raging winter storm, thinly veils outright despair: ' "The Rescue: A Romance of Shallow Waters", spreads itself,

more and more shallow, over innumerable pages.' As the novel grew
fitfully, Conrad learned that Karol Zagórski, his second cousin once
removed, had died in Lublin. His heartfelt condolences to Zagórski's
widow include the poignant comment 'And now I feel quite alone.'
Made by a man who had a family and lived near friends, the statement, however much occasioned by bereavement, reveals something
of his essential core.

Not surprisingly, given his adjustment to fatherhood and his worries
about making ends meet, 'nerve trouble – a taste of hell' came just
before the Conrads, with Dolly and Borys, went to the Cranes at
Ravensbrook in Oxted, Surrey, for a ten-day visit, only a month after
Borys's birth. 'Stevie' had invited several people to meet Conrad,
including Harold Frederic, an American working in the *New York
Times*'s London bureau and a minor novelist whose *Damnation of
Theron Ware* Heinemann had brought out in 1896. He had also just
reviewed *The Nigger* for the *Saturday Review*, finding in it the sea 'as
no other story-teller of our generation has been able to render it' and
'substantial promise in Mr. Conrad's steady progress'. Sick with worry
over debts, Crane proposedthat he and Conrad collaborate on a play.
According to Garnett, it was to be 'on the theme of a ship wrecked on
an island', an unlikely project that took a while to die. In any case,
Conrad had 'Stevie's' best interests in mind, introducing him to 'old'
William Blackwood at a lunch at the Garrick Club. The introduction
proved useful, and his writing appeared in *Blackwood's Magazine* later
in the year. More immediately, the advance Crane received from
Blackwood would meet his expenses for a trip to Havana to cover the
Spanish-American War, finally declared, after much noisy sabre-
rattling, in April; in that month Crane had left to cover it for the New
York *World*. The visit to Oxted went so well that Conrad suggested,
in a vague way, a three-month stay in Brittany with the Cranes. Jessie
presumably got along well with Cora, unconcerned by her hostess's
colourful history. And she must have known something of it.
Recalling Cora Crane, Conrad revealed to Hamlin Garland his
awareness of 'some gossip of a particular kind', but had only kind
words for Crane's companion, who 'nursed him devotedly during his
illnesses'.

Conrad returned to Stanford-le-Hope behind in his work, although

Crane soon came for a visit, which coincided with the publication of *Tales of Unrest* in New York on 26 March 1898. (Unwin brought it out on 4 April.) The reception was promising, although even successful story collections then, as now, sold only moderately. Amidst the praise there was also stiff criticism of the style and narrative method of the five stories. The *Times* reviewer slated 'The Return' for prolixity; found 'Karain' too 'overloaded' with description; and observed that 'The Idiots' lacked the virtue of conciseness. He paid a backhanded compliment to Conrad on 'An Outpost of Progress', a work having 'more of matter to the amount of words in the rest'. His overall judgement, however, possibly reflected the tastes of the common reader: 'Mr. Conrad is always only too conscientious; he has "thought himself weary," and having no great gifts of narrative he buries even that gift under mountains of words.' Characteristically, Conrad celebrated the book's appearance with a bout of 'beastly nervous trouble' that forced him to take to bed; the pressure of writing *The Rescue* was literally making him ill, and illness also justified the escape from it. In the weeks that followed, his sense of loneliness became a reality, as Garnett left for spring holidays in Italy; Ted Sanderson got married ('the despotism of the baby', 'wretched health', and pressures of work prevented Conrad from attending the wedding); and Crane left to cover the Spanish-American War for Joseph Pulitzer's *World*.

Nailed to his desk, Conrad bemoaned his situation to Aniela Zagórska: 'We live with difficulty from day to day – *et c'est tout*! My reputation grows, but popularity remains behind. The work is not easy and every day seems more difficult to me. How cruel and stupid life is!' Even spring's arrival was greeted with a snarl: 'Spring! *Che coglioneria!* [Balls!] Another illusion for the undoing of mankind.' Whatever the exaggeration here, the period was an intensely unhappy one, brightened by Garnett's unwavering belief in his writing.

In the midst of this creative crisis, Conrad managed to dash off a review of a book of Malay tales by Hugh Clifford, requested by the prestigious *Academy*, and ground out an article on his childhood enthusiasms, James Fenimore Cooper and Captain Marryat. *The Nigger* and *Tales of Unrest* were both in the bookshops, and completing *The Rescuer*, if he could just do so, would mean a turn in fortune. The

American firm of McClure, the publisher of Mark Twain and William Dean Howells and with an influential house magazine, offered £250 for its American serial rights and £50 for book rights, more than fifteen times what Conrad had received for *Almayer's Folly* a mere three years earlier. The cold reality, as Conrad confided to Garnett, was that the novel was stalled: 'In the course of that working day of 8 hours I write 3 sentences which I erase before leaving the table in despair.'

This bleak mood persisted until late spring, when Blackwood and McClure mooted Conrad's writing more short stories. This seemed to promise financial salvation, because the lesser effort yielded higher returns; creatively, it would be a relief from the sluggishly developing novel. 'Youth' was either written now, in May, or begun earlier and now returned to. In either case, it was followed quickly by the beginning of 'Jim, A sketch' (which eventually became *Lord Jim*) now planned as a 20–25,000-word story. The £35 Conrad received from Blackwood for 'Youth' was certainly welcome, and more was promised. Once an author proved 'a fit' with the firm, Blackwood repaid loyalty with generous encouragement backed up by advances. And unlike Heinemann, Blackwood's had an attractive and long-established venue for serialisation. *Blackwood's Magazine* (known familiarly as *Maga*) offered solid, sometimes stodgy, fare – politics and serious articles on a variety of issues in addition to fiction – but it was widely read at home and in the colonies and distributed in the United States. In the late 1890s, its circulation reached nearly 50,000 in Britain, with a further 12,000 copies being sold in the United States through McClure. (By contrast, the first edition of *Lord Jim* ran to 2,500 copies.) Publication in Henley's *New Review* may have bestowed glory; publication in *Maga* brought attention.

McClure's regular advances on *The Rescuer* for its American publication proved a mixed blessing. Aware that he could not meet the deadline, Conrad by taking the money was committing himself to producing. Playfully he mentions his dishonesty, but his humour thinly papers over a shabby reality. Things were, in fact, going so badly for him that he began to think about a return to the sea, a possibility he raised with Cunninghame Graham in the hope that his friend might be able to pull strings in Scotland. At that point, the string to be pulled was attached to Sir Francis Evans, owner of the Union Line, which ran passenger steamers to South Africa. Conrad had an interview – really a courteous gesture to Graham – that went nowhere. His last service, in the *Adowa*, dated back more than four years, and the market was flooded with younger men with more recent experience.

His spirits flagged badly as he picked away at *The Rescuer*, laying 'Jim' aside. His confession of early August to Garnett – who was still receiving dribs and drabs of the novel and responding with encouragement – that 'I am suicidal' requires considerable salt. Although dramatically unhappy, he was not yet that desperate. The very same day he consoled Graham over *his* sorrows: his large family estate, Gartmore, on Loch Lomond, was proving too expensive to maintain. The letter is not that of a man holding a gun to his temple – he asks if he could help Graham by reading proofs of his new book on Morocco – and within weeks Conrad returned his own proofs of *The Rescuer*'s first three chapters to Clement Shorter, who had bought the novel from McClure and scheduled it for the *Illustrated London News*.

The novel not only refused to die, but was showing signs of life, if not quite as vigorously as Borys, now teething. Conrad took refuge at Garnett's home The Cearne, near the small town of Edenbridge on the Kent–Surrey border, for a fortnight's peace, intending 'to do a monstrous heap of work'. The change of scene would also provide intellectual company. He saw Garnett's friend E. V. Lucas, and reconnected with H. G. Wells, if only by correspondence, defending 'Youth' against charges that Wells had laid. Noting their differences, he told Wells, with both percipience and hyperbole: 'Some day You will perhaps deny me – cast me out – but it will be too late. I shall always be yours.'

During this working holiday at The Cearne, Conrad met Ford Herman Hueffer (Ford Madox Ford as of 1919), who, with his wife, Elsie Martindale, leased a house nearby in 'Dostoevsky Corner', the name given to that part of the village inhabited by simple-lifers and Russian political exiles. Garnett had probably known Hueffer for years, even perhaps as a child, and his sister Olive was particularly friendly with Hueffer until his marriage collapsed in 1909.

Whether an introduction or a reacquaintance (Jessie Conrad locates their first meeting at the Cranes' in February), the encounter proved a revelation. Then twenty-four, Hueffer fell under Conrad's spell. As *The Times* put it as early as 1894, Hueffer had 'already achieved a certain measure of distinction' as a young poet and novelist. Born in Surrey, he enjoyed playing the bull in the English china shop, burnishing his German credentials when it suited him (his father, a music critic for *The Times*, born in Münster, had immigrated to England in 1869), and cocking snooks at English philistinism. He had impeccable, if second-generation, avant-garde credentials. His grandfather, Ford Madox Brown, a minor Pre-Raphaelite painter, had made his home in Fitzroy Square a gathering place for artists and writers. Hueffer spoke French well, and despite his unattractiveness (photographs suggest a drooping walrus suffering from chronic fatigue), attempted to pose as a rakish continental. Jessie disliked him intensely, managing to conceal her distaste for some years. Inclined to be haughty, Hueffer less successfully hid his dislike of her. Fountaine Hope's daughter, who encountered Hueffer as a teenager or young adult, remembered him as 'a real calamity', 'conceited', and 'palpably unstable'. His personal appearance was 'deplorable': his 'nails in perpetual mourning' and a toothbrush 'a luxury unknown to him'.

The meeting had immediate consequences, the writers discussing possible collaboration. Moreover, the Conrads were ready to leave Ivy Walls, and Hueffer was willing to sublet The Pent,* an eighteenth-century farmhouse set in attractive rolling countryside in Kent in the parish of Postling, about 3 miles north-west of Hythe and 5 miles from Folkestone. Essex's bleak marshes could be left behind; the accommodation was not, as was Ivy Walls, shared and would thus allow greater privacy; there would also be more room: 'Five bedrooms above, two and the long kitchen below', a small outer building, and an outdoor privy.

---

* 'Pent' is an Old Kentish dialect word meaning 'incline', or 'sloping land', possibly derived from the French *pente* (a slope or declivity). Pent is also an English and Scottish surname – not, however, common – and as the past participle of 'to pen' means 'confined' or 'shut in', as one pens flocks of sheep. By extension, the name may refer to closed-in views, true of Pent Farm. The house is mentioned in a document related to land title dating to 1787. In the 1841 Census of England, the first to include family names and householder details, it appears under the name Pent House, inhabited by John Broadley, a farmer, and his wife and children.

Before committing himself, Conrad made a brief trip to Glasgow, part of his on-going and doomed attempt to find a ship. While there he met Neil Munro, part of Blackwood's stable and a friend of Graham's. A now forgotten journalist and a writer of Scottish fiction, Munro had the popular touch and reached a wide audience. Conrad read his collection of stories, *The Lost Pibroch* (1896). Munro's *John Splendid*, a 'highland romance' set in seventeenth-century Argyll, appeared in *Maga* concurrently with 'Karain'. Unreadable now, the book sold out on the day of publication and was reprinted four times within a year. Conrad's lightning visit to Glasgow included a call on Dr Robert MacIntyre, a friend of Munro's and Graham's, who took an X-ray of his hand, and with whom he listened to Paderewski on the gramophone. After dining with Munro at the Art Club, the writers rambled 'through the sleeping city' until the early hours. Throughout the visit Conrad wore two hats: sea captain by day, writer by night.

Returning home, he immediately wrote to Hueffer confirming his interest in The Pent, sight unseen. Leaving Stanford would mean leaving the Hopes, but H. G. Wells lived in nearby Sandgate, Henry James at Lamb House in Rye, and Stephen Crane was rumoured to be returning to the south coast, while Canterbury was just 12 miles away. The Conrads' immediate neighbours would be farmers. Conrad went down to Kent to inspect his family's future home, staying overnight with the Hueffers, with whom his ties were strengthening. With plans for the move under way, he did little work but was much improved in mood: 'I've destroyed all I did write last month but my brain feels alive and my heart is not afraid now.' Oblivious to the disruption occasioned by the move, he read James's 'The Turn of the Screw', which he admired, and 'The Covering End', which he described as 'unutterable rubbish'. The former, a masterpiece of psychological and narrative subtlety, must have struck him. On his desk *The Rescuer* lay groaning for attention, and he left it there.

The move, which forced Conrad away from his interior pre-occupations, occurred in stages: Conrad and Jessie's sister Ethel arrived at The Pent first; Jessie and Borys the following day; the furniture van two days after that. Just prior to the Conrads' arrival, Conrad and Hueffer agreed to collaborate. Crane and Conrad had flirted with the idea, and there were precedents, even noble ones.

Writing to Henley, who himself had collaborated on four plays with Robert Louis Stevenson (and famously quarrelled), Conrad invoked Alexandre Dumas, who had relied upon a number of writers. Their immediate target was 'Seraphina', an adventure novel that Hueffer had partly drafted. As the Spanish-American War continued to rage, its Cuban and Caribbean settings were topical. Laboured on mightily, the story was set aside for another damp squib, *The Inheritors*, and eventually emerged, under the title *Romance*, only in October 1903. Overly long, its plot, involving pirates and smugglers, is also unduly complicated. Like their other joint productions, all artistically unconvincing, it is hopelessly hybrid, mostly Hueffer topped with a drizzle of Conrad.

Why collaborate at all? Conrad was blunt as to his reasons: 'The affair had a material rather than an artistic aspect for me.' Laid out to Henley, the plan does not lack bold naivety. Hueffer would act as a goad on Conrad to produce, a kind of superior secretary with a stick. Conrad would use his connections to draw publishers to Hueffer. Conrad held to his part of the bargain, talking up Hueffer to Meldrum of Blackwood's and broadcasting news of the collaboration. Henry James likened the collaboration to a 'bad dream' recounted at breakfast. Also hostile to the idea, H. G. Wells lectured Hueffer during a walk in Regent's Park Zoo, as the erstwhile collaborator later recalled in a letter: 'you began by warning me that my association with Conrad might damage my career. You went on to say that all this talk about Literary [*sic*] technique was deleterious or nonsensical.'

Conrad was also reaching out to others at this time, reading Graham's proofs while he was away, again in Morocco, generously responding to Cora Crane's requests to help 'Stevie' financially, and more often in contact with Wells. By early November, and settled in at The Pent, his entanglements with the wider world and friends proved a tonic: 'I feel hopeful about my own work. Completely changed.' This was but another swing of the pendulum, but the mood held for a time.

Conrad may have had a rare sense of having at last found his intellectual milieu. He was reading Graham's *Mogreb-el-Acksa*, about Morocco, enthusiastically; had dutifully read Hueffer's first novel *The Shifting of the Fire* (published by Unwin in 1892); and received a copy of the recently published *The Invisible Man* from Wells. Galsworthy, now himself embarked upon a literary career, came to stay for a night in mid-December, and Garnett was also asked to visit. Remoter from London than Stanford-le-Hope, The Pent, with access to Charing Cross via the South Eastern Railway, was proving to be no backwater. Amidst the reading and the visitors, the neglected *Rescuer* hobbled forward tentatively, but was then once again laid aside as Conrad took up 'a narrative after the manner of *Youth* told by the same man dealing with his experiences on a river in Central Africa'. With this news, addressed to Blackwood, who, coincidentally, had requested a contribution to *Maga*'s thousandth issue, Conrad's long period of creative fallowness during which he picked at *The Rescuer* as at a scab he could not leave alone was at last drawing to a close.

5

'The Fatal Partnership': Collaborator and Friend (1899–1904)

Conrad set to work on a new African tale, eliciting a £40 advance from Blackwood. The welcome 50-guinea prize from the *Academy* for *Tales of Unrest* (the equivalent of more than two years' rent on The Pent) eased a financial strain that had become increasingly acute. Stephen Crane, just back in England from Cuba, wired his congratulations on the prize and received a bleak account of Conrad's emotional life during his absence: 'I've been nearly dead and several times quite mad since you left.' The consoling news was that Conrad would come to him directly after he completed 'a rotten thing I am writing for B[lack]wood'. Self-dramatisation merged with excitement at 'Stevie's' return. The Cranes planned to settle nearby in the Sussex village of Brede, about midway between Hastings and Rye, renting a fourteenth-century manor house known locally as 'The Giant's House'. On a visit there, J. M. Barrie supposedly found the inspiration for *Peter Pan*'s Captain Hook: Brede Place is reputedly haunted by a child-eating ogre, gleefully sawn in half by locals after he had eaten too many village children. The Conrads, who called on the Cranes several times, became closer to their friends.

Mentally, Conrad was revisiting the Congo; he made progress on 'The Heart of Darkness' (the serial title), completing it in February 1899, shortly after the novella's first instalment had appeared in *Maga*. On seeing the second, his publisher commented how much he admired the work: 'It is very powerful and a wonderful piece of descriptive word painting with the weird African nightmare sensation sustained all through in a marvellous manner.' An artistic development of singular importance, the novella displays Conrad's mature artistic voice and method, its final title, moreover, providing a catch-phrase for the darkest sides of the modern experience. With 'Youth' out and 'Heart of Darkness' appearing in *Blackwood's*, prospects for a collection of stories became real. Some 10,000 words of 'Tuan Jim: A Sketch' still lay on his desk. Completing it for serialisation – Conrad then believed it was half-written – forced him to confront *The Rescuer*. Seeing Clement Shorter, editor of the *Illustrated London News*, he learned that the novel had expanded too much for serialisation.

An attack of gout, which he blamed on 'agitation, exasperation, botheration', followed a pre-Easter visit by McClure and a helter-skelter stay by the Hueffers, who came with their eighteen-month-old daughter, Christina. The period after Easter, with the house again restored to him and his family, found Conrad moody and pessimistic, once again seriously depressed: 'my memory is good and sane even if my mind is diseased and on the verge of craziness'. Yet he worked to some effect; and one might wonder – although his depression was real and struck with regularity – whether at times he tended merely to take refuge in a passing bad mood. Repairs on The Pent occasioned a return visit to Brede Place with Jessie's sister, Dolly, 'living in' to help with Borys.

Conrad, back at work on a 'long short story to complete a vol: of three' (the story was now retitled 'Lord Jim'), was behind in his writing as pressure was building for the publication of a book in 1899, but as 'Jim' continued to grow throughout the summer, hopes for that faded. Conrad went sailing on *La Reine*, a boat he had bought from Crane, at a critical moment in the story's evolution. He had reached Chapter 5 of 'Lord Jim', a crucial point where the narrative method shifts from omniscience to Marlow. The introduction of the sea captain as narrator, both involved in *and* telling the story, altered 'Lord Jim' in a way that Conrad himself could not predict. Originally planned to be around 20,000 words, the story's length suddenly doubled, and over the following year it gradually developed into a full-length novel more than six times its originally estimated length. Its writing advanced, although Conrad almost ritually complained about the progress of his work, telling Garnett: 'I am writing – it is true – but this is only piling crime upon crime: every line is odious like a bad action . . . I am like a man who has lost his gods.'

The East to which he had returned imaginatively in 'Lord Jim' became real for a moment when Hugh Clifford and his wife called in late August. *Maga* provided a connection, with Clifford's work in the August issue. Not long after, Conrad read Clifford's recent collection *In a Corner of Asia*, craftsmanlike Malay stories that stimulated reflections about his own work precisely at the moment when he was working on 'Jim''s early Marlow chapters. The tale's first instalment appeared in *Maga*'s October 1899 issue even as the narrative, still planned as a short work, continued to evolve. Over the next months Conrad was engaged in a delicate balancing act: sending copy to Meldrum at Blackwood's London office – sometimes typed up by his wife or even sent in manuscript – correcting a second typescript made through Meldrum's office, correcting serial proofs, and hammering out still more of the story. In the larger world, the outbreak of the Boer War provoked news copy and vivid emotions. Conrad followed the conflict closely, deeply distrusting both the motives behind it and its conduct, and worrying about Ted Sanderson, who although a new father and in delicate health, was liable to be called up. He did in fact go out, and, after the war, he and his wife stayed in Africa for nearly a decade.

Meanwhile, Hueffer and Conrad put 'Seraphina' aside to concentrate on *The Inheritors*. A topical and brief political satire fused to a sentimental plot, the novel was mainly written by Hueffer, as Conrad later revealed: 'Very little writing in this book is mine. Hueffer practically held the pen. The discussions were endless.'

Progress on 'Lord Jim' came to a sudden halt in early December. On 29 November 1899, Hope's eldest boy, 'Jack' (officially, Fountaine) had been found dead in the Garland Marshes off Stanford-le-Hope. The circumstances, which Conrad characterised as 'appalling' and 'peculiarly abominable', more than hinted at sexual foul play: the seventeen-year-old's body, bruised and 'in a nude condition', was discovered in a creek about a mile from Ivy Walls Farm. Conrad uses the word 'murder' to Garnett, but the inquest, despite noting 'distinct signs of a struggle' in the wet earth, suspicious scratches on the body's mid-section (and not upon the hands and feet), and the appearance of an anonymous letter that made certain unspecified allegations – which the coroner confidently declared to be false – returned an open verdict, as the coroner had vigorously recommended. (His conduct of the investigation strongly raises suspicions of a cover-up.) The Conrads, who had known the boy from childhood, immediately hurried to Stanford-le-Hope to console their shocked and grieving friends, and in mid-December the Hopes came to The Pent for a three-day visit of recuperation.

By desire, Conrad's Christmas was 'very solitary', spent only with his wife and child, the emotional upheaval of the 'mysterious' death of his friend's son spoiling the festive season. At Brede Place, the Cranes' year-end celebrations included *The Ghost*, a playlet produced at Brede School House about the famous ghost that had intrigued Barrie. In addition to Crane and Conrad, the playlet's authors included Henry James, H. G. Wells, and Rider Haggard. How this entertainment about a child-eating ogre affected Conrad's mood remains in question – that is, if, in fact, he attended the performance. Another cloud darkened the time: already in poor health as the result of thirty hours in a dinghy after a boat wreck (the material for his well-known story 'The Open Boat'), Stephen Crane suffered a lung haemorrhage shortly after the Christmas festivities at Brede Place. The time was also soured by jingoistic reports of what the press referred to as the Boer War's 'progress'.

Unfavourable to work or a good mood, these events did not, however, prevent 'Lord Jim' from growing steadily. An artistic achievement without parallel in his earlier work, financially it proved a millstone round Conrad's neck. Regular advances continued to flow from Blackwood, but the publication of the planned volume of stories had to be put off as 'Jim' grew, and no book by him appeared in 1899. He dangled embryonic ideas for future work before Meldrum – an astonishing list of what would eventually become *Typhoon*, *The Shadow-Line*, and, possibly, 'The End of the Tether' – even as he was posting more of 'Jim' to him.

These ideas for more fiction literally tumbled out, but they would need both time and good health to develop; however, work on 'Jim' came to a halt as Conrad came down with bronchitis, malaria, and gout. He emerged from his sick-bed to deal with proofs that had been piling up, and by mid-February 1900 had recovered sufficiently to visit H. G. and Jane Wells in Sandgate. On the Channel between Hythe and Folkestone, the village provided bracing sea air and a desperately needed change. Jessie accompanied him, her sister Ethel remaining at The Pent with Borys. Conrad's convalescent visit may have been strained, an adjective that characterises much of his contact with Wells, whose *The Plattner Story and Others* (1897) he had received as a New Year's gift. His praise for its 'lucidity of expression' came with a backhanded compliment on Wells's 'wonderful "easiness"', which, while making Wells popular, condemned him as a minor writer.

The Inheritors, the novel Conrad had written with Hueffer, found a home with Heinemann, where Garnett, having finally escaped the prickly Unwin, was now employed. Encouraged by McClure, Conrad even had fantasies of American serialisation, despite the book's specifically British *roman-à-clef* satire. The critics mauled it gently when it appeared in June 1901. *The Times*'s charitable verdict was that it was an 'unsuccessful' experiment 'full of intelligence astray'.

Marguerite Poradowska arrived for a week in the early spring. The Hueffers in Hythe – Elsie in the last stages of pregnancy with Katherine, their second daughter – were invited to meet her. Hueffer's fluent French was, no doubt, welcome. For her part, 'Tante' Marguerite took a practical hand in helping settle Jessie Conrad's sisters Dolly and Eleanor ('Nell' or 'Nellie'), aged sixteen and fifteen respectively, into a small, recently opened convent school in Slough, Berkshire, run by nuns of the Bernardine Cistercian Order. Conrad, despite his precarious finances, generously paid part of their annual school fees, although, by favour and with Poradowska pulling strings – the Order had connection in Lille – these were reduced.*

Lord Jim continued to balloon, even through an attack of gout, with Conrad doggedly using a paperweight to hold down the sheets as he wrote with a pained wrist. Unaware of the rapid turn of Crane's illness – his tuberculosis aggravated by malarial fever contracted in Cuba – Conrad planned to go to Brede Place for a week. The visit was

---

* With this kindly act, Poradowska, as far as surviving evidence goes, gently fades out of the Conrads' life. Thereafter, they met in Marseilles and in Paris in 1906; a letter from her dated April 1907 survives; and there was contact with her through Karola Zagórska in early 1920.

cancelled as his friend's condition worsened. Cora needed money to cope with their situation and even appealed to Conrad. He went briefly to Dover to take leave of the Cranes, staying at the Lord Warden Hotel on the seafront. Cora had arranged for care in Switzerland's curative mountain air, and like many before them (Dickens had stayed at the hotel), they were waiting for improved weather to cross the Channel. Years later Conrad remembered the occasion, Crane sending his love to Jessie and Borys and then turning away to stare 'wistfully out of the window on the sails of a cutter yacht that glided slowly across the frame, like a dim shadow against a grey sky', He died in Germany, en route to Switzerland, early on the morning of 5 June 1900, aged twenty-eight. Conrad mourned him deeply, his feelings spilling over into the last ten chapters of *Lord Jim*. His extreme closeness to 'Stevie', like most intimacies, is ultimately inexplicable; coming from different worlds, they also harboured very different literary ambitions, but the personal connection was intense, and the response to Jim's death in the novel Conrad was then completing serves, in part, as a tender eulogy for his lost friend.

His tale of the novel's ending, at dawn on 14 July after twenty-one hours of steady writing in an empty house accompanied only by the family dog, a gift from 'Stevie' to Borys (and named after *Carmen*'s toreador), has a fictional quality:

I sent wife and child out of the house (to London) and sat down at 9 am, with a desperate resolve to be done with it. Now and then I took a walk round the house out at one door in at the other. Ten-minute meals. A great hush. Cigarette ends growing into a mound similar to a cairn over a dead hero. Moon rose over the barn looked in at the window and climbed out of sight. Dawn broke, brightened. I put the lamp out and went on, with the morning breeze blowing the sheets of MS all over the room. Sun rose. I wrote the last word and went into the dining room. Six o'clock. I shared a piece of cold chicken with Escamillo (who was very miserable and in want of sympathy having missed the child dreadfully all day). Felt very well only sleepy; had a bath at seven and at 8.30 was on my way to London.

The 'end' (revision was to extend into early September) was

celebrated with a three-week working holiday with the Hueffers in Belgium. Lodged at first in the rue Anglaise in the centre of Bruges, the party found the old medieval town wiltingly hot and quickly decamped for the Grand Hôtel de la Plage in Knocke-sur-Mer, the coastal town's charms having been talked up by Poradowska. The collaborators managed little writing. The ménage included two girls – three-year-old Christina and three-month old Katherine – and two-and-a-half-year-old Borys, who fell seriously ill with dysentery. He required constant care, and the whole hotel was sent into panic. Jessie Conrad remembered the holiday as 'nightmarish' and 'terrible', adjectives perhaps coloured by time spent with Hueffer. Back at The Pent, she nursed Borys to health on a diet of 'raw beef, dry toast and the whites of eggs in water', as Conrad's thoughts turned to completing the volume of stories for Blackwood. They had no respite from troubles as Jessie, anxious and exhausted, was felled by neuralgia, and Conrad struck by a 'cold, cough, piles and a derangement of the bowels'.

His affairs muddled on, but he now took an opportunity to put his career on a more businesslike footing, responding to a second overture from the literary agent James Brand Pinker, by offering him a specimen of *Romance*, which he and Hueffer had recently taken up again. The collaborators met Pinker in London in early October, and Conrad outlined plans for *Typhoon* and 'Falk', characteristically underestimating both their length and the time required to complete them. The connection with J. B. Pinker & Sons survived Pinker's and Conrad's lives, and proved highly profitable both to the agent and the writer. The business relationship, in time, became a genuine friendship, Conrad taking to the self-made man, six years younger than he. The son of a Camberwell-born stonemason, Pinker climbed the economic ladder high enough to send his first son, Eric, to Westminster School and for the family to live in Burys Court. A rambling late-Victorian Gothic pile with substantial grounds near Reigate in Surrey's commuter belt, it had been completed in 1876 for the brewer Edward Charrington. At the cutting edge of changes on the literary scene, Pinker cannily marketed clients of established reputation, including Henry James, and those making a name for themselves: Joyce, Bennett, Galsworthy, Wells, and – very unhappily

– D. H. Lawrence, who characterised him as 'that little parvenu snob of a procurer of books'. Short (a mere 5 6), bespectacled, somewhat over-dressed, and indefatigably energetic, Pinker galvanised London's literary world.

Published in book form in early October 1900 to favourable reviews, Lord Jim even sold moderately well, although, once again, it proved to be a novel destined not for large sales but for the appreciation of an elite. Reviewers grumbled about its length and complex narrative method, but in general responded intelligently. The Speaker's anonymous reviewer welcomed Conrad into 'the front rank of living novelists', and William L. Alden, London correspondent for the New York Times, hailed Lord Jim as 'a great book, a wonderful book, a magnificent book . . . no book like it has ever been published before in the English language'. Arnold Bennett in an unsigned review for Pall Mall Gazette characterised Conrad's realism as 'graphic, vigorous, conscientious, and full of knowledge and penetration', although he lashed the novel's 'formlessness'. Conrad crowed to Meldrum about an 'absolutely enthusiastic' letter from Henry James. As this flattering attention arrived, he was already back at work, beginning Typhoon, a novella that again mines his nautical and Far Eastern experience. Set in the South China Sea aboard ship, the novella focuses on man's puniness and indomitability in the face of a tremendous typhoon that threatens the life of the hapless SS Nan-Shan. By the time he and Hueffer completed 'Seraphina' in November, Conrad had Typhoon well in hand.

Conrad's social calendar suggests a career that was on the boil and better managed: 'I have to see Watson, Pawling, Meldrum, Pinker, McClure and desire greatly to see Garnett.' In London to see his banker (Watson) to take out life insurance, he arranged for Galsworthy to meet Meldrum. The gesture was to lead to Blackwood's publishing A Man of Devon, the next year, with Galsworthy moving from Duckworth's, which had published his collection of short fiction Villa Rubein.

As the new century was about to begin, Conrad's greetings went to William Blackwood, who had made 'the last year of the Old Century very memorable' by 'the production of Lord Jim'. He may have grasped that this was also a farewell of sorts. The connection with Pinker would soon cause a frost in Conrad's relationship with Blackwood, who insisted upon being on clubbable terms with his writers, precisely the old gentlemanly way of doing business that Pinker, A. P. Watt (the founder of the first literary agency in London in 1875), and Albert Curtis Brown, established in 1899, were eagerly putting an end to.

Aside from outstanding commitments (the book of short stories and *The Rescue*), Conrad was drifting away not only from Blackwood but also from Heinemann and Pawling, his amicability being replaced, under Pinker's rational regime, by a clearer and more disciplined way of earning a living from his writing. Even before Pinker had come on the scene in the mid-1890s, Heinemann had bridled at the new professionalism: 'This is the age of the middle man. He is generally a parasite. I have been forced to give him a little attention lately in my particular business. In it he calls himself the literary agent.' The new century was, indeed, ushering in a new era.

The year 1901 began with a good omen. Conrad had completed *Typhoon*, delivering it to his agent the next day. He established a *modus operandi* with Pinker, sending a revised typescript to be typed by a professional 'typewriter' and asking for an advance. Responsible for placing Conrad's work with the highest bidder, Pinker received 10 per cent commission on the sale price. He also acted for his interests in America, where he dealt through the New York agent Paul Revere Reynolds, who had established his agency, the first in the United States, in 1893. The hard-nosed search for the best possible terms, for all its advantages, meant that Conrad was shunted from publisher to publisher both in England and in the United States. In due course Pinker acted for Conrad with William Heinemann, Harper, Methuen, J. M. Dent & Sons, and T. Fisher Unwin, and in America, with McClure, Harper Brothers, and Hodder & Stoughton until with *Chance* in 1914 Doubleday, Page became Conrad's American publisher for the remainder of his career. Pinker could at times arrange a contract for three books, but when these lapsed, time-consuming negotiations had to be entered into, there being little sense of commitment on either side. The system also forced Conrad frequently to adjust to unfamiliar production procedures and in-house personnel.

(Not surprisingly, when it came time to issue a collected edition of Conrad's work, negotiations proved complicated and protracted.)

After a short hiatus, Conrad began 'Falk', a long story he had mentioned during his first meeting with Pinker. Its ungenteel subjects – shipwreck, cannibalism, and urgent sexual desire in a narrative set on Bangkok's Chao Phraya River – ensured that no magazine editor would touch it. Again, writing that would in time prove significant met with scant response from his contemporaries. The national mood was, in any event, inimical to such work: Queen Victoria died on 22 January 1901; and the new monarch's accession dominated the news as the Boer War continued to drag on. Editors proved squeamish. *Typhoon*, with its gripping story – will the ship survive? – should, by contrast, have been an easy sale, but it was too long and too expensive. Conrad's sense of the market was developing, but he remained, more than ever perhaps, committed to a high artistic vision that meant appealing to a small public. The materials of *Typhoon* – a tremendous storm and the fate of Chinese coolies returning home in a ship threatened with sinking – has popular elements, but Conrad used them in such a way as to construct a wry tale that, as so often with him, employs several perspectives and shifting centres of authority. A subtle sense of humour and an appreciation of the interplay of the shipboard characters vie with the vivid action for attention, and, tellingly, the precise moment when the ship manages to weather the typhoon threatening her is presented only indirectly. With disarming honesty, and, in the event, prophetically, Conrad told Pinker: 'No doubt You'll find me difficult to handle very profitably. At any rate at first.'

This productive period was interrupted in February and March, when illness once again visited The Pent. Jessie was again down with neuralgia, a peculiarly painful condition involving the nerves of the face; even a slight breeze was capable of triggering it. (She was particularly unlucky, as its onset is normally in middle age and she was not yet thirty.) To compound matters, her visiting mother fell seriously ill and took to bed for a week, while Conrad, weakened by an 'extremely bad' attack of gout, complained of toothache and had an extraction, then took to bed himself. The mayhem was aggravated by that terror of Victorian and Edwardian middle-class life, 'a servant crisis', which hovered and then fell as the husband of their servant, Mrs Nash died. If these accumulated misfortunes were not enough, the winter weather was 'too horrible'.

Needing to escape, Conrad contemplated visiting the Hueffers as soon as they had settled in at Winchelsea, where they were moving to be near Elsie's widowed mother. With tongue in cheek, Hueffer recounted plans for the visit: 'Conrad talks of coming over . . . he is going to drink some waters in early morning, wander round the church, and imagine himself doing a continental cure. If he does, it would do him good, I think, and we could all make merry together.' Whether Conrad was capable of this much is questionable, for yet another problem loomed: his landlord (or, technically, Hueffer's from whom the Conrads were still subletting The Pent), Richard Hogben, who already loathed the Conrads' dog, Escamillo for chasing sheep and chickens, wanted to end Hueffer's tenancy, which would force the Conrads to search for a new house. In the end, that storm blew over, but Conrad's work languished until he joined the Hueffers in Winchelsea in May for work on 'Seraphina'.

During the stay Hueffer must have embroidered an anecdote in his book, *The Cinque Ports: A Historical and Descriptive Record* (published by Blackwood's the previous year), giving Conrad the germ for a story. 'Amy Foster', the tale of a castaway swept up on the Kentish coast and abused and rejected by the local population, draws upon memories of his illness during his honeymoon in Brittany and, surprisingly, features the actual names of the Conrads' neighbours in Postling. Conrad made its central tragic character a *góral*, a Polish highlander from the Carpathian mountains, and wrote its 10,000 words at top speed, completing a draft by mid-June. The story later appeared in the venerable mass-circulation *Illustrated London News* at Christmastime, accompanied by 'a fine drawing of Amy on her day out giving tea to the children at her home, in a hat with a big feather'. Amy's wavering sympathy for a man from another culture has pro-voked comparisons with Jessie Conrad, whereas she herself identified Amy's plodding simplicity of character as that of her long-serving housemaid, Nellie Lyons.

In an attempt to complete 'Seraphina', Conrad soon returned to Winchelsea for a week to work, but he was still 'hard at it' in late June, just as reviews of *The Inheritors* were about to filter in. He believed that the book would sell, writing to Hueffer of the 'shekels' it would 'extract' from the pockets of the British public. His optimism was not only ill placed but even reckless. The reviews were mainly middling, although he grasped at their positive points, particularly when communicating with his collaborator. Heinemann, which published the book on 26 June 1901, advertised it hopefully with a quotation from the *Daily Telegraph*: 'A work to be read and well weighed by the thoughtful, and of no small interest to the student of the times.' However much or little the book belonged to Conrad, it involved a bold shift in subject: his last public appearance had been with *Lord Jim*, with its 'exotic setting' and psychological intensities.

The small public that did read *The Inheritors* had ample grounds for confusion. The short novel mixes topical satire about imperialism gone madly awry, newspaper connivance in the imperialist adventure, financial chicanery, and futuristic science fiction with a romance plot involving a girl from the Fourth Dimension. The fun, so to call it, depends upon recognising the press baron Lord Northcliffe (later a friend of Conrad), Belgium's Léopold II, and the British politicians Joseph Chamberlain and Arthur Balfour. There are also portraits of T. Fisher Unwin, Edward Garnett, and Ford Madox Brown (Hueffer's grandfather) recognisable only by a very small in-crowd. Conrad attempted to defend the novel in the *New York Times Book Review* in a letter to the editor that bears evidence of close work. Syntactically and stylistically complex, it is, in some ways, a more compelling performance than the novel it seeks to defend, as if Conrad's artistic conscience had belatedly rebelled against the joyless task he had set it: topical satire was not a vein for his talent. But 'The Fatal Partnership', as he jestingly characterised his collaborative arrangement with Hueffer, continued, dominating the coming months as 'Seraphina' (later *Romance*), another 'fatal' work, was completed and then revised. At this stage, through Pinker, he submitted a sample of it – with an eye to serialisation – to Blackwood. Meldrum, who played go-between, discerned it as 'Hueffer's story and Conrad's telling', confessing to find the dramatic intensity 'a little forced'. Blackwood, whose nose was keener, returned it to Pinker within ten days. With so much already done, it proved difficult to abandon the book, and

Conrad, who announced its completion for early November, felt forced to keep returning to it until March 1902, when it was finally completed.

The Conrads spent the Christmas holidays with the Hueffers, Conrad intending to move 'Seraphina' forward, but fate intervened yet again when Hueffer swallowed a chicken-bone at his twenty-eighth birthday dinner on 17 December. He was unable to dislodge it until Boxing Day; the accident caused an attack of nerves, followed by an abscess in the cheek. Hueffer remained incapable of work, but Conrad made progress, staying on in Winchelsea until early January. Although he had written *Typhoon*, 'Amy Foster', and 'Falk', and part of another short story, titled 'To-morrow', again based upon an idea of Hueffer's, Conrad described 1901 as a 'disastrous year' that had been 'wasted' in 'tinkering here, tinkering there'. Again, one wonders if this is mere self-dramatic posturing. Apart from their intrinsic artistic quality, the three stories brought in £200 (more than twice the national average income of £96 in 1902). He had also received £40 from Pinker as an advance on 'Seraphina' (its end now looming), payment for *The Inheritors*, and royalties on *Lord Jim*, which had been reissued during the year. His intense dissatisfaction with his accomplishments for the year seems unjustified in another way: his rate of production ought to have pleased him. But Conrad found himself – or claimed to find himself – in a financial crisis, and he dreamt up an elaborate scheme to insure his life. Pinker declined to give him a requested further £40 advance, and his first communication of 1902 to his agent is filled with a frustration that borders on hysteria: 'Really all these anxieties do drive me to the verge of madness – but death would be the best thing. It would pay off all my debts and there would be no question of MS. Really if one hadn't wife & child I don't know———.'

But even in the midst of these gloomy thoughts, he was projecting future work, mentioning to Meldrum an idea for autobiographical sketches 'about Ships, skippers, and an adventure or two' (the germ of *The Mirror of the Sea*), and offering him a finished piece comparing Elizabethan to contemporary literature, to be printed unsigned. (If written and published, it has not been traced.) He laid aside 'Seraphina' to complete 'To-morrow'. Focusing on Bessie Carvil, a young woman tyrannised by her blind father, the story is also that of the return of a Prodigal Son, Harry Hagberd, and a study of paternal obsession. Captain Hagberd, who has developed a mania about his sailor son's return, has mentally degenerated to the point that he is unable to recognise the young man, who on arrival attempts to seduce the sympathetic Bessie. She responds to his appeal in a desperate attempt to escape her death-in-life existence, but, then, frightened by Harry's stolen kiss, returns to her ogre father's thrall as Captain Hagberd madly mutters about the return of his son 'to-morrow', which, of course, never comes. A harrowingly powerful tale of emotional entrapment and paternal brutality, as a psychological self-portrait, with its veiled recollection of Conrad's father's possessiveness and fixed idea, the story contains the seeds of a future breakdown. In addition to bringing ready cash, the story's completion liberated Conrad from the long-delayed volume of stories for Heinemann.

He contemplated the end of another overdue project, the book of stories for Blackwood, displaced by *Lord Jim*'s evolution, and attempted to deal directly with George Blackwood, a much more 'business-minded man' than his uncle. He offered the firm 'Falk' for serialisation, and met with a refusal that must have stung. He continued with the third story for the *Youth* volume, 'The End of the Tether', about a sea captain whose attempt to conceal his increasing blindness ends with his ship sinking under him as he, in effect, commits suicide to recover his lost honour. The story once again returns to the Far East and to Conrad's experience in the *Vidar*, as Captain Whalley's *Condor* makes a ceaseless round of visits to the same backwater ports. The plot, which draws upon Hugo's *Les Travailleurs de la mer* and borrows from *Madame Bovary*, may have a more immediate source in the recent suicide of Hueffer's sixty-one-year-old father-in-law, William Martindale. Suffering from melancholia, the Pharmaceutical Society's past president and Winchelsea's former mayor had taken prussic acid. Hueffer claimed to have offered Conrad advice, but if he did so, it was about narrative method, not plot.

Work on 'The Troubles of Captain Whalley', as Conrad mockingly referred to 'The End of the Tether', went hand in hand with the financial troubles of Captain Conrad. He had gone to Blackwood's on bended knee, even offering to sell his copyrights (aside from *Almayer's Folly*, which Unwin had bought), only to be reminded that he had been a loss for the firm. His spirited defence of his work and viewpoint – 'I am *modern*, and I would rather recall Wagner the musician and Rodin the Sculptor who both had to starve a little in their day – and Whistler the painter who made Ruskin the critic foam at the mouth' – fell on deaf ears. *Blackwood's Magazine*, if anything, had become stodgier, and its publisher was irritated at having to deal with 'his' author through a middleman. Conrad, who turned to Galsworthy and Pawling for help, lamented that 'all my art has become artfulness in exploiting agents and publishers'. Shifts to survive had to be made, but he found trips to London cap-in-hand repugnant. He was no longer a fledgling writer but a man with a family to support, and yet was still appealing for cash to live on and to cover his debts.

A few days later he reported to both his publisher and collaborator that a substantial part of 'The End of the Tether' had gone up in a fire in his study as he and his family were dining. The sceptically inclined have considered this version of events a canny subterfuge spun for his publisher to excuse a missed deadline, with the exploding lamp that set off the blaze a mere fiction. But a carpet was ruined; a table charred; and a wire went off to Hueffer, who was still legally responsible for the condition of The Pent. Conrad also informed Galsworthy of the event (a man he regarded highly and dealt with honestly), and, almost twenty years later, he still owed Hueffer for damages to The Pent. If Conrad was lying, his mendacity was truly elaborate. Fires and illuminations were, as it happened, topical: bonfires to celebrate Edward VII's coronation, scheduled for 26 June 1902, were being lit in some parts of the country, although the coronation was postponed until early August because the King was suffering from appendicitis.

A grant of £300 from the Royal Literary Fund, established in 1790 to help authors in need, came none too soon to help Conrad with his troubles: the windfall amounted to twelve years' rent on Pent Farm. The moneys disbursed by the Fund came from subscriptions, donations, legacies, and its annual fundraising dinner, at which a cheque form was placed beside each plate. Introduced by a fellow writer, an applicant was assessed on the basis of both literary merit and financial need, and then recommended by sponsors. Edmund Gosse –

Heinemann's literary adviser and soon to become Librarian of the House of Lords – served on the committee and championed Conrad's cause by garnering supporting letters from Henry James and the novelist Mrs Craigie (who wrote as 'John Oliver Hobbes'). On the application form, Gosse wrote in the space headed 'Cause of Distress': 'Slowness of composition and want of public appreciation.' Responding warmly to Gosse's call to come to Conrad's aid, James praised *The Nigger* as 'the very finest & strongest picture of the sea and sea-life that our language possesses – the masterpiece in a whole class; & *Lord Jim* runs it very close', concluding wistfully, 'Unhappily, to be very serious & subtle isn't one of the paths to fortune.' Conrad's case was dealt with at the meeting of 9 July, and he signed a receipt for the grant two days later. The financial relief was immediate: he was able to post Hueffer a cheque for overdue rent.

His moods still swung unpredictably; better after a break in Winchelsea, he was soon characteristically complaining to Galsworthy of being 'Quite broken backed and very low spirited'. Completing 'The End of the Tether' was taking its toll, and its conclusion, in late September, came after some sleepless nights. Insomnia then gave way to depression, an increasingly frequent visitor. Again he evaded his black mood by decamping, with Jessie and Borys, to the Hueffers and then to Galsworthy's bachelor quarters in Chelsea, where he sat for a portrait by Galsworthy's German brother-in-law, Georg Sauter. With 'The End of the Tether' delivered to Edinburgh, he started work on a new short story – called 'Nostromo'.

'Constantly promised, and as constantly postponed,' as one reviewer put it, *Youth, A Narrative; and Two Other Stories* finally came out on 13 November 1902. Reviews of the volume trickled in as a winter storm pelted The Pent, and as Conrad's thoughts, incredibly, turned to completing *The Rescuer*. Opinion predictably differed on which story succeeded best. Writing anonymously in *Academy and Literature*, Garnett, ever a stalwart support and perspicacious critic, notably hailed 'Heart of Darkness' as 'the high-water mark of the author's talent'. 'Youth', however, captured the lion's share of attention, and several reviewers had yet to warm to the Modernist methods that Conrad was so boldly exploring. The poet and novelist John Masefield, in the *Speaker*, praised the brilliance of Conrad's style but found the narrative line 'most unconvincing'. Sir William Beach Thomas, whose unsigned review in the *Times Literary Supplement* faulted the 'indulgence in poetic rhetoric' (already a long-standing 'problem' in some views) preferred 'The End of the Tether' to 'Youth' and 'Heart of Darkness'. Shockingly to modern taste, some other contemporary reviewers shared his preference. George Gissing gushed to a friend that Conrad was 'the strongest writer – in every sense of the word – at present publishing in English. Marvellous writing! The other men are mere scribblers in comparison.'

The Christmas holidays of 1902, like those of the previous year, were spent in Winchelsea with the Hueffers, with Hueffer playing Father Christmas for his two little girls and Borys. Henry James, who came to give toys but may have arrived after the Conrads had left, pronounced 'The End of the Tether' the finest of the stories in *Youth*, but was unimpressed by the narrative method of 'Heart of Darkness' and objected to Kurtz as elusive despite 'all the talk about him'. Conrad grumbled at convention, observing that since adolescence he had 'disliked the Christian religion, its doctrines, ceremonies and festivals'. Scrooge-like, he grumpily feared that 'the Bethlehem legend' would prove hostile to the *Youth* volume and that stories titled 'Heart of Darkness' and 'The End of the Tether' contrasted too vividly with the annual outburst of sentimentality and good cheer. Despite these gloomy prognostications, Meldrum could report that the volume's sales were good. Indeed, piles of the book were to be seen at Bumpus, the long-established Oxford Street book shop, and delighted by the 'very proper appreciation' of reviewers, the ever good-natured Pawling promised to re-advertise *The Nigger* to take advantage of the press frenzy. Mudie's Lending Library and W. H. Smith's, however, remained unconvinced and did not take the book, but Conrad was tasting something approaching success, even if again mainly a *succès d'estime*.

The Hueffers' planned arrival, with five-year-old Christina, to celebrate Borys's fifth birthday in mid-January engendered an uncharacteristically playful mood, with Conrad making elaborate plans imitating the Great Durbar held in Delhi on New Year's Day 1903 to proclaim the new king Emperor of India. (Conrad's wit reveals a more delicate and more highly developed sense of humour and even high-jinks than the quite rare and sometimes laboured jokes in his writings.) Having lent Hueffer *The Rescuer* some weeks before, Conrad may have renewed the possibility of collaboration. The next month would bring a contract from Smith, Elder for *Romance*, and there was yet more evidence of success: the publication of *Typhoon and Other Stories* by Heinemann in April, with a simple dedication to Cunninghame Graham, was toasted in coffee by Hueffer and Olive Garnett at fashionable Gatti's in the Strand.

Coffee was an excessively modest way of marking the occasion, for in a scant six months Conrad had placed two collections of stories before the public. Gissing, who had thought highly of the *Youth* volume, wrote to the author with unbridled enthusiasm, commenting on each of *Typhoon*'s stories: 'Of "Typhoon" who can speak adequately? It is tremendous. The terror of it haunts me in the night-season.' He acclaimed 'Amy Foster' as 'pathetic a thing as can be found in literature', but 'Falk' staggered him even more: 'this is fine work & anyone who does not shout in delight over it I call a thistle-munching ass!' 'To-morrow' occasioned praise of Conrad's poetic powers. In *Bookman*, the Cornish short-story writer and literary journalist, Arthur Quiller-Couch, repelled by Captain Falk's cannibalism, proved himself 'a thistle-munching ass' in selecting 'To-morrow' as the finest story of the four.

'Nostromo', intended as a 35–40,000-word story to be completed in June, continued to expand, and Conrad was falling into a habit, begun with *Lord Jim*, that would dog the remainder of his career. Ever poor at estimating expenditure, he was unable to estimate a work's length with any accuracy, or the time needed to write it. He hacked out 'Nostromo' from books, his memories of the Caribbean, and his brief glimpse of the South American coast in 1876. As the summer progressed, relief from constructing a fictional world almost *ex nihilo* came as he advised Elsie Hueffer on her translations of Maupassant stories. The task proved congenial, Conrad's admiration of the French writer witnessed in the cadences of his own prose and in many turns of phrase.

Conrad lunched with Hugh Clifford, who was on home leave, at the Wellington Club, where he also met Thomas Hardy for the first time. Other notables at the lunch included Edmund Gosse and Sir

Frank Swettenham, a distinguished colonial administrator in Malaya and Clifford's collaborator on a Malay–English dictionary. Clifford ruefully recalled that 'Conrad did not greatly shine in this company. He was naturally extraordinarily reserved, very shy; and moreover he was embarrassed by a simplicity and lack of confidence.' Separate visits from the painter William Rothenstein and Galsworthy provided yet another break from 'Nostromo'. An accomplished portraitist introduced to Conrad by Cunninghame Graham (they had travelled together in Spain and Morocco in 1894), Rothenstein came to The Pent sketchbook in hand. Of German-Jewish extraction, Rothenstein, who had trained at the Slade and in Paris, where he knew Degas, Toulouse-Lautrec, and Whistler, was cosmopolitan in outlook, and also known in the 1890s 'Yellow-Book' London of Wilde and Beardsley. Conrad and he got on well, and an enduring friendship began that connected Conrad, if intermittently, with the art world. (Rothenstein's pastel of Conrad now hangs in London's National Portrait Gallery.)

When forwarding the proofs of *Romance* to his collaborator, Conrad seems to have had a mild case of cold feet about the novel. He suggested that it bear an explanatory note assigning its inspiration and original elaboration to Hueffer, and haggled over the dates of its writing, worrying that '1896–1903' would suggest seven years of work. He must have been at least unconsciously aware that his involvement in the book was beneath his talent, and renewed gout and depression were a response to several dissatisfactions. Although 'Nostromo' had been progressing well, he had been pushing himself and the result was a brief collapse, compounded by toothache: 'The end of all things is not far off for me,' he lamented to Hueffer. Such confessions pepper Conrad's revelations to friends, their true import difficult – and often impossible – to judge. Conrad had a tendency to shy away from confidence into alternating bouts of bravado and showy despair. As a correspondent, he could be variously chary and revealing, but he was almost always calculatingly guarded even when appearing to wear his heart on his sleeve.

Another constant thread is his need for more money. Despite the recent £300 grant from the Royal Literary Fund, he coolly borrowed – or received as an extraordinarily generous gift (the evidence is unclear) – £150 from J. M. Barrie, who was then just about to begin *Peter Pan, or The Boy who wouldn't Grow Up*. Conrad had mentioned Barrie's work to friends on a few occasions, but this is the first indication of a personal connection. How he and Conrad fell into this degree of intimacy remains a mystery, and there must surely have been somewhat regular contact and prior correspondence; Conrad speaks of 'old time regard'. On record are Barrie's reported recollections of lengthy conversations in his study. He remembered Conrad as 'Always so nervous and intent on the subject at hand. I used to like to imagine that he was really a pirate, who at any moment was likely to leap from his chair and stick a knife into me!'

Presenting Conrad as a model for *Peter Pan*'s Captain Hook or the immortal Mr Smee burbling before the Eternal Boy tends to undermine Barrie's memoir, although others vouch for Conrad's nervous intensity and physical hyperactivity. Barrie's projections – the sense of latent threat, with Conrad about to stab him with a knife – hint at deep anxieties. Barrie's freakish height (he was only 5 1) made him somewhat childlike, and Conrad, even at only 5 8 , towers though seated. The outlaw image (Conrad as pirate) is likewise more revealing about Barrie than Conrad: Barrie's marriage was long troubled, and his interest in boyhood and boys warmer and more vivid than considered 'normal', then as now. Conrad's letter of thanks to Barrie for the loan (or gift), courtly rather than intimate, is frustratingly opaque.

Closer but, as we have seen, troubled by considerable differences, was Conrad's friendship with H. G. Wells. The bluff persona of the fantasist of the future often abraded Conrad's 'over-sensitised receptivity'. Resentment and anxiety lurk in Wells's acid-etched thumbnail portrait that pits Conrad the poseur against Wells himself posing as the average man: 'I found . . . something ridiculous in Conrad's *persona* of a romantic adventurous un-mercenary intensely artistic gentleman carrying an exquisite code of unblemished honour through a universe of baseness.' The Grub Streeter's philistine disdain for 'high' art combined with an exaggerated working-class pragmatism do Wells little credit, while the mud cast upon Conrad falls off lightly. It is scarcely surprising that the friendship ebbed and, over time, undramatically faded out altogether. The temperamental difference yawned too wide, and T. S. Eliot's recollection of Conrad as 'a Grand Seigneur, the grandest I have ever met' goes some way to explain why the two drifted apart.

Mental fatigue, an inability to concentrate, and nervelessness followed an early winter attack of gout: 'I *feel* a perfect wreck,' Conrad confided to Wells. But he felt sufficiently restored to invite Roger Casement to call. Having read 'Heart of Darkness', Casement was not merely a social caller; he saw in Conrad a potential ally in his tireless efforts to mobilise public opinion against atrocities in the Congo Free State. Casement's recent report to Parliament on the subject had led to a public outcry. The men had last seen each other by chance in 1896 at the Johnson Club, a group formed by Fisher Unwin to discuss Samuel Johnson. Now the gaunt, quietly intense Irishman came to The Pent for an overnight stay. In the light of Conrad's later characterisation of Casement as a man 'of no mind at all. I don't mean stupid. I mean that he was all emotion', the visit was affable, Conrad being punctiliously courteous (*correct*, as the French say) but presumably withholding his real sentiments. He subsequently replied to a direct enquiry from Casement that he had not himself witnessed the cutting off of hands that figures so appallingly in Casement's exposé and begged off becoming involved in the protest: 'I would help him but it is not in me. I am only a wretched novelist inventing wretched stories and not even up to that miserable game.' Instead he effected an introduction to Cunninghame Graham, believing that Graham's well-honed political sensibility, wider connections, and journalist friends might be more useful to the Irishman. Conrad's later statement that he and Casement had 'never talked politics' can presumably only refer to Irish affairs, Casement's other great commitment, and, as it proved, his undoing.

Christmas brought no brightening of his mood, and looking back on 1903, Conrad once again complained that he had had 'an awful year of it', feeling that his work had advanced little. Jessie, 'chilly and languid' and 'very much run down', needed a change but was hostage to The Pent until an invitation came to spend a fortnight near the Hueffers, now relocated to London at Airlie Gardens, not far from Galsworthy's. The Conrads settled into rented quarters nearby, at 17

Gordon Place, just off Kensington Church Street. Town life presented opportunities for distractions from *Nostromo*, with Conrad now delivering chunks of the novel to Pinker. In the event, disaster struck. Out to do some early morning shopping at John Barker's department store in Kensington High Street while her husband was breakfasting with Galsworthy, Jessie took a bad fall and dislocated both knees, already weakened from an earlier accident. Pain and medical expenditure ensued, and Borys had to be looked after. Conrad tried to work, but then more bad news came: his bank, William Watson & Co., had failed. His overdraft with them was £200 (today £76,500) or possibly £250, and the bank's creditors circled.

Sidney Colvin, a friend of Robert Louis Stevenson's and Keeper of Prints and Drawings at the British Museum, whom Conrad had met recently through H. G. Wells, urged Conrad to turn the bleak story 'To-morrow' into a one-act play (eventually titled *One Day More*), a suggestion Conrad eagerly took up, working on the adaptation in Galsworthy's study as Galsworthy himself laboured on *The Man of Property*, the first novel of the Forsyte Saga. On the surface Conrad's new departure seems to come out of nowhere for a writer so concerned with both stylistic effects and his characters' inner states, neither of which triumphs on the stage, and this venture was mainly a grasping at straws for hard cash, as was composing sea sketches for the popular press. Some of these were now being dictated to Hueffer, who pitched in by extracting dialogue from 'To-morrow.'

With the sea sketches, Conrad soon had an eye on an eventual book, but his attitude to the material is revealing: 'I can dictate that sort of bosh without effort at the rate of 3000 words in four hours.' His own era was to receive *The Mirror of the Sea*, part reminiscence and part grappling for belletristic effect, enthusiastically. Galsworthy wept on an omnibus (or train) while reading it. Conrad was falling back into old habits, juggling several projects competing for his time and attention: the day was reserved for *Nostromo*, while the 'bosh' occupied the hours between 11 p.m. and 1 a.m. The juggling act continued in London as the fortnight's break stretched, Jessie Conrad's fall demanding rest and 'doctor's care', and as expenses multiplied she and Borys finally returned to The Pent, with Conrad remaining behind to dictate sea articles to Hueffer.

By the time Conrad returned to The Pent, his wife's leg was causing her severe problems, and permanent paralysis, and even amputation, seem to have been mooted. She was also suffering from a defective heart valve, and within a few weeks her neuralgia returned yet again, further complicating a miserable situation. Conrad responded to the continuing strain with fever and headache. Steady work was, however, an absolute necessity, and through Pinker, a Miss Lilian M. Hallowes, a thirty-four-year-old 'typewriter' born in Penrith in the Lake District, was engaged. Working with Conrad on and off for the next twenty years, and remaining unmarried, she became at times almost a member of the family. Borys Conrad, who described her as 'tall' and 'willowy' and wearing a bun that kept coming apart, notes that his father 'not only tolerated her presence in the house but even developed some affection for her . . . due, I believe, solely to the facts that she was a good typist and possessed the ability to sit quite silent and motionless in front of her machine, hands resting tranquilly in her lap, for long periods, reacting promptly to a word, a phrase, or a sudden outburst of continuous speech, hurled at her abruptly as he prowled about the room or sat hunched up in his big arm-chair.' A photograph of her in later life, posing jauntily with a feather in her hat, suggests geniality, intelligence, and a self-contained air. She and Conrad became close, but the suggestion that she became his mistress is the product of vivid imaginations.

His wife's dismal condition, their dire financial straits, and the hard necessity of producing fiction in unfavourable circumstances suggest The Pent's atmosphere. Conrad was by now reduced to outright begging. He called on Galsworthy for 5 guineas to pay the growing medical bills, and Pinker, who had already taken on Conrad's insurance premiums, was also touched for Miss Hallowes's salary (25 shillings a week). She was now optimistically put on a six-month contract, with Conrad dictating *Nostromo* as well as the sea 'bosh'. The quality of the resulting prose, particularly the end of *Nostromo*, shows the strains that he was labouring under: 'Half the time I feel on the verge of insanity,' he informed David Meldrum, who was not even a close friend. The other half of the time he clearly managed to write, as chapters of *Nostromo* were still being sent to Pinker, and the sea sketches accumulated. Hueffer, who helped with both projects, could do so no longer, as, on the brink of a nervous breakdown himself, he and his wife left town to live in the New Forest.

Pressures, though they did not dissipate, suddenly eased slightly. Jessie Conrad regained some mobility thanks to successful electro-massage therapy to her leg muscles, and Conrad contemplated an escape to the nearby seaside resort of Deal for sailing and a change of atmosphere. Galsworthy provided crucial emotional support at a trying time, and Conrad responded to his continuing loyalty by writing a brief preface for Ada Galsworthy's translations of Maupassant stories. (Divorced from Galsworthy's first cousin, she therefore bore the same surname and had long been in a relationship with John, although they were not to be married until the following summer.) The task of reading the translations allowed Conrad to revisit a writer he admired and had drawn on in his own early work. Will Rothenstein proved another stalwart friend, lending 'another' £50 (suggesting a previous loan), and Cunninghame Graham, down for a visit, showered Conrad, an inveterate smoker, with strong throat-scraping Brazilians and books. The latter gift included W. H. Hudson's recently published fantasy *Green Mansions*, set in what today is called Amazonia, a timely gift as *Nostromo* expanded.

Despite his friends' support at this difficult juncture, Conrad's moods remained wavering. He groaned to Garnett that 'The sands O Brother are running out', and informed Hueffer 'I have been half dead.' He called upon deep reserves and discipline to accomplish as much as he did, and then another unpleasant storm broke. A rumour spread that Conrad's appalling financial state was due to Pinker's niggardliness and tight management. Wholly unfounded, it none the less ruffled feathers that required smoothing. Pinker assured H. G. Wells that Conrad, who had been offered £7 in royalties at Heinemann's and a £70 cheque from himself, was in no need of the loan of a pound to return home. Gosse, then actively waging a campaign to secure a Royal Bounty grant for Conrad, was corrected upon this point, about which he claimed to know nothing. (Gosse, now Librarian at the House of Lords, not only saw Balfour, but also lent the Prime Minister some Conrad books to read on his summer holidays to advance the cause.)

The whole affair has an ugly character. Conrad seems to have lacked perspective on his situation, the fecklessness of youth still present in the family man at mid-life. Dependency seems to have been an intrinsic need, and he was constitutionally unable to economise. Was he living beyond his needs, or like the legendary boy, crying wolf? In the days before the National Health Service, unexpected medical expenses could deal a crippling blow, and, obviously not to be blamed for his bank's failure, Conrad was in real financial difficulties, but these were surely partly of his own making. Rothenstein, when arranging financial help for his friend, felt that Conrad was 'a pathetic person, & he seems to me, like so many artists, to have muddled his life quite unnecessarily'.

The Conrads travelled by chauffeur-driven motor car to Stanford-le-Hope, via Rochester, for a few days in late August 1904. And there, after a thirty-six-hour assault on *Nostromo*, with an interruption for a tooth to be pulled, the novel's final pages were scrawled out. The end came at three in the morning, Conrad announcing to Galsworthy in what for him was the equivalent of a whoop: 'Finished! Finished on the 30th in Hope's house in Stanford in Essex, where I had to take off my brain that seemed to turn to water.' Fresh from his desk, and the worse horrors of the dentist's chair – Conrad had what the French call *une peur bleue* (a 'blue fear') of dental work – he coolly asked Pinker for £100 (roughly £38,200 today), average wages for a year. The novel's completion was timely, Harper's having sent a stiffly worded enquiry about the book, which they had contracted: 'We really must ask you to let us have the completion of the "copy" at once, as the delay is getting very serious, as not knowing how much the book makes we cannot order the paper.' Conrad's retrospective and deliberately charming account of writing the final word is a continuation of the fiction, with its obvious nod to Jonathan Swift: 'my sojourn on the Continent of Latin America, famed for its hospitality, lasted for about two years. On my return I found (speaking somewhat in the style of Captain Gulliver) my family all well, my wife heartily glad to learn that the fuss was over, and our small boy considerably grown during my absence.'

Despite the immense effort and the pains of writing, Conrad had cut corners: 'Personally I am not satisfied. It is something – but not *the* thing I tried for,' he told Will Rothenstein. Sending moneys due for Hueffer's work on dictation of *The Mirror*, he was even blunter to Elsie Hueffer about the artistic sleight of hand: 'The finishing for TP's horror [*T.P.'s Weekly*, the magazine serialising the novel] was no end at all in *any* sense. 'Twas a necessity. I am sick and tired to death.' Relief at being 'finished' intermingled with a sense of having just missed something finer and larger, his artistic conscience bruised by monetary need.

He contemplated wintering in Morocco, much loved and no doubt talked up by Graham, and went so far as to make enquiries of a hotel-keeper in the Atlantic coast town of Mogador (now Essaouira). He also enquired into Capri, mentioning to Graham a house with an orange grove and a sunny situation. Either destination would reduce daily expenses, and going south seems to have been doctor's orders. Laying plans for a change of scene, Conrad picked away at things, and planned more *Mirror* sketches. In early October, he hurriedly wrote a 2,500-word appreciation of Henry James, for which the *North American Review* paid £25. Receiving nearly a year's rent for a mere week's work must have been both flattering and frustrating: journalism paid well, but was not his *métier*, as he said when looking back on his occasional essays and journalism, collected in *Notes on Life and Letters* (1921): 'After all the things in that book – it is not my trade!' (The diction suggests the line was written with a Gallic shrug.)

Nostromo, published on 14 October 1904, was to meet with a cool and even hostile press, and Conrad ruefully admitted to Pinker that the novel had had 'a bad sendoff'. E. V. Lucas, normally a Conrad partisan, paid only a backhanded compliment in the *Times Literary Supplement*: '*Nostromo*, though a shapeless work, is yet a shapeless work by a man of genius, satisfying only occasionally, but never undistinguished.' More forthrightly, and devastatingly, he judged that 'Many readers will never survive it.' John Buchan, then a novice short-story writer with contributions to *Blackwood's* to his name, wrote anonymously in the *Spectator*, warning that despite the novel's undoubted strengths 'It would be a thousand pities if an author who has few equals in talent should habitually spoil his work by an inability to do the pruning and selecting which his art demands.'

Congratulations and praise from Garnett, whose signed review in the *Speaker* brims with intelligent appreciation, meant something personally, but sales, not the praise of friends, were the greater need. In retrospect, Conrad characterised the novel, which many now regard as his undisputed masterpiece, as 'the least lucky of my reveries – badly printed, obscurely published and generally ignored'.

The book was a printing disaster – Conrad complained of 'the slovenliness . . . the horrid misprints, the crooked lines, the dropped punctuation marks'. Harper's, yet another new publisher for him, had served him ill, but he alone was responsible for the faulty Spanish, smoked out by Graham, and for the novel's lack of popular appeal. Set in a composite South American country plagued by endless cycles of corrupt and inefficient rule, the novel dealt with topical subjects: imperialism, colonialism, the growing influence of the United States in South American and even world affairs. It was also more narrowly topical in drawing loosely on Panama's separation from Colombia with the aid and connivance of the United States, a subject much in the news during 1903 as Conrad was writing. An unhappy marital relationship and a swashbuckling title-character give human interest to the play of political and philosophical ideas the novel explores, but in two years of close labour Conrad had produced a densely layered, lengthy, intricate masterwork dealing with politics, morality, and the cycles of human history, and had again written for posterity rather than for the average reader of his own day. As far as these readers were concerned, he had also blurred his image: having set his fiction in the Far East, Africa, and at sea, he had suddenly turned to South America. And then, as now, readers tend to prefer consistency in an author's profile. Conrad's own shift to a new publishing house also suggests a refusal to settle, although Pinker now had control over where Conrad's work appeared in print.

Rather than Morocco or Capri, the 'broken-down crocks', as Conrad referred to himself and his wife, went first to Bayswater, at 10 Princes Square, and then into a flat at 99 Addison Road off Holland Park. They had at least two other goals in mind than the change of atmosphere: extensive treatment for Jessie, and Conrad's presence in town when *Nostromo* came out. Conrad had had breathing attacks (his self-diagnosis), one so severe that he wondered how he would get home, and, unwell and anxious, his wife was nursing Borys, then being tortured by tonsillitis and high fever.

When Conrad felt better, he began dictating more *Mirror* papers to Miss Hallowes and drafting a South American short story. Turned down and later incorporated into 'Gaspar Ruiz', this was a potboilerish tale set in South America, shards of *Nostromo*, which he seems not to have been able to shake off. He now characterised the novel as 'accursed', whether for the huge labour it cost him or for its middling reception, or both. He desperately needed to take time off, but had no paid holidays, no pension, nor any guarantee that he could maintain the pace he had set. As he was to write in the essay 'Tradition' (1918), 'Work is the law', and so it was even when circumstance militated against the peace of mind necessary for it.

Jessie entered a private nursing home for treatment on her knees. Considering Conrad's financial circumstances, the costs for her care were staggering: the physician charged 58 guineas, and the nursing home near Harley Street was to cost 8 guineas a week. (A month's stay was mentioned.) Conrad had to cadge again, borrowing £30 from Rothenstein and £25 from W. P. Ker, Professor of English at University College, London, presumably introduced to him by the painter. The only good news was that Jessie's operation was successful and her recovery so rapid that her time at the nursing home could be curtailed. As Christmas 1904 approached, Conrad managed to work, again dictating to Miss Hallowes. His wife's recovery revived plans for a stay on Capri, a perverse destination for an invalid learning to use crutches, for the island town is all curves and steep inclines.

In what was generally a self-absorbed period of his life, Conrad's eyes turned to the outer world. He followed the progress of the Russo-Japanese War closely in the daily and illustrated papers. With his labours on *Nostromo* (a novel about several empires, the old Spanish one and the coming American one) over, he contemplated with interest Tsarist Russia's first death throes. Financial difficulties continued to beset him. By luck, the accountant handling the winding up of Watson's bank was an old acquaintance, W. B. Keen, with whom he had shared outings on the *Nellie* with Hope and whom he had fictionalised as the accountant in 'Heart of Darkness'. The word 'bankruptcy' was mentioned, but Pinker was proving both compassionate and practical in keeping Conrad's head just above water, although now and again kicking over the frequent demands on his purse. In a moment of frustration, Pinker – the highly successful self-made man, who no doubt had arrived at his position in the world partly through self-discipline – pronounced the word 'extravagance', apparently qualified by the adjective 'mad'. Conrad rose in self-defence, but he had now thoroughly established a pattern of borrowing from his agent against future writing, and Pinker could be counted on, whatever the occasional unpleasantness. Conrad was, essentially, still dependent upon others, despite a solid critical reputation and a body of work that included, in the judgement both of his contemporaries and of posterity, several masterpieces. He owned no property; had no steady income; his disabled wife required medical treatment; and he had a son whose education would have to be paid for. Despite his efforts, and his achievements, the future must have looked as insecure as ever.

6

The Analyst of Illusions

(1905–1909)

The cry 'Italie! Italie!', both a stern call to duty and a prospect of future happiness, punctuates Berlioz's mid-nineteenth-century masterwork Les Troyens, and was Conrad's watchword during the first months of 1905. He promised Pinker that he would return from a planned four-month excursion to Capri with 'a good 2/3ds (at least) of a novel', and, though fending off a cold and the return of depression, he was engaged in a flurry of preparations to leave. On the island itself, lodgings were negotiated through a cleric, a friend of Henri-Durand Davray, Conrad's French translator, while Conrad arranged for tickets and settled the passage to Naples via Paris with Thomas Cook's. He kept Pinker abreast of his activities and plans, the latter including the writing of an article on the Russian Empire, an idea that sprang from coverage of the Russo-Japanese War by newspapers and the serious monthlies. Begun the previous February over the rival imperialist ambitions of Russia and Japan, the war offered further evidence of a Russia facing political turmoil, and for Conrad probably stirred memories of his childhood and youth. More immediately, his imagination, as Nostromo indicated, was exercised by both abstract and immediate political questions.

Inauspiciously, on Friday, 13 January, the Conrads – with Borys and a Miss Jackson, a trained nurse in tow – left on their first trip abroad since their honeymoon nearly nine years before. They arrived in Paris in the early evening, staying overnight in the St-Petersbourg Hôtel in rue Caumartin near the Opéra. At midday on Saturday they were in a sleeper bound for Rome, arriving in Naples at two in the morning of the 15th to snow, a cold north wind, and no transport. Not only had the private carriage ordered in advance given up on them, but the longed-for warmer weather had failed to materialise. More bad luck struck immediately. Rough seas prevented the short crossing to Capri, and their stay at the elegant and expensive Hotel Isotta e Genève, whose driver, seeing them in the lurch, had virtually kidnapped them on their arrival, stretched to five days at £2 a day for the hotel alone.

The party finally reached the Marina Grande on a moonlit evening, and after the great commotion and agitation of unloading *la signora* and her invalid chair – a delicate, even hair-raising operation – was greeted by no fewer than three priests, evidence of the vigilance of their local contact, Canon Ferraro. Conrad had done little work on the Russian article in the week since leaving London. The rosy hope of writing 60,000 words in sixteen weeks was unattainable, and he was also already over budget. He emitted the usual cries for help, and touched Galsworthy for a loan to cover the unexpected hotel bill. As a sign of worse to come, Miss Jackson, to whom Conrad had rapidly taken a dislike, fell ill with flu, which turned into pneumonia. In the face of gathering adversity, Conrad's determination remained unshaken, and he expanded his domestic arrangements at the Villa di Maria to include a room to write in.

The Conrads settled into a smallish, two-storey house with a tiny garden on the then-named via Giardini di Augusto. On the island's Marina Piccola side, it stood below the crest of a hill and beneath the famed Grand Hotel Quisisana and other fashionable hotels. But even peace and a room of his own to write in did not necessarily lead to productivity. Conrad either avoided his writing-room or spent his time in it staring at blank pages. A month after arriving he was producing at the pace that Gosse had diagnosed as a 'cause of distress'. His 'Slowness of composition' had extenuating circumstances: years later Conrad recalled the villa's leaky roof and inadequate heating, complaining that the family had all 'nearly died of cold'. As a consequence of the inclement weather, there were bouts of the flu, bronchitis, and insomnia; between these he dictated to his wife an early draft of an essay that was to expand into 'Autocracy and War'. The complexly structured discussion takes up current events in Russia, particularly the war in Manchuria, and its 10,000 words would be the only writing Conrad completed during the entire four months of his time in Italy.

The weather continuing to be 'impossible', with 'rain, hail, thunder', the only bright spot was meeting Ignazio Cerio, whose brother Giorgio treated the ailing Miss Jackson and gave electrical treatments to Jessie. (Giorgio, who later married the American portraitist, philanthropist, and bird enthusiast Mabel Norman, must have spoken at least passable English, although Conrad probably possessed a smattering of tourist Italian.) The father of Edwin Cerio, a notable architect and Capri's most distinguished writer, Ignazio, a medical doctor, was a historian and specialist in the island's geography. In addition to his huge collection of antiquities, fossils, and shells and plants gathered both on the island and during extensive travels, Cerio possessed a good library, which he generously made available to Conrad. But this kind act was to prove partly responsible for the birth of a monster of remarkably protean character. Conrad now conceived the plan of a 'Mediterranean' novel that would obstruct, and occasionally strangle, his creative energies for the next two decades. In time, the original idea – he proposed to treat French and English rivalry over Capri in 1808 – evolved into *Suspense*, set during Napoleon's exile on Elba. Endlessly picked at, the work occupied his last years and was left unfinished at his death.

Yet another month passed with little in the way of improvement, and with Conrad sinking into the lethargy typical of depressive personalities: 'I've done nothing. Nothing at all,' he lamented to his French translator. This was not quite the whole truth since 'Autocracy and War' advanced, if not on paper, then in his head. As Jessie Conrad convalesced, Conrad made two friends, the writer Norman Douglas, who the year previously had seen into print a small book on Capri's famed Blue Grotto and another on the island's forest cover, and Count Zygmunt Szembek, a Pole settled in southern Italy for his health. The island's foreign population frequented a café not far from the Conrads, the 'Café Zum Kater Hiddigeigei' run by the beautiful Donna Lucia Morgano. According to Compton Mackenzie, a later visitor, 'to receive from her hands a glass of vermouth was to drink deep from the prodigious breasts of Mother Earth'. (Conrad went there with his '*petite famille*' for chocolate.) Another social butterfly, Muriel Draper, an American who met Douglas in 1905, witheringly observed the 'motley crew of English, Danish, Polish, German, American strays', who chattered 'from tea-party to tea-party' at the 'little grand opera piazza'.

Austrian-born, Douglas, then thirty-seven, a man of cosmopolitan tastes and interests, had been educated at Uppingham and Karlsruhe before finding employment with the Foreign Office. His introduction to Conrad came through Harold Trower, the British consul, who apparently combined his official duties with acting as an unofficial welcome committee. An enthusiast of the island's history, geology, and flora, Douglas would have met Conrad in time in any case, being friendly with Dottore Cerio. With his five-year marriage to a cousin ended, Douglas began exploring an interest in very young men in Capri and Naples (where he owned a villa), the latter city famed as an Arcadia regained, and Wilde's destination with Lord Alfred Douglas on his release from prison. The male nudes of the German photographer Baron von Gloeden, who lived in nearby Taormina, give an idea of what lured Douglas to an area also renowned for its supreme natural beauty and superb climate. E. M. Forster, the vivisectionist of the English abroad, had made comparable discoveries a couple of years earlier, although only in his fiction did he possess the young Italians he so warmly admired. Conrad proved extremely helpful to Douglas, introducing him to Pinker and to Garnett as a 'find', and offering Douglas detailed advice placing his writing.

The sixty-one-year-old Szembek, the Conrads' near neighbour, had, like Douglas, escaped a repressive culture for the arms of Italian youths, who to some were one of the island's special charms during this period. Conrad drew upon Szembek for 'Il Conde', a tale that in the highly coded terms of the day deals with homosexual prostitution and attempted blackmail, its elderly hero eventually retreating from Naples in disgrace to a certain death in the cold climes of the North. Conrad explicitly acknowledged his indebtedness for the story's kernel to a 'very charming old gentleman' he had met in Italy, to whom, he claimed, the '"abominable adventure" did really happen'.

As 'Il Conde' reveals, Conrad either knew of or sensed Szembek's (and Douglas's) sexual proclivities. Like any adult on the island, he was fully aware of what he referred to as 'The scandals of Capri –

atrocious, unspeakable, amusing scandals, international, cosmopolitan and biblical flavoured'. Two such, no doubt still a topic of gossip, had broken out in 1902. The one involved a German painter, Christian Allers, who fled as far as Samoa after the police began to probe rumours of orgiastic parties at his villa; the other, even more high profile, involved Friedrich Alfred Krupp, then the world's richest man. The subject of international attention because of its protagonist's fame and wealth, the scandal broke with such violence that the Kaiser's throne wobbled, Wilhelm II having visited 'Fritz' Krupp aboard his yacht off Capri. (In some versions the Kaiser had also enjoyed the favours of young men there.) 'Lo scandalo Krupp,' as the outraged Italian press called it, involved 'un circolo di degenerati' living off the German industrialist. Heir to the long-established family armaments enterprise Krupp of Essen, Krupp, like Count Szembek, had initially retreated South for his health and there found other diversions. Forced to leave Italy, and with his wife in a mental asylum, he took his own life on returning to Germany, a suicide variously covered up in newspapers as a heart attack or apoplexy.

In revealing the scandal the Italian press loudly cried out against orgies, and peppered its revelations with words such as porcheria (obscenities) and vergogna (shame). The press conveniently omitted to cry out against the thriving circle of blackmailers upon which it had relied for information, none of it given for free. Another major 'international' scandal involved the Franco-Swedish poet and diplomat Jacques, Count d'Adelswärd-Fersen (a descendant of Marie-Antoinette's Swedish lover, Axel de Fersen), who fled Paris for Capri in 1903 at the age of twenty-three after charges were brought against him for holding orgies and black masses involving under-age youths. (Count D'Adelswärd-Fersen lived openly with his 'secretary' Nino Caesarini, a fourteen-year-old Roman, who had been a construction worker.) His engagement broken off and career ruined, in consolation he was building himself Villa Lysis, taking its name from Plato's dialogue on friendship, near the Villa Tiberius. It was under construction during the Conrads' stay.

Good news came from Will Rothenstein in late March. Through Edmund Gosse's good offices, Conrad had been awarded a £500 Royal Bounty grant (£190,000 in today's terms), a one-time bursary given on the Prime Minister's recommendation to worthy persons in distress. Widows of writers, civil servants, and officers figured prominently among recipients, although there were no strict guidelines and indigent persons engaged in work thought to be valuable to the nation – a category that included writers, scientists, and scholars – could also apply. Conrad met the only other formal requirement – British nationality (though Gosse was initially uncertain about this and had to enquire of Newbolt). Owing money for rent, medical bills, and income tax, not to mention the overdraft at Watson's, his failed bank, his debts accounted for all but £130 of the grant. Not awarded in a lump sum, the grant was to be disbursed through Rothenstein and the novelist and patriotic poet Henry Newbolt as trustees. Instead of gratitude, the arrangement provoked resentment and a fit of furious and even unbridled anger. Conrad complained to Gosse that the trusteeship gave 'the appearance of "Conrad having to be saved from himself"', and he blamed Capri for undermining his sense of identity and thus preventing him from writing. Apart from the consul, his only known English acquaintance on the island was a Colonel Bryan Palmes, retired from the Somerset Light Infantry. (Douglas is at once too cosmopolitan and too 'local' to count.) Conrad had lost his cultural bearings: 'I, in my state of honourable adoption,' he wrote, 'find that I need the moral support, the sustaining influence of English atmosphere even from day to day.'

With his time in Italy coming to a close, Conrad twice went to Naples for dental treatment. His fear of dentists was so paralysing that on the first occasion he went to the city but in the end did not see a dentist. For moral support and to give his family a change of scene, he was accompanied by the entire party, including Miss Jackson. A 'whiff of tainted air' during a tour of nearby Pompeii gave Borys a severe sore throat and high fever. Conrad visited with Galsworthy, then passing through Naples after finishing *The Man of Property* in Amalfi, and either now or on his previous stay went to the Museo Archeologico to see the treasures of Pompeii and Herculaneum, which, like Count Szembek, are recalled in 'Il Conde'.

Amidst this flurry of activity and toothache, Conrad possibly sent 'Autocracy and War' to Pinker on schedule. A topical piece, its timely publication was an issue, but Pinker never received it, and Conrad lamented its loss in the mail. There is, however, some justification for believing that story invented, for in late April he let slip to Wells that he had been trying to 'get something off to Pinker for dear life', a revealing phrase. When the essay finally arrived in England – Conrad either sending or, as the case may be, re-sending it – Pinker had no trouble placing it speedily with the prestigious *Fortnightly Review*. Its acceptance emboldened Conrad to enquire about writing more journalistic pieces on politics for the *Monthly Review*, which Newbolt had founded and until October of the previous year had edited. His response is unknown, but as an essayist Conrad's originality is marked. 'Autocracy and War' draws on several devices more common in fiction; it is complexly, even idiosyncratically structured; and it suggests an observer whose deep meditation on the nature of autocracy, particularly its history in Russia, establishes his impeccable credentials. When the piece was collected in Conrad's essays, *Notes on Life and Letters* (1921), one reviewer found it severely lacking in balance, qualifying it as 'condemnation in the form of rhapsody'.

Home beckoned, but the Conrads lingered as spring set in. Jessie was still receiving electrical treatment, and the holiday, whatever its additional expense and the lack of progress in Conrad's work, had at least helped her. For his part, Conrad was heartily sick of Capri, and when the annual visitation of beer-drinking German tourists descended on the island, he had had enough: 'this climate, this sirocco, this transmontana, these flat roofs, these sheer rocks, this blue sea – are impossible'. As he wrote to Pinker just before leaving by boat for Marseilles in mid-May: 'I *am* glad to be off at last.'

In prospect lay the staging of *One Day More* by the Incorporated Stage Society, a group that specialised in 'difficult' work and plays likely to fall foul of the Examiner of Plays, dramatic censorship being enforced by the office of the Lord Chamberlain. Before leaving Capri, Conrad toyed with the notion, and had even blocked out a sample, of a series of short stories, possibly about the Boer War, 'of extracts from *private* letters of a war correspondent. Imagine him writing to his girl – the inner truth of his feelings – things that *don't* go into his war correspondence – that *can't* go into it'. This Kiplingesque fantasy developed no further, but as a symptom of creative anaemia it sets off alarms.

Of Conrad's feelings on revisiting Marseilles and the haunts of his youth, last seen in 1878, we know nothing. It had changed as much as he, with steam replacing sail in the Vieux Port. Some of his time in the city was spent in the company of Marguerite Poradowska, who was wintering in the Midi. He arrived at The Pent fatigued by the boat-train journey to Folkestone. News of the successful sale of 'Autocracy and War' came just as gout struck, perhaps in part caused by a return to an English diet, more heavily meat-based than that on Capri. With Pinker about to leave for New York on business, and after an absence of nearly five months, Conrad hastened to London, where he also intended to see Meldrum (about *Maga* and some *Mirror* sketches), Colvin (about the staging of *One Day More* planned for June), and Rothenstein and Newbolt (about the Royal Bounty grant). He completed only part of his ambitious schedule before running back home ill, his meeting with Rothenstein having been marked by ill-temper. (Rothenstein twice refers to Conrad's attitude as 'hysterical' about the method of paying out the grant.)

Galsworthy, who saw him in early July, reported that Conrad was 'especially well just now', his recovery obviously complete. He went to town several times to see *One Day More* in rehearsal. Given the production's non-commercial nature, the opportunity mainly offered insights into the theatre for future use. *One Day More* was a resounding flop. Its four performances brought in a beggarly amount of money, but focused the attention of stage managers and what Conrad called 'an exceptionally intelligent audience', on him. George Bernard Shaw, at the crest of his career, was enthusiastic, but as Conrad later recalled with a humour that only thinly covers disappointment: 'the freezing atmosphere of that auditorium . . . was cold enough to preserve a dead sheep to the end of ages'. Later still, he considered a performance by the Stage Society as 'a sort of cheerful funeral ceremony, or at any rate a certificate of unfitness to live as far as the large public is concerned'.

One Day More shared a double bill at the Royalty Theatre with Laurence Alma-Tadema's *The New Felicity: A Modern Comedy*, and the pairing of plays was unhappy. Conrad's stark vision of domestic tyranny and a woman adrift sat oddly with a comedy; the play was hardly summer fare even for a select audience; and the actors, at least in his view, were 'awful'. Whether in self-defence or in a bout of realisation that dialogue was not his strong suit and that West End plays were mainly concerned with domestic, and specifically English, situations, Conrad judged the experience a waste of time. Journalism still seemed an outlet, and he managed, during a period of creative drift, to land a £25 commission from the *Standard* for an article celebrating the centenary of Trafalgar; in due course he awkwardly tagged the piece on Nelson on to *The Mirror of the Sea*.

Juggling projects, Conrad became preoccupied with *Chance*, though it was not to be completed until seven years later. He seems to have found his vein once again, but a tempest in a teapot now rose up: Conrad got into a huff about the editing of his Nelson essay, complaining about cuts. The *Standard*'s editor, H. A. Gwynne, stood his ground, begging to inform Conrad of 'the exigencies of newspaper production'. Conrad's response to the whole affair was off balance, possibly the result of stress. His wife, who had made a good recovery during and after the stay in Italy, had a 'nervous breakdown of a sort', which was complicated by a heart condition. As for himself, Conrad diagnosed sheer boredom, punctuated by attacks of gout, as part of the reason for his pique. However glad he was to leave languorous Capri, daily life at The Pent seems to have been taking a toll. Much as the Conrads liked the house, its isolation offered few diversions and it was impossible socially. 'Amy Foster' suggests the limited views and experience of those living in the Kentish countryside. Positive as The Pent had proved for Conrad's work and as a brake on expenses, when he was not at his desk the place could induce a sense of claustrophobia. Occasional escapes to town were necessary, but they drained a purse that was too often nearly empty. Jessie Conrad required more bustle and more company, and, gregarious and fun-loving, she must have found the relative seclusion burdensome at times: becoming ill was one way of rebelling against it.

The Conrads went up for a week's stay in lodgings in Kennington, in south London, in mid-November. Overcrowded and not entirely 'safe', the location was chosen for its proximity to Jessie's mother, and in order that they might take medical advice about Jessie's nervous trouble. Rather than proving salutary, the visit to town once again proved calamitous, as Borys contracted scarlet fever and dysentery, followed by complications that affected his kidneys. Professional care was required; costs mounted; the strain on the boy's already stressed mother increased; and the usual cycle of overspending set in as the one-week stay stretched to six.

Unable to see friends for fear of spreading contagion, Conrad dictated two short stories for ready cash, 'The Anarchist' and 'The Informer', dry runs for *The Secret Agent*, which he began shortly after. These 'anarchist' stories are a further development of the political interests evident on Capri, and at this point Conrad may, indeed, himself have harboured a secret longing for radical change, not least in the patterns of his life. He also finally completed 'Gaspar Ruiz', a long short story about tyranny, liberation, and revolution set in South America. Its acceptance by the *Pall Mall Magazine* for £126 (£47,900) was welcome news as the money, which signalled his now solid reputation, would cover Borys's medical expenses and the London stay. Before Christmas, again felled by gout, Conrad took to bed in all likelihood feeling like Job as tribulations gathered without cease: 'constant invalidism and persistent calamities' is the phrase he used in writing to David Meldrum. Amidst these, his wife became pregnant for the second time.

When Borys was well enough to return to The Pent, the Conrads arrived home just after the turn of the year accompanied by a nurse. But 1906 began badly: poisoned by a disinfectant she had used, Borys swelled up and ran a dangerously high pulse, forcing Conrad to search for a doctor in driving rain. The experience may well have encouraged thoughts of a winter escape, and he soon argued that six weeks in Montpellier would not be a 'luxury' but 'a necessity of life'. It would also be an opportunity for a change before Jessie's pregnancy became too advanced. The university town, which Conrad may have visited during his distant youth in the South of France, offered fewer diversions than Marseilles, and, although gracious, was not 'fashionable' like glittering Biarritz.

The Conrads arrived from Paris to find Carnival in full swing alongside full-scale riots occasioned by a bill presented to the Chamber of Deputies that proposed separating the French state from the Roman Catholic Church. They settled into the handsome Hôtel

Riche et Continental on the Place de la Comédie, also the location of the Opéra. It was warm and sunny, and Conrad took to writing in the elegantly laid out Jardin du Peyrou, beginning a story called 'Verloc', another excursion into the territory of two of his recent short stories and to be roughly the same length. In time, it expanded into *The Secret Agent*, as Conrad laid *Chance* aside. Aware that his previous time on the Continent had been a complete failure in terms of work done, Conrad regularly sent copy to Pinker and knocked *The Mirror of the Sea* into final shape as Borys took riding and French lessons.

Conrad lost (or claimed to have lost) his wallet, and requested £25 from Pinker. The arrival of another child would entail more expense and demand more steady work, and he announced the forthcoming change in his life to his agent. Conrad had been a dutiful rather than doting father to Borys, who celebrated his eighth birthday in mid-January. Jessie, who turned thirty-three a month later, was recovering from the previous autumn's nervous troubles and coping with her new condition. One wonders if her pregnancy was planned, or if it signals an attempt to smooth over a troubled relationship. Her husband was undoubtedly highly strung and, as she told her sister Dolly, 'always very difficult to manage'. Jessie did so partly through pluck and a keen sense of humour, but these are not infallible remedies for testiness, and, as a number of observers have noted, Conrad remained more often than not mystified by 'the English sense of humour', which tends to the subtly ironic and self-mocking. At times he found his wife's easy humour irksome. And not surprisingly, the writings of a man who once claimed that the whole history of humanity could be written on a cigarette-paper – 'They were born, they suffered, they died' – little testify to a highly developed sense of play, although they evidence an appreciation of the ironic and the grotesque. Conrad's rare jokes, on the other hand, tend to be somewhat clumsy and overly self-conscious. (Of a childhood friend who had become a successful beetroot producer, he wrote: 'The beet grown from this seed contained more sugar to the square inch – or was it to the square root? – than any other kind of beet' and 'Mr Verloc, steady like a rock – a soft kind of rock – marched now along a street which could with every propriety be described as private.')

As the prospect of the Conrads' return home loomed, Conrad was predicting that 'Verloc' would reach 18,000 words and already had in mind another story, about a bomb in a hotel, a motif subsequently much reworked as the centrepiece of *The Secret Agent*. The months in the South of France had proved a success: his family's health and his own had improved; a better mood had resulted; and he was writing steadily. He returned home to proofs of *The Mirror of the Sea* in mid-April and to news that Edward Garnett's father, Richard, had died. Meanwhile 'Verloc', as happened with 'Jim' and 'Nostromo', continued to stretch beyond its originally planned length.

As Jessie Conrad's delivery neared, plans for her confinement in London, where medical care was better than in rural Kent, were finalised. The Galsworthys generously offered their flat at 14 Addison Road, a 'wide, tree-lined' street in Kensington, while they went abroad. Conrad repaid the favour by setting up a luncheon at which Pinker successfully proposed to take on Galsworthy as a client. The Conrads' arrival in London in early July, with much luggage, was meticulously planned, with dinner for four (the family were bringing a maid) ordered beforehand, but when Galsworthy suggested strawberries, Conrad vigorously spurned the idea: 'by a merciful dispensation of Providence I detest the things'.*

He worked to good purpose on 'Verloc' in the 'detached house of light stone behind green railings', a haven of calm not far from Notting Hill's slums, where at 9.30 a.m. on 2 August 1906, John Alexander Conrad Korzeniowski ('J-A-C-K'), arriving only a few days late, made an easy entrance into the Conrad family. The new father had an attack of paternal nerves during the week leading up to his son's birth, but he seemed happy, as was Jessie. A girl had apparently been hoped for, but from the first, Conrad took to this son, 'of an amiable and unassuming disposition', as he described the newborn. Not only were his two sons to remain very different in temperament and achievement, but also held distinct places in their parents' hearts. John was his father's favourite; Borys, until the early 1920s, his mother's. Considering that he was an only child until the age of eight and a half, Borys proved remarkably free from immediate sibling

---

* His attitude was less hostile a few summers later when he thanked another friend for 'strawberries – the most Excellent fruit'.

rivalry, celebrating 'Brother Jack's' birth by allotting him a half-interest in Escamillo (affectionately, 'Millo'), the family dog.

Conrad seems to have increasingly enjoyed family life after his second son's arrival, although another child of course added pressures to an already strained income. Denied much of a childhood himself, he grew into the role of father slowly, with Borys almost serving as a preparation for John, although his children's physical needs and bursts of energy seem at times to have perplexed him. By necessity a bookish child and by temperament an introverted one, Conrad found Borys's more typical boyish extroversion and enthusiasm for the outer world and John's love of nature causes for curiosity and even wonderment. Conrad shared his sons' fascination with machinery – he enjoyed building Meccano models and playing with toy ships with John; Conrad's own leisure activities were reading and chess. At a time when childhood itself was undergoing redefinition – with children less often treated and dressed as small adults and less frequently on the lower rungs of the ladder of gainful employment – Conrad as father, as in so many things, stands on the cusp of the late Victorian and the Modern.

Amidst the disruptions caused by John's birth, 'Verloc' somehow grew. A gulf opens up between Conrad's desk and his part as paterfamilias: he was writing about a dysfunctional family and a riven society. Despite now ritual cries about not getting on quickly enough with his writing, he seems to have been comparatively happy, perhaps even needing a pretext to feel discontented. Thus, although lodging near Holland Park, an oasis in overcrowded London, he complained to Will Rothenstein about 'the wilderness of bricks' that oppressed his spirit and Borys's, yet almost as soon as he was back in Kent he seized the opportunity of a London break to attend the opening of Galsworthy's *The Silver Box* at the Court Theatre on Sloane Square (later the Royal Court Theatre), where he saw Garnett and Wells. The play's director, Harley Granville-Barker, then *the* power on the London theatre scene, urged Conrad to write a play, an idea he tucked into the back of his mind.

In addition to this nod of encouragement, he could celebrate *The Mirror of the Sea*'s excellent reception, accompanied by a loud chorus of praise from friends – the Galsworthys, Garnett, Lucas, Henry James,

Conrad on a horse

Conrad in Cracow by Walery Rzewuski (1874)

Ewa Korzeniowska (née Bobrowska), Conrad's mother

Apollo Korzeniowski, Conrad's father

Marguerite Poradowska, Belgian writer, Conrad's 'Aunt'

Conrad's relative Aniela Zagórska, with her daughters Aniela and Karola

Apollo Korzeniowski (right) in exile (1860s), with two unknown Poles

Conrad's maternal uncle Tadeusz Bobrowski

Conrad in Le Havre by Charles Potier (1882)

Late-nineteenth century Marseilles: the Cannebière with the Vieux Port in the background

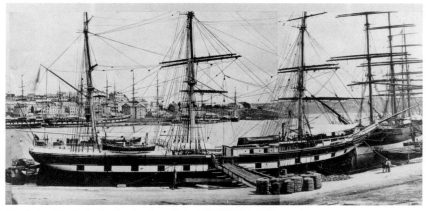

The Duke of Sutherland, Circular Quay, Sydney (12 January 1871)

Inside the London Sailors' Home, Well Street, near the Tower of London

Looking across the Thames from the Tilbury Hotel at Gravesend, showing ships at anchor

The SS Stanley, similar in construction to the SS Roi des Belges, which Conrad commanded on the Congo River, from a painting by Frans Hens

John Galsworthy (c. 1895)

T. Fisher Unwin

Stephen Crane

H. G. Wells (1903)

R. B. Cunninghame Graham
(c. 1890)

Conrad by Charles Beresford
(1904)

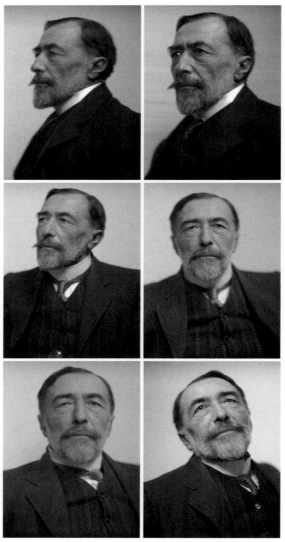

Conrad by Alvin Langdon Coburn (11 March 1916)

and Rothenstein. Even Kipling was moved to write a congratulatory note. Happy with the 'really appreciative' reviews, Conrad, in curmudgeonly fashion, felt that some critics had, with pleasure, exiled him to the ocean even as he was completing a novel about London. *The Secret Agent*'s serial ending, like *Nostromo*'s, was so rushed as to be botched, and, wanting to revise the novel extensively for its book form, Conrad complained of serious depression and general ill health. As an antidote he planned another trip to the South, with departure for Montpellier planned for mid-December. *En passant*, there would be dinner in Paris with Marguerite Poradowska and lunch with Davray, who had recently seen his translation of 'Karain' published in the magazine *Le Mercure de France*, and the poet and playwright Rémy de Gourmont.

Only eight months after they had left it, the Conrads were back at the Hôtel Riche. Hopes of staving off gout, saving on expenses, and enjoying good weather were sufficient excuses for leaving England in December. As regards the weather, the arrival was a partial failure: cold over Christmas, the temperature dipped to as low as minus 4°C on the 30th, but Conrad was simply glad to escape gloomy Kent, revelling in what he called the 'cold, calm dry brilliant' weather. He loafed in the sunshine, picked at Davray's translation of 'Karain' for its publication in book form, and, although nothing actually got on to paper, contemplated future work. Jessie, whose eyes had lately been bothering her – yet another in a seemingly unending series of ailments – received £25 for a cookery book from the publisher Alston Rivers and set to work. *The Handbook of Cookery for a Small House* did not, however, see the light of day until Heinemann published it in 1923. There were now two writers in the family. (She also later wrote on food for various newspapers.)

Conrad's own plans were to get on with *Chance*, and there were no entertainments to distract him – the opera went on strike after *Tosca* on 3 January 1907 and remained dark for the rest of the Conrads' stay – but the weather made him languid. To Hueffer, like himself an ardent Francophile, he reported on the land's 'inexpressible' beauty and he went about 'entranced' and 'drunk with colour'. He must have been tempted at least to think of resettling in an area that so stimulated his senses and that held old memories, but his ties to England had strengthened. Suddenly the languor lifted, and he was writing: 'I'm at a piece of work that utterly absorbs me,' he told Davray. It was inspired by newspaper accounts of a duel in Paris between two military officers. The staunch refusal by both the principals and seconds to reveal its cause encouraged sensationalist press coverage. 'Le Mystérieux Duel' revived an old story of a duel between two of Napoleon's officers. Conrad somehow came across a version of it and immediately began fleshing out its bare bones, temporarily completing 'The Duel' as Mardi Gras began. Wandering about the town with Borys, Conrad was relieved of his wallet by a pickpocket when they alighted from a tram-car to help a woman who had been struck by it. What he had gained on the one hand ('The Duel' had virtually written itself and the incident of the tram may have provided material for the close of *Under Western Eyes*), he had lost with the other. He passed his spare time taking Spanish lessons and doing background reading at the Bibliothèque Municipale for the projected Mediterranean novel conceived on Capri. He also picked away at *Chance* – or at least claimed to have done so.

Borys resumed riding and French lessons and was also learning to fence. Over a game of dominoes with him, Conrad suddenly realised that his son was seriously ill. Adenoids were diagnosed, and an operation was in prospect, but then Borys came down with measles, followed by bronchitis, fever, and anaemia. The boy simply melted away, and concern gave way to outright alarm as problems with his lungs were detected. He rallied but remained weak. Having been a sickly child himself, Conrad may have bitterly recalled the well-meant but barely adequate care provided to him as his own parents moved from one temporary home to the next. Despite the help of Elena Wright, a relative of Jessie's who took dictation and typed, as well as a girl to help out, the situation proved emotionally draining. Dispirited, Conrad slept badly and fell behind in his work, eking out a mere 500 words a day, as his friends flourished. Galsworthy, who had completed *Joy*, a new play, had another novel published, *The Country House*, and saw *The Silver Box* revived, while Hueffer celebrated the publication of *Privy Seal*, the second novel in his *Fifth Queen* trilogy. The Conrads now had the spring weather to console them, but, unlike the previous spring's outing abroad, this stay was proving a mixed success. Even 'The Duel', which had begun so well, was taking longer to finish than Conrad had contemplated.

With the story finally done, *Chance* again moved to the centre of Conrad's desk, only to be dislodged by gout, lethargy, and depression. Retreating to a spa seemed advisable, and the Conrads left for Geneva on 15 May 1907, leaving a trail of debts behind them. The baby, suffering from whooping cough, sickened dramatically during the journey. Fearing contagion, La Roseraie, where Conrad had stayed during his water cures in the 1890s, cancelled their reservation and the family took refuge in the Hôtel de la Poste. The full force of another disaster struck shortly after the Conrads' arrived: Conrad, who had intended to revise *The Secret Agent* extensively, found page rather than galley proofs waiting for him. He turned to them despairingly as John began to mend in the hotel garden's fresh air.

There was, however, to be no respite from paternal anxieties. Borys fell ill yet again, this time with rheumatic fever. Perhaps remembering Titus Andronicus, who laughs because he has 'not another tear to shed', Conrad told Pinker that he would not be offended if he laughed at the news. Helping to nurse Borys, Conrad began a hydropathic cure himself, drinking quantities of mineral water to stave off gout. As he did so, Borys, already weakened, now developed pleurisy. Conrad comforted his son by making paper birds and reading him James Fenimore Cooper and Captain Marryat, his own boyhood favourites. Trying to maintain a cool head amidst family troubles, he somehow added nearly 30,000 words to *The Secret Agent*, opting for his sense of artistic integrity rather than expediency.

He began to think about returning to England and 'a fresh start' at the end of July. With considerable rent overdue on The Pent, 'damnably expensive to live in', the 'start' would mean finding a new home. Conrad planned to complete *Chance* by his fiftieth birthday in early December, and meanwhile every word sold counted, for he was now deeply in debt to Pinker. Including medical expenses, this continental excursion (now 'this damnable outing') had entailed runaway costs.

Back at Pent Farm in August, the Conrads would not leave England again until the summer of 1914. Almost immediately, Conrad went to

Winchester to look at a house on what proved to be a wild-goose chase as he learned only on the spot that the town's climate encouraged gout. His characterisation of London as a 'wilderness of bricks' suggests a preference for country life, not least because of its lower costs. An advertised 'old Farmhouse 2½ miles from Luton' inspired enquiries. The £60 rent, including rates, was, in fact, higher than he was paying for The Pent, but, by way of compensation, London was much closer, with a whole hour shaved off travel time. The property of Sir Julius Wernher, the lord of the manor, who had made his fortune in diamonds and gold in the Transvaal, the roomy eighteenth-century house set on high ground in a quiet, agricultural area was adjacent to the ruins of Someries Castle. Cora Crane, who visited in mid-November, described it as 'a heavenly old farm' with a 'beautiful walled garden'.

With movers arranged and furniture purchased, the Conrads moved as planned, but met with utter chaos on their arrival. Furniture was scattered everywhere; the workmen were still about; a pump was in pieces; and – the back-breaking straw – one of the removal vans had gone missing. In the midst of this confusion, Borys was to begin school at St Gregory's in Luton. The turmoil made work impossible, and Hueffer, badly needing the money that Conrad owed him, was pleading for payment. The move coincided with the publication of *The Secret Agent*, on 13 September 1907. The mixed reviews motivated Conrad to proclaim the book 'an honourable failure', and again he had to take consolation in the intelligent response of his friends. Graham 'liked' it; Garnett reviewed it favourably, and to Conrad's unconcealed pleasure; and Wells, its dedicatee, wrote a close and intelligent appreciation. Arnold Bennett confided in his diary that in *Nostromo*'s wake it gave off 'a disappointing effect of slightness', although it was precisely the 'simplicity' of its telling that motivated *Truth* to proclaim it 'a book to read'. By the time the press had had its say Conrad had convinced himself that the reception was 'distinctly good', and retrospectively he somewhat exaggerated the hostile comments on the tale's 'sordid surroundings and moral squalor'.

As Borys settled into school, the Conrads played host to the Galsworthys, and Conrad resumed work on *Chance*. At the request of

Garnett, whose play *The Breaking Point* had been refused a licence for production, he added his voice to a protest against dramatic censorship. The Lord Chamberlain's prudery, exercised through his Examiner of Plays, the paid incarnation of Mrs Grundy, stirred Conrad into a long letter of 'stately invective and contemptuous derision'. Ruthlessly mangled, first by Garnett, whose cuts received Conrad's begrudging permission, and then by the *Daily Mail*, 'The Censor of Plays' takes on bumbling officialdom and takes a stand on artistic freedom. Conrad also became a signatory, with Barrie, James, Hardy, Hueffer, Shaw, J. M. Synge, and Wells, to a letter to *The Times* demanding the outright abolition of censorship. Characteristically wary of public political commitments, he was moved to defend the position of art in the nation's life, repelled by the history of autocracy and ideological containment long practised, as his protest observes, by Imperial China and Imperial Russia.

As he was taking this public stance Conrad's circle widened to include twenty-eight-year-old Stephen Reynolds, later a social critic and short-story writer. At this point the young man had to his credit an illustrated guide, *Devizes and Roundabout*, and was working on *A Poor Man's House*, a hotch-potch of dialogue, rumination, poetry, polemic, and sea shanties based in part on his experience of lodging with a fisherman's family in Sidmouth. (Published the following year, it was praised by Conrad, Galsworthy, and Arnold Bennett.) Reynolds was a Garnett discovery, but the introduction to Conrad apparently came through Pinker. ('I'm a Pinkerite,' Reynolds declared when Garnett was attempting to place Reynolds' novel *The Holy Mountain* with Heinemann.) Reynolds settled in Devon, his love for his married fisherman friend, Bob Wooley changing the course of his life.

Another sexual outcast invited to Someries at this time was Cora McNeil, the former Cora Crane. Coming up from London on Jessie Conrad's invitation, she arrived with a 'Mrs Barrett', one of the 'girls' who worked for her in the brothel she now ran, as a bluestocking madam, in Jacksonville, Florida, where she had disastrously remarried: her new husband, a younger man, was an alcoholic of highly unstable temperament. The 'proper big welcome' Jessie promised might have been rather less warm had the hostess been fully aware of the sources of her guests' income. Henry James, by contrast, had firmly rebuffed

Mrs McNeil's attempt to re-establish contact. In common with H. G. Wells, who entertained her and her travelling companion, nine-year-old Borys had no qualms about her, meeting the party at Luton station on his way home from school. (His mother's description identifying him as 'a fair haired school-boy with a fawn overcoat and a school cap' echoes the description of Stevie, the youth who is blown up by a bomb, in *The Secret Agent*.) He picked violets for the guests, before Cora, after a 'good lunch' provided by her hostess, whom she found 'fat & an invalid', returned to London.

A good train service from St Pancras both encouraged visitors and trips to town. Conrad visited the Hueffers and his old friend Ted Sanderson, on home leave from South Africa. He invited Pinker to lunch, which suggests the development of a warmer personal relationship with his agent; Sidney Colvin came for a week; back from Italy, Will Rothenstein was also invited to call. Amidst this social whirl and attacks of gout (the latter most likely the result of the former) his work languished. A day after his fiftieth birthday, Conrad sent pages of *Chance* for typing, and revealed to his agent that he had in mind a new short story, 'Razumov', about a revolutionist blown up by his own bomb. Like several of Conrad's short stories, it was destined to take a different shape and to displace his main project, still *Chance*, and in due course it grew into the full-length novel *Under Western Eyes*. Conrad soon began sending instalments of the new story to Pinker for typing, as its plot was being fleshed out. To Galsworthy he mentioned that he was writing a story involving betrayal, love, and confession, and to his agent that the story concentrated on 'the very essence of things Russian'. The political involvements of the autumn had taken an unexpected turn, and Conrad, ever the chameleon as a writer, was yet again venturing into new artistic territory.

Stephen Reynolds was invited for Christmas, 'a kind notion', about which his guest felt 'all sorts of things, all good'. The holiday brought bad weather and more gout, which struck with full force on Boxing Day, lingering, with intermittent severity, until after New Year's Day. The attack probably accounts for Conrad's only known bout of vegetarianism; it is as if he suspected he was being poisoned at his own table. His doctor prescribed *Colchicum autumnale*, a medicinal plant popularly known as 'Naked Ladies'. Eating red meat and seafood is responsible for an accumulation of uric acid crystals in the joints, especially in the extremities, and causes the condition, but at the time the relationship of gout to diet was not fully established and myths about the effects of over-indulging in port and heavy wine-drinking substituted for scientific knowledge. Conrad did enjoy wine and spirits in moderation, and in his later years, when he was again living in Kent, favoured Bridge's Fleur-de-Lis Taproom as his local for a peg of gin of an evening. A man whom Norman Douglas characterised as 'the greatest stickler for uprightness I have ever known' was by temperament little inclined to over-indulge, and alcoholics in Conrad's fiction (notably the chief engineer of the *Patna* in *Lord Jim*) are treated without sympathy.

Conrad attempted to deal with his almost alarming financial situation by appealing to Pinker yet again. His timing was ill chosen, for, irritated by several writers in his stable, Pinker proved less than fully responsive. Conrad none the less refused to cancel a planned birthday treat for Borys, taking him to London to see the famous illusionist John Nevil Maskeleyne. Spending his 'last loose shillings' on the outing, he told Galsworthy that he was shivering in his study because he was unable to pay his coal bill. Begging letters once again went off to Pinker and to Galsworthy, and he refurbished and amplified, for quick sale to *London Magazine* 'The Black Mate', a jokey story apparently written for a competition held by the enormously popular *Tit-Bits* back in 1886. (In *Ulysses*, Joyce expresses his contempt for the magazine by having Leopold Bloom use its pages as toilet-paper.) Whatever the story's origins – his wife's version is dramatically at odds with Conrad's own – it deals with deception exposed.* A sailor dyes his prematurely whitening hair to get a job, loses his hair dye at sea, and then claims to his captain that his hair has turned white as the result of his having seen a ghost. Perhaps the tale's only notable aspect is the ghost itself, which migrated to the opening section of

---

* Jessie Conrad claimed to have supplied her husband with the story's kernel, which rules out its having been written nearly ten years before they met. The story's interest in 'jaunty tricks' is, on the other hand, un-Conradian and appears to have been cut to measure for *Tit-Bits*; the magazine did offer a 'Special Prize for Sailors' in 1886 that may well have attracted Conrad to try his hand at writing.

'Razumov'. Stories were very much Conrad's focus at this time, as he tinkered with copy for A Set of Six, a new collection scheduled to appear in the autumn of 1908, bringing together the stories that had appeared over the past two years: 'Gaspar Ruiz', 'The Informer', 'The Brute', 'An Anarchist', 'The Duel', and 'Il Conde'.

A winter excursion in 1908 was not an option. Claiming that his agency was having problems, Pinker, as Conrad knew, would balk at the expenditure and be likely to have bitter recollections of the previous year's disaster. Furthermore, Borys was attending school, and a careful eye had to be kept on his health. Staying put, Conrad made steady progress on 'Razumov', which was now growing into a novella, but payment for the work would only come in time, and again he applied to the Royal Literary Fund for relief. His application states that his income for 1907 had amounted to £427. His case came up at its 8 April 1908 meeting, supported by letters from Wells and Galsworthy, the latter informing the committee that Conrad's 'life ever since he became a writer' had been 'one long struggle to keep his head above water'. There was campaigning before the event, and the committee was packed with supporters. Barrie put the motion, seconded by E. V. Lucas, and Conrad was granted £300 (£109,000 in 2005 terms). Economies were planned, and moving from Someries had already been discussed. Taken to reduce costs, the new house had, to the contrary, proved expensive, and Conrad openly regretted leaving The Pent.

'Razumov' continued to expand, but Pinker's growing frustrations with his client provoked a minor skirmish. Anxieties, quietly accumulating, may have helped bring on 'an attack of gouty dyspepsia' that was, as so often, compounded by depression. Over the next year and a half Conrad's mental state began slowly to unravel. The first worrying signs, read by himself, were manifested over the summer: 'I have been ill in body and am too diseased in mind to say anything about myself . . . Everything is very bad here,' he confided to Hueffer. Complaints thread intermittently through observations to friends, but the tone subtly shifts in this uncharacteristic revelation of his inner feelings.

A Set of Six, published by Methuen on 6 August 1908, was widely noticed – a testimony to Conrad's solid reputation – and not badly received. Garnett's approval caused pleasure, but one review upset and even angered Conrad. Reviewing the volume for the *Daily News*, Robert Lynd characterised the author as 'a man without country and language'. Lynd's real complaint, which Conrad preferred to ignore, was about his use of English. Lynd makes only general statements of principle, however, and not specific comments: 'A writer who ceases to see the world coloured by his own language – for language gives colour to thoughts and things in a way that few people understand – is apt to lose the concentration and intensity of vision without which the greatest literature cannot be made.' As regards country, the journalist asserted that Conrad had found 'a new patriotism for himself in the sea. His vision of men, however, is the vision of the cosmopolitan, of a homeless person.' Given Conrad's recent and continuing bouts of depression, Lynd's insult – as Conrad saw it – could hardly have come at a worse moment. Insight into his psychological state, even discounting his characteristic exaggerations about it, can be garnered from a comment to one of his physicians: 'My brain may be all right but as I have an unconquerable impression that it is going to pieces, the look out is not cheery. A sort of horrible disillusion with everything has mastered me or all but. I am still struggling feebly but I feel the net is over me, and the spear is not very far.'

Unable entirely to brush off Lynd's comments as uninformed and merely stupid, as he could Orzeszkowa's attack on him at the outset of his career, Conrad was wounded and self-wounding, so much so that he was evidently unconsoled by the *Times Literary Supplement*'s observation that the stories were 'characteristically English' in their humour. He also crossed swords with Garnett, who ground an old and blunted axe in referring to his typical 'Slavonism'. To some degree, Conrad took Lynd's observations out of context and exaggerated their intent; he saw real offence (perhaps even malice) where none seems intended. Rejecting the press's facile categorisations, he understandably bridled at being pigeonholed as a writer of the sea. Personal feeling *was* involved – he must have been tired of critical misunderstanding and popular neglect – but he was also concerned, needlessly perhaps, about the impact such comments might have upon his readership, still 'the happy few' rather than the vast public.

Lynd had hit a sore point. Conrad had remade himself, adopting a language not his by birth and likewise choosing his nationality. In 'Poland Revisited' (1915), writing touchingly of leaving Britain to set out on a continental journey, he is moved by the gentle landscape of Kent to a confession: 'I felt that all this had a very strong hold on me as the embodiment of a beneficent and gentle spirit; that it was dear to me not as an inheritance but as an acquisition, as a conquest in the sense in which a woman is conquered – by love, which is a sort of surrender.' Rarely has patriotic feeling, too often seen in its brutish, tribal forms, been more tenderly expressed. Whatever his foreign accent and courtly manner, his odd turns of phrase and outright grammatical errors, Conrad had made English and England his 'home', and here was a representative of the host culture, a Little Englander, telling him that he did not 'belong', whereas he felt strongly that he did.

Conrad's awareness that some people would always think of him as 'a sort of freak, a bloody amazing furriner writing in English', although it may have impinged upon, did not alter the way he saw himself. His integration into English life had been preceded by his integration into French life. Arriving young in France, he felt no stranger there, and indeed insisted on the essential Western character of Polish culture, which allowed him to make the required mental and emotional shifts, if not quite seamlessly, then with a degree of ease: 'Nothing is more foreign than what in the literary world is called Slavonism, to the Polish temperament with its traditions of self-government, its chivalrous view of moral restraints and an exaggerated respect for individual rights: not to mention that the whole Polish mentality, Western in complexion, had received its training from Italy and France and, historically, had always remained, even in religious matters, in sympathy with the most liberal currents of European thought.' Conrad's claim to be British *avant la lettre* is made on the basis of shared values and political ideologies. He viewed himself as a Western European culturally, rejecting the claims of the East, with its traditions of autocracy and religious orthodoxy; however much the sceptically inclined might wish to find Conrad's claims exaggerated and his vision of Polish history rose-coloured, it was deep and even fundamental to Conrad's sense of himself. Some insecurity is natural to immigrants, but, with time, it tends to ease and in certain cases, as links are forged and the unfamiliar becomes banal, it can dissipate.

Some have seen the Lynd affair as goading Conrad into writing *A Personal Record*. He began it in September during a visit to the Hueffers, now settled in the small Kentish village of Aldington, on the northern edge of Romney Marsh. If so, he responded in no immediate way to Lynd, choosing to claim English as his language and the Republic of Letters as his country much more subtly. He returned to 'that damned Luton place' with a plan to spin out some recollections, as he had the essays in *The Mirror of the Sea*, assuring Pinker, somewhat disingenuously, that this would not distract him from 'Razumov'. Conrad may actually have felt in a reminiscent mood (he was, after all, now of an age when some looking back is normal), but Hueffer, his ambitious plans advancing for a literary monthly, the *English Review* – 'a supplement indispensable to intelligent men and women' – identified a vein that could be mined for money. Hueffer felt that Conrad's regular appearance in a journal devoted to new and challenging writing was essential. Recollections that touched little upon his life at sea would be a new departure and would usefully keep his name before the public's fickle eye. Throughout the autumn, composition of his memoirs pushed aside 'Razumov', then, in truth, stalled, although Conrad put on a brave face to his agent (and perhaps even attempted to deceive himself) about this. In the end, his monthly total of words was about his average, but was devoted mainly to autobiography, not fiction.

Back at Someries, he began dictating his recollections to Miss Hallowes, now re-engaged for work on 'Razumov'. By early December, and after another attack of gout, he had completed four of the eventual seven chapters of 'Some Reminiscences' (later *A Personal Record*)* and drafted his only story on a Polish subject, in due course titled 'Prince Roman'. His ambitious plans 'to make Polish life enter English literature . . . To reveal a very particular state of society, bring forward individuals with very special traditions and touch in a

---

* Conrad's recollections, serialised in the *English Review* from December 1908 to June 1909 under the title 'Some Reminiscences', were published in book form in January 1912 in England as *Some Reminiscences* but in the United States appeared as *A Personal Record*, a title Conrad adopted for all later printings.

personal way upon such events as for instance the liberation of the serfs' had changed completely. The volume as finished concentrates on the writing of *Almayer's Folly* and the beginning of Conrad's sea career, with his own and his family's experiences in the Ukraine taking a minor role. At mid-life, he had wanted to look back and give coherence – both publicly and privately – to his diverse life but temperamentally shied away from self-revelation. Still less do these deliberately episodic reminiscences amount to an over-anxious *apologia pro vita sua* or a taking up of the sword against Lynd.

Eager to leave Someries but ever deeper in debt to Pinker, Conrad was caught in a vice: 'I can't think of anything or decide on any point.' Involvement in the *English Review* renewed his connection with Hueffer, brought in cash, about £20 per instalment of 'Some Reminiscences' (exempted from Pinker's 10 per cent commission), and confirmed Conrad's place among the leading writers of the day. Hueffer's inaugural issue, which appeared in late November, was a who's who of the writers that counted: Conrad's reminiscences rubbed shoulders with Hardy, Henry James, Galsworthy, W. H. Hudson, Cunninghame Graham, Wells, and a translation by Constance Garnett of a Tolstoy story. Had he wished, Conrad could have basked in glory and recognition, but storm clouds gathered. A fire that broke out in his study just before Christmas entailed bother, repairs, and expense, and could be read as a sign of a coming conflagration.

As the prospect of escaping Luton for a house in Aldington became real, Conrad returned to work on 'Razumov' and even talked of completing *The Rescuer*. In addition to saving on rent – the house there cost only £30 a year, half of the rent of Someries – the 'little hole', draughty and lacking modern conveniences, offered proximity to the Hueffers, a welcome development as the *English Review* got on securer financial footing. (Hueffer originally had financial backing for only four issues.) Variously described by Conrad as 'a little cottage without charm or beauty', 'our cage', and 'impossible', the house soon proved an aggravation, and nearness to Hueffer illusory. Then involved with Violet Hunt, a writer ten years his senior (her tendency to stage dramatic temper tantrums earned her the nickname 'Violent Hunt'), Hueffer was spending little time in Kent, and retreating to London as his troubled marriage finally collapsed.

As Conrad's finances deteriorated, his tone with Pinker became increasingly peremptory and then aggrieved. He flatly stated that life on £600 a year (£218,000 in 2005) was impossible; again made overly optimistic plans for economising; and considered applying for a Civil List pension, which, unlike a one-time Royal Bounty grant, was granted for life and would provide a regular income. Tired of the cramped and unsuitable house and otherwise unhappy, he announced to Stephen Reynolds that his nerves had 'gone to pieces'. The danger that they would actually do so was growing frighteningly, as he had to force words out on a regular basis to keep a roof over his and his family's head. The financial pressures were relentless, but given Conrad's temperament and his writing to date, Grub Street offered no realistic alternative to Mount Parnassus.

The escape from Someries finally occurred in mid-February 1909, with Conrad completing another instalment of 'Some Reminiscences' amidst the disruption. The shortest of the eventual book's seven 'chapters', it is an artistic manifesto in a belletristic mode and sits oddly in an autobiography, with Conrad lapsing into his *Mirror of the Sea* manner. It appeared in the same issue of the *English Review* as 'The Nature of a Crime', a story he and Hueffer had written in the spring of 1906. Published under the puerile pseudonym 'Baron Ignatz von Aschendrof' (the surname incorporates 'Conrad' and 'Ford'), the tale, characterised by Hueffer as 'awful piffle' even as it was being composed, involves embezzlement, sexual adventure, and threatened suicide. (As regards infidelity, potential public disgrace, and financial fiasco, it perhaps vividly prefigures the end of Hueffer's marriage.)

In the midst of a productive period, with two further instalments of 'Some Reminiscences' in view and 'Razumov' being picked at, Conrad had a falling-out with Hueffer over arrangements for a call by Dr Robert Mackintosh, who was then treating his gout. Hueffer, a drawing-room autocrat, had overstepped the bounds once too often, and his sometime collaborator muttered darkly about Hueffer's 'mania for managing the universe', a characterisation echoed in a comment to Norman Douglas: 'The fact is that H[ueffer] loves to manage people.' With Conrad's dander now raised, nothing would calm him, and Elsie Hueffer, deliberately or not, threw fuel on a vigorously smouldering fire, calling upon her friends in an attempt to enlist them on her side of her collapsing marriage. She met with a friendly welcome, but her 'horrible details and revelations' about Conrad's and Hueffer's mutual friend Arthur Marwood, whom she accused of making advances to her and with whom Hueffer had broken off relations, deeply upset the Conrads.

Marwood arrived to present his side of the story. Although he called on Conrad regularly, almost weekly, for some years, Marwood is one of Conrad's friends about whom frustratingly little can be said because of a lack of documentation. Conrad admired his friend, who, like his cousin 'Lewis Carroll' (Charles Dodgson), had read mathematics. He provided the writer with a reliable 'sounding board' for developing ideas, but Jessie Conrad reportedly 'detested' the Yorkshire squire, and Borys found a man whom others thought a brilliant conversationalist of encyclopaedic knowledge both 'unintelligent and bovine'. As regards the immediate issue, Conrad was inclined to trust Marwood rather than Elsie Hueffer, but the tale was unsettling, and he brooded over Hueffer's personal and professional muddling: the *English Review*'s finances were becoming nearly as embroiled as Hueffer's because Hueffer had paid his contributors generously, and even over-generously, given that magazine's circulation was low.

Far from being able to manage the universe, Hueffer proved incapable of competently and decently handling his own affairs. The end came when he tried to arrange a meeting between Conrad and the American journalist and poet (and later novelist), Willa Cather, who was acting as a go-between for McClure in the United States and the *English Review*. Guilty again, in Conrad's eyes, of attempting to 'manage' him, Hueffer, who seems to have effected the introduction clumsily, merely succeeded in irritating Conrad, who later fulminated about McClure's enterprise: 'I am too English and even too European a writer for my prose to fit in with the dreary crude stuff he prints.' Patronised once too often by Hueffer, Jessie Conrad may also have stoked scattered fires. She had memories of his sometimes appalling behaviour, especially at The Pent, and seeing the last of Hueffer would certainly have pleased her.

Gout caused Conrad to miss the deadline for July's instalment of 'Some Reminiscences'. He deeply regretted the loss of income, earmarked for Borys's school fees. Elsie Hueffer continued to call, retailing gossip and the travails of her broken marriage, and Conrad, curious about the *Review*'s fate, was vitriolic about its management by 'that horrible Jew' David Soskice, Hueffer's brother-in-law. Given his statements about the issue elsewhere, the anti-Semitism, however crude, was casual. Conrad's hostility had deep roots: Soskice was Russian. And Conrad, had he been eagerly looking for excuses to break with Hueffer, had now found one. At a low point emotionally and determinedly inept at personal relationships, Hueffer complained that Conrad's failure to meet his deadline left 'Some Reminiscences' in a '*Ragged condition*'. Conrad defended the work as artistically complete as it stood, and when Hueffer announced in the *Review*'s July issue that his contributor's 'serious illness' prevented the continuance of the series, Conrad slammed the door on the friendship. Fully aware that Hueffer's nervous problems were causing him to spiral out of control, Conrad, unwell himself, was nevertheless exhausted by his collaborator's megalomania and '*impossible*' conduct. The mismanagement of an enterprise in which he had placed high hopes contributed to his touchiness, and on this sad and sour note the 'fatal partnership' dissolved. By winter, things had gone so badly between the two men that Conrad referred to 'that infernal Ford . . . going about raving'.

Other friends filled the gap left by Hueffer. The poet Arthur Symons, who had written favourably on Conrad's work and was then recovering from a complete mental collapse, was in touch, as was 'Reggie' Gibbon, a journalist and short-story writer who had seen service in the Merchant Navy. Conrad's friendship with the handsome thirty-year-old Welshman, which possibly came about through Pinker who acted as Gibbon's agent, became closer through Garnett's weekly lunches at the Mont Blanc restaurant in Gerrard Street. The luncheon club brought together younger talents and more established writers, and although Conrad attended infrequently, he came to know several young writers through it. Contact with Gibbon, who then lived in Wrotham (locally pronounced 'Rootem'), about 30 miles from Aldington, seems to have been particularly close at this time, and Conrad spoke with him 'for hours on end' about his work. As a sign of deepening ties, the Conrads spent their summer holidays in Trottiscliffe (locally 'Trosley') about 10 miles from Rochester, with

Reggie and Maisie Gibbon. Jessie, whose knees had deteriorated, had a break from domestic duties, while Conrad, who could not settle to writing, took a busman's holiday, looking through Gibbon's notes of an assignment in St Petersburg. True to form, the holiday proved troubled as John, who suffered mild heat stroke, required a doctor.

At a moment when Conrad needed a change of perspective, he received a long letter from a New Zealander who had lived in Malaya for years and had married a high-born Malay in Penang. Writing partly in appreciation of *The Mirror of the Sea*, Captain Carlos M. Marris, in England for medical treatment and to visit his family in Durham, vividly recalled Conrad's time out East, conjuring up bygone ships and bygone days. Moved to invite the 'soft-eyed black-bearded' sea captain to call upon him before he returned to Penang, Conrad, after the event, declared that his readers in the colonies would get 'more of the stories they like'.

The return to Far Eastern materials was soon realised: 'The Secret Sharer' – '*Quite* a good enough story' – poured out of him in early December as 'Razumov' still lay unfinished on his desk. Set in the Gulf of Siam, the story meditates intensely upon loyalty and justice, themes with which Conrad was wrestling in his longer project, and perhaps allowing him to make progress on it. If his history of its writing is reliable, he wrote its nearly 15,000 words in a fortnight (double his *monthly* average). The very welcome money went to cover the treatment of the Conrads' housemaid, Nellie Lyons, at Folkestone Hospital. Buoyant and attributing his change of mood to Dr Mackintosh's effective treatment, Conrad was excited at the prospect of writing further stories and completing either *The Rescuer* or *Chance*. Cold water was suddenly thrown upon this mood when Pinker, with whom he had apparently been somewhat out of touch, seems to have complained about time diverted from 'Razumov'. Worse, he issued an ultimatum – or what Conrad, at any rate, took to be one: the novel had to be completed within a fortnight, or cash advances would stop. Conrad threatened to 'fling the MS of Raz in the fire', or so he told Gibbon and Galsworthy. To his agent, he more temperately defended his rate of production and adduced chronic ill health.

The stage was set for a débâcle, with Conrad once again losing a sense of perspective. Pinker's communication had the opposite effect to that intended: it brought Conrad's writing to a dead halt. Conrad told Galsworthy that he had been 'nearly out of my mind' on receiving it, and whatever the reality of Pinker's tone and language, the ultimatum, coming as 'Razumov' entered its final phase, was badly timed. But the affair blew over, Conrad putting aside his exasperation and doggedly returning to his desk just before Christmas, although ill-feeling lingered. A jaunty promise to show up at Gibbon's with 'Pinker's scalp' hanging at his waist betrays his deeply wounded feelings and an anger that continued to seethe.

7

Breakdown and Recovery
(*1910–1914*)

For the Conrads, 1910, a year of family crisis, opened with an outbreak of influenza, at the time an epidemic throughout Kent. Conrad was unable to write, and Pinker, on hearing this, seems to have concluded that his client was up to old tricks. In communications with his agent, Conrad focused on plans for a volume of stories, with the promise of his new novel's penultimate batch of copy almost an afterthought. Making slow headway, he gave 'Razumov' its new and final title: *Under Western Eyes*. A promise to deliver the last chapters in person to Pinker on 17 January, was, in the event, cancelled, with Conrad again pleading illness. Ill or not, he simply had not finished his work and wrote furiously over the next few days. Telegrams were sent announcing the novel's completion on the 26th and Conrad's arrival in town the following day. At their meeting, the two men had words. Exasperated with Conrad, not fully aware of his shaky mental state, and perhaps feeling that the writer, massively in debt to him, was not being sufficiently open, Pinker precipitated an outright quarrel. Conrad seems to have taken particular offence at his agent's remark that he 'did not speak English' to him. After spending a restless night at Galsworthy's, he returned to Aldington and fell into a high fever accompanied by chills. Clifford Hackney, a doctor from Hythe, diagnosed 'a complete nervous breakdown' that had been 'coming on for months'.

Sentimentalists have attributed the breakdown to Conrad's 'confrontation' with his 'Polish ghosts' in *Under Western Eyes*, a work concerned with issues of national identity, personal loyalty, abandonment by the father, and betrayal and deceit, set in Russia and in Russian revolutionary circles in Geneva. This 'nationalist' reading of an emotional event relies upon the assumption that Conrad was no longer able to bear the terrible burden of 'betraying' the Polish dream of independence and that he nursed a deep-seated sense of guilt that had taken its long overdue revenge. The facts suggest a temperament overstrained for years and a series of choices, both recent and past, that had led to a dead end. Now a desperately ill man, Conrad had for some time been on a collision course with reality in regard to his everyday responsibilities. He had struggled under emotional and financial stress before he took up writing; was working as hard as he could to feed and to provide shelter for himself and his family; and had finally run out of options. Pinker, the source of his security, such as it was, and a quasi-paternal figure, had not only rebuffed but had also rejected him. And there are areas of Conrad's carefully guarded emotional life that remain too dark to allow for easy gauging of how rewarding in mid-life he was finding marriage and fatherhood.

Those attributing this crisis to Conrad's 'confrontation' with his past in his fiction have tended to neglect several pieces of evidence of greater weight. His history of 'nervous troubles' extended back to his deeply unhappy childhood; Marseilles and the Congo were notable trigger-points that suggest an underlying emotional malady; 'nerves' and depression plagued his adult life, and he had resorted several times to water cures to recover from them. The surprise, perhaps, is that a full-blown crisis had not occurred much earlier. More immediately, the break with Hueffer, for all its complications, was a neglected warning signal. Conrad had quarrelled with the world and urgently needed an escape from gathering pressures. His breakdown was a way of finding this. His debt to Pinker had swollen unmanageably, and the established pattern of overspending, dependency, and stopgap borrowing to make ends meet, whatever its several and partly excusable causes, had run its course. At the time of their quarrel, Conrad's debt to Pinker – not yet the close personal friend that he would later become – had increased to £2,700 (worth £973,000 in 2005), a figure so staggeringly large as to call seriously into question Pinker's business acumen and practices.

Conrad was more or less incapacitated from late January until early

April, when Edward Garnett called to find him recovering but still bedridden, and there were minor relapses thereafter – moments of panic and inertia. He appears only to have put the nervous illness, attended by a series of severe attacks of gout, finally behind him in May. His wife nursed him tenderly through the crisis, and whilst acutely anxious herself, coped as extremely difficult circumstances assailed the entire family. Aged twelve at the time, Borys glosses over his father's breakdown in his memoirs, either not wishing to air family laundry or wanting to avoid revisiting a traumatic episode. (Boarding at St Gregory's in Luton, he, in fact, witnessed little of it at first hand.) Not yet four, John was possibly too young to remember much about it, but he responded to his father's incapacity in a way that nevertheless reveals its distressing impact on him: 'Jackolo imitates my extinct tones, whilst scolding his favourite Teddy-bear, to perfection. The other day, I understand, he gave to some yokels an exhibition of my limping which astonished them not a little. All this is done in the innocence of his heart. He goes through these performances with the utmost gravity.'

At the outset, the situation, as Jessie Conrad described it, looked bleak, even hopeless: 'Gout everywhere, throat tongue head. There are two swellings on the back of his head as big as my fist. Poor boy, he lives the novel, rambles all the time and insists the Dr and I are trying to put him into an asylum. He is not to be allowed the least mental exertion or to see anyone at present.' Conrad, in delirium, 'spoke all the time in Polish, but for a few fierce sentences against poor J. B. Pinker'. Part of the time, he lived 'mixed up in the scenes' of his novel, holding 'converse with the characters'. Despite Conrad's paranoia, temporary seclusion and continual professional care might indeed have been sensible options, but they would also have been costly ones and the lack of ready money foreclosed them. Jessie, level-headed, had to do duty as a nurse. Galsworthy's generosity kept the family afloat during Conrad's breakdown, and Robert Garnett, Edward's elder brother, a solicitor, took charge of Conrad's affairs, continuing afterwards to act in his stead, especially with Pinker, with whom relations remained cool for some time.

Conrad woke to find himself being cared for, perhaps exactly the 'medicine' he desired, in a reversion to patterns going as far back as

Tadeusz Bobrowski's guardianship. When his powers and energies returned, he faced revising *Under Western Eyes*. There seems to have been some talk of taking sea air, but that plan was laid aside as he completed the novel. Robert Garnett, a translator of Dumas *père*, looked over the corrected typescript, and even Borys pitched in, helping to put its muddled 600 pages in order. Conrad was aware that he was liberating himself mentally in returning to his task: 'I am . . . coming back to the world,' he told Galsworthy. Another positive sign, despite the effortful concentration it involved, was inspiration for a new short story, already given a title, 'A Smile of Fortune'. Like *Under Western Eyes*, it was a backward glance, dramatising and embroidering Conrad's tangled romantic experience on Mauritius. His past was a vein Conrad repeatedly mined for his fiction, but it may be noteworthy that, upon recovering, he took up the theme of unhappy love.

Another liberation offered itself in the prospect of an escape from the awful cottage in Aldington, which Conrad disliked and had found small and noisy from the outset. A 'picturesque and roomy' seventeenth-century farmhouse, with orchards and surrounded by woods, had been located in Orlestone, a village about five miles from Ashford and only a mile from Ham Street, the closest railway station. The new home, Capel House, rented for £45 a year, was not far from The Pent, allowing the Conrads to return to an area of Kent that they liked. The move, scheduled for late June, would ensure that Conrad, who was still shaky, would not be overly disturbed during the final two months at Aldington, and the new short story grew.

At this time of much change in his life Conrad made a new acquaintance, Warrington Dawson, a thirty-two-year-old American, 'an engaging and interesting personality', of colourful background and literary interests. In England to cover the funeral of Edward VII, who had died suddenly on 6 May, the aspiring novelist carried an introduction from the Sandersons, whom he had met in East Africa while on a big-game hunt with Theodore Roosevelt. A 'confirmed bachelor', Dawson had been living in Versailles with his widowed mother, Sarah Morgan, a journalist and diarist, who had died the year before. Dawson was invited to Aldington for a day, Conrad's hospitality motivated, perhaps, by his current inability to go to London, and by the need for stimulation. Marwood, on his regular

Thursday call, also met the Southerner. Although Dawson remained in intermittent contact until the end of Conrad's life, Conrad maintained a polite distance from his acquaintance's literary work, for Dawson had grand ambitions but scant talent. Roosevelt, who sent greetings to Conrad through him, begged off from calling, citing a heavy schedule. 'Very safe bunkum that,' Conrad observed of the former President's courtesy.

Shortly after moving to Capel House, Conrad made his first excursion alone since January, visiting the Gibbons in nearby Trottiscliffe, not working but running about in the side-car of Gibbon's 'fiendish' twin-cylinder motor-bike, an experience he found so enjoyable that, in due course, he bought a second-hand 12-horsepower Cadillac. His driving skills were redoubtable, and in his younger son's estimation he treated the motor car like 'a pony and trap'. A keen motorist who enjoyed going at high speed, he landed the little car in ditches on occasion and had several near-accidents. Borys Conrad, who thought his mother, despite her disability, the better driver, remembered his father, who 'never took a map', treating the car as a substitute ship, Conrad characteristically saying, 'We're too far to the South – we better head back that way a bit.'

As Conrad pressed on with 'A Smile of Fortune', his relationship with Pinker remained cool. His first surviving communication after his breakdown, written in late May, addressed formally to 'Dear Sir' and closing with the formulaic 'Yours faithfully' (replacing his customary 'Yours ever' or 'Yours always'), flirted with barely concealed ironies. His business affairs largely remained in his wife's and Robert Garnett's hands. Just before leaving Aldington, fortune did indeed smile but in such a way as to aggravate the friction with Pinker. Conrad received an invitation from Lindsay Bashford, the *Daily Mail*'s literary editor, to write a weekly Saturday book review. At 5 guineas per thousand words, the attractive offer would potentially add over £250 to Conrad's annual income. Pinker was not informed of the arrangement, and, learning of it, assumed that Conrad was acting behind his back (and thus swindling him out of his commission). He became incensed. Galsworthy served as a cautious intermediary between his own agent and his friend and helped to put out the blaze before it could rage too destructively.

Jessie Conrad's version of the end of this affair is that Conrad was not promptly paid, which caused his patience to snap; Borys's that his father, sent for review books that the famous murderer Dr Crippen had been reading during his attempted escape to Canada, refused in pique and broke with the paper. As it was, Conrad had already written to his neighbour, the poet Edward Thomas, asking if he would ghost-write for him at a pinch. If true, Conrad's outrage over the Crippen business gave him an excuse to wriggle out of a commitment that, shortly after it was undertaken, proved burdensome: he had always found it impossible to write to a deadline; the books sent to him were for a popular, middlebrow readership, decidedly not his own; and the newspaper had high-handedly treated him as a mere employee. The arrangement also met with increasingly firm objections from Pinker, who believed Conrad should concentrate on his real work. In the end, only three reviews – chatty, left-handed pieces – were published by the paper, and another was killed by the editor.

Conrad made significant public engagements in mid-1910, consenting to join the Academic Committee of English Letters for the Royal Society of Literature and adding his name to a petition addressed to the Prime Minister, H. H. Asquith, in support of a bill extending the suffrage to women. Formed by Edmund Gosse to 'take all possible measures to maintain the purity of the English language and to hold up a standard of good taste in style' and otherwise encourage serious writing, the Academic Committee held its first meeting as Conrad was slumming in Grub Street for the *Daily Mail*. The petition to Asquith, signed by Galsworthy, Hueffer, and Shaw, among others, played a very small part in the public agitation for the bill's passage, massive demonstrations having taken place in London.

Conrad now planned to return to work on *The Rescuer*, abandoned a decade before, and then *Chance*, which had been simmering since the 1905 stay on Capri. Mention of the former ruffled Pinker, to whom Conrad wrote, again addressing him as 'Sir', with open displeasure, stating that 'As you have thought necessary to hint gratuitously that I am trying to get further advances on work delivered, I beg you to take notice that I shall write "Chance" when it suits me, exactly, and at my own pace.' The frost had not thawed. Welcome news came (not publicly announced until the following summer) that an application for a Civil List pension of £100 per year had been successful. Indefatigable in Conrad's cause, Galsworthy had been behind this. Just before its public announcement Conrad acknowledged that it was 'in a sense a confession of failure', although he preferred to concentrate on 'its other and honourable side'. And after all, Byron, Tennyson, and Wordsworth had been Civil List Pensioners in their day. He only resigned it in 1917, somewhat belatedly given his success by then.

Another happy event was a promised visit from Ted Sanderson, on home leave early in the summer. His return proved permanent, with his appointment to the headmastership of Elstree School in November. The old closeness was never quite re-established, but Conrad and he remained in contact. The past was vividly present in other ways, too, as Conrad turned neither to *The Rescuer* nor *Chance* but to 'Prince Roman', drafted during the composition of 'Some Reminiscences'. His only story to deal directly with a Polish subject, it centres on the exploits of a heroic and self-sacrificing aristocrat committed to the struggle for independence. Its straightforward narrative and simple conception of heroism presage the tone and approach of later, less complex work.

Hugh Clifford proved highly influential in determining the direction of Conrad's future projects. The year previously while dining in Colombo with Gordon Bennett, owner of the *New York Herald*, he had talked up the novelist and lent three of Conrad's books to Bennett for his voyage to Bombay. Impressed, the highly successful news-paperman was now looking for a Conrad novel to serialise. Given the paper's positive attitude to Russia, *Under Western Eyes* was an unlikely choice. *Chance*, into which Conrad was weaving topical matter, the social and political status of women and large-scale financial fraud, was likewise a more obvious choice than *The Rescuer*, set in the Eastern Seas and done in Conrad's early manner: dense prose, moral complexities (divided loyalties and an adulterous attraction), and an 'exotic' setting.

As prospects looked good for selling *Chance*, Jessie's leg was causing her nervous and physical strain. The severe pain caused insomnia and nervous stress, neither fought off by mere pluck, and her better leg was showing signs of fatigue from stress. She bore the affliction heroically, the pain so intense that even amputation began to seem a more attractive alternative to keeping her leg.

Feeling 'flat and sceptical', Conrad did not or could not immediately turn to *Chance*, frittering away time on 'The Partner', a short story begun around the time of the Sandersons' call. He may have hoped that the story's topicality (financial swindling and patent medicines) would make it marketable, although it also touches on the lugubrious: mental illness (certainly topical at Capel House) and murder. A diversion from more pressing work, its writing may have helped him see more clearly the subject of financial chicanery that he was to develop in *Chance*. But Conrad was mainly inclined to play the tortoise during the autumn, dawdling over 'The Partner' until early December and editing and polishing 'A Smile of Fortune' for the *English Review*, a rate of production that he could ill afford.

As the 'vigorous agitation' for the cause of women's suffrage filled the news, Conrad stored up reflections for *Chance*, which continued to languish: 'I can't get on terms with the thing somehow.' The suffragettes had turned violent, attempting to force their way into the House of Commons, breaking the windows in government buildings, mobbing the Prime Minister and Mrs Asquith, and laying siege to Downing Street. 'Black Friday' saw some hundred women arrested, and the issue played a role in the election fever that gripped the nation in the next few weeks, with the Liberals returning to power in December.

Just before Christmas 1910, Conrad lamented his 'miserable mental state', but on Boxing Day he suddenly began a new short story, 'Freya of the Seven Isles', a melodramatic tale set on an island group off Sumatra and inspired by Captain Marris's call. The 'silly story', about an unhappy love affair and an intense and ultimately fatal romantic rivalry, occupied him on and off for the next two months. His claim to Pinker that he had done some work on *Chance* needs to be weighed against a comment he made to Hueffer at the end of March 1911: 'I am just now trying to make a fresh start with a thing called *Chance*.' To Galsworthy he was more forthright about his mental condition: 'no two consecutive ideas, no six consecutive words to be found anywhere in the world'. At best, his writing limped forward, and like 'The Partner', completing 'Freya' took an inordinate time, considering its length. It was, however, well recompensed: published in New York's *Metropolitan Magazine* and the *London Magazine*, the story earned £60, more than a year's rent.

Conrad made halting progress on *Chance* – 'Slow. Dam' slow' – throughout the spring of 1911, and there was a reconciliation of sorts with Hueffer, now living in Germany. Thanking him for a book of short stories (not by him), Conrad poured out his heart: 'I did not write before simply because there was nothing to write – nothing good, nothing new . . . since last June I have been fairly well. Only – no elasticity. Life an awful grind. The feeling that the game is no longer worth the candle.' Condemned to playing that game, he was spinning himself out as 'a disillusioned spider' spins his web 'in a gale'.

Fisher Unwin, with whom Conrad had recently had a tussle over the sale of French rights to *An Outcast of the Islands* without his consent, expressed an interest in acquiring the copyright to Conrad's *An Outcast* and *Tales of Unrest*. (He already owned *Almayer's Folly* outright – a point of friction for years between the two men.) The suggestion set Conrad thinking for the first time about a collected edition of his work. At the same time he definitively gave up a plan to add to 'Some Reminiscences', a book dangled before Unwin with the comment that he was already involved in negotiations for its appearance. The move is odd considering how much he disliked his first publisher, but the volume lay outside his agreement with Pinker, and he had to refresh old skills to place it. Eventually he signed a contract with Eveleigh Nash, whose autobiography list influenced his interest in the book, but how well Conrad's memoirs sat on a list mainly made up of the recollections of aristocrats, military gents, and sportsmen is a moot point.

In late spring, as if a blocked dam had broken, the writing of *Chance* came more easily; Conrad calculated that he had written 12,000 words in a fortnight, and begged off an invitation from Edward Thomas in order to continue working at Capel House: 'I can't, positively can't, get away from the table for more than a few hours – and even this with fear and trembling lest it should mean losing my grip (my writing grip – not the musing grip) on the silly subject.' The deprecatory word 'silly', also used of 'Freya', is troubling. Consciously reaching out for popularity, Conrad had at last learned new tricks to please a less discriminating audience, one contented with genre fiction and demanding a clear narrative line. In the process, he was ploughing well-worn literary furrows, including the damsel-in-distress motif and allegory. And he was also over-elaborating his material. Whereas he had been proud of the fact that there were 'No damned tricks with girls' in 'The Secret Sharer', he now had mastered these somewhat too thoroughly, ensuring that his work would, both in its subjects and its themes, gain wider appeal among the majority of fiction-readers, for whom sea life and so-called 'masculine' problems like honour were of little interest.

Visiting Dymchurch for a break while Capel House's drains were opened up, he caught a summer cold as the nation revelled in the festivities and traditional bonfires celebrating George V's coronation, the event itself falling on a very rainy 22 June, a rare break in a summer famously hot. After a sluggish period, save for a brief excursion to Ramsgate to look over St Augustine's Abbey School for Borys, Conrad tied himself to his desk again. Another possibility for his elder son, now thirteen, was the HMS *Worcester*, the training-ship of the Thames Nautical Training College, docked off Greenhithe. (Originally built as a three-decker in Portsmouth in 1833, under a new name and altered to accommodate 150 cadets, she had arrived there in 1877.) Conrad interviewed the Captain-Superintendent, and decided on this more practical course of education as a good training for a career in engineering. Borys would enter in the upcoming Michaelmas term, with his proud father taking time off to settle him into the ship. At the last minute, Cadet Borys Conrad had to be fitted with spectacles, which occasioned 'a good cry' on his part. Although he got high marks for his studies in the *Worcester*, his poor eyesight put paid to certain career opportunities, and, keen on motoring, as was his father, he was later to enter the rapidly expanding motor-car industry.

A momentous event in mid-July 1911 was a call from the French novelist André Gide, accompanied by the poet Valéry Larbaud and Agnes Tobin, a rich bluestocking from San Francisco, who wrote poetry and translated from both Latin and French. The three, who arrived by motor car, spent a Sunday in animated discussion with their host, returning for lunch the following day before going to call on

Conrad's near neighbour, Arthur Symons. A pleasant social occasion, it reflected Conrad's growing stature in France and laid the foundations for a long-lasting, if mainly epistolary, friendship with Gide, who later translated *Typhoon* and directed Conrad's translations for the Parisian publisher Gallimard. The connection established with Tobin was also a turning-point, for she provided an introduction to John Quinn, a wealthy New York lawyer specialising in tariff law, who was eagerly amassing an unparalleled collection of Modernist art – sculpture by Brancusi, works by Matisse and Rouault, and no fewer than fifty Picassos. He was also a serious collector of literary manuscripts, especially those of Pound, Yeats, and Joyce. (In due course, he became the owner of the manuscript of *Ulysses*.) The connection with Quinn provided cash for work both long done and recently completed, and Jessie Conrad soon began hunting down old manuscripts and typescripts for dispatch to New York, whence came back cheques and a regular flow of correspondence from Quinn, who dictated long, rambling letters about his interests and activities.

Just as relations with Pinker were returning to normal, Garnett, now a reader for *Century* magazine, mistakenly claimed that he had first seen 'Freya' years ago. His slip made it look as if Conrad had been deceiving his agent over the pace of his work, and Pinker's ruffled feathers once again needed smoothing. At about this time, Norman Douglas, recently arrived from Italy, came to Capel House for a weekend. He turned up with a seriously high fever, and his condition soon became life-threatening. In addition to nursing a sick friend, the Conrads feared contagion for their boys. Jessie found the experience 'like a nightmare', and Conrad, upset and unable to work, even feared having to pay Douglas's funeral expenses. They got him into hospital in Ashford, and after the immediate strain eased, Douglas returned for a brief period of recovery.

The publication of *Under Western Eyes* in early October 1911 occasioned a congratulatory telegram from Hueffer, a further attempt to patch up their friendship. What should, however, have been a happy event provoked brooding. Conrad worried over the fact that the novel was his first book to have appeared in three years; his absence from annual booklists had, however, not dented his reputation, and stories had appeared in the meantime. But he was making little progress on *Chance*, and, when touching Norman Douglas for £10 to cover an overdraft, he lamented that work was unremitting: 'Never, never a moment to breathe and forget.'

He was at least moderately buoyed by the reception of *Under Western Eyes* and news that Tauchnitz wanted to print the novel in a continental edition. Garnett's ardent Russophilia did not make him a good choice as a reviewer (his unsigned review appeared in the *Nation*), and Conrad was moved to a prickly response to his old friend: 'I suppose one must make allowances for your position of Russian Ambassador to the Republic of Letters. Official pronouncements ought to be taken with a grain of salt.' The *Pall Mall Gazette*'s reviewer found the novel 'entitled to rank with the best work that Mr. Joseph Conrad has given us', an opinion seconded by the reviewer of the *Morning Post* who judged *Under Western Eyes* 'written with that intensity of vision, that complete absorption in and by the subject, and that astonishing mastery of the subtleties of language which have ever distinguished its author's best work'.

Gaining momentum from the novel's reception, Conrad began to make headway with *Chance*, producing under pressure but for once without panicking, although, characteristically, the novel's end was being forced: 'It positively pains me not being able to do with the end what I should like to do.' Its conclusion kept him at home, and as the novel was finally coming to an end, he cried: 'The last 2000 words! Horrors!' In fact, it required considerably more than that, and the ever-patient Pinker received a batch of 3,000 words in mid-January 1912, not long before the novel's first instalment appeared in the *New York Herald*. Conrad, vexed about the delayed completion, discussed it with Pinker, first by telephone, and then by letter, addressing him for the first time since their quarrel as 'Dear Mr Pinker' rather than 'Dear Sir'. The latter formula recurs from time to time, but Conrad was relenting and finding emotional balance, while Pinker's steady loyalty had worn away at his author's grudge. Just as crucially, for both his family's well-being and his art, he was producing regularly and roughly to schedule. There was, as he had said to Norman Douglas, never any respite, and his thoughts, as he was finishing off old projects, turned to new ones: he revised three stories for a new collection, '*Twixt Land and Sea* ('A Smile of Fortune', 'The Secret Sharer', 'Freya of the Seven

Isles'); toyed with writing further reminiscences (though he never did); and contemplated the long-delayed Mediterranean novel, which still lacked a subject: 'I hesitate between the occupation of Toulon by the fleet – the Siege of Genoa – or Napoleon's escape from Elba', none, for that matter, promising topics for his pen.

Appreciative reviews of *Some Reminiscences*, which came out in January 1912, could not prevent a case of the winter doldrums, as Jessie Conrad and five-year-old John came down with the flu, sore throats, and high fevers, and Borys, spared while at home for the Christmas holidays, contracted a fever on returning to the *Worcester*. Amidst these travails *Chance* continued to grow: the final '2000 words' predicted at the end of December came closer to 20,000, and, visits from Stephen Reynolds and Reggie Gibbon apart, Conrad valiantly stuck to his desk. The national coal-miners' strike demanding a minimum wage, begun in late February, may have encouraged him to do so, railway schedules being disrupted until Easter; London's transportation was in even greater chaos when cab-drivers staged a week's sympathy strike in March. (The miners' strike also inconvenienced the *Titanic*, then coaling for her maiden voyage.)

As he had with *Lord Jim*, Conrad 'finished' *Chance* early in the morning after a long stint at his desk: at 3 a.m. on the rainy morning of 25 March as his 'working lamp began to burn dimly' and 'the fire in the grate' began 'to turn black', he brought it to a close. He celebrated the event by lunching with Pinker at the Waldorf near the agency's office and with Hueffer's successor as editor of the *English Review*, Austin Harrison, who was invited to hear Conrad's case for the novel's serialisation. His two-hour campaign on its behalf failed: the commercially savvy editor objected to its length and to its method of development, fearing readers would have difficulty following the story in monthly instalments. Harrison dithered, or out of misguided politeness held out hope, but in the end he remained unpersuaded. Conrad's tenacity had one aim: the monthly's glory days under Hueffer's inept financial but superb artistic management had passed, and he wished to bring down his still substantial debt to Pinker (once again 'My dear Pinker', an acknowledgement of his generosity as regards the pace and length of *Chance*).

Finishing that novel, Conrad told André Gide, had left him 'stupefied for a fortnight', arguably a brief period considering the effort it had required. During this break from his desk he posted 'The Brute' and then 'Karain' to Quinn. The latter story, travelling in the *Titanic*'s mail-pouches, had gone off uninsured. Considering the horrors of that night in the North Atlantic, Conrad's loss was minor. The event stirred him deeply, and in the flood of public interest he offered an article on the sinking to *Nash's Magazine*. Learning that publication would be delayed until its next issue, he cabled William Randolph Hearst's *American*, only to be declined, and next appealed to Pinker to contact Harrison. Unlike *Nash's Magazine*, Harrison was even willing to delay publication of the May issue for an essay by Conrad, and the seaman-turned-writer immediately started work following an overnight visit from Garnett, and wrote most of its 5,000 words at white heat on the night of 24–25 April.

'Some Reflexions, Seamanlike and Otherwise, on the Loss of the *Titanic*' is an assault on sensationalist journalism, outdated Board of Trade regulations, and the 'very new and "progressive"' shipping ethos that had sacrificed safety for 'pretty-pretties' and luxury. Conrad's sardonic '*J'accuse*' was noticed, and in some quarters criticised. The desire to reply to his critics and comment on the *Titanic* Inquiry held in London in May afforded the subject of a polemical follow-up, published in the *English Review*'s July issue, as public interest in the disaster remained high. He did not, however, feel impelled to attend any of the sessions of Lord Mersey's Inquiry, as, for example, were Leonard and Virginia Woolf, and mainly relied upon accounts of it in *The Times* for his second piece. The essay rails against the spirit of the age, mumbo-jumbo in various guises (trade 'arrayed in purple and fine linen'), sensationalist journalism, and trumped-up sentimentality. Galsworthy and Stephen Reynolds both sent letters of appreciation. This foray into topical journalism brought a windfall of £30 (£10,400 in 2005) for the second article alone (half the advance he had received for the 55,000-word *A Personal Record*), more than recouping the £20 he had expected from Quinn for the manuscript of 'Karain'.

Conrad again left 'the Mediterranean novel' to one side, embarking instead on a novella set in the Far East with the working title 'Dollars'.

Conceived on narrow lines, with an initial target of some 10,000 words, it developed into *Victory*, another full-length novel. In the meantime, as the novella was simmering in Conrad's head rather than advancing on paper, he declined Galsworthy's invitation to spend a week in Devon. As the new 'long short story' began to sputter, Arthur Symons who lunched with Conrad found him 'somewhat less nervous, but with all his vitality'. They ate Italian food, drank Graves and coffee, and Conrad drove the poet back to Wittersham in his Cadillac, 'a worthy and painstaking one-cylinder puffer' of some 'antiquity'.

As the new 'Dollars' story grew, Conrad was contemplating the publication of another collection of short stories in the autumn, following Pinker's negotiations closely and making a few revisions to the texts. Reading up on Napoleonic history filled his leisure hours, and at the end of July the Conrads, as doting parents, went with Reggie Gibbon to the *Worcester*'s prize day, the event also marking the College's sixtieth year of operation, with Lord Brassey, Lord Warden of the Cinque Ports and the founder of the *Naval Annual*, giving out the prizes. When the summer holidays began, Borys Conrad and his father raced about the countryside in the family motor car, and Capel House opened its doors to streams of visitors. Conrad provided Warrington Dawson with an introduction of sorts to Pinker: 'I don't know what you have got hold of there – a swan or a crow.' (The cawing allowed no real doubt; this was a friendly gesture.) Galsworthy stopped by at a moment that saw work 'formally' begin on the Mediterranean novel.

On the newly promoted Senior Cadet Borys Conrad's return to school, his father at the puffer's wheel left with Jessie and John for a restorative tour, stopping with the Gibbons at Trottiscliffe and then with the Hopes in Stanford. On returning home, Conrad paid for the holiday in gout and depression, and after some time in bed, had to hobble about on crutches. He was sufficiently well to grant an interview to James Huneker, an influential American literary journalist, and one-time acquaintance of Stephen Crane. Three years earlier Huneker had sent Conrad a copy of *Egoists: A Book of Supermen* (1909), a book not only about Nietzsche but also several continental writers including Stendhal and Anatole France, and had received gracious thanks. The warmth of Conrad's invitation to Capel House suggests a possible earlier meeting, in the autumn of 1909. In the pen-portrait commissioned by the *New York Times*, Huneker comments on the writer's accent and voluble French, and on the mixture of the continental and English in Conrad's manner. Huneker, who informed Conrad of the favourable reception of *A Personal Record* in America, proved a success.

Another literary journalist with whom Conrad became friendly at this time would play a large role in his later years. Garnett, who thought well of Richard Curle's laudatory article on Conrad for the magazine *Rhythm* – 'quite the best thing . . . not in details' but in 'appreciation & insight' – effected an introduction. Conrad unreservedly admired the piece ('All that went before seems mere verbiage in comparison') and quickly took to the man. The friendship deepened over the following year and then became a habit, as the practical Curle took on the roles of publicist, investment adviser, dining companion, and sometime adoptive son. A Scot with an English education and literary ambitions, and in Garnett's view 'a big sort of boy (aged 30.) egoistic but quite a nice chap', he offered Conrad both manly camaraderie and the kind of intellectual com-panionship for which he yearned and had to find outside his immediate family. As a replacement for the oft-times volatile Hueffer, Curle was more down to earth and decidedly less gifted though emotionally more stable. He saw himself as 'rather a sceptical person, & at the same time, rather easily hurt'. He got on well with the whole family, playing 'Uncle Dick' to Borys and John, and appreciative of Jessie's cooking.

Also moving into Conrad's circle at this time was Józef Retinger, a Pole in his mid-twenties who had become acquainted with Arnold Bennett in Paris and may have paid particular notice to Conrad's letter to *The Times* on the First Balkan War proposing complex international arrangements to oversee the city, a dry run, as it were, for Conrad's later highly idealistic suggestion that a multinational protectorate be entrusted with establishing an independent Poland after the First World War. Engaged in enlisting British support for Polish affairs, Retinger was invited to Capel House where his attempt to recruit Conrad for the cause of a constitutional monarchy for Poland was received rather less warmly than he himself. Even before they met, Conrad observed that 'Rousing sympathy for landowners must be about the hardest task anyone can set oneself to do at the present day.'

For his part, the controversial young enthusiast – one pundit dubbed him 'the Talleyrand of Notting Hill', another 'arrogant and stupefyingly tactless' – found Conrad's 'attachment' to his former country 'objective, passive, and reticent'. Rivalling Hueffer in inaccuracy and exaggeration in his memoirs of Conrad, Retinger seems reliable at least on this point. Having acquired an English identity by dint of effort and choice, Conrad's 'reticence' on the subject of his origins could only be surprising to someone who failed to understand, or who resented, his many-layered but essentially quite simple decision. Distrustful of politicians, sceptical about politics, wary of popular 'isms', Conrad nevertheless allowed a personal friendship to develop, and both he and his wife became friendly with Retinger's wife, Otolia. 'The very type' of a 'Polish country girl', she helped engineer their trip to Cracow in the summer of 1914. Retinger's experience, in the end, was comparable to Spiridion's earlier: he repeatedly failed to involve Conrad in issues that were his life's blood, and aside from writing a memorandum to the Foreign Office in Retinger's stead (as he was not a Briton, Retinger had no right to), Conrad remained cool towards Retinger's enthusiasms. He dropped the Pole altogether not long after the war, by which time Retinger's marriage had collapsed; his political machinations had also veered so wildly out of control that by October 1917 he was *persona non grata* in England and the following year was deported from France.

The now familiar descent of gout and depression brought 'Dollars' to a halt in the autumn of 1912. 'The more one is anxious the less easy it is to get anything out of the inkstand,' Conrad gloomily (and without much originality) observed to Pinker; upon recovering, he interrupted his main work to write 'The Inn of Two Witches' for the *Pall Mall Gazette*. Set during the Peninsular War, the story somewhat clumsily relies upon Gothic effects, with suffocation by a killer bed, its central plot element, suspiciously reminiscent of one that Wilkie Collins used in 'A Terribly Strange Bed' (1852). Conrad later claimed not to know Collins's story.

This piece of cynical commercialism brought in £40 from England and another £40 from the United States, while the manuscript could be sold to Quinn, who did indeed buy it for £15. Conrad bitterly warned Norman Douglas, then working for the *English Review*, that Douglas had yet to plumb 'the vapid depths of public imbecility'. Lashing out at the magazine's audience 'as having neither minds nor gullets', Conrad advised 'You must dilute your stuff', and was, albeit resentfully, taking his own advice. His contempt for the revamped *English Review*, now advertising itself as 'indispensable to the City worker who has little time for the study of books, and to the dweller in the country who wishes to keep in touch with the whirlwind changes of modern life', was thorough, but this readership, which he had done little to woo earlier in his career, was precisely the one at which he now was casting longing glances.

Shortly after Conrad turned fifty-five, Curle came and conquered Capel House, the first of many visits over the next dozen years. The more intellectually stimulating André Gide, arriving from Brighton after spending Christmas Day with Edmund Gosse and Henry James, must have found Conrad's domestic arrangements a vivid contrast to his previous days spent with aesthetes, both inclined, like himself, to high art and young men. Borys was home for the holidays; John, aged five, prepped to say '*Bonjour, Monsieur. Comment allez-vous?*' played with his toys; and Mrs Conrad bustled over the servants' preparations for lunch. Gide gave John a Meccano set that Conrad also much enjoyed, although his son recalls that he grew easily frustrated, his gouty hands too large and clumsy for the nuts and bolts. After Gide's call Conrad came down with neuralgia, succeeded by mild depression, and Gibbon, during a call, found him with his 'face, lips, nose swollen to a monstrous size'. As he aged, the attacks of gout became more frequent, wearing down his system and nerves and making him increasingly, and even notoriously, irritable. He struggled, with varying success, particularly at home, to maintain his impeccable manners, but crotchetiness could force even these to slip. When annoyed, he had a habit of flicking bread pellets at table, even in restaurants, and, once served a calf's head by his wife, he refused to eat it by pettishly turning his chair round until the offending dish was removed.

Ill humour dominated his contractual negotiations for *Chance*. Disappointed by J. M. Dent's decision not to serialise the novel in its house magazine, *Everyman*, Conrad was displeased that Methuen, which he had not forgiven for causing him to revise *The Secret Agent* in page proofs, would bring out the book. Conrad addressed a stiff letter to the firm – 'I don't shake novels out of my sleeve' – recalling that it had declined a book of short stories not many months previously and indicating a desire to put an end to an unpleasant association whilst fulfilling the terms of a three-novel contract arranged through Pinker. Methuen replied no less starchily that they wished only to deal with Conrad through his agent. He found the revision 'a killing job simply'. It was finished during another cigarette-fuelled night at his desk, but he was pleased to think it his 'biggest piece of work' since *Lord Jim*, implying a lesser opinion of *Nostromo* that suggests a loss of touch with his artistic wellsprings, for *Chance*, for all the brilliance and verve of its opening sections, does not rival *Nostromo* in scope or depth. Carping at Methuen, he predicted only modest success for the book, but his judgement also proved faulty on that point: its serialisation in the *New York Herald* alone paid £1,400, clearing half his debt to Pinker in one fell swoop.

Conrad, who had undoubtedly 'arrived' on both sides of the Atlantic, was now being paid in terms commensurate with his well-established reputation. From the outset his writing had been mainly well received, but the sums he got for it tended barely to cover the costs of maintaining himself and his family. The rise in payments had been somewhat slow but generally steady. In 1894, nearly twenty years before, unknown and unproved, he had sold *Almayer's Folly* to Unwin for £20; he could now get three-quarters of that amount for the holograph manuscript of a short story, whatever its quality.

Given his growing popularity in America, Conrad briefly contemplated a short business trip to New York (eventually accomplished ten years later). Further evidence of American interest came during F. N. Doubleday's annual spring business trip to London. The now highly successful New York publishing firm had extensive connections and a large list. A partnership between Doubleday and Walter Hines Page, sometime Ambassador of the United States to the Court of St James's, it had an office in Manhattan and owned extensive printing works in Garden City, Long Island. A man of practical talents and signal determination, Doubleday had, for instance, done particularly well by Kipling, who nicknamed him 'Effendi', an Arabic title of deference punning on his initials.

During his 1913 visit, Doubleday broached the idea of a collected edition with Pinker and Conrad, an ambitious venture that would require the obtaining of rights from several firms both in England and the United States, Conrad having been shuttled from publisher to publisher throughout his career. It also meant dealing with the prickly Unwin who had tied up Conrad's earliest books. Doubleday set about his goal with an American gusto that Conrad was to find baffling and even irritating as Doubleday clumsily stepped on several toes. Out of pocket for £400 of unearned advances for *The Rescuer*, Heinemann nursed a long-standing grudge, bluntly referring to Conrad's dealings with him as 'very unfair & ungentlemanly', but promising to overlook this should the English version of the collected edition come to him. If it did not, he made clear, it would not appear at all. At this juncture such an edition proved a will-o'-the-wisp in any case as the war intervened to postpone it. Another attractive prospect that likewise rose and vanished at this time was an approach from Sir George Alexander, the well-known actor-manager who had played Jack in Wilde's *The Importance of Being Earnest*, about the possibility of Conrad's writing a play. A first act (its subject unknown) was roughed out with 'Reggie' Gibbon, but the project foundered, its lasting impact being to reawaken Conrad's interest in the stage – or, rather, the possible profits to be derived therefrom.

Warrington Dawson and the pianist John Powell, a fellow American Southerner, were busy establishing a Fresh Air Art Society, whose tenets included affirming the Oneness of Life and the Oneness of Art and the clear Light of Truth. They attempted to interest Conrad in it, but, temperamentally wary of cranks and nonsense, however nicely dressed up, he declined to attend its inaugural meeting at the Small Queen's Hall on Langham Place, a concert hall used for recitals and smaller ensembles. His enjoyment of serious music, which played a mystical role in the Society, led to a nodding acquaintance with Powell, who gave a series of 'Fresh Air' concerts at the Æolian Hall in the early winter of 1913, attended by

Conrad and Jessie. Powell, who tended to conflate ideology and music, later expressed openly racist views and ardent support for Eugenics.

A considerably more momentous meeting took place in August 1913 with Lady Ottoline Morrell, whom Borys collected from Ashford in the family car. An ardent Conradian, the flamboyant aristocrat and social gadabout had been forewarned by Henry James that Conrad, having lived a rough 'life at sea', had never met with 'civilised women'. She seems thus to have carefully chosen an unconventional dress for her descent on Capel House, upon the advice of her 'Bloomsbury' friend the newspaper critic Desmond MacCarthy. Reading *Some Reminiscences* on the way down, she found their author in the flesh 'electric' in his intensity. She later recollected Jessie as 'a good-looking fat creature', who provided a 'reposeful mattress for this hypersensitivity'. 'The mattress' from Camberwell served lunch to the 'civilised' woman, and after talking with Conrad about his writing and of their mutual friend, Henry James, she left. What the Conrads made of her call – perhaps more a visitation from another world – is unrecorded.

Its far more lasting effect was to bring about a meeting between Conrad and Lady Ottoline's then lover, Bertrand Russell, already well launched on his philosophical and mathematical career at Cambridge, who called upon Conrad in her wake. Russell described the encounter in excited, passionate prose: 'The emotion was as intense as passionate love, and at the same time all-embracing. I came away bewildered, and hardly able to find my way among ordinary affairs.' Both of them intellectually audacious iconoclasts and non-believers, Russell and Conrad shared views, although the intense and serious philosopher had also shuffled off conventional morality. Drawn out by Russell's personality, Conrad feared he had talked 'all the time with fatuous egotism', but sensed that he had been understood, confirmation of that coming in the philosopher's invitation to call on him at Cambridge. The friendship proved durable, and the depth of Russell's admiration can be gauged from the fact that he named his only son after the writer.

Conrad's compliment pre-dates Russell's: beginning a new short story, 'The Planter of Malata', a tale of unrequited infatuation, he cast as one of its characters a philosophy professor, possibly subtle homage to his new acquaintance. As so often, Conrad optimistically predicted a quick conclusion to this side effort, but his turn to a short story in the midst of a major project characteristically signalled that the 'real' work in hand was blocked, and just as typically the story grew, reaching 25,000 words. Schizophrenically both an unhappy love story and a ghost story, 'The Planter' takes up themes being explored in the languishing novel whose tropical setting it shares. Taking advantage of the mood for short fiction, Conrad promised Pinker that he would write another story to complete a volume, eking out 'Because of the Dollars' ahead of schedule, despite a 'horrible' Christmas during which the whole household fell victim to 'a mysterious epidemic'. This Dickensian narrative of murder and mayhem, in which a self-sacrificing former prostitute is bludgeoned to death for informing on a trio of thieves, anticipates, much like 'The Planter', ideas and plot elements used in *Victory*, as Conrad circled round and variously tried out his material.

Certainly, the lugubrious material he was exploring in his fiction would suggest to the psychoanalyst a period of disturbance of some severity, as he killed off one protagonist after another. He was also plunging into deep waters in *Victory*, whose characters include a girl on the edge of a social and moral abyss and an extravagantly misogynistic homosexual, plain 'Mr Jones', inspired, in part, by the man he had run across on Sankt Thomas so many decades before. His real knowledge of the homosexual temperament was based on recent friendships, with Norman Douglas and Gide, both of whom were attracted to young men, although the latter kept up social pretences in a marriage disastrous to his wife and himself. Conrad may have sensed that Powell and Dawson were likewise moved by men; the latter was so self-repressed that he was soon to acquire severe physical ailments, becoming a semi-invalid before the onset of middle age. A psychoanalytic approach might find in Conrad's portrayal of the Jones–Ricardo ménage in *Victory* a means of dealing with (or of brushing to one side) his growing closeness to and dependence upon Curle. He was at the same time creating a protagonist, Axel Heyst, who, warned off emotional attachments by his philosopher father, is, to his peril, busy making them.

Chance finally appeared in January 1914, shortly after a visit from Cunninghame Graham, who brought his recent miscellaneous collection, *A Hatchment*, and the Ranee of Sarawak's recently published autobiography. A high-born socialite on the London scene, some of whose French ancestors had been guillotined during the Revolution, the Ranee, also known as Lady Brooke, was married to a descendant of the first Rajah of Sarawak, Sir James Brooke, on whom Conrad had partly modelled the character of Lord Jim. She was a friend not only of Graham but also of Henry James and moved in several intersecting artistic circles. The book came at a good moment, as Conrad ventured again to the East in his fiction; later he confessed to Her Highness that he had lifted a plot element for *The Rescue* from her 'delightfully ladylike' *My Life in Sarawak* (less dramatically titled than her daughter-in-law's later *Queen of the Headhunters*).

Conrad was moderately buoyed by Graham's generally favourable response to *Chance*. Russell, who had 'qualms' about its happy ending, claimed that it held his interest 'intensely & increasingly as it went on'. Precisely this narrative thrust, and its less than typically complicated intrigue, urged Sidney Colvin, now a close friend first met over the staging of *One Day More* in 1905, to predict for it the popular success that had so long and so frustratingly eluded Conrad. The novelist and naturalist W. H. Hudson, on the other hand, disliked the novel, finding Marlow grown into 'a bore', and burst out laughing at the over-egged denouement: 'It was so hugely comical, all that laborious leading up to the melodramatic finish *à la* Hardy in his . . . early novels.' But perhaps the most hurtful response – Conrad claimed to be pained by it – was that of the aged Henry James, who in a controversial essay on 'the younger generation' in the *Times Literary Supplement*, slated the novel's narrative method, memorably describing Marlow's narrative as a 'prolonged hovering flight of the subjective over the outstretched ground of the case exposed', and (surely a case of the pot calling the kettle black) claimed that the work placed Conrad 'absolutely alone as a votary of the way to do a thing that shall make it undergo most doing'. James confided to his disciple Edith Wharton that *Chance* was 'infinitely more practicable, more curious and readable, (in fact really rather *yieldingly* difficult and charming), than any one of the last three or four impossibilities, wastes of desolation, that succeeded the two or three final good things of his earlier time'. The vast public ignored 'The Master's' strictures, some attracted to the book's dust-jacket, which portrayed a seated girl being offered a shawl by a gallant and good-looking ship's officer. As the novel went into its fifth printing, Conrad informed Doubleday that 'It had a remarkable reception'; that had what is now called a 'knock-on effect' as Doubleday laid plans to reissue *Almayer's Folly* and *The Nigger* in the United States.

This alone should have provided Conrad with sufficient encouragement to complete *Victory*, but even greater pressure came when the associate editor of New York's *Munsey's Magazine*, lunching Conrad at the Savoy, struck a deal for delivery by 1 May. Begging off a visit to Cambridge, Conrad told Russell that he had sold his soul to 'the devil in the shape of a Yankee editor'. The sale price was $6,000 (now $100,000), and the devil was Frank A. Munsey, whose highly successful mass circulation magazine with few literary pretensions had a readership of half a million. *Munsey's Magazine* was edited by a man credited with transforming 'a once noble profession into an 8 percent security', and eulogised as having 'the great talent of a meat packer, the morals of a money changer and the manners of an undertaker'. But did that matter? Speaking with the American regional novelist Hamlin Garland several years later, Conrad saw the deal as his career's financial turning-point, recalling that from this viewpoint his 'early books were all failures. Each one proved a "frost"'.

The prospect of serialisation galvanised Conrad, and *Victory*, then provisionally called 'The Island Story', 'a long dreary machine', suddenly lurched forward after lying on Conrad's desk for two years. Conrad took time off to read Garnett's *Tolstoy: A Study*, and used the Russian writer as a whipping-boy to vent long-standing reservations about Christianity to a friend who shared his indifference to it: 'I am not blind to its services but the absurd oriental fable from which it starts irritates me', adding that its impossibly demanding standards had brought 'an infinity of anguish to innumerable souls – on this earth'. A spring cold and an attack of gout, followed by a relapse, meant that Conrad could not meet *Munsey's* looming deadline, although he doggedly kept up the flow of copy as his health improved.

With his usual optimism, he foresaw a month's further work on the book, but that stretched to nearly two, and he completed the novel only in late June.

He took time off to write an article for the *Illustrated London News* on the recent sinking of the *Empress of Ireland* in Quebec's St Lawrence River. Although the loss of life rivalled that of the *Titanic* and the catastrophe generated much press attention, the public, not indifferent, was less excited than it had been about the earlier disaster. Accompanied by Richard Curle, Conrad hurriedly read proofs for the article at the magazine's offices, and then spiritedly replied to the several criticisms it received before leaving for Sheffield with Borys. Having left the *Worcester* in April with a first-class certificate, he was to sit the university's entrance exams. Curle tagged along, and he and Conrad spent a few days in Harrogate visiting Curle's friends, Ralph Wedgwood, a railway director and the great-great-grandson of Josiah, founder of the famed china house, and his wife, Iris. On the evening of 28 June 1914 – the day on which the Archduke Franz Ferdinand, heir apparent to the throne of Austria-Hungary and his wife, Sophie, Duchess of Hohenburg, were assassinated in Sarajevo – Conrad dined with Curle's brother-in-law, the historian H. A. L. Fisher (Sheffield University's Vice-Chancellor) and various other professors.

The night before returning to Capel House, Conrad took Borys to see the music-hall star George Robey, the famed 'Prime Minister of Mirth', who had Conrad in convulsions. Once home, two projects occupied him: correcting the typescript of *Victory*, and preparing for a visit to Cracow, about which he openly confessed 'mixed feelings'. Retinger and his wife had urged the visit, and an invitation to the estate of Retinger's mother-in-law had been issued. On the eve of the Conrads' departure Conrad told Galsworthy that instead of visiting the scenes of his youth he had 'much rather' be in Devon at the novelist's country house. It would certainly have been the wiser choice; Galsworthy wondered aloud about the family jaunt to a highly troubled area of the Continent.

Accompanied by the Retingers, the Conrad family set out for Harwich from Liverpool Street station on Saturday, 25 July, for the overnight crossing to Hamburg, where, after resting, they took in the famed Hagenbeck Zoo. They arrived at Cracow's Grand Hôtel, via

Berlin, on the 28th, the day Austria-Hungary declared war on Serbia. Conrad marked his arrival with an evening walk about the town centre with Borys and the Retingers, confronting scenes he had last seen forty years before. The next two days were taken up with visits to his father's grave in the Rakowice cemetery, to the Jagiellonian University's library, Wawel Castle, and to an old friend in the countryside, as Europe rushed headlong and relentlessly towards war. General mobilisation, declared on 1 August, the day on which Germany declared war on Russia, found the Conrads alien enemies on Austro-Hungarian soil in a town in uproar and swirling with rumours.

With their hotel requisitioned and future developments far from clear, the Conrads decided to take refuge in the small resort town of Zakopane in the Tatra mountains. On John's eighth birthday, they arrived at 'Willa Konstantynówka', a pension run by Conrad's cousin Aniela Zagórska, with the help of her two daughters, Aniela and Karola, who entertained their distant relative from abroad. Unencumbered by children and a disabled wife, Retinger, who managed to escape to England, told Galsworthy that Conrad was working on *The Rescue*, probably a misunderstanding, as Conrad, eager to return home, made plans to 'rescue' himself and his family. By mid-September, a time when the Conrads had intended to be back in England, the trip had become an unmitigated disaster: 'We are here destitute of means, without warm clothing and indeed in a very deplorable plight.'

Pleading for money from his agent, Conrad detailed an escape through Italy by way of Vienna where he planned to appeal for emergency funds from the American Ambassador, Frederic Courtland Penfield, a widely travelled and wealthy Philadelphian then also representing Great Britain's interests in the Austro-Hungarian Empire. In England, Ambassador Walter Hines Page also worked behind the scenes on the Conrads' behalf. At Zakopane, known for its cool, mountain climate, the company of the Zagórskis mitigated the stress, as Conrad spent his time discussing the war's course, dipping into contemporary Polish literature, and mixing with writers and artists, including the novelist Stefan Żeromski, the young Artur Rubinstein, who practised on Konstantynówka's piano, and the anthropologist Bronisław Piłsudski, the famous marshal's elder brother.

A return journey to Cracow in early October snow by trap and then by night train ended with the Conrads' stranded for eleven hours in the railway station's waiting-room, which also served as a makeshift field hospital where they witnessed blood and suffering. After a tedious and lengthy train journey to Vienna in cramped conditions, Conrad spent a few days in bed exhausted by gout, before calling upon Penfield and arranging the journey to Italy. He also took Borys to a shooting-gallery, where, to their shock, the targets were kilted Scottish infantry, which he instructed his son to make sure to miss. Unknown to them, the family's escape had been exceedingly narrow: a government order, gone astray, had been issued to detain Conrad for the war's duration.

He telegrammed Pinker from Milan on 20 October, begging for money for the voyage from Genoa; from here, five days later, the Conrads left for England in the Dutch mail-boat SS *Vondel*, which made her way through an English Channel already bristling with warships. Arriving at Gravesend on 2 November, Conrad ambitiously made plans to clear up arrears of business and see friends. After meeting with Pinker and Arnold Bennett and being introduced to Edmund Candler, a journalist and short-story writer whom E. M. Forster had met in India and would draw upon for the character of Mr Fielding in *A Passage to India*, Conrad virtually collapsed. Begun with mixed feelings, the journey to Poland and the past had proved costly emotionally and financially and had come within a hair's-breadth of disaster. As the Europe he knew fell apart like a flimsy house of cards, Conrad, tired and ill, was unable to settle to a commissioned essay about his recent experiences. Like his articles on the sinking of the *Titanic* and the *Empress of Ireland*, this article would allow him to pronounce upon (and profit from) events of moment. With Pinker's elder son, Eric, already in uniform (and by April in Egypt), and with posters asking for volunteers appearing in public places, sixteen-year-old Borys fretted bitterly at being too young to enlist. His father, suffering mental and emotional fatigue, retreated further into illness as the war that was to be over by Christmas showed no sign of concluding soon.

8

The Englishman
(1915–1919)

The shadow lies over this land. This is a time of great awe and
searching of hearts and of resolute girding of loins.
Conrad to Eugene F. Saxton, 17 August 1915

Recovering from the ill-judged and nearly disastrous excursion to
Cracow, Conrad was unable to work despite blandishments from
newspaper editors that the war would make lucrative copy. His was a
case of more than simple exhaustion. He was wearing out, as one
severe attack of gout rapidly followed another. Drained of vitality, his
face had long taken on the leathery look of the heavy and inveterate
smoker, the habit also slowly corroding his heart. The 'sort of sick-
apathy' he complained of upon returning from the Continent
ominously extended over several months. In January 1915, he finally
settled down to work for the first time since the previous summer's
revisions of *Victory*, writing a series of four articles, brought together
under the title 'Poland Revisited', commissioned even before his
return home. He had immense trouble in starting, and in the end the
articles, a kaleidoscopically structured reminiscence dealing with his
recent trip, his childhood, and, briefly, his early life at sea, were
rejected by the *Saturday Evening Post*, which had commissioned them,
because they failed to relate 'actual war experiences'. Conrad's market
sense was once again faulty. Only a concerted campaign by Pinker in
England and by Doubleday's Eugene F. Saxton in the United States
(where there were several rejections) saw the long autobiographical

essay finally appear in London's *Daily News* and Boston's *Evening Transcript*.

His right hand gouty, and behind in his work, Conrad faced the task of settling Borys, travelling up to Oxford for a couple of days to arrange for a half-year's coaching to prepare the youth for another attempt at Sheffield's entrance exam, which he had failed the previous July. Boyishly keen to enlist, Borys, who had turned seventeen in January, was too young. Preoccupied by his son's future, Conrad fell into a reminiscent mood and laid out tentative ideas for two new short stories whose roots lay in his youthful experiences and enthusiasms. 'First Command', eventually *The Shadow-Line*, was to be a story in the manner of 'Youth', with its narrator looking back on his initiation into adulthood; the other idea, reaching further back to a 'Carlist war episode of my *very* young days', evolved into *The Arrow of Gold*. As ever when broaching new projects, Conrad ritually promised to advance on *The Rescuer*, which, health permitting, was now to be 'finished by end October'.

Conrad spent ten days in London at the Norfolk Hotel in late February. Off the Strand, the hotel was just around the corner from Pinker's office, a street away. The stay in town was in effect a low-key publicity tour coinciding with Dent's publication, on 24 February 1915, of a new short-story collection *Within the Tides*, bringing together 'The Planter of Malata', 'The Partner', 'The Inn of Two Witches', and 'Because of the Dollars'. Intending to make progress on 'First Command', Conrad used the occasion to catch up with friends, seeing Curle, Norman Douglas, the Colvins and Fountaine Hope's brother, Linton, the yachting architect.

The volume of stories, the last published in his lifetime (another came out after his death), was mainly well, if not enthusiastically, received. Conrad was irritated by W. L. Courtney's review in the *Daily Telegraph*, which carped at the puppet-like characters and 'false realism'. Telling Galsworthy that the collection was 'not so much art as a financial operation', Conrad, who openly referred to the stories as 'second rate efforts', was bewildered by the amount of money they had brought him. Even taking inflation into consideration, the serialisation of 'The Planter' had earned six times what 'Heart of Darkness' had. His work now clearly marketable, Conrad was yet painfully aware that potboilers were beneath him; in 'First Command' he was planning to return to a more ambitious treatment of his material; not long after arriving back at Capel House, he sent Pinker what he thought to be 'not quite half' of the story (some 5,000 words). It was to expand, as usual, evolving into a novella as its themes and narrator developed depth, and Conrad again took to exploiting what for him was his most congenial genre in terms of length.

The war, an 'ugly and desperate adventure', grieved him, and he retreated into work, fussing over *Victory*'s galley proofs, which had been badly set by Methuen. 'Wretched and coughing dismally', he found 'the very sunlight . . . grim, sinister'. Reggie Gibbon on a visit to Capel House brought first-hand news of Italy, where he was a war correspondent. Home for the Easter break, Borys was full of enthusiasm for enlisting; he was angered as women cried 'Shame' after him in Oxford's streets because he was not in uniform and amateur recruiters handed out white feathers for cowardice. Deeply repulsed by the recourse to armed conflict to settle the affairs of nations, Conrad sided firmly with Britain, where he said his 'strongest feelings' were now 'deeply rooted'. Temperamentally reticent about public involvements, he had no qualms about adding his name to those of well-known authors (Bennett, Galsworthy, W. W. Jacobs, Rider Haggard) puffing a book on the Red Cross, prefaced by Queen Alexandra and sold for the benefit of 'the sick and the wounded': 'There's no doubt of its being just the thing. Wonderfully selected, admirably arranged, it's bound to move one with any vestige of entrails. Yes, I think it is a most effective book.' But he declined, with firmness, an invitation by the pianist-politician Ignace Paderewski to lend his name to the Polish Victims Relief Fund that Paderewski was organising, on the lofty grounds that 'Russian names' were to appear on the committee, his scepticism about Russian involvement in European affairs deep and unrelenting.

Remaining level-headed while the war effort became confused and jingoism increasingly dominated public sentiment, Conrad brooded as bad news arrived from the Dardanelles and the stalemate in Flanders continued. As *The Times* reported, the intelligentsia and literary world were preoccupied by events: 'Under one guise or another, the war is the subject or the occasion of nearly every article in every review.' This preoccupation led Conrad to craft a cautious note to

Victory, a novel completed before the war's outbreak, distancing his work, with its possibly confusing title, from the prevailing anti-Hun hysteria. Although Schomberg, its villain, displays 'indubitably the psychology of a Teuton', he is, Conrad argued, a fundamental human type, self-seeking and malice never being absent from the course of human history: 'far from being the incarnation of recent animosities, he is the creature of my old deep-seated, and, as it were, impartial conviction'. His sensitivity on this point was not exaggerated. At a Mont Blanc luncheon shortly after the war began, Garnett, a pacifist, responded to a remark that the Germans were afraid of cold steel by remarking that everyone was. Ralph Hodgson accused him of being pro-German, and he lost a friend.

Taking refuge in the vanished maritime world of his youth, Conrad made progress on 'First Command' and even picked up *The Rescuer* once again, returning to a past yet more distant. And as Jessie lived with increasing pain, her runaway weight compounding her health problems, he became increasingly involved in John's life, taking pleasure in reading to his nine-year-old son and joining him to play with his large collection of toy cars and boats. In London, he took him to the circus and to Maskelyne and Devant's Mystery Show at St George's Hall, where the famed conjuror once pulled a string of sausages out of John's sailor suit.

As a precaution, in early June Conrad sent Pinker pages of the evolving *Shadow-Line* 'for *Safe keeping*'. The night before, Capel House had been rattled by the force of an explosion in the Channel, six miles distant. As casualty lists lengthened, the war began to bite deeply even in the depths of Kent, and, Conrad's precaution was sensible: Ashford, a major railway centre, threatened to become a target for enemy action. Meanwhile at Oxford, Borys, becoming acquainted with a recruiting officer whose motor car he had repaired, decided to enlist immediately, as recruitment officers began to wink at statements about a recruit's actual age and men below the legal age limit began to find their way into the army. His father counselled against this, insisting that the youth wait for a commission and placing his hopes on the Army Service Corps, a branch responsible for transport where Borys's mechanical abilities would be valued and his poor eyesight of little concern.

Sketch of Conrad by John Singer Sargent (1911)   Portrait of Conrad by A. S. Kinkead (1924)

Etching of Conrad by Walter Tittle (1924)

Conrad standing at his desk by De'Ath & Condon (c. 1913)

F. N. Doubleday (1930)

Richard Curle on the *Berengeria* sailing from New York (1925)

Ford Hueffer (1915)

Edward Garnett in the Friends' Ambulance Unit (1917)

Borys Conrad (1922)

John and Borys Conrad during the Great War

John Conrad as a boy

John Conrad with his sons Richard and Peter with their dog, Nero

John Conrad, Jane Anderson, and Jessie and Joseph Conrad at Capel House (1916 or 1917)

The Conrads at Capel House, September 1913

Jessie Conrad (mid-1920s)

Lilian M. Hallowes, Conrad's secretary, in the New Forest (1930s)

Conrad in Corsica with J. B. Pinker (left) and an unidentified person (February 1921)

Conrad seated in a deckchair aboard the *Tuscania*, arriving in New York (1 May 1923)

Conrad's funeral cortège in Canterbury Cemetery, 8 August 1924 (left to right: undertaker, John and Borys Conrad, their uncles Albert and Walter George, R. B. Cunninghame Graham, Jean Aubry, Richard Curle, Count Edward Raczynski)

Conrad at Oswalds (June or July 1924)

Conrad's summer reading suggests almost an obsession with developments in the momentous and historic conflict. His books included Frederick Scott Oliver's *Ordeal by Battle*, a plain-speaking attack on recent British foreign policy; Lord Eversley's *The Partitions of Poland*, an analysis of old animosities once more galvanised into life; and Frederic Harrison's *The German Peril*. A two-day visit in June from Hugh Clifford, now Governor of the Gold Coast (present-day Ghana), could have offered little relief from the topic of the war. His aide-de-camp had died of his wounds in December 1914; his eighteen-year-old son Max and two of his nephews had been wounded; and his brother Henry was in uniform. And shortly after Clifford's visit, the Conrads hurried to Trottiscliffe to say farewell to Gibbon, who was again leaving to cover the war after a five-month stint at the Russian front.

Borys and Conrad then made their way to Sheffield, as they had the year before, for Borys to re-sit the entrance exams. Again, its Vice-Chancellor, H. A. L. Fisher, although plunged into war activities, hospitably opened his home to Conrad. This time Borys passed, but deferred entrance. Returning to Capel House via London, Conrad saw Curle, now in the Naval Reserve Anti-Aircraft Corps, and caught up with Cunninghame Graham, who was back from Uruguay where he had been buying horses for the war effort. (His ship home managed to make it to port after being torpedoed.) Busy at the War Office, Graham had influence, and Conrad asked him to pull strings for Borys. Their *rapprochement* effected, Pinker visited Capel House. The two men, long successful business associates, were drawn even closer as Conrad's other friends were called away by the war, and Pinker was now a confidant and a true friend. John Conrad, through a boy's eyes, thought of him as Beatrix Potter's Pigling Bland, for his 'fresh complexion; rather pink and white' and his 'neat and tidy attire', tending to the overdressed.

Conrad continued to pick away at 'First Command' through the war's second summer, but to Warrington Dawson in Paris he characterised his mental state as 'deplorable', a code-word for enervating depression. Dawson himself was retreating into invalidism, experiencing episodes of hysterical blindness and paralysis that made a walking-stick necessary.

Conrad worked on and off, with Jessie again typing for him, but the 'war atmosphere' made writing difficult: 'Reality, as usual, beats fiction out of sight,' he observed to Doubleday. As though anticipating the final scene of Shaw's *Heartbreak House* (completed in 1917) where the old world is smashed to pieces, the Conrads spent an August evening in their garden 'listening to the hum of an airship's engines filling the still night air' before the sound of booming guns faintly punctuated 'the dark quiet fields'. They retired not knowing what had happened: 'Zepplin – or English patrol airship?' Wells's *The War in the Air* (1908), which predicted such attacks, had proved chillingly accurate. Added to the general uncertainty and growing anxiety was the list of departing friends and acquaintances; Fountaine Hope's son, Conrad (named after Conrad), and Hueffer, who, at the age of forty-four, had joined the 19th Welch Division, were both leaving. Moved by events, worried about his son, and lonely, Conrad for once let his guard down to Hueffer, lamenting: 'Yes, mon cher! Our world of fifteen years ago is gone to pieces.' Borys enlisted in the Royal Engineers field telegraph and wireless section, but, with Graham's support and helped by his certificate from the *Worcester* (his first class was in both scholastics and seamanship and his conduct 'very good'), received the hoped-for commission as second lieutenant in the Army Service Corps and was to report for duty towards the end of September. Conrad accompanied him as far as Bromley station, where Borys was as excited as if the 'Portal of the Seventh Heaven open[ed] on this earth'.

Victory was published towards the end of September 1915, in the same season as Hueffer published his masterpiece *The Good Soldier*. Conrad's novel sold out its first and second printings on the day of publication. He had seen fame, fortune, and achievement come, perhaps later than he had hoped. On a flying visit home, Borys brightened a house where even the new dog, Hadji ('Millo' had lived to the age of twelve), moped. Conrad celebrated his novel's publication with a short stay at the Norfolk, seeing Gounod's *Romeo and Juliet* in Thomas Beecham's 'Opera in English' season, while John was taken to Maskeylne's 'House of Mystery' again. It proved the last outing for some time as Conrad, who caught a chill in town, came down with 'an alarming attack of gout' that forced him to bed, where he fought off insomnia. In the midst of these physical trials, came news that Borys, who had been transferred to Portsmouth, would leave for France sooner than expected. His mother was felled by neuralgia, partly brought on by news of the death of a neighbour's only son in the trenches as anxieties about her own child became acute, and her youngest brother, Frank, went out to Palestine and Egypt.*

Attempts to place *The Shadow-Line* in the large circulation *Land and Water* brought its editor to Capel House in early November, with Conrad promising a conclusion soon. An attack of gout (yet another) put paid to this hope, and he engaged a typist for dictation. Not long after completing the novella, he began a new story, 'The Humane Tomassov' (later 'The Warrior's Soul'): set during the 1812 Retreat from Moscow, it deals with the morality of men caught up in a great conflict. Meditated over for so long, it seemed to Conrad 'to be running off the pen by itself'. Despite this turn to new work, sorrows arrived, as Shakespeare has it, in battalions: Curle underwent several minor operations; Jessie, whose ailing and ageing mother had to be cared for, was having heart problems; Borys, who came home on short leaves, developed shingles; and *Land and Water* rejected *The Shadow-Line* for serialisation because it lacked action. In a dark mood and even unconsoled by *Victory*'s runaway success, Conrad balked at sending conventional Christmas greetings for 1915, 'this year of fire and slaughter'.

In early January, the Conrads went to the fashionable watering-hole of Southsea, having taken leave of Borys at Portsmouth. For someone with Conrad's interest in the Napoleonic period, the towns were rich in naval lore and history. The anchor of Nelson's *Victory* was then displayed on Southsea's esplanade, adjoining their hotel, the Queen's, and the ship herself was anchored in Portsmouth's Royal Naval Dockyard. The town boasted Dickens's birthplace museum, and scenes of the first work of English literature he had read were set there: 'It is extraordinary how well Mrs. Nickleby could chatter disconnectedly in Polish and the sinister Ralph rage in that

---

* Conrad's later report that 'All my wife's brothers are gone to the front' is apparently wrong. Walter had a game leg and would have been unfit for military service, while Albert did not participate in the war.

language.' Conrad's unrevealing 'It is very interesting here' suggests an enjoyable excursion, whatever grim purposes lay behind the dockyards' bustle.

Not long after the Conrads returned home, eighteen-year-old 'Mons[ieur] Borys' left for the front. His 'incoherent' joy would soon undergo some dampening, although his tone remained 'absolutely boyish' even on reaching Armentières. As Lieutenant Conrad buoyantly crossed the Channel, the last troops had only recently been evacuated from Gallipoli. His son's boundless enthusiasm, as Conrad transmitted it to various friends, appears to have been that of a fool, but on the subject of the war and its conduct there was more than one fool in England. To Graham, Conrad conceded that '*cette guerre a été bien mal engagée*' – but whether the French phrase means 'ill-fought' or 'botched' is ambiguous.

'The Humane Tomassov', a first draft complete, was held back for revision as Conrad energetically plunged into planning his collected edition. Garnett was out of touch for some time; returning from Italy, where he had served in the Friends' Ambulance Unit, he made efforts to renew a friendship begun in another age, and Conrad was reminded of the past, too, as he generously helped his mother-in-law financially, with Jessie herself ailing. At a time of general loss, word came that Arthur Marwood, long tubercular, was dying. As long ago as 1888, ill health had prevented his taking his degree at Cambridge. One of Conrad's closest friends – 'We have been very, very intimate,' he told Pinker – he seems to have reserved him to himself, sharing him less with his family than other members in his circle. Marwood died on 13 May 1916, aged forty-eight. An attack of gout prevented Conrad from attending the funeral.

With Marwood's death, and Curle invalided out of the Royal Naval Air Service and leaving for South Africa for his health, Capel House became quieter, but not as remote as *Victory*'s island of Samburan, for the world kept intruding upon it. The trial of Roger Casement, who had been arrested on a charge of high treason, began in late June. Having remained in Germany when war broke out, Casement was arrested on arriving in Ireland with a cache of arms and charged with collaborating with the enemy. He was also accused of saying that Germany would win the war. A smear campaign based upon diaries whose authenticity has long been contested,* played up the fact that Casement was homosexual, and, perhaps even more shocking at the time, had a highly pronounced interest in young Africans. Ireland naturally saw *Albion perfide* at her dastardly work. John Quinn was personally acquainted with Casement; as the son of Irish immigrants to America and privy to information in high legal circles, Quinn characterised the diaries as 'too filthy and nauseating to even think of'. Their impact on Casement's trial and subsequent appeal remains uncertain.

Casement, condemned to death for treason and his appeal denied, was hanged at Pentonville Prison on the morning of 3 August, the day after John Conrad's tenth birthday. Calling Casement's actions 'a stab in the back', Conrad had declined to sign an appeal for clemency got up by Sir Arthur Conan Doyle. Motivated by a belief that Casement had been mentally incapacitated by his years in the tropics, Conan Doyle feared to see him a martyr for the Irish cause. Subject to much comment, Conrad's refusal to join his voice to those appealing for clemency is complex. He was, as we have seen, habitually hesitant in making public pronouncements about politics, and he strongly identified with an England that was seriously threatened by her enemies. As the Conrads listened to the guns booming day and night in Flanders, word came from Borys that he would soon advance as the heavy bombardment prepared for the Battle of the Somme; the issue of Ireland's status could, in Conrad's view, wait until the war was over and the nation's safety secured. Casement's patriotic activities and allegiances seemed tragically misplaced, and as the death toll from the Somme rose, Conrad's circle was not spared. Hugh Clifford's brother and his son Max both died in the carnage; Ralph Wedgwood lost a cousin (and in 1917, his younger brother). In 1915, Sir Maurice Cameron, whose acquaintance Conrad had made through Hugh Clifford, had lost his son Ewen. Richard Curle's wife lost three of her brothers.

One of the war's most fervent supporters, Lord Northcliffe, owner of *The Times* as well as more populist papers, entered Conrad's life

---

* After an extensive forensic inquiry, the diaries were pronounced genuine in 2002. According to some, however, the investigators overly relied upon handwriting analysis, and the case remains open.

about this time. Seeking out a meeting, he arrived from his country house in Broadstairs where he took refuge from the heavy (if self-imposed) burden of the world's work. Born into a family of ten children and of humble origin, he now figured among England's richest and most powerful men. Conrad, who maintained the connection, had a 'curious impression' of the press baron, who seems to have had greater success in playing distant uncle to John and to Robin Douglas, then living with the Conrads.

Another new acquaintance was Northcliffe's mistress Jane Anderson Taylor, an American journalist then aged either twenty-eight or twenty-three – sources differ – born in Atlanta and married to Deems Taylor, a journalist (and later a composer and music critic). Arriving alone in England in September 1915 as a war correspondent for the *New York Herald Tribune*, she placed her journalism in *The Times* and the *Daily Mail*. She had first met Jessie at the April unveiling of the American sculptor Jo Davidson's bust of Conrad. According to John Conrad, she came to what she herself described as a 'small house with its beamed ceilings and its little crowded rooms' to interview his father; her own version was that she arrived with an introduction from Northcliffe, in the company of the *New York Tribune*'s Gordon Bruce. The uncertainty is typical of her personality and life. A lion hunter, she had bagged H. G. Wells (who later thought her 'fishy'); arrived to conquer George Harvey of *Harper's Magazine* with an introduction from Buffalo Bill Cody (a friend of her father); and, according to legend, made her way to Northcliffe bearing a note from Theodore Roosevelt. The novelist Rebecca West, Wells's lover, found Jane Anderson 'very beautiful, with orange hair . . . a slender figure, a ravishing complexion, and a great charm of manner'. She might have added that the young American had few conventional moral scruples and was naïve when it came to politics.

Anderson later offered sufficient cause for the break-up of the Retingers' marriage, and flirted (and probably more) with Borys Conrad in Paris. The 'dear Chestnut filly', as Conrad called her (to his wife), seems to have trained her sights on him. The biographer Jeffrey Meyers characterises her as Conrad's 'lover' and 'mistress', with the speculation quickly hardening into fact. Jane's tendency to hero worship (later extended to Franco and Hitler) and her need for male admiration, particularly from successful middle-aged men, were powerful. Conrad pronounced her 'quite yum-yum'. At fifty-eight, his sexual instincts, as *The Arrow of Gold* and *The Rover* suggest, had not fallen asleep, but whether he was moved to adultery and carried on a full blown extra-marital affair under his wife's watchful eye is, on balance, unlikely. Jessie, for her part, claims to have sniffed and quickly put an end to any possible trouble. On the other hand, Anderson seems to have been manic and disoriented, perhaps emotionally over-extended and also suffering from what we would now call 'culture shock'. Her husband's biographer goes so far as to say that she suffered 'a nervous breakdown' this summer. Highly strung, she tended towards the histrionic, a talent she later developed when touring the United States to rouse support for General Franco. During her speeches she 'clenched her fists, and closed her eyes, and sobbed with nearly every sentence', appearing to one observer as 'a small-time actress giving an imitation of Hitler and Eleanor Duse rolled into one'.

She seems to have impeded Conrad's work very little; he looked over a rough dramatic version of *Victory* by Basil Macdonald Hastings, whose own plays had seen West End and Broadway runs and who also dabbled in short fiction. Conrad made meticulous suggestions about the adaptation, and although not associated with it publicly, advised Hastings on lines, casting, and even scenery and costumes. Lord Northcliffe, then in France to observe the war at first hand, saw soldiers in the trenches reading the novel. A French translation was in progress, as Gide, taking over from Davray, put real energy into overseeing Conrad's translations and enlarging his French readership.

The war came even more close to home as the Chief Censor, Captain Sir Douglas Brownrigg, an old friend of Hugh Clifford, approached Conrad about publicising the war effort; several writers had lent their talents to this. The assignment, which required him to write three articles, entailed touring ports and meeting men in active service. Conrad enthusiastically accepted the offer and began planning his itinerary. The 'great void' created by Curle's departure for South Africa was being filled with business, writing, new interests, and new friends. The evening before he left for Lowestoft and Yarmouth (now Great Yarmouth), Conrad dined at Jane Anderson's London flat, an event dutifully related to his wife, then in Folkestone on a holiday of her own. He inspected ships, lunched with officers, and took his first and only flight; he disliked the experience, which he wrote up for a little magazine edited by Macdonald Hastings.

Perhaps an even more dramatic event was sailing out into the North Sea in a minesweeper, HMS *Brigadier*. Although feeling 'very strung-up' and with his head 'in a whirl', he got on well with the men and enjoyed the bustle and attention. It may be that Conrad was glad to escape Capel House's emotional pressures, the world of male camaraderie and action appealing to a part of him long stifled by domesticity and close work at his desk. After a brief return home, he set out for Liverpool, Glasgow (where he caught up with Cunninghame Graham), and Edinburgh for more touring of ships and naval bases. As he was doing so, Jane Anderson, whom Northcliffe had dropped, was at Capel House keeping Jessie company in Conrad's absence. Her own husband arrived in London in late September to cover the war, but had left for France almost immediately; the cracks in their marriage were widening irrevocably.

Conrad's northern tour directly inspired a new short story, eventually titled 'The Tale'. Set at sea in the war's early days, it is a troublingly ambiguous rewriting of 'The Secret Sharer', dealing with tested loyalties and the limits of moral knowledge. Before completing it, he was preparing to set out again for the Admiralty, travelling to Ramsgate and Dover, and then seeing Brownrigg and Northcliffe in London before heading for Edinburgh. This second northern tour was more intense than his first. He spent ten days on the HMS *Ready*, a Q-ship (a boat posing as a merchant vessel but in fact on naval reconnaissance and a decoy for submarines). Encountering a mine or being torpedoed was a real risk, which Conrad undramatically and squarely confronted as he broached with Pinker the possibility that the ship might go missing. Arriving in a stingingly cold and wet Edinburgh, he plunged into his 'duties'. Again, the ship's company proved congenial, even galvanising, as Conrad was alternately interested in and repelled by the technological changes that had taken place since his own, now long ago, days at sea.

At the end of the mission, he was put ashore at Bridlington in Yorkshire, and, according to Jessie's somewhat garbled version, there fell foul of officialdom. His foreign air roused suspicion, and he was not, as required, carrying his identity papers. He managed to calm fears, and *en route* to Capel House, spent a few days in London at the Norfolk Hotel off the Strand, during which he and Northcliffe had an 'almost tempestuous' discussion about naval matters. The great man was under the usual strains of greatness, but the intensity of the dust-up, soon patched over, may have owed something to recent news of a nephew's death at the front. Before returning home, Conrad stopped in Greenhithe to read letters from 'Old Worcesters' for one of the articles the Admiralty had commissioned him to write.

Arriving at Capel House in late November, Conrad was soon privy to the news, conveyed by Sidney Colvin, that Norman Douglas had been arrested at South Kensington station for indecently assaulting a sixteen-year-old boy. Bail had been refused. Conrad, who had already counselled Douglas to constrain his sexual adventurism, now had to confront his friend's fourteen-year-old son Robin, expected at Capel House for Christmas, with news of his father's arrest. His loyalty to Douglas extended to his taking official responsibility for the boy, then just completing his first term in the *Worcester*, so that his father's disgrace would have no repercussions on him.* Possibly facing additional charges relating to even younger boys, Douglas took a wiser course on his release than had Oscar Wilde: he broke bail and, on the advice of Conrad and Compton Mackenzie, left for Capri.

Making little headway with writing for the Admiralty, Conrad had begun a new short story by mid-December. Envisaged as around 10,000 words, the story is possibly his first serious attempt at *The Arrow of Gold*. The novel's focus on sexual tensions and rivalries and a femme fatale seems to have been nourished by recent news in Conrad's immediate circle: Gibbon and his wife, long unhappy, had decided on a divorce, and Jane Anderson announced from Paris her husband's impending return to New York. (He left in January, and they officially separated eighteen months later.) Conrad, who in August had helped her revise an article for the *New York Tribune*,

---

* Although without official consequences, the scandal seems to have affected Robin Douglas psychologically. He received 'V. Poor' both in 'scholastics' and conduct during this term, and earned a rating of 'Poor' for conduct from the Captain-Superintendent in every subsequent term except Michaelmas 1918 (his last), his certificate being held back for stealing.

attempted to interest Pinker in her as a client. To her credit were a dozen stories in American magazines, mostly set in the country's south-west, then still lightly settled, where she had lived adventurously with her father. She now fancied herself both a fledgling novelist, with a stock of autobiographical material to draw upon, and a poet. As to the stories, Conrad's literary antennae remained unimpaired – 'It's very Young stuff of course' – and he was no less clear-sighted about her character: 'she lacks judgment and determination in the conduct of her life'.

The rhythms of war coloured the year-end holidays. Edward Thomas, then a second lieutenant on Christmas leave to see his wife and two children, spent a night at Capel House. It was the poet's last visit: in April 1917, he was killed in the Battle of Arras. Conrad learned from Hueffer, who had suffered a concussion in the autumn, that he was in hospital in Rouen recovering from the delayed effects of gas poisoning. Reading *Chance* 'rather deliriously' (with delight or a light head is unclear), he unerringly caught the novel's tone: 'The end is odd, you know, old boy. It's like a bit of Maupassant tacked onto a Flaubert façade.' Due home but not heard from since before Christmas, Borys finally turned up a few days before his nineteenth birthday in mid-January 1917. His anxious mother experienced the wait with almost frantic anticipation. Conrad found his son more mature, even something of '*un homme à femmes*' (ladies' man); taking pleasure in the 'really fine officer', he confided to Cunninghame Graham, who was about to leave for South America again, that although Borys lacked brilliance he had '*des idées de gentilhomme*'. Gibbon, who had seen the youth in France, thought that 'this business made a man of him', his 'calm competence and appetite' evident as was his thorough mastery of 'bad language'. Lieutenant Conrad was also putting out warning signs of future problems: the dupe of a clever gambler, he had got into debt and was overspending. In this respect, at least, he was proving rather too much a chip off the old block.

Conrad's struggle to write the three articles for the Admiralty proved unavailing, and he produced only 'The Unlighted Coast', an essay that opens with generalities about the nature of combat and then focuses on a seaman's anecdote about strafing a zeppelin. Even it proved too 'Conradian' to be usable, and first appeared in *The Times* a year after the writer's death. Eager to make progress with the embryonic *Arrow of Gold*, at that time a short story, he was by his own admission 'without much grip on' his writing, and apart from giving further detailed advice to Hastings on the staging of *Victory*, settled into a fallow period that extended over much of the first two months of 1917. Involved in Hastings's adaptation, the well-known actor-manager H. B. Irving asked for revisions and rewriting to accommodate his new wish to play Heyst. (He had originally thought to play the villain, Mr Jones.) Hastings completed his work in mid-March, and Conrad, who found the play 'curiously prosaic and tending to the obvious', suspected that Irving, in fact, simply wanted to wriggle out of the project. He himself was barely coping as gout prevented *The Arrow of Gold* from advancing: 'I creep on with the story.' Not long after, he lamented again that it 'still crawls', metaphorically transferring his malady to his writing.

Preoccupied with his own affairs, Conrad professed 'no interest whatever' in the fate of Russia, where the Bolshevik Revolution had broken out, its course and influence on the conduct of the war were still highly uncertain. The call from the Duma for the Tsar's abdication was a signal of a world in upheaval, but whether Conrad's indifference was genuine or a matter of protesting too much is impossible to tell. Commenting on the death of Ralph Wedgwood's younger brother in action, in the same breath he noted his own son's 'tone of elation' as his battery advanced. In the midst of the continuing blood-letting, *The Shadow-Line*, dedicated to Borys and his generation, received a 'very respectful' reception, the first printing (5,000 copies) selling out in a month. As ill luck would have it, a wartime paper shortage delayed a second printing.

The strain of the prolonged conflict was now beginning to tell on Conrad – he spoke of the war's 'never-ending sorrow'; it even prevented him from working: 'who can be articulate in a nightmare?' The war also meant isolation as Capel House lacked visitors, apart from the occasional presence of Colvin, too old to do any war work. Conrad had no energy to go to town and idled away his hours, as his wife's health began to deteriorate seriously. Her knees made walking increasingly painful, and, stout for some time already, she was now morbidly obese, the result of decreased mobility and a calorie-rich diet, supplemented by chocolates, cakes, and spirits. Conrad's gift to celebrate their twenty-first wedding anniversary, on 24 March 1917, was a self-propelling invalid-chair. As he commented to Colvin: 'I saw her just now creep painfully across the room and could have cried.'

The United States' declaration of war on Germany on 6 April was, Conrad thought, a 'warlike caper', one he responded to with mixed feelings, as he vented his characteristic scepticism (dating back at least to the Spanish-American War) of the Great Republic's motives. He was none the less pleased that Britain should receive greatly needed support, and to an American correspondent reported enthusiasm for the event as 'not noisy but very deep', noting that the service at St Paul's marking the occasion had been 'very fine'. Scathingly ironic about the imperialist adventurism of the United States, Nostromo had warned of the honey-coated rhetoric upon which she habitually relied, a mask for raw ambition and money-grubbing. Conrad was also inclined to an aversion to her citizens, at least in the abstract: 'O! those Americans! They all seem to have something just a little wrong with their brains.' He even cautioned his son about the Americans he had fallen in with in France – '5 words from an Englishman are worth 5000 from an American, any time' – and philosophically shrugged off Borys's short-lived infatuation with Jane Anderson: 'if he must meet a "Jane" it's better he should meet her at 19 than at twenty-four'. Retinger, who observed Conrad's 'dislike of Americans and the American mentality', suggests that his friend's attitude was to become more positive after his trip to New York City and New England in 1923.

Suspicious about the United States, which had amassed huge profits at sea while the war battered Britain's economy, Conrad also now grew anxious about the import of the Russian Revolution, a subject to which he had claimed to be indifferent. Fearing to appear 'qualified to speak on things Russian', he even hesitated over Garnett's request for a foreword to his book on Turgenev, a collection of his prefaces to his wife's translations. In the end, he asked his old friend to Capel House to discuss the matter, and cast the preface as an informal letter. Praising a writer he greatly admired, he used the occasion to take a sideswipe at Dostoevsky, whose emotionalism and politics repelled him, although, as *Under Western Eyes* indicates, he had read *Crime and Punishment* carefully.

Garnett's request was a reaching out, and Conrad and he again drew close, recognising their deepest affinities and papering over their long-standing political differences. Events in Russia, which had descended into anarchy as the Tsar abdicated in March, may well have cooled Garnett's Russophilism. With Conrad's friendship with Pinker also deepening, no doubt owing in part to their sons being in the trenches, the associations of his earlier career revived with greater intensity as fame and success drew round him. Further evidence of his rise in reputation was André Gide's translation of *Typhoon*, and a second English edition of *Lord Jim*, a novel that sold well throughout the war, at a time when courage and fidelity were issues both of private and of public concern.

Even as he sent notice of relinquishing his Civil List pension at the end of the government's fiscal year, Conrad took on a regular financial commitment to assist his sisters-in-law, and his mother-in-law, who had recently turned seventy. As with so many areas of Conrad's personal experience where documentation is scant, it is difficult to typify his relations with his wife's family. He liked Frank, her youngest brother, and when young, Jessie's sisters had often pitched in at Stanford-le-Hope and The Pent. He later tenderly recalled to her sister Dolly, widowed by the war and remarried and settled in South Africa: 'Certainly I carried you to bed more than once. Generally you would be fast asleep and as insensible as a stone, but, of course much more pleasant to carry.'

A more immediate family concern was Borys, who after his stint as Parisian *boulevardier*, was back at the front. Jane Anderson, too, had moved on and acquired more serious interests, including Retinger, whose wife, in Lausanne, had recently been delivered of a baby girl. Borys's ten-day home leave in September cheered his parents, at a time when his mother was suffering from bronchitis and his father from a gouty hand, as illness continued to be Capel House's most frequent visitor. Conrad felt a strong tug at his heart when he said farewell to his son at Ashford station, finding their parting 'even harder than the time before'. John, who had turned eleven in August, was also gone, having entered Ashford Grammar School as a weekly boarder. He was desperately homesick, and his mother missed him so much that weekend visits proved wrenching for them both.

The Arrow grew throughout this summer, as Conrad wrote with oddly uncharacteristic ease, or at least complained less about making slow progress. His health continued to hold, aside from the gout during Borys's home leave. He made important deletions to *Nostromo* for a new edition, retreading old ground almost with enthusiasm: 'I am attending to the proofs, and I rather like it. Jolly good stuff. But I had a bad time writing it.' Confronting work he had done fifteen years before not only revived the past but also confirmed how prescient his observations had been about the fates of nations. As in his imaginary South America, men just across the Channel were indeed fighting and dying for 'material interests' and politicians' dreams, and the United States, as his character the crude and bullish Holroyd predicts, was on the rise, relentlessly: 'We shall be giving the word for everything; industry, trade, law, journalism, art, politics, and religion, from Cape Horn clear over to Smith's Sound, and beyond too, if anything worth taking hold of turns up at the North Pole. And then we shall have the leisure to take in hand the outlying islands and continents of the earth. We shall run the world's business whether the world likes it or not.'

Bedridden with pain, Jessie possibly had bone disease in her knees, as her condition was little improved after a month's complete rest. She hobbled on crutches, and one of her sisters came to help with chores. The Conrads settled in for nine days at the Norfolk Hotel to hunt out accommodation for a prolonged stay in town for her operation and recovery. They opted for a spacious flat in Hyde Park Mansions on the Marylebone Road, with easy access to Regent's Park, Hyde Park, and Edgware Road tube. Arriving at the flat in a Rolls lent by a friend, Jessie enjoyed the ministrations of a titled surgeon, Sir Robert Jones, England's most distinguished orthopaedist. Conrad laid on wine (Beaune and Chablis) and engaged Miss Hallowes for *The Arrow*, his first novel to be composed mainly by dictation. As in the 1890s, he shared the evolving work with Garnett, but both had seriously lost their touch, Garnett as critic and editor and Conrad as stylist and storyteller. He dictated the work without enthusiasm: 'I am chilly,

chilly. Still I do something every day but it all seems without relief and colour and strangely remote – directly I lay it aside.' It grew by 600 words a day, but its writing gave little pleasure as Conrad only intermittently felt in touch with his subject. Dictation, which lends itself to prolixity, tended, moreover, to loosen his style.

The war now came home in a particularly intimate way as Jessie's sister Dolly lost her husband in late November 1917 in the Battle of Cambrai, a conflict Borys would become involved in a month later. The capital experienced occasional air-raid warnings, which seem not to have hampered Conrad's enjoyment of city life. As his wife underwent treatment, he visited friends – the Colvins, Galsworthy, Garnett, and E. V. Lucas; took in Ibsen's *Ghosts* in which Catherine Willard had a role; and, though in small measure, he poked at the fashionable literary circles he had generally avoided. The social whirl took its toll and while dining out, Conrad was struck down by gout.

This period in town also brought new acquaintances. At a lunch with Colvin, Conrad met Hugh Walpole, a rising writer of popular fiction, with the first two of his 'Rogue Herries' series selling well. In his mid-thirties, the square-jawed intellectual with the 'right' background (The King's School, Canterbury, and Emmanuel College, Cambridge) was a self-conscious and self-confident charmer. His then lover, Percy Anderson, an artist and costume designer, took advantage of the introduction to sketch a chalk-and-wash portrait of Conrad. One of the elderly Henry James's favourites – The Master found Walpole 'delightful and interesting' and of 'blooming, bursting, bounding vitality' – Walpole was favourably struck with Conrad: 'even better than I had expected – looking older, very nervous, rather fantastic and dramatic somehow – his eyes I think – "an intellectual Corsair."' He proved an ardent admirer, having a penchant for father substitutes and older gentlemen. (Anderson was then almost seventy.) With Marwood dead and Curle in South Africa, Conrad may have wanted a new friend, a surrogate older son, although he seems always to have kept Walpole at a remove or two from real intimacy. Shortly after their first meeting, Conrad sent him a copy of the recently reissued *Nostromo* and a jokily phrased invitation to dine with him and Garnett: '*un repas quelconque* [a scrambly meal] . . . probably Red Herring' served on 'chipped plates'. As Conrad discoursed on Poland, Walpole found Garnett 'As melancholy and drooping as ever.' Conrad himself described his former mentor as 'a moody and somewhat freakish personage' who belonged to 'a past, the glory of which has passed away'. Cecil Roberts, a new acquaintance favoured with this description of Garnett, was a rising journalist and war correspondent and was being flattered as the man of the moment.

Another stage in Conrad's life as a father was now marked, as John was sent off to board at Ripley Court, Surrey. A stiff 15 guineas were owed to Ashford Grammar School for the lack of notice; Jessie protested about the distance from Capel House, but an eleven-year-old's needs and energies were proving more demanding than she would admit. Now chronically unwell and old enough to be the boy's grandfather, Conrad, who was planning to take Miss Hallowes back to Capel House on a three-month contract, may also have needed a quieter home for his writing. He greatly enjoyed playing with John, who was sensitive to his father's moods: 'there were times when his work didn't satisfy him, and then his temper would become slightly frayed. But you could always tell this as soon as we met, and on these occasions I kept quiet.' Just before returning to Capel House, Conrad, seeing John at Ripley Court, felt sad at the sight of 'the dear little pagan' encased in an 'Eton jacket and horrible round collar'. He had cause to recall his own very different education, and quickly write an essay titled 'Tradition', commissioned by the *Daily Mail*. Treating the Merchant Service generally and praising its conduct during the war, the loosely organised piece is part reminiscence and part unabashed propaganda. Northcliffe's 250 guineas for it (£262.10; in 2005's terms nearly £42,000), in effect a lordly and quite lavish gift, were accepted '*de bon cœur*'. The press lord's generosity also extended to paying Conrad's £40 membership dues to the Athenaeum, to which, as an 'eminently distinguished' person – terms of membership that Conrad recalled to Pinker – he had been elected.

On his return home Conrad suffered yet another attack of gout, blaming his 'feverish symptoms' on the area's 'chill clay' rather than his change of diet. Missing London's whirl, he invited Walpole to stay, promising that work could be done 'in this silence and solitude'. Miss Hallowes was expected, and John returned home for Easter. Conrad was distressed by the 'horrible time' at the front, with Borys and Eric

Pinker 'in the thick of things' in the Battle of Saint-Quentin, the latter having won the Military Cross for valour. Back from France, Will Rothenstein invited Conrad to his exhibition of war pictures, 'On the Peronne Front'. Before the opening, Conrad suffered through a 'very bad' lunch (the war had limited supplies of foodstuffs) with the Rothensteins and H. A. L. Fisher, now Minister of Education, who opened the exhibition. The *Times* reviewer found the paintings 'the best documents of the war yet produced', and hoped that future ages would glimpse in them 'the horror and beauty of our time'. For his part, Borys was still greatly enjoying his time in service, Conrad indulgently discerning 'a military vein imbedded [sic] somewhere in that child's temperament'. Garnett, who refused to participate in the war, asked Conrad to pull strings for him so he could avoid repercussions for his attitude, which differed so sharply from that of Conrad's son: 'I have no earthly objection to killing the responsible people who engineered the war or who are prolonging it, but I refuse absolutely to do military service for objects I do not believe in – such as the conscription of Ireland, the break-up of Austria, the recovery of Alsace-Lorraine, or other such objects (open or secret) of our ruling caste!'

With John's return to school in May, Conrad could report to his agent work done on *The Arrow*: 'The beastly thing is like an india-rubber band. Stretches' – a comment he could have made about several of his works. To Ted Sanderson's wife Helen, he dropped the show of bravado altogether: 'It's probably rubbish.' In mid-month, he went to see Congreve's *The Way of the World*, an excursion mainly engineered to see Catherine Willard, a young actress with whose journalist mother Grace (or 'Mama Grace') Willard, the Conrads had become friendly. A comedy of a much grimmer kind played itself out as Conrad was drawn into denying that he was Jewish. Frank Harris, a journalist and the biographer and friend of Oscar Wilde then living in the United States to edit *Pearson's Magazine*, made the claim. Writing to a rabbinical student that he had no 'racial prejudices', Conrad laid out 'long descent' from 'an "Old Christian"'. He went on the counter-attack, assailing Harris for his untruthfulness and pro-Germanism and taking the occasion to attack Wilde, too: 'he sent me a copy of his book on Oscar Wilde which I didn't care to have, both on account of the author and of the utterly uninteresting subject'. When the suggestion of Jewish ancestry resurfaced in the *New York Times Book Review* after Conrad's death, Curle, in a letter to the editor, stated that Conrad was 'purely Polish, apart from one ancestor who was either French or Italian'.* (This information, presumably from Conrad, has never been mentioned elsewhere, but then Curle also fantastically asserts that Conrad as a child had a private audience in Vienna with the Emperor Franz Jozef.)

Another new acquaintance, Jean Aubry, a French journalist and critic, entered Conrad's milieu at this time. 'G. Jean-Aubry', as he most often styled himself in print, had written the previous autumn when Conrad was travelling in the north for the Admiralty. This time he received an invitation to Capel House. Well connected in Paris's literary and musical circles, he knew Debussy, Ravel, Manuel de Falla, and Albert Roussel (the latter two setting some of his poems to music), and Paul Valéry. In London, he edited the *Chesterian*, a magazine on musical matters, and moved in the circle of the Swedish-born soprano 'Madame Alvar', offstage Mrs Louise Harding, the wife of a well-to-do barrister. (One of Conrad's intimates characterised Aubry as her 'lapdog'.) The friendship with the austere-looking Frenchman, then in his mid-thirties, developed rapidly, their shared intellectual and cultural interests developing into a personal close-ness. The contact revivified Conrad's French and his enthusiasm for French culture at a time in life when nostalgia for one's youth would have been unsurprising.

Just before the Conrads left for London as Jessie faced yet another operation, Walpole visited; he found Conrad 'simply superb. A child, nervous, excitable, affectionate, confidential, doesn't give you the idea anywhere of a strong man, but *real* genius that is absolutely *sui generis*.' Conrad returned the compliment, judging Walpole's *Green Mansions* 'fine'. Returning again to Hyde Park Mansions for two

---

* The allegation of Jewish origins took the ugliest of forms in 1936 when in a lecture at Munich University (subsequently published), Wilhelm Stapel, the pro-Nazi director of the monthly magazine *Deutches Vokstum*, denounced Conrad's work and its dissemination as part of the Jewish 'infiltration' of German intellectual life. Stapel alleged that Conrad's work, published in Germany by the prominent Jewish publisher S. Fischer Verlag, was a 'Polish Jew' living in England.

months, Conrad was pleased by the change of scene: friends were near at hand, and Miss Hallowes was readying *The Arrow* for publication at Pinker's office. Borys, on a special ten-day leave, lifted his parents' spirits at a difficult juncture, but almost on arrival he fell seriously ill with the flu and had to extend his stay. In the year of the great influenza pandemic, Conrad himself escaped with only a mild case. With costs mounting and Jessie's medical bills coming in, he arranged to write ' "Well Done!" ' for the *Daily Chronicle*, an article praising the wartime effort of the Merchant Service. It lived up to its title, its 5,000 words earning him £100. Pinker placed *The Arrow of Gold* for serialisation, at a time when Conrad's sales were buoyant in the United States. The successful author, however, felt 'beastly seedy' with gout, and back in Capel House in mid-August, 'doing nothing' and 'not fit for anything', he had an attack of lumbago followed by depression. A visit from that 'charming person', Walpole, improved his spirits, and the new friend also made inroads on Jessie's affections, becoming her confidant.

Miss Hallowes arrived to start work on *The Rescue*, just as Conrad toyed with the possibility of writing an article on the Bolshevik Revolution. World events continued to impinge, as Retinger, having busybodied himself out of France and now ill and in straitened circumstances in Fuenterrabia, in the Spanish Basque country, in desperation called on Conrad for help, addressing his pleas via Jessie, whom he informed of his desire 'to go to Capel House and stay with you for a time'. He requested that Conrad intercede with the Foreign Office or the Prime Minister for his re-entry into Britain: 'both as a man and as a Pole I am suffering and passing through great "malheurs" '. This dramatic appeal fell upon deaf ears, Conrad having by now, at least to his own mind, definitively broken with Retinger, no doubt objecting not only to his extremist political machinations but also to his personal life.

With John at school, and Jessie's condition worsening, the three Conrads again left for a fortnight in London for medical treatment. Conrad with Miss Hallowes checked into the Norfolk, close to Pinker's office, where Conrad planned to dictate more of *The Rescue*. The hotel afforded good underground connections to Jessie's Baker Street nursing home, where she was to be operated on, pending Sir

Robert Jones's return from the Italian front. To cover these unplanned expenses Conrad resorted to selling the original fragment of *The Rescue* to Thomas J. Wise, a noted bibliographer and collector, a contact apparently made through Aubry. It later emerged that Wise was also a forger and a thief, fraudulently producing literary rarities and cutting pages out of first editions in the British Museum's Library to increase the value of his own imperfect copies of Renaissance works. Conrad too was acting underhandedly: the transaction with Wise occurred behind Quinn's back, the New Yorker having a 'moral claim' on first offer of any manuscript; however, this payment avoided transatlantic communications and was swift, as Wise showed himself keen to add anything in Conrad's hand to his magnificent Ashley Library (a collection named after the street in which he lived).

At home again, the Conrads received news that Borys was in hospital in Rouen. Pinned under a collapsed wall, he had breathed in chlorine gas on the Menin–Cambrai road, the work of a German howitzer, and was also suffering from shellshock. Perhaps for his parents' benefit, he made light of his experience, but nevertheless remained in hospital for a month, suffering from insomnia and feeling shaky, before being moved to Le Havre. Conrad seems to have suffered quietly from depression, anxious about his son and also facing the task of finding a new home as the landlord of Capel House had died the previous December and his son wished to take occupancy.

On 11 November 1918, Conrad and Jessie listened 'soberly thankful' as the village bells rang in the peace, and were stirred by the solemnity of the occasion. Conrad looked cautiously towards the future that the war had ushered in: 'Great and very blind forces are set free catastrophically all over the world.' Borys's arrival home for a fortnight's leave was a vivid reminder of these, and Capel House became a virtual field hospital, as Borys coughed from the gassing, Jessie suffered from the flu, bronchitis, and a swollen throat, and Nellie Lyons, whose service with the Conrads dated back to The Pent, was so dangerously ill that she was taken to hospital. (She died, aged thirty-six, in January, Conrad paying for her funeral and mourning her deeply.)

The Conrads found their eldest son changed, but underestimated the severity of his mental condition. His mother, who sympathetically recalls his nightmares and 'moody fits' in her memoirs, thought a change of air (for some reason opposed by Conrad) would help. Her naïvety in facing her son's serious and chronic depression is unblameable and, with hindsight, understandable. Shellshock was little understood at the time and had been treated barbarically, to the point that mentally ill men had been shot for cowardice. As late as 1921, a *Times* leader bullishly commented 'Shellshock comes from soft men.' Troubled by the 'detestable atmosphere thick with gloom' clinging to the house, Conrad cancelled a planned visit from Siegfried Sassoon, whose poetry he was reading in anticipation of it, and also put off Garnett. As Christmas approached, Conrad's mood was dark: 'A cloud of unreality hangs about men, events, discourses, purposes.'

During this gloomy time – brightened only by John's return for the Christmas holidays – he managed to dictate 'The Crime of Partition', partly cobbled out of a pamphlet Retinger had published in French in 1916. Rehearsing somewhat conventional views about Poland's partition, including that she was blameless for her weakened condition, it seeks to mobilise support for a reconstituted nation-state. It had taken a world war to loosen the Austrian, German, and Russian yokes, a goal Conrad's father had fruitlessly dreamt of in an earlier age. Interested in the abstract principles in play, Conrad was sagely aware of *Realpolitik*. Meanwhile, his friend Cunninghame Graham was even more politically active; running as a Socialist in Stirlingshire, he had come third in the election held on 21 December 1918.

Conrad was full of plans for completing *The Rescue* and nailing down the delayed collected edition with Doubleday, who was then in England for some months, combining business with his honeymoon. (His first wife, a writer, had died during a trip to China earlier in the year, and he had married again in November.) Negotiations with the American publisher, still in London in February, did not run smoothly: Conrad came away feeling that 'Effendi', preoccupied with the mechanics of the edition, did not 'care a damn' what he had written. Unwin, who had to be courted for the edition to be complete, was proving predictably tetchy, and Doubleday's business methods had vigorously rubbed salt into old wounds. The publisher also seems to have revived Conrad's prickliness about things American; he fretted over the nation's pushy prominence at the Versailles Peace Conference: 'American influence in European affairs cannot possibly be good on account of those people's crudeness and ignorance backed by great material strength and an awakened sense of their power. Luckily there is a sense of futility about them which will probably make them less dangerous than they might be.'

Unfinished business dominated the New Year of 1919, as Conrad, confined to bed, worried about finding a new home. Jessie's knee was again demanding medical attention, and while she was being treated, Conrad, Miss Hallowes, and Borys moved into the venerable Durrants Hotel in Manchester Square near the Wallace Collection and a ten-minute walk from Oxford Street. Conrad took the opportunity of being in town to inspect Dr Robert Mackintosh's Surrey Scientific Apparatus Company in the south-western suburb of Mortlake, in hopes of giving Borys a start. A job offer would also permit his immediate demobilisation. In the event, these plans proved premature: Borys was ordered to the Maudsley Hospital in Denmark Hill, south London, for the treatment of neurasthenia.

Returning to Capel House, Conrad relentlessly dictated and then corrected The Rescue, dictation to Miss Hallowes again encouraging prolixity. Contemplating the long-delayed Mediterranean novel, he boned up on the period, as negotiations for a new house progressed in fits and starts. With most of their belongings in storage, the Conrads finally vacated Capel House on 25 March 1919, for nearby Spring Grove, a large seventeenth-century manor house on the outskirts of Wye, about four miles from Ashford. They took the house on a six-month lease at £7 7s. a week (£1,025 in 2005) as Conrad negotiated for a lease on Oswalds in Bishopsbourne, a small village nestled in rolling countryside about four miles south of Canterbury. Named after a blacksmith whose covered-over forge in its study dates to the early sixteenth century, the house, featuring extensive gardens and wide views, was the former dower house of Bourne Park, a stately home where the nine-year-old Mozart once played. 'Georgianised' and then extended during the Victorian period (a billiard room and ballroom tacked on before Conrad's time have since been demolished), it boasts its own historical associations: it abuts St Mary's Church, whose rector Richard Hooker worked on his classical statement of Anglicanism, *The Laws of Ecclesiastical Politie*, during his tenure in 1594.

There was yet more to-ing and fro-ing including a visit to town to consult with Macdonald Hastings and the actress Marie Löhr, who had taken up an option on Hastings's adaptation of *Victory*. The play opened on 26 March 1919 at the Globe (now the Gielgud) Theatre in Shaftesbury Avenue. Conrad declined to attend, whether from tiredness after the move the day before or to mark a distance from Hastings's work. Colvin, Pinker, Walpole, and Borys were in the opening-night audience, which greeted every act 'with great and increasing applause' and 'loud enthusiasm at the end'. The King and Queen went to see the play on the 31st. Opening the same week as Somerset Maugham's new comedy, *Caesar's Wife,* and a revival of Rostand's *Cyrano de Bergerac*, Hastings's adaptation had a *succès d'estime*, attracting respectful reviews and the attention of the illustrated papers. By the time it closed in mid-June, it had brought profits in which Conrad had a share. His financial situation was now not only settled but even good, the trajectory of his success charted in the home he was contemplating moving into, a far cry from cramped lodgings in Gillingham Street.

Another financial windfall came when Northcliffe commissioned an article for the *Daily Mail*'s 'Golden Peace Number' to mark the signing of the Treaty of Versailles. Overcoming his initial reluctance to interrupt work on his novel, Conrad rapidly wrote 'Confidence', yet another paean to the Merchant Service and its economic and moral importance to the nation. A heavy attack of gout struck after he completed it, leaving him 'very weak and unwell', and delaying work on *The Rescue*, even as pleasant spring weather set in. Perhaps his continuing ill health contributed to his animosity towards Spring Grove, which he initially found a 'charming house' in 'a very charming spot', but which, by July, he was calling 'odious'. Borys, still jobless and considering more tutoring to improve his prospects, remembered the family's time there as extremely social, the house attracting numerous visitors, although Conrad claimed to feel 'savage and misanthropical, and pessimistic'.

Health is a typical obsession of ageing, the past another. The latter returned in two forms in the late spring. Jane Anderson was busying herself on Conrad's behalf in Hollywood, attempting to stir up interest in the sale of film rights and keeping in touch about her efforts. One wonders, however, how she reported these as Conrad confided to Pinker: 'Jane seems slightly distracted.' The other visitor from the more recent past was Richard Curle, who returned home after three years in South Africa, where he had been writing leaders for the *Pretoria News*. And meanwhile, a chapter begun in the very distant past had finally closed: Conrad could celebrate completion of *The Rescue* (now given its definitive name), begun nearly twenty years before.

Negotiations for the sale of film options flourished; after Hueffer's and Pinker's shares were deducted, Conrad received £3,080 (roughly £430,000) from the Laski Film Company for rights to *Romance*, *Lord Jim*, *Chance*, and *Victory*. He celebrated the deal and his somewhat improved health with a well-earned break, going to see Reggie Gibbon, the Colvins, and the Hopes. The fly in the ointment, however, was the reception of *The Arrow of Gold*. The *Morning Post* reviewer declared its story unlocatable and that the characters were presented at 'double and treble removes', yet it confessed to a fascination with the workmanship. More bluntly, the *New Statesman* observed: 'The story is, in itself, a little unfortunate', the promised gun-running 'the merest and vaguest background' and the love interest 'touched on so lightly' as to be underdeveloped. Conrad, who now held that newspaper reviews were simply a matter of boosting sales (or not), dismissed the bad reviews as 'very poor, puzzle-headed hesitating, pronouncements', and took comfort in friendly remarks. Peevishly, he blamed Unwin for bringing the novel out in August. At the same time, however, he admitted to Colvin, who had yet to write his review, that 'the plot cannot be told for there is none' and claimed that the novel was a study of a woman. He consoled himself that the critics had not discerned 'failing powers', but the muted response had, in fact, registered these, and whatever Miss Hallowes's famous patience, the *mot juste* did not drop to the clack of a typewriter key.

In America, Doubleday's publicity machine operated in over-drive, and the novel, published in 15,000 copies, achieved bestseller status. An advertisement in *Publishers Weekly* seems oddly to concede that

Conrad was in the main a difficult read: 'Never, even in "Victory," has Mr. Conrad written a story so direct and free from circumlocution, and never has he portrayed a character, either man or woman, so fascinating or so elusive as Doña Rita.' The same trade journal excitedly reported orders by booksellers in New York, Chicago, Philadelphia, and Boston in quantities of 1,000, 750, and 500 copies. Whether the books that were sold were, in fact, read (in today's terms, the Man Booker Prize phenomenon) is another matter. Attempting to read it, E. M. Forster's mother dubbed it '*The Arrow of Lead*'.

The monotonous themes of gout, Jessie's excruciating pain, and Borys's search for employment dominated the Conrads' summer. Invalided out of the army, Borys received an annual disability pension of £150, quite adequate for the time, but never close to meeting needs that became increasingly extravagant. In late August, a stay at the Norfolk revealed that yet another operation was required on his long-suffering mother; it was scheduled to take place in Liverpool before the year's end. Circumstances had already conspired against work and with the move to Oswalds imminent, Conrad, realising he would get little done, again began to consider a theatrical venture. Pinker came down with Frank Vernon, a producer and translator, to discuss dramatising *The Secret Agent*.

The move to Oswalds in early October 1919 occurred in stages. A railway strike and gale force winds complicated matters, but Borys, still with his parents, managed ably. John reached Ripley Court before the trains stopped running, but food supplies, which quickly became scarce, were rationed, and horses and carts (not yet gone from rural England) clogged the roads to Canterbury market. The first night in the new house was spent camping 'with a few sticks of furniture without curtains and carpets'. Amidst these upheavals, Conrad made inroads on his new project, reporting the first act of *The Secret Agent* 'well advanced'. Eager to escape Oswalds' chaotic arrangements, he fled to Burys Court, Pinker's spacious 'Victorian gothic' pile in Reigate (now the home of a private school). With its extensive grounds and turrets, it provided concrete evidence of Pinker's success much as Oswalds, though rented, symbolised Conrad's.

With Conrad nibbling at dramatic adaptation, a proposal from J. M. Dent focused on another aspect of his activities: Dent, who saw a latent opportunity in Conrad's scattered essays, wanted to bring them together. Conrad's initial response was cool – 'I have a great dislike to have a collection of fragments of my prose in volume form even when the object of it is educational' – but left the door open for negotiations should the project have 'some good inducement of a material kind'. Deferred for the time being, *Notes on Life and Letters* eventually came out in early 1921.

On a quick run into town, Conrad saw Cunninghame Graham, but 'between "Rebecca" & "Doris"' got no chance of a word with him. It is unlikely that these lady companions graced the staid Wellington Club where the friends had lunched the previous week, and a faint whiff of the *louche* clings to this tantalisingly vague reference. Conrad occasionally went to the '43' Club in Gerrard Street, opened in November 1921 by Kate Meyrick, 'London's Nightclub Queen', but then so did much of the fashionable capital. (Meyrick bagged no fewer than three peers for her daughters.) The arts crowd – including painters such as Jacob Epstein and Augustus John and writers including J. B. Priestley, as well as the raffish end of the smart set – paid court. 'Cocaine girls, gangsters, and neurasthenic post-war criminals' frequented Soho, but Conrad's visits to the '43' occurred during its early and tamer period.

Questioned later about his father's sex life, Borys Conrad laconically declared it 'normal', and then frosted over. As for Conrad's emotional life, he grew increasingly dependent upon younger men: Curle, Aubry, and Walpole. On leaving for a long American lecture tour in September, Walpole got a farewell warmer than their acquaintance might seem to merit: 'I feel my approaching loneliness deeply. I shall try to hold on to the lifebuoy till you return.' Conrad's loyalties, however, could affect his judgement, and around this time what should have been a minor molehill grew into a mountain, involving Gide and Aubry. Quite regularly assigning Conrad's texts for translation without consulting their author, Gide had selected Madeleine Maus, whom he had long known, to translate *The Arrow of Gold* after she had submitted satisfactory samples of her work. Aubry, however, expressed to Conrad his keen interest in translating the novel, and fulminating that 'a woman has just got hold of *The Arrow*', Conrad sent Gide an insensitive and wounding letter insisting that

Mme Maus stop her work forthwith and that Aubry be assigned the task. His (specious) grounds were that the novel's nature demanded a male translator. Gide, the innocent party who had energetically been working on Conrad's behalf, was understandably upset and returned Conrad's letter to him. (It does not survive.) Gallimard had entered into a contract with Mme Maus and was probably left out of pocket; for her part, she protested to Gide about having to throw away two months' work.

In the end, Conrad and Aubry got their way, but the whole affair has an unpleasant flavour that suggests more than the crankiness of chronic ill health and advancing age. Conrad, who had been petty, had jeopardised his friendship with Gide, who deserved a better return for his mainly selfless efforts. Not long after, although partly, no doubt, under pressure to get on with his own writing, he turned over the entire project to the indefatigable Aubry, whose inferior Conrad translations had a stranglehold on the French market until they were finally systematically replaced during the 1980s.

In the midst of this squabble, progress continued on the dramatisation of *The Secret Agent* under Frank Vernon's close supervision. An experienced man of the theatre, Vernon corresponded with Conrad about the staging and came to Oswalds to discuss it. Conrad's initial reservations about the project – 'Personally, I cannot defend myself from the dread of the whole thing turning out repulsive to average minds and shocking to average feelings' – in the end subsided, although he feared that stripped of its persistently ironic presentation, as staging would require, the story might appear 'merely horrible and sordid'. His objections, including a sense that there would be 'very little glory or profit in the production', were strong but not dissuasive. Nor did he seem to consider the mainly sad history of 'novelists' theatre', forgetting Henry James's infamous opening night of *Guy Domville* when the Master appeared before the curtain to catcalls and boos. By the time he had begun the third act in mid-November, news came that J. E. Vedrenne, once Harley Granville-Barker's partner, would produce the play at the Royalty Theatre. He also began to yield on another point about which he had first had qualms, asking Curle, then in touch about the sale of Conrad pamphlets to 'keep a list of your discoveries in view of a Vol: by and bye'. The reprinting of Conrad's essays in limited editions, tentatively begun by Clement K. Shorter was pursued more ambitiously, and lucratively, by T. J. Wise, the bibliographer and book collector.

While he perspicaciously managed his career, Conrad's domestic affairs remained mixed: his wife's condition preoccupied him; Oswalds, however, was finally being properly furnished, its few sticks being added to with a Broadwood piano for the parlour and other 'necessities', acquired through the good offices of 'Mama' Grace Willard, whose daughter Catherine was still busily establishing her stage career. (Borys suspected that his mother fancied her as a daughter-in-law.)

With the third act of *The Secret Agent* behind him, Conrad prepared for the planned six weeks in Liverpool for Jessie's operation. Borys, assigned the task of keeping his father company there, found them lodgings at 85 Kingsley Road in Princes Park. Conrad took an instant dislike to the city – 'Life is rather impossible here' – and even signing the agreement for Doubleday's collected edition, finally arranged by Pinker after considerable negotiation, little improved his mood. A stomach ailment bothered him, followed by gout and prostate trouble; expenses proved 'rather heavy' in the 'dratted town', and work turned out to be 'impossible'. Coming to Liverpool to lecture at the city's Royal Institution on 'Verlaine et les musiciens', Aubry provided some consolation. Even better, in Conrad's view, was Jessie's rapid improvement, which allowed the trip to be cut to half its projected length.

Arriving home for his first Christmas at Oswalds, John's impression of the house, judged perhaps with the eye of the future architect, was that it possessed an 'air of faded gentility' and neglect. His father was otherwise preoccupied: felled by the prostate infection, 'a beastly complaint', that had come on in Liverpool, he was also depressed and suffering from a gouty wrist when an old acquaintance, Major Ernest Dawson, a contributor to *Blackwood's* and an old Burma hand, turned up just before New Year. Dispirited by the past month and a half of idleness as regards his work, Conrad felt that he would 'never do anything any more'.

9

'Smiling Public Man'
(1920–1924)

'. . . where is his like today, Joseph Conrad!'
James Huneker to John Quinn, 30 June 1914

The mood of despondency that had plagued Conrad began to dissipate as he started to prune *The Rescue* and considered collecting his occasional essays for the press: the handful of book reviews written in 1910, the polemics occasioned by the sinking of the *Titanic*, and the pieces on Poland and the Merchant Service written during the war. The preface to *Notes on Life and Letters*, as he called the collection, gently, and somewhat poignantly, reminds the reader that the project was, in effect, a case of 'tidying up' before he himself quitted the scene. It was one of several testamentary acts, with Conrad now concerned about the image he would leave behind him. Another reminder of the passage of time was Borys's twenty-second birthday in mid-January, for which Catherine Willard came down. Conrad's valedictory mood continued as he became involved in the specifics of the long-delayed collected edition, which Doubleday was to bring out in America and Heinemann in England. Karola Zagórska's arrival at Oswalds for a six-month stay put Conrad back into contact with his mother tongue and stimulated memories. The distant relative to whom he had become close in Zakopane was a trained singer, and Zagórska brought music to the house. Whatever Conrad's reminiscent mood, he declined an invitation to become associated with the Anglo-Polish Club on the grounds that he knew no influential people in England who could further the Polish cause and lacked sufficient knowledge of Polish affairs.

But his eyes remained fixed on the past in other ways. In March, while writing an 'Author's Note' to *The Secret Agent* for the collected edition, even as he was putting together a dramatic adaptation from the novel, he must have recalled his days in Montpellier. On the other hand, the long-ago failure of *One Day More* seems to have been forgotten, or at least brushed aside, and dramatic adaptation proved a new and invigorating departure. Conrad's self-satisfied report to Galsworthy that he had 'managed to ram everything' into the play 'except the actual cab-drive' ominously suggests, however, a lack of aptitude for writing for the stage. He had, in fact, attended the theatre infrequently, and adapting a complex ironic novel demanded not only compression and the wholesale rethinking of plot but also a thorough knowledge of contemporary theatrical conventions. Conrad, as *The Arrow of Gold* had sadly suggested, was growing out of touch with his talent.

Blithely happy with progress on his play, Conrad also had to cope with a domestic drama. Still in severe pain, Jessie faced another operation, this time in Canterbury, where she would stay for her recovery. Intended as the final operation to end an old problem, it provided only immediate and temporary relief and occasioned short-lived optimism. Conrad himself, wearing a gout boot, hobbled about the house, cheered by Karola's presence, but he had to report to Pinker, recently back from the United States, that the operation had failed. Ice-bags eased Jessie's pain, but 'more knife-work' – painful, expensive, and emotionally disruptive – was in prospect, and Conrad's nerves grew frayed as the unhappy situation continued. Another costly operation in May, 'a four-inch cut below the knee down to the bone' under local anaesthetic and involving a major nerve, again failed to alleviate Jessie's horrible suffering.

With still another operation in view, Conrad retreated into himself, too depressed to see anyone, even Walpole, who had just returned from an American lecture tour. But his mood then shifted and an invitation went off to Aubry. His wife's ill health caused more tension than he confessed to, the misanthropic mood lingering as he laid plans to call upon the Colvins in London: 'I have grown so stupidly nervous,' he told Lady Colvin, 'that at times a mere railway journey scares me out of my wits.' Even allowing for hyperbole, Conrad was profoundly and obviously unhappy, both domestically and as an artist. He fretted now about the Mediterranean novel: 'why should I suffer from such a state of funk about that book?' And he dug deep to write 'Author's Notes' to *Under Western Eyes*, *Chance*, and *The Shadow-Line* despite the onset of depressive symptoms, including, typically, difficulty in concentrating.

A respite from this moody self-absorption came when Curle and Walpole arrived for a weekend. Returning to town with his friends, the party lunched fashionably, at Frascati's in Oxford Street, with Conrad then going off to pass a few hours in the nearby British Museum Reading Room to burrow into a few books on the Napoleonic period. The price he paid for the day's outing was gout and the 'depth of the dumps'. To compound the latter, Conrad was about to lose Curle again, this time to Burma for six months with the *Rangoon Times*.

He consoled himself with the favourable reviews of *The Rescue*, published on 24 June 1920, reading them closely and cheered by those tending to boost sales. That in *Punch*, which found the novel likely to be 'the greatest novel of the year' and 'in the authentic manner' of Conrad 'at his unapproachable best', was one such. As was that in the *Sketch*: '*The Rescue* is a thing so massive, so profound, so beautiful, so masterly, that this faint emotion is entirely submerged in the sense of complete absorption.' Virginia Woolf, then a veteran reviewer but a fledgling novelist, in her unsigned review for the *Times Literary Supplement*, disagreed, finding the story 'long and elaborate' and judging that its tragic elements, although abundant, 'fail to strike one unmistakable impression upon us . . . because Mr Conrad has attempted a romantic theme and in the middle his belief in romance has failed him'.

Posterity has mainly shared Woolf's view. Set in Far Eastern waters, partly aboard an English ship and an English yacht but centred on a plot of native intrigue involving the recapture of power and an adulterous, but unconsummated, relationship, *The Rescue* combines elements of early Conrad (the sea, ships, the exotic, betrayal and loyalty, an adventurer hero) with a love plot that smoulders but stubbornly refuses to catch fire. The novel appealed to Conrad's contemporaries (and was even made into a silent film starring Ronald Colman), but, like most of his late work, it dates badly and has faded from view.

As Jessie Conrad finally began to improve, and the Mediterranean novel (then known as 'The Isle of Rest' and eventually called *Suspense*) moved forward, there were reasons for momentary contentment. In the mood for company, Conrad invited John Powell to visit; he was in England at the time, for a performance with the New York Symphony under Walter Damrosch. The pianist, whose *Rhaposodie nègre* for piano and orchestra, based on 'Heart of Darkness' had premiered in 1919, was swiftly followed by Cunninghame Graham, who arrived with T. E. Lawrence ('Lawrence of Arabia') and Lord Northcliffe. Impressed by Conrad's 'flashing eyes' and laughter, Lawrence felt 'uneasy' with his host, who carped at Hueffer and marked the occasion by presenting Lawrence with a copy of *The Mirror of the Sea*.

Out of the blue, the head of a Liverpool shipping firm, Lawrence Holt, asked Conrad to comment on a scheme to fit out a sailing-ship to train cadets. Moved by a request that brought back memories of his sea life, he plunged into a project that not only promised an honorarium but also distracted him from the Napoleonic novel once again being picked at, with its history extending as far back as 1905 and the stay on Capri. Holt came to Oswalds to discuss the scheme, just as proofs of Heinemann's collected edition began to arrive. Having no intention to embark upon the kind of thorough revision Henry James had done for his famous 'New York Edition', Conrad nevertheless intended to look them over, but in the end gave only a cursory glance to the first couple of volumes and delegated Miss Hallowes to hunt out misprints in the rest. Although handsomely produced, the volumes put paid to any hopes of a 'definitive' edition: Heinemann's editors had gentrified Conrad's prose, regularised his punctuation and spelling, and smoothed out his grammatical lapses. Doubleday's editors were, on the whole, much less intrusive, mainly content to pour old wine into new bottles.

As Karola Zagórska was leaving for Italy, Ralph Pinker visited for Canterbury Cricket Week. Interested in agricultural training, he made arrangements with Colonel Matthew Bell at Bourne Park (Oswalds' owner), and lodged on and off with the Conrads for the next year. The arrangement reflects the strength of Conrad's relationship with Pinker, mutual business advantage having, as we have seen, blossomed into friendship. The falling-out of a decade ago had long been forgotten. Pinker joined the Conrads for part of their late summer holiday in nearby Deal in early September 1920. The journey was an easy one, and the seaside town, about 20 miles from Canterbury, not dauntingly fashionable. Staying at the South Eastern Hotel near Deal Castle, Conrad pulled together and lightly polished *Notes on Life and Letters* and wrote a film scenario based on 'Gaspar Ruiz', with Pinker's help. Already the least inspired of Conrad's short stories, it was chopped up into *Gaspar the Strongman* in hopes (that in the end proved vain) of making quick money. On their return to Oswalds, the Conrads learned that Sir John Millais, son of the painter and a Kentish neighbour with whom Conrad played chess, had died. Distractions – writing the preface to *Notes on Life and Letters*, lunch with Frank and Nelson Doubleday, visits from Walpole and the Australian poetess Dorothea MacKellar – tended to soften the blow, but Conrad grieved, writing to Millais's mother: 'I was grateful for the liking he had for me and I am deeply grateful to you for the gift by which you are good enough to recognise my great regard and affection for him. My dear Lady Millais I can hardly bear to write about this!'

Excuses to avoid the manuscript once again on his desk multiplied as Conrad became involved in an attempt to settle Borys at Dr Mackintosh's Surrey Scientific Apparatus Company. The firm, which specialised in wireless telegraphic equipment, offered an opening that suited Borys Conrad's practical bent, and, although it was unstated, Mackintosh, with whom Conrad was friendly, could keep an eye on him. In the event, Mackintosh's impractical nature was to clash with Borys's youthful ambitions for the firm, into which Conrad and his son had both put money.

Conrad had other distractions from the work in hand: he 'Englished' an article for the *Fortnightly Review* that Jean Aubry had written on him; was interviewed by Ernest Rhys for New York's *Bookman*; called on the Pinkers at Burys Court; and sat to Max Beerbohm for a sketch, friendly to an artist who so memorably sent up

Conrad's early somewhat overwrought style in his 'The Feast', one of the parodies in *The Christmas Garland* (1912). At the same time, the prospect of a production of *The Secret Agent* involved him in counting chickens before they hatched. Norman McKinnel, an actor-producer, took an option on the play, and negotiations and scenarios for its casting occupied Conrad for the next several months. Now seriously interested in the theatre, Conrad accompanied by Pinker attended a matinée performance in the Little Theatre's Grand Guignol season, one of the two plays featuring Lewis Casson and Sybil Thorndike. The outing inspired Conrad to dramatise 'Because of the Dollars' under the title *Laughing Anne*. Catherine Willard and Jean Aubry were Christmas guests; Ralph Pinker was intermittently around; and Sam Everitt of Doubleday's, on a business trip to England, was fêted with oysters as Oswalds hospitably opened its doors to guests.

The gap between a social calendar bristling with engagements and Conrad's private feelings, shared with Garnett, yawns wide: 'I have done nothing – can do nothing – don't want to do anything. One lives too long.' Too much can be made of this world-weariness. Borys was settled with a job; John was to begin at Tonbridge School in the new year; and the Conrads' home bustled with preparations for a continental holiday, the Conrads' first trip abroad since the ill-fated Polish expedition of 1914. Feeling guilty about neglected work, Conrad deserved a rest, although even 'the conquest of Corsica', as he playfully called their journey south in search of sun, was partly intended to kick-start the Napoleonic novel. Miss Hallowes, after dispatching the final proofs of *Notes on Life and Letters*, which appeared in late February, was to make her way to Ajaccio, portable typewriter in tow.

For the Conrads the journey to the mountainous island of Napoleon's birth began happily, and concluded, true to form, in ill-temper and self-recrimination. In vogue with English tourists to the extent that it boasted an Anglican church, Ajaccio, where the Conrads intended to put up for 'two or three months' at the ultra-fashionable Hôtel Continental, was scarcely a leap into the unknown. Pinker, his wife Mary, and his daughter, Œnone, were to join the Conrads, and Cunninghame Graham and his companion Mrs Dummett were also scheduled to arrive. Conrad's taste, as usual, was impeccable and extravagant: the large hotel, featuring a palm-treed exotic garden, had been graced by the then Archduke Franz Josef of Austria and the Archduchess Elisabeth before their elevation to the Austro-Hungarian throne.

With Borys as chauffeur for the initial leg to Rouen, and Aubry as travelling companion to Marseilles, the excursion had the character of an ambitious and well-planned junket. The party, including the Conrads' usual chauffeur, Charley Vinten who was to take over from Borys, and Jessie Conrad's nurse-companion Audrey Seal, left for Calais on 23 (or 24) January 1921. A small cloud darkened its departure: Conrad had learned from Pinker, in effect his banker, that he was spending £4,000 a year (£515,000), and that economising would truly have to begin. (Where all that money went is a question likely to remain unresolved with the documentation surviving.) En route to the south, the party met Aubry's parents, who lived near Le Havre. Although the motor car broke down twice, near Chartres and then just outside Montélimar, the journey proved enjoyable. The party did get lost one night, a potentially dangerous experience when street lighting was patchy. On arrival in Marseilles, which Conrad had last seen in 1878, the Conrads put up at the Hôtel Splendide near Gare St-Charles.

On the eve of the crossing to Ajaccio, Conrad enthusiastically urged his agent to 'Throw care to the winds and come out south with punctuality and dispatch.' As bad weather set in, this buoyant mood was to prove short-lived: 'Cold. Wet. Horrors,' he recorded. And the 'beastly hotel', where 'intense good form prevailed' among its polo-playing colonels and 'rather better class' frumps, proved rather too elegant: 'A lot of rather smart people are staying.' The 'confounded island' turned out to be larger and 'wilder' than Conrad anticipated, and he judged its inhabitants 'dirty rather'. (In writing to Aubry, about a people at least nominally French, he referred to the Corsicans as 'charmants'.) What began as a Forsterian idyll à la Room with a View occasioned ill-temper and strained nerves, although these were soothed by a ceaseless round of activities and by friends.

Always keen for excursions and company, Jessie enjoyed their trips round the island as far as Bastia. Through Sir Maurice Cameron, an old friend of Hugh Clifford's, the Conrads became acquainted with a young Irish artist, Alice S. Kinkead, who later painted oil portraits of them. Conrad also met the French playwright Henri-René Lenormand, who offered to lend him Freud to read, believing that his work revealed particularly relevant insights to a creative writer. Conrad politely declined, sceptical about technical explications of the human character, which he had observed with an artist's eyes. The time was one of true relaxation, spent in cafés and in boating with Pinker, who, to his daughter's accompaniment, sang in the evenings. There were also visits to the Maison Bonaparte, Napoleon's birthplace in the rue St-Charles, as well as to the château of his arch-rival, Pozzo di Borgo, some half-dozen meandering miles out of town. Its charms, architecture, and noble vistas drew the Conrads no fewer than four times. The other notable event was the Conrads' twenty-fifth wedding anniversary, celebrated shortly before they left for Marseilles.

Fearing a railway strike at home and tired of hotel life, the Conrads returned to Oswalds via Caen in early April. The writer met with a summons from Pinker for an immediate clarification of his finances and spending. The Conrads' lifestyle was undoubtedly comfortable: Oswalds required a large staff, including cooks and gardeners; John enjoyed private schooling as well as a tutor; a chauffeured motor car was available; there was Miss Hallowes; London stays were always in the best hotels. Moreover, Conrad was generous to the Zagórska sisters, affording Karola, who lived in Milan for healthier weather and vocal training, a regular allowance, and he helped maintain his ageing mother-in-law. Jessie had her own allowance apart from housekeeping expenses, which were not small as visitors called regularly and were entertained at table and with wine, and Borys also made various calls upon his father's purse. Income tax came as a regular and nasty surprise. Grudgingly, Conrad promised to be more pound wise.

He foresaw box office receipts and further sales of film rights, as the theatre cast its spell, and hurried to London to see the actor Norman McKinnel in a now-forgotten play, with possibilities for the dramatised *Secret Agent* in mind. But just as his finances were placed on a new footing, clouds again gathered round Borys. Mackintosh's company, its success uncertain almost from the outset, teetered and then, in July 1921, finally collapsed. Out of pocket for £300 (£37,000),

Conrad angrily broke with the physician-inventor. Borys, unemployed again, also turned out to be in debt to the tune of a further £300. (His mother blamed her son's spendthrift habits on his romantic involvement.) In these circumstances, Curle's return from the Far East, where he had been working for the *Rangoon Times*, was timely, and from now until Conrad's death, he proved a stalwart emotional and practical support. Genuine though the friendship was, Conrad used Curle to attract notice to his work, while Curle, happy to play the insider, obliged with glowing reviews and exploited his connections with the newspaper world to boost Conrad.

Just as Conrad's interest in theatre was deepening, Bruno Winawer, a Polish physicist turned playwright and journalist, wrote to him about his play *The Book of Job*, a satirical comedy with Shavian elements, recently staged in Poland. Conrad reported that he found the play entertaining, but (not entirely truthfully) claimed that he lacked connections in London's theatrical world. All of a sudden, he set about translating the play, and, assurances to Pinker to the contrary, neglected his own languishing writing. Why the play, a dullish affair dealing mainly with local issues, appealed to Conrad remains a mystery. He may have wanted to hone his skills as a theatrical adaptor to apply them to his own fiction. *The Book of Job* led nowhere – apart from a welcome £100 from Wise, who eagerly acquired the typescript for his growing collection.

In the meantime, Jessie Conrad's portrait had been painted by Alice Kinkead, and Conrad sat for Theodore Spicer-Simson, an American sculptor who took photographs for a portrait medallion, for inclusion in a volume on *Men of Letters of the British Isles*. Commissioned by *The Times*, Conrad quickly wrote a short essay to celebrate the Dover patrol's contributions to the war effort, to be published on the day that the Prince of Wales unveiled a memorial to the men and women who had kept guard on the Kent coast. A period of summer diversions ensued, as Conrad in effect took time off. He went to Burys Court, returning with J. B. and Ralph Pinker for Canterbury's Cricket Week, an annual early August event held since 1842. Conrad's interest in the game itself is unrecorded, but, playing the gracious host, he laid plans for putting up Pinker's entourage of servants and arranged lavish luncheons near the grounds. The party arrived at Oswalds in grand style, with Pinker, in top hat, driving a four-horse mail-coach. The Galsworthys motored down for bank holiday luncheon, and with John home from school and Aubry expected, the house bustled.

When Conrad returned to his Napoleonic novel, he did so mainly to tidy the little he had then written so Pinker might have an extract to hawk about for serialisation. The revision stimulated a return to actual writing, and in a show of bravado Conrad predicted adding some ninety pages during a month of 'close sitting'. In truth, he was written out, and, truncated as it is, *Suspense*, as the novel was finally called, is a sad, better forgotten, ending to his career. Some paragraphs are directly lifted from the *Mémoires de la comtesse de Boigne*, a celebrated account of the Restoration and the July Monarchy; others are undigested research, in the manner of George Eliot's *Romola*; and the prose, almost consistently flabby and mechanical, suffers greatly from having been dictated. However much Proust may have admired the Countess de Boigne's memoirs, chit-chat about salon life was ill suited to Conrad's talent. Sadder still, he was unaware that he was slumming intellectually. A much more exacting mental excursion was his grappling with Bertrand Russell's *The Analysis of Mind*, presented to him by its author on a recent call.

A series of false starts and disappointments mark this period. Conrad fussed over proofs of his wife's cookery book, which was not published until 1923. A volume of plays for Doubleday, containing *One Day More* and *The Secret Agent*, was cancelled (why is unclear), although Conrad had read proofs for it. A new edition of *The Mirror of the Sea*, illustrated by John Everett, a marine landscape painter and engraver and a friend of Will Rothenstein's, was raised by Pinker, and Conrad, deeply moved by Everett's exquisite pictures, responded with enthusiasm: 'Those things are, properly speaking, marvellous, in truth, in sentiment, and in rendering. What an accurate and imaginative vision!' In the end, Everett ran out of patience, and the idea, so enthusiastically embraced, died a slow death.

'Seedy and often in pain', he now learned of Norman McKinnel's decision not to stage *The Secret Agent*. Conrad put a good face on his disappointment, vainly hoping that Pinker would seek out other possibilities. Suddenly, in mid-December he told his agent of a new work, 'within the long short-story limits', which he planned to have ready for Pinker's annual late-winter business trip to New York. Conrad, not unusually, was wrong on both counts: *The Rover* grew into a novel, and he completed it only in July 1922. Curle spent Christmas at Oswalds, preoccupied with his marital troubles, which ended in a divorce in early 1922.

As so often, Conrad's year-end proved unhappy: exhausted by a raging cough (which would rack him on and off over the next two years), he was vexed when the car broke down as he was on his way to see Jessie's physician Sir Robert Jones in Canterbury. Conrad coughed throughout a New Year's visit at Burys Court, and Pinker himself was recovering from a bout of ill health. The visit was coloured by intimations of mortality as Conrad apparently discussed making his will and proposed Pinker as his executor. ('Not good friends' with his father's agent, Borys registered his objections about the choice to his mother.) Still with a persistent cough, Conrad now came down with gout and the flu, which prevented a visit to town before Pinker left for New York. What proved to be their last meeting took place at Oswalds, Pinker being uncharacteristically dispirited. Gravely ill during the crossing in the *Aquitania*, he died of pneumonia on 8 February 1922 at New York's Biltmore Hotel, his daughter Œnone by his side.

Usually reserved, Conrad owned up to a 'sense of irreparable loss', and, according to his wife, became 'a bundle of nerves and indecision'. Pinker had been his virtual business partner, a friend, his *de facto* banker, and quasi-father figure for nearly twenty years. His death marked the end of a long era in Conrad's life, and the pattern of psychological dependency would suddenly have to cease. Hugh Walpole, the author of Pinker's obituary tribute in *The Times*, singled out 'kindliness of heart' as the primary reason for the literary agent's huge success, pointing out how much the careers of Henry James and Conrad owed to his canny management. Whatever Conrad's personal loss, he mourned a wise and steadfast business counsellor. Considering his inability to control his spending and make the hard decisions required for a major international career, Conrad had done extraordinarily well out of Pinker. In testimony both to his personal closeness to his father and to Conrad's importance to the firm, Eric called at Oswalds shortly after news of his father's death had reached the family. Initially hesitant about Eric's capacities, Conrad gradually conquered his doubts, remaining loyal to J. B. Pinker & Sons and falling into many of the patterns – excepting the personal intimacy – established with 'J. B.'

Walpole, who passed a tension-filled weekend at Oswalds a few days before Pinker's death, had found both Conrads suffering from poor health and frayed nerves. Arriving to what he characterises as the 'Usual atmosphere of whisper and ailing on at the Conrads', he was distressed: 'State of things really awfully bad. J. C. much worse – shrivelling up, looks like an old monkey and does nothing all day. The house divided absolutely into two camps and who is speaking the hints I really don't know . . . Got through the day somehow. Jessie in hysterics in the evening.' Walpole discovered the cause of these tensions a few months later. Like her elder son, Jessie, too, had run up debts – perhaps through backing the horses, or by over-generously opening her purse to Borys. Whatever the case, she had been unwise and was unable to cover her debts from her regular allowance; looking about for cash in a desperate attempt to conceal her situation from her husband, she, like Borys, turned to the successful young writer for 'help'. Privy to the situation, Lady Colvin discussed it with Walpole, and even Sir Robert Jones somehow became involved. However sympathetic to Jessie, Walpole's deeper and unshakeable loyalty was to Conrad: 'I love him dearly and his tenderness to me during these years, to me and to my work has been a help to me I simply can't describe. Therefore I must not in any way at all do anything behind his back.'

Conrad, now temporarily managing his own career as Eric Pinker was establishing himself, made progress on *The Rover*, which had displaced *Suspense* and was typically expanding. In April, his health and mood improved as John's presence brightened Oswalds, and Conrad's interest in adapting *The Secret Agent* was rekindled. Allan Wade, an actor with Harley Granville-Barker who had produced for the Stage Society, read the play carefully, sniffing out its strengths and weaknesses. He also graciously took on the task of reading Conrad's translation of Winawer's comedy. As Conrad recovered from another attack of gout, he was ebullient, sending Eric Pinker a batch of *The Rover*: 'I have my dear fellow worked well . . . I am feeling better than I have felt I may say for years.' With few lapses, the mood stretched into the summer as Conrad revised *The Rover*, his last completed novel. It rises above weak writing in its mid-section (again the effect of dictation and, possibly, hurry) to end triumphantly, the old seaman Jean Peyrol going nobly to his death in a skilful battle with the elements, sacrificing his life for values he believes in and people he has come to care for. The themes of commitment and fidelity have a final outing that falls just short of greatness, and Conrad was aware of his achievement: 'The story will make a good volume. Perhaps a remarkable one.'

He seemed, however, fated never to be happy long. In late July, Borys, no longer able to fend off his creditors, appealed to his father. Lawyers became involved; costs spiralled; Eric Pinker and Curle were consulted; and Conrad was several hundred pounds the poorer. The fuss, strain, and the trips to town drained him: 'I am feeling still a little sick at heart for that will not be the end of it.' He was increasingly unable to protect his son against himself, and his fears proved prescient. Borys steadily ran up debts with an insouciance that outstripped even Conrad's own in his youth; by the time his father died, he was in hock for £3,000. His once doting mother could not avoid altering her feelings as he grew more spendthrift: 'The foolish boy Borys seems to have no moral sense, no idea of the value of money.' However 'foolish', Borys was mentally fragile to an extent both his parents consistently failed to realise. Conrad's lifelong habits of heavy spending and exaggerated expectations of his income may also have provided what today would be called a 'negative role model'. As Conal O'Riordan, an Irish playwright with whom Conrad was friendly in the 1910s, commented when Borys was cadging money in the 1930s: 'I was very fond of his father but I cannot pretend to think he was a wise parent.'

Even as he coped with private grief, Conrad, his fame stretching across the Atlantic, was forced to play what Yeats would call the 'smiling public man'. He judged American artist Walter Tittle's lithographic sketch of him 'very successful', and entertained Hamlin Garland, who was spending the summer in England. The now virtually forgotten regional novelist, arriving for lunch with one of his daughters, an introduction from Sir James Barrie in hand, was gathering material for an article and for his regular lecture tours. The stately Midwesterner found Conrad more disconcertingly 'continental' and nervous than he had anticipated: 'His body radiates energy. His arms fly about like flails. His face was alight with welcome and his words came mumbling, tumbling out. He was altogether continental. He gesticulated like a Polish Jew, but his speech was filled with cockney accents.'

Conrad drew up and signed his will at his solicitor's, asking Curle and Sir Ralph Wedgwood, a friend he had made through Curle, to act as executors. The document provides only for his wife and children, leaving no gifts or legacies; his generosity to the Zagórska sisters took the form he had already arranged: they were to own the copyright in his works published in Poland. The settling of his affairs may have been urged on by Borys's latest troubles, but Conrad felt no equanimity about his family's situation. The consolation of this stressful time seems to have been re-reading Galsworthy's *Forsyte Saga*, recently issued in a single volume. Congratulating his old friend on 'a great art-achievement', he reflected that the last couple of years 'had in one way, or another' been 'a pretty bad time'.

There were other reminders of time's passage. On 14 August 1922, Lord Northcliffe died, followed a few days later by W. H. Hudson. Although close to neither, Conrad had had dealings with both men, and he comforted Garnett, an intimate of the naturalist-writer, that with Hudson's passing 'Something unique is gone out of the world.' He later joined Cunninghame Graham and others on the committee to put up a memorial in Hyde Park. (The eventual statue of Rima, the heroine of his novel *Green Mansions*, was by Jacob Epstein.)

In a rare break from routine, the Conrads travelled from Dover to Liverpool in mid-September to visit Sir Robert Jones. On the evening of their arrival they listened to the gramophone after dinner, an experience Conrad disliked. The party made a brief excursion to North Wales, in an Armstrong Siddeley limousine and Rover Tourer. Jessie and John enjoyed the jaunt, but the cough that had plagued Conrad earlier in the year returned in force. The party stopped at

Oswestry School in Shropshire, where Conrad met the headmaster and boys.

On returning home, Conrad seriously contemplated giving notice on Oswalds, and then abandoned the idea. The house was proving too costly, but economies, as he appears to have impressed upon his elder son, were not really in his line. Tadaichi Hidaka, a Japanese academic on leave in England, made contact, was met at the station by Conrad and John and offered lunch, tea, and hours of conversation. Although not lavish, such entertainments were over-frequent – and mainly time-wasting. With a small Japanese readership (*One Day More* had been translated in 1914 and 'Because of the Dollars' in 1921), Conrad either appreciated this testimony to his fame, or was curious about a region of the Far East he had not himself visited. Absorbed in 'constant meditation' about *Suspense*, he was also distracted from the project by J. Harry Benrimo, an American actor turned theatrical producer, who was expressing an interest in the dramatic version of *The Secret Agent*. Benrimo, who shared Doubleday's sense of urgency, quickly arranged a production; Conrad invited him to Oswalds, and planned to meet the company. In mid-October he signed a contract providing, on a sliding scale, for 5–10 per cent of gross receipts on London and provincial performances and a New York run, and energetically threw himself into suggestions for casting.

Conrad attended two rehearsals and made some cuts and changes, and even as the press promoted the upcoming play – featuring his photograph with the actors – its author grew apprehensive. The playbill featured the celebrated Miriam Lewis as Winnie, something of a draw, and Sybil Thorndike's brother, Russell, as Ossipon. Conrad highly praised the boy playing Stevie, but thought Inspector Heat too young and the Professor miscast. The opening on 2 November 1922 at the Ambassadors Theatre was a gala event. Suffering with his cough, Conrad remained at the Curzon Hotel and was interviewed by *Teacher's World*; Jessie in her box had '*the* evening of her life'. Arriving to pick her up, Borys saw most of the last act. A full house of friends, acquaintances, and the literary elite applauded warmly, and congratulations rained down by wire, but neither could cover over the professional critics' merely polite and respectful reviews.

Conrad, who judged some of the response 'rather silly', railed at the press response as so much chattering in a 'noisy parrot-house'. Some of it undoubtedly was. Whatever the problems deriving from under-rehearsal and some merely adequate acting, the play itself was found 'challenging', Benrimo's experiments with lighting effects compounding the impression. But, in the end, Conrad had only himself to blame: he had tried to impose his vision on theatrical conventions rather than working within them, and traditional expectations ruled a relatively conservative form. Fatally static, and, according to one cartoonist, full of 'volumes *and* volumes of talk', the play closed after only eleven performances. Conrad's expectations of ready money were disappointed, and he had wasted his time and energy, both of which were growing short. Disillusionment, regret, and ill-temper, variously masked, lace his comments on the fiasco. Like *Suspense*, the adaptation had proved a wrong turning, and, grasping at straws to avoid self-criticism, he blamed the concurrent Annual Motor Show and the recent general election for damaging the play's prospects.

Another vexation, minor by comparison, arose to re-focus his ire. He had allowed a friend, Harriet M. Capes, a writer of children's stories, to produce an anthology with the title *Wisdom and Beauty from Joseph Conrad* in 1915. The volume of snippets, which had attempted to make Conrad into La Rochefoucauld, had long embarrassed him. (For instance, a quotation culled from *Nostromo* reads: 'A woman with a masculine mind is not a being of superior efficiency; she is simply a phenomenon of imperfect differentiation – interestingly barren and without importance.') Miss Capes's publisher, more familiar with printing Sunday School tracts than contemporary fiction, had reissued 'the damned thing'. Already irritated by his play's failure, Conrad staged a full-blown temper tantrum, fuelled by the suspicion that the publication would benefit neither Miss Capes, as he sincerely hoped, nor himself.

More bad news came as Hearst's syndicate rejected *The Rover* for serialisation in the United States, but its prospects soon revived, with the mass circulation *Pictorial Review* expressing interest. Another money-making American venture was also mooted: Doubleday felt a trip to New York would boost Conrad just at the right moment. His company had been preparing the terrain for a few years, with strategic advertising, and sales of recent Conrad titles, as well as the backlist, had been good. Naïvely, Conrad told his publisher that Galsworthy had suggested that he arrive in Halifax and make his way to New York by train to avoid 'excessive publicity' – precisely, of course, the trip's point. Conrad seriously considered going, imagining a few private lectures rather than the usual whistle-stop tour of nightly readings, a rigorous programme inappropriate to an aged lion such as himself. Among his closer friends, Galsworthy and Walpole had laboured mightily on the American lecture trail, and he doubtless knew of Hamlin Garland's successful reading tours. Aware, however, that his marked accent would be the subject of comment and curiosity, he drew the line at being exhibited like a carnival freak, however well paid. In anticipation of the trip, he sent Doubleday the 45,000 words he had written of *Suspense*, a piece more fretted about than actually worked upon. He now predicted its completion in March 1923.

In a businesslike Christmas Day missive to Eric Pinker, Conrad breezily dismissed a 'regulation winter fit of gout', while John's holidays were ruined by the mumps. Conrad was now flirting with the idea of moving to France to save on income tax. The end of 1922 was fraught with emotional ructions, illness, and financial worries, the latter surely exaggerated given the sum he left upon his death. Aubry's arrival put an end to none of these but at least brightened his mood, as did the news that Borys, well settled into his new job in the Trading Department of Daimler's Manchester concern at Rusholme, had received a raise. (Borys's annual after-tax salary of £85 (£14,600), even topped up by his £150 disability pension, still proved well below his needs, as his debts were again mounting.) Able to work, Conrad laboured on *Suspense*, whose long evolution was proving fatal to any sense of plot. Even as he promised to economise and to find a less expensive home – not quite New Year's resolutions – he was making plans to send John to France for a year to improve his French.

A break from *Suspense* came in early March when Conrad turned to a proposal to write a foreword to Thomas Beer's biography of Stephen Crane, the first undertaken. Aged thirty-three and a noted short-story writer in the United States, Beer, carrying introductions from Hamlin Garland and Garnett, hurried to Oswalds to discuss the project just before returning to New York. Criticised at the time, his biography has more recently been exposed as partly a fraud – Beer fabricated 'evidence', quoting letters that had never been written – and Conrad's long, affectionate memoir prefaces a discredited book. Eager to benefit from Conrad's name, Beer, a lawyer from a well-to-do legal family, apparently paid the £400 fee for the introduction out of his own pocket. Garnett, long a champion of Crane's work – 'I have tried to rub into those blasted Americans that Crane was a master' – encouraged Conrad, who drafted the 8,000-word piece in a fortnight. Initially excited by the project, Conrad characterised the preface as 'mostly twaddle' and 'hack-work'. Again he had strayed from *Suspense*, his spleen possibly vented because he was yet again squandering his talent. He was, however, certainly not wasting his time from the financial perspective, earning £50 for 1,000 words (£8,600 in 2005 terms). He promptly sold off the manuscript to Thomas J. Wise for another £110. The sums are high but not extravagant: Eric Pinker had sold the 80,000-word *The Rover* for £4,000.

'Blasted' or not, Americans were on Conrad's mind as he ordered new clothes for his trip, arranged his passage, and was interviewed by the *Philadelphia Ledger*. He was to leave from Glasgow on 21 April 1923, and remained reluctant about the venture to the very last, telling Karola Zagórska that it held no appeal and remarking to Sir Robert Jones that he was going 'without enthusiasm'. Curle would accompany him only to Scotland, and not, as Conrad had originally hoped, on the trip itself.

He made the trip north in stages, visiting Fountaine Hope, who was recovering from a stroke, in Colchester, and in London made his first public speech (a five-minute dry run for public speaking in the States), seconding a resolution at the 99th National Lifeboat Institution meeting, chaired by Admiral Beatty, at New Bond Street's Æolian Hall. At the home of Jean Aubry's friend Madame Alvar, he saw Ravel (met the previous summer), who was in London to conduct his compositions at the Queen's Hall, and then saw Pinker's widow and Ralph and Œnone before leaving the Curzon Hotel. The artist Muirhead Bone (his brother David commanded the *Tuscania* in which Conrad would go to New York), who would provide company during the voyage, met Conrad and Curle at St Enoch station. In the evening, Neil Munro, an old acquaintance, and yet another Bone – John, editor of the *Glasgow Herald* – joined them for dinner.

Muirhead Bone proved companionable, and Conrad, who spent time on the bridge and stayed up with the Bones until the early hours, enjoyed himself. He even spun money out of the voyage, writing 'Ocean Travel', which Curle placed in the *Evening News*. In curmudgeonly fashion, the article rails against changes at sea since Conrad's day a quarter of a century before, as his two articles on the *Titanic* had fulminated about excessive luxury. When his own moment of modern 'ocean travel' came, he had few qualms about travelling first class and dining in full fig at the captain's table.

Any illusions about a quiet arrival already dissipated, he was none the less ill prepared for the onslaught that greeted him at Quarantine on 1 May. He rose early and dressed impeccably and formally, to greet Doubleday, his host and the visit's stage manager. Eric Pinker, then in New York on business, the pianist John Powell, and Christopher Morley, a journalist indefatigably enthusiastic in the Conrad cause, made up the welcoming committee. They were helpless when it came to shielding him from the mayhem at the dock where two 'mobs', one of photographers and another of reporters, had assembled to greet the famous writer. Abashed at the photographers' scrum some forty strong – one kept shouting 'Take your hat off, Mr. Conrad' – Morley himself wrote several articles about the event, describing Conrad as a 'spare, almost fragile figure, garbed with clerical sobriety in a black overcoat, white muffler, and a round bowler hat, his left arm bandaged'. The editor of the *Polish Daily Telegram*, with a group of Poles, came forward with 'enormous nosegays', promptly handed to Eric Pinker as in a royal walkabout, to greet (and stake a claim on) the author.

The exact opposite of sneaking in by the back door, the arrival beggared even Conrad's descriptive powers: 'I will not attempt to describe to you [his wife] my landing, because it is indescribable. To be aimed at by forty cameras held by forty men that look as if they came out of the slums is a nerve-shattering experience.' He was bemused by the outpouring of American energy, simultaneously pleased and taken aback. As we have seen, prior to his visit, his attitude to Americans, partly formed by his dealings with Doubleday and by his objection to the nation's intrusions into world affairs, was mainly negative, perhaps partly a claim to Englishness. (Walpole reports of one of his visits to Oswalds that Conrad 'Got very angry as usual at the mere mention of Americans or Russians, both of whom he detests'.) The visit to the United States, during which he was flattered, praised, and lionised, appears to have softened his feelings.

Conrad stayed at Effendi Hill, Doubleday's sumptuous Long Island estate in the town of Oyster Bay, where his hostess installed him in a ground-floor bedroom to spare what she judged to be his 'very delicate state of health'. That, however, prevented neither gala dinners – Powell played Chopin and Beethoven after one – nor Doubleday's invitation to nineteen reporters to 'tea' to interview Conrad. His host also laid on a lavish dinner for the political set, which was attended by 'Colonel' Edward House, an adviser to President Wilson and an influential political figure, and John W. Davis, former Ambassador to the Court of St James's and 1920 presidential hopeful. (He lost to Calvin Coolidge in 1924.) Conspicuously absent from any guest list was John Quinn, either by Conrad's desire or his own, Conrad's shifty selling of his manuscripts to Wise forgotten by neither. On the other hand, Quinn had somehow never managed to meet Conrad on his trips to England even before their relations had cooled.

Muirhead Bone casually sketched Conrad after an intimate Sunday dinner, and the author toured Doubleday's elaborate printing works at Garden City, a factory done up like an Oxford college complete with well-manicured gardens. Graciously, Conrad addressed his 'fellow employees', but they found his accent impenetrable, and the secretaries assigned to take down his every word in shorthand abandoned the task in despair. Conrad then moved from Effendi Hill to Doubleday's town house on West 58th off Central Park. Harriet James, the wife of railway magnate Arthur Curtiss James, one of the country's wealthiest men, dined with Conrad, and arrangements were made for him to read at her palatial East 69th Street home. The expected audience of fifty blossomed into nearly two hundred; invitations for the glittering affair were highly sought after and even intrigued for. In the library the Doubledays waited with Conrad, who shook 'like an aspen leaf' from stage fright as the audience gathered, and Doubleday then introduced his author's only public reading. It lasted an hour, with 'audible snuffling' accompanying the reading of

Lena's death scene from *Victory*, before New York's elite retired to a midnight supper.

After a few quiet days, Doubleday took Conrad off on a ten-day motor tour of New England. The trip was favoured by good weather, but Conrad later railed against the scenery – 'stony, unkempt and disused, astonishingly wild' – and American cities, which he judged 'overorganized'. The party stopped in Springfield, Massachusetts, at Yale, and in Boston, where Conrad, staying at the Copley-Plaza Hotel, visited 'Mama' Grace and Catherine Willard, now re-established in America. Press interest continued unabated, and the press corps dutifully reported the writer's visit to the South Boston fish pier and Harvard, noting what had impressed him (the university, and the houses of James Russell Lowell and Longfellow) and what had not (the Charles River, Radcliffe College, and Harvard Bridge).

The tour closed with two days at the country home of Elbridge L. Adams, a New York lawyer and avid book collector with whom Conrad had been in friendly correspondence. Apart from inscribing Adams's collection of his work, he rested for the trip home. *The Times* oddly reported that Conrad's stay in the United States was being curtailed because of illness, whereas he was leaving as planned, sailing from New York on the *Majestic* on 2 June 1923. He left 'with a strong impression of American large-heartedness and generosity', perhaps intensified by the Doubledays' decision to accompany him home. The press reported his parting words, which may have been calculated to appeal to the quintessentially American desire to be 'liked': 'I am leaving this country with a very strong feeling for its people and its institutions. I found everything very much greater than the dreams of America I had as a boy.' In the farewell he could not resist a plug for Doubleday's forthcoming Concord edition of his work, named for 'the peculiar connotation the word has with American and British ideals'.

A week later, a tired Conrad arrived home to a family crisis, learning from his wife – and given her vivid displeasure, her delivery of the news is unlikely to have been calculated to soothe – that Borys had secretly married the previous September. (And more secrecy was involved: at the time they married at St Giles Registry Office Borys and his bride were living at the same address in Bloomsbury.) The news brought on an attack of gout; the concealment of the wedding suggests, in addition to the distance between father and son, the degree to which Borys had become unmoored. His inability to handle money had already given Conrad ample reason to distrust him, and now Borys was openly a 'disappointment'. Deeply offended, Conrad, however, wanted no break, and even increased his feckless son's allowance, philosophically telling his agent: 'Marrying is not a crime and one can not cast out one's son for that. I believe that this particular marriage is foolish and inconsiderate.'

Jessie, who had herself learned of the marriage just before Conrad left for New York but judged it wiser to let the news wait for his return, took against her new daughter-in-law, Joan King, who had apparently been on the scene since the war: 'Apart from the secrecy, which was not necessary, it was a most disastrous marriage from every point. To begin with she is not even of a good working class, in fact she belongs nowhere.' Relatively little is known about Joan King or her background. The daughter of a manufacturer's agent, she was an only child, born in 1894 in Leyton, Essex, on London's north-east fringe. Her parents married in early 1893. Her father, James Edward King, died when she was quite young, and her widowed mother, Ada King (née Taylor), brought her up alone, while working as a dressmaker. By the time Borys Conrad got to know her she had, in effect, long been a Londoner. Her marriage certificate gives no profession, and nothing is known of her education. Her mother-in-law's class-based hostility seems, in any event, disproportionate to the case.

Doubleday, in England until late June, visited Oswalds and turned Conrad's mind to future plans. In the short term, Conrad dictated to Miss Hallowes an article on 'Christmas Day at Sea' – a breezy reminiscence, written for easy money, about holiday celebrations he remembered from his seafaring days – and returned to *Suspense*, which was groaning for attention on his desk and was now attended to 'with clenched teeth', arguably not an ideal way to approach creative work.

Borys, accompanied by John, came to Oswalds to introduce his wife to his parents. Initially stiff, and with Jessie on high dignity, the ceremonious occasion was mercifully interrupted by the impromptu arrival of Lewis Ricci, a writer of naval fiction and sketches then at nearby Chatham. By late July, tempers were sufficiently in control for

Borys and his wife to stay at Oswalds while they searched for London digs, the couple now leaving Manchester as Borys took up a post as manager of Daimler's Vauxhall depot. It was John's turn for attention as his parents took him to Le Havre in mid-September to settle him with a Protestant clergyman's large family. Aubry accompanied the Conrads, who were introduced to his parents, but Conrad, oddly, missed seeing Gide, arriving unannounced at Gide's home in nearby Cuverville, and merely leaving a message with the servants that he had dropped by. Given his punctilious habits, this *sans façon* call is curious. He made his excuses to Gide, praising his charming home, but had he truly wished to see his translator and (supposed) friend, prior arrangements could have been made. A more successful contact with French literary life was made in late October, when Paul Valéry lunched at Oswalds, the party including Walpole, Curle, Aubry, and Valéry's hostess, Madame Alvar.

At this time, Conrad responded to an offer from the magazine *Countries of the World* to write an article on geography, an unusual subject for his talent if yet more evidence of his well established position. He produced 'The Romance of Travel' (later titled 'Geography and Some Explorers'), a 5,000-word essay sold for £200 (£34,400 in 2005), recalling his youthful interest in exploration and paying homage to several intrepid personalities, including Captain Cook and Abel Tasman. In due course, the essay made its way into *National Geographic*, accompanied by comically irrelevant photographs, including one of polar bears.

Not long after completing it, he suffered so severe an attack of gout that his doctor ordered a general examination. It revealed 'a pronounced flabbiness of heart'. Conrad, whose early life involved physical labour, sometimes strenuous, had led a mainly sedentary life once he settled to his desk, with even sailing excursions apparently limited after about 1900. The cult of exercise and sports, which set in during the mid- and late-Victorian periods, seemingly held few attractions for him, and, a keen motorist, he is not known to have indulged in walking or cycling, popular pastimes of the day. Jessie, whose knee was causing grave concern, was now seriously worried about her husband who, although looking 'shaky,' refused to follow doctor's orders, probably including advice to curtail his heavy smoking or change his diet. To add to her troubles, she had recently learned of the death of her brother Frank. Employed as chief steward of the Union Castle Line's *York Castle*, he had died in East London, South Africa, of influenza caught during a terrible storm in which his ship had nearly foundered. The task of breaking this news to her nearly eighty-year-old mother fell to Jessie.

Declaring himself a 'crocky, groggy, tottery, staggery, shuddery, shivery, seedy, gouty, sorry' wretch as Borys and his wife descended on Oswalds for a week, Conrad was given further cause for his bad mood by John Quinn's sale of his manuscripts, auctioned off in New York at record-breaking prices. Quinn had promised to keep his collection intact, but no single buyer could have afforded it, and he wanted money to buy modern pictures, his other great passion. Conrad, who admitted that he had 'nothing to complain of', none the less jibed at the action as 'a wonderful adventure to happen to a still-living (or at any rate half-alive) author', and ironised about Quinn's either lying low 'like Brer Rabbit' or graciously giving 'his hand to kiss to the multitude of inferior collectors who never, never, never dreamt of such a coup'. The real rub was his estimate that Quinn had made a thousandfold return on his investment, and a further cause for annoyance, if one were needed, is that Conrad's recent triumphal visit to America might well have boosted the prices.

The Rover appeared in England on 3 December 1923 (Conrad's sixty-sixth birthday) to generally good reviews. Galsworthy had praised the novel to its author, and Conrad was particularly moved by Garnett's 'enthusiastic' response, conveyed in a private letter. The novel's publication recalled times past in another way, since Unwin was the publisher: in a sense, Conrad's literary life had come full circle. The novel's reception marked a shift in Conrad's critical fortunes that would dominate the decade or so immediately following his death. As the Bloomsbury journalist Desmond MacCarthy later summarised: '*The Rover* was greatly enjoyed and not a little carped at – respectfully of course . . . I enjoyed it immensely myself; yet when a friend said to me casually, "I have just finished listening to a performance on the Conrad," I saw what he meant, and recognized the justice of the criticism. Artistically, it resembles more a voluntary on a powerful organ to show its compass than a musician's constructed masterpiece. All the famous Conrad stops are pulled out one after another.'

The Christmas holidays were spent partly with Muirhead Bone and his family, in Canterbury, and with Aubry; Jessie, confined to bed, made it downstairs for the festivities. Now that his heart ailment was more systematically treated, Conrad's health had somewhat improved, but he remained ill-tempered: 'I have been captious and "*grincheux*" [grumpy] for days, as is always the case when I am not well.' Illness goes some way towards explaining his increased irascibility and hypersensitivity during his final years. Hamlin Garland, on an extremely tense call in the autumn, found him prone to monopolise the conversation: 'in the rush of his speech he spread his hands, flapped his elbows, and shrugged his shoulders as if in an agony of haste. His face twitched. At our previous visit he had been a poor listener, but on this day he could not listen. He was on the war-path.' They just avoided a heated quarrel – about the state of the American railways.

Unable to sleep, Conrad passed the first night of 1924 reading Arnold Bennett's *Riceyman Steps*. Optimistic about the course of treatment he was undergoing, he could not fail to realise that his health was seriously deteriorating. He suffered high temperatures for days on end, as well as from a bronchial cough and a 'semi-asthmatic condition'. Conrad toyed with escaping for part of the winter by renting a small villa not far from the writer Edmund Candler and his wife in the French Basque country. Even as he expressed the thought, he felt reluctant to leave Jessie, in need of her surgeon's care. Curle proved temptingly loyal, willing even to throw over his job to accompany his friend.

In the end, Conrad jettisoned plans to get away, and, vaguely hoping for an excursion to the South of France in the autumn, also cancelled plans for a trip to Brussels, managing only to run about in the family's new motor car. Arranged through Borys, the handsome 1912 Daimler (formerly the Duke of Connaught's and purchased for £200) offered spacious room for Jessie whose mobility was increasingly curtailed. For once, Conrad's son had done something that pleased him, although Borys, showing a 'curious restraint and reserve' to his mother, had mainly a distant and respectful relationship with his father. Soon to move from Coventry for a year's posting in London, Borys, in his father's view, was being rewarded for his managerial skills, but these did not extend to his own life, the capital offering even wider opportunities for spending. Jessie welcomed her son's proximity, hoping to see more of her first grandson, Philip James Conrad, born on 11 January 1924. As babies often do, he effected a thaw in relations that had cooled.

Buoyed by reports of *The Rover*'s excellent sales in America and enjoying a spate of better health, Conrad once again settled to work. This was briefly interrupted by two visitations – no other word seems quite apt – the first from his grandson, with nurse and parents in tow, the second from Ford Madox Ford (as Hueffer had become in 1919). Conrad noticed that Borys, during his visit, was again displaying worrying 'neurasthenic symptoms'. Ford made a flying visit to Oswalds between trains to discuss republishing *The Nature of a Crime* in his *transatlantic review*, a venture partly funded by John Quinn. The two 'talked pleasantly of old times', the reception correct if not warm. (Asked to propose trains, Jessie, in pain, had chosen late ones, thus allowing only a brief call.) In the spring, Ford again turned up unannounced en route to London, the letter proposing his call arriving after his departure. (Conrad suspected it had been posted late deliberately.) Ford was still fussing about the collaborations in view of an eventual collected edition of his own work, and Conrad ironically observed that such an edition would 'sweep all Europe and devastate Great Britain'.

Even as the business with Ford was being settled, Doubleday proposed publishing a collection of Conrad's short stories. Initially reluctant to tear things out of their original contexts, the selection occupied Conrad for the next few months; perhaps he was responding to the sense, conscious or not, that this was another valedictory task. Ford's proposal that they collaborate and Doubleday's new idea offered to keep Conrad in the public eye and bring money from recycling old work. A 5,000-word introduction to the collection of stories would itself, Conrad reminded his agent, bring in £250 (not to mention the typescript's sale to Wise), and he speedily quashed Doubleday's suggestion that Muirhead Bone should write it. Far more startling is his initial selection, which included 'The Brute' and 'The Inn of Two Witches', weak pieces, among the most derivative he had written. At the same time his thoughts turned to earlier writings, he was contemplating two stories to complete a new volume, but confessed to Galsworthy that he was 'incapable of finding a subject – even for one. Not a shadow of a subject!', a problem that also beset *Suspense*, on which he optimistically claimed to have had 'a better grip'.

A more permanent artistic achievement of the time was Jacob Epstein's portrait bust of Conrad, a commission arranged through Muirhead Bone. Epstein settled into an inn at the nearby village of Bridge with his wife and daughter. Conrad was edgy during the sittings, and, feeling faint at one, had what Epstein describes as a heart attack. Not the best remedy for a heart condition, a whisky was brought to help the spell pass. As the author openly lamented that he was 'played out', Epstein viewed his difficult subject as 'crippled with rheumatism' (presumably gout) 'crochety, nervous, and ill'. During some sessions, Conrad dictated letters to Miss Hallowes. Even as the bust was being done, Conrad thought it 'marvellously effective'. The bronze sculpture suggests inner reserves of power as well as detachment and intense loneliness, Epstein surmounting what in his account almost appears an aversion to his subject. Hugh Walpole, a possible buyer of one of the castings, disliked the bust's 'Semitic-appearance and thick lips'.

Whatever the reasons for Conrad's edginess during the sittings for Epstein, he was well enough to invite Aubry for a weekend, to remind Alice Gachet (a relative of Marguerite Poradowska's then at the beginning of her long career as a theatrical coach at the Royal Academy of Dramatic Art) of a promise to call, and to issue invitations to Curle and to Commander Frederic Cooper, a naval officer who had written about him for the *Nautical Magazine*. Distractions from his writing, this burst of activity counterbalances Epstein's view of a self-indulgent neurotic bemoaning his state, and reading between the lines of Jessie Conrad's account of the sittings, it appears that the transplanted New Yorker and his family, entertained at meals, proved difficult guests. Conrad's optimism after a prolonged period of illness – he was 'better' and 'doing some work, slowly.

Mentally I feel still languid. But all this is improving' – offers a very different view of this period.

Shortly after Epstein had completed his bust, Conrad, although gout-ridden, sat for another portrait. In contrast to Epstein's bust, which suggests latent energy, Alice Kinkead's oil, though obviously the work of a minor artist, emphasises nobility, tenacity, and strength of character, Conrad's dark brown eyes hawk-like and confronting the world almost aggressively. With Miss Hallowes on leave, Conrad, unable to write by hand, idled away his days. He and Jessie ran up to London for yet another consultation with Sir Robert Jones. Her pain now 'constant', she faced another operation in the late spring.

A welcome call from Hugh Clifford, on home leave from Lagos, seems to have proved tonic, and as Miss Hallowes returned to her duties, Conrad settled to his desk. Apart from catching up with arrears in his correspondence, the first result was a preface to his shorter tales followed by another brief preface, to *The Nature of a Crime*. As he was yet again revisiting old work, the newly elected Labour government of J. Ramsay MacDonald proposed him for a knighthood. Graciously, he declined this recognition of his achievement, recalling his early life in Britain of 'hard toil' with 'working men'. He had ample recent precedent for turning down the honour (Kipling and Galsworthy had also done so), and it was consistent with his refusal of honorary degrees from Oxford, Cambridge, Edinburgh and other universities, although he longed to be awarded the 1923 Nobel Prize for Literature. (He was never officially nominated for it, and in that year it went to Yeats.)

The operation on Jessie's knee scheduled for early June was postponed for a fortnight, but John hurried over from France and Borys from London to keep Conrad company. The delay allowed Conrad to attend lunch at the Polish Legation, an invitation he had declined several times in the past. His acceptance had a practical aim: he thought it might provide business contacts for Borys. On 13 June, Sir Robert Jones, after spending the night at Oswalds with Conrad and Aubry, operated on Jessie Conrad at St George's Nursing Home in Canterbury. The procedure, aimed at improving her mobility and relieving pain, involved shaving the bone to rid it of disease while also excising an old scar. Shortly after it, Conrad's acute bronchitis returned, a cough plaguing him day and night and tiring him. Dr Fox ordered him to bed, and put off limits the four-mile trip to Canterbury to see Jessie.

Despite John's company, Conrad was fighting 'a fit of severe depression which has taken me by the throat as it were'. His invitations to Curle and to Jean Aubry strike a lonely note. Miss Hallowes was on holiday, and when John left for France Oswalds felt even emptier. Grace Willard, who called towards the end of a holiday in England, proved overly vivacious. For her part, Jessie remained 'chirpy', although the prolonged draining of her wound kept delaying a return home.

At a bleak time Conrad got yet more bad news: Lady Colvin, nearly eighty-five, was dying. The only positive note was the *Daily Mail*'s offer of some well-paid hack-writing. Conrad took up his pen for the commissioned piece, 'Legends', originally conceived as treating 'Sailors Saints University Dons etc. Subjects of Legend'; in so far as he completed the essay, it once again mainly concerns the Merchant Service. He was aware that he had in effect stopped writing, telling Sir Robert Jones that a year and a half had passed since he had 'done any work that counts'. This kind was of the money-making sort, 'Conradese', as he had mocked a similar effort; discussing it with his agent, he mentions Jessie's dressmaker and John's tailor and mathematics tutor and laments this 'damnable month for unexpected bills', several of which came from doctors. This fretting is wholly out of proportion: had need arisen, he could have called upon some £20,000.

Jessie, again experiencing pain, was unable to return to Oswalds, and Conrad resumed his daily journeys to see her in mid-July, working on his article, even as he was hit hard by another attack of gout. On the 24th, Jessie could finally come home, although a week in bed was ordered. Within the next few days Conrad invited Curle for the August bank holiday weekend. Borys and his family were coming from London and John from Le Havre.

Arriving at about eleven in the evening on Friday, 1 August, Curle found Conrad in bed reading. He descended to a late supper and then re-entered Conrad's bedroom to chat for an hour and a half, a habit they had fallen into on similar occasions. He found Conrad looking 'very well and in singularly good spirits', eager to describe the new house that Charley Vinten, the Conrads' chauffeur, had discovered as the plan to quit Oswalds was revived. Conrad raised the question of publishing his fragmentary novel 'The Sisters' and, stimulated by a recent article in the *Times Literary Supplement*, they discussed the Second Empire. Mention was also made of John Quinn's death from cancer a few days earlier (on 28 July).

In the morning – the day of John's eighteenth birthday – talk focused on *Suspense*, with Conrad proposing 'about six different lines of treatment', and before he and Curle left in the car at around eleven, Conrad picked at 'Legends' in his study. About half-way to their destination along the Dover Road, Conrad felt pains in his chest, a repetition of what had occurred a few days before. Curle urged their immediate return to Oswalds, and Conrad went up to his room as soon as he arrived home. By the time the doctor appeared, his breathlessness and arrhythmia had passed, but they returned, and Curle was called in. Conrad felt shooting pains down his arms, a symptom of heart attack, but not, seemingly, one that alarmed the doctor when he came again later in the day. A telegram announcing Lady Colvin's death arrived, but to spare him stress, Conrad was not informed of the news. At about eight, Conrad's sons, daughter-in-law, and grandson arrived by motor car, and were summoned to his bedside.

As Conrad's breathing became laboured, Dr Fergusson, called in from Canterbury, ordered cylinders of oxygen from Canterbury Hospital. The night of 2–3 August passed in discomfort and fitful dozing, with Conrad intermittently sitting up in his chair or taking to his bed, attended by his manservant Arthur Foote. Used to long nights of work in the past and to insomnia when unwell, Conrad spent his last night restless and struggling for sleep.

At about eight in the morning of Sunday, the 3rd, Audrey Vinten, who had trained as a nurse, found his pulse normal, and Foote left his post to go on an errand. Half an hour later, Conrad's labours ended. Awake in her room, his wife heard him cry out, 'Here' – possibly 'Here you.' Long overstrained, Conrad's heart had stopped, and his body fell from his chair to the floor. Later, Jessie found comfort in the fact that his death was so sudden, Conrad unaware of its approach. For a man who had confronted his fate alone, his life's end was appropriately solitary. Foote and others ran to the bedroom, and Borys, shocked, broke the news to his brother: 'Your father is dead.'

After

Sleepe after toyle, port after stormie seas,
Ease after warre, death after life does greatly please.
Spenser, *The Faerie Queene* (1590)*

As Conrad's widow gave way to grief, it fell to Curle, ever level-headed and practical, to announce the news to the world. He busied himself with telegram forms, as Jessie's local physician, Dr Douglas Reid, arrived to comfort her and complete the formalities. As Reid and Foote laid Conrad's body on his bed, stillness settled over Oswalds. With little first-hand experience of mortality, John recalled the 'all-pervading' silence enveloping the house, the hours after his father's death passing in 'a soundless, shapeless void'.

During the night it rained, in times past, a sympathetic gesture of nature's collaboration in human grief. Conrad had joined the voices silencing this world-view, and looking at life steadily, he knew that no one sees it whole. His life was over, and, as rain pelted Canterbury, it fell to posterity to make what it could of him. Its first attempts were fumbling. Few of the Monday morning papers – taken up with the bank holiday crush at the railway terminals and recalling the declaration of war a decade before – got his 'real name' correct.

---

*The quotation appears as the epitaph on Conrad's tombstone, which John Conrad designed. Conrad had used it as the epigraph to *The Rover*, where, despite its origins (Giant Despayre is counselling suicide), it pays homage to good and faithful service. Several critics find evidence of Jessie Conrad's impercipience about her husband in her use of such a quotation as his epitaph, whereas she had Conrad's authority for seeing it in a positive light.

Several emphasised Conrad as a sea writer (long a sore point with him): Edinburgh's *Weekly Scotsman* noted the passing of 'The Skipper-Novelist'; the *Daily Sketch* wrongly placed his birth in Cracow; others remembered the failure of the dramatic version of *The Secret Agent*; Cork's *Weekly Examiner* took a swipe at *Romance* as 'the poorest' work 'with which Conrad's name is associated'. In Bayreuth for the first Wagner Festival after the war, Hugh Walpole was disappointed by the 'rather mediocre' coverage in *The Times*, which said 'all the obvious things'. As it did so, it also reserved judgement on his final or eventual stature, mentioning, in a vacuous phrase, that his volumes possessed 'the shifting glamour of mystery and beauty'. Many obituary writers did, however, venture that Conrad had made a permanent mark on English literature as a great stylist.

Recovered enough to deal with practicalities, Jessie sent news to close friends. On Tuesday, Nellie Lyons's brother, Charles, employed by the undertakers Messrs. J. Hunt & Sons of Mercery Lane, Canterbury, arrived. When the professionals had finished in Conrad's bedroom, they carried the coffin down to the drawing-room, and Jessie was moved downstairs to be able to greet callers. The decision to give her husband a Roman Catholic burial was ultimately hers, although probably made in consultation with her sons and family. Not too much should be read into it as regards Conrad's religious beliefs: he had been born and baptised a Catholic, and the Church's ancient rites proved convenient. The small church next to Oswalds would have accommodated the number of mourners with difficulty, and its distance from Canterbury for those coming from London would have proved awkward. Conrad, for that matter, had even less an affiliation to the Church of England than to that of Rome.

On Thursday, 7 August, comforted by her mother and her sister Eleanor, Jessie Conrad took her last farewell of her husband. Still recovering from her operation, she could not have attended the funeral had she wished to. (At the time, it was, in any case, not usual for the widow to attend the service.) At 11.15, the hearse left for Canterbury, preceded by a police cyclist and followed by a car carrying flowers and three others accommodating the principal mourners – Borys and John, Curle and Ralph Wedgwood (Conrad's executors), Edward Garnett, and Jessie's two surviving brothers, Albert and

Walter. As the cortège moved off, Bishopsbourne's church bell tolled solemnly.

Making its way into the town, which was overflowing with visitors and festooned with flags for the 79th Annual Cricket Week, the procession ended at the small Roman Catholic church of St Thomas of Canterbury in Burgate in the town centre. Father Edmund H. Sheppard, vested in black and accompanied by altar boys and the processional cross, met the coffin at the door. It was placed in the central aisle, draped in purple and flanked by tall lighted candles. A choir of four sang the high requiem mass for a congregation of around sixty intimates and friends. 'Blessed are the departed' from Spohr's 1826 oratorio *The Last Judgement* was sung at the Offertory, and the final procession moved into the bright sunlight to the Dead March from Handel's *Saul*.

At Canterbury cemetery, the number of mourners swelled to about a hundred, official representatives and others having arrived on the 10.30 train from Victoria, which reached Canterbury East station at 12.29. Met there, they were taken directly to the cemetery for a service commencing at 1.15. Among the dignitaries were representatives of the Polish Ambassador (Count Edward Raczyński) and of the Royal Society of Literature, as well as the Dean of Canterbury, who, in his Sunday sermon, had paid tribute to 'a great and noble-minded man'. There was a moment of silence, and in addition to the prayers in Latin, one was said in English. The whole event was understated and intimate, and John Zelie, an American academic present, saw it as particularly and even peculiarly English.

The wreaths testified to a varied life. They came from those of modest station – the staff of Oswalds, 'Florrie and Sarge' (Jessie's elder sister and her husband), Miss Lilian M. Hallowes; from Fountaine Hope and his family and the Sandersons; and from those with their hands higher up the ropes: Sir Hugh and Lady Clifford, Lady Millais, Madame Alvar, Colonel and Mrs Matthew Bell of Bourne Park (Oswalds' owners). Jean Aubry's observation to Cunninghame Graham that 'all Paris' would have turned out for the funeral of Anatole France widely misses its mark. Leaving aside the fact that the old market town was not Paris, the lack of show, the ramshackle good form and dislike of display, even the diversion of an annual sporting event are quintessentially English. It is as if the orphan boy from an impossibly provincial backwater had been taken to the country's heart. Graham's *riposte d'escalier* to Conrad's fashionable French friend was the right one for the moment, and also speaks for posterity: 'Well, well Conrad to my way of thinking was far above Anatole France in sheer genius.' The number at the graveside matters less than those who gather after the moss has grown. The crowds at the funerals of Victor Hugo and of Balzac celebrated great political moments as much as they did major literary achievements. All England did turn out for the death of Lord Northcliffe, who, born in modest circumstances, died worth £2 million (£258 million in 2005). He was lionised at Westminster Abbey, and 'miles of reverent crowds' lined the route to St Marylebone cemetery in Finchley. Today, 'The Napoleon of Fleet Street' is remembered mainly by cultural historians.

Death often enough engenders squabbles over legacies, whether of 'moveable property' (as the law calls it) or of the more intangible, spiritual kind. Conrad's last will and testament obviated any contest over his belongings: it advantageously set up trusts to be administered by Ralph Wedgwood and Richard Curle, his executors, for his wife and sons, with provisions for the disbursements of annual income from his copyrights, which expired, in England, only in 1974. As *The Times* duly reported, he left an estate, after death duties, valued at £20,045 (£3.4 million in 2005 terms). Pinker had left nearly twice as much; Galsworthy, who died in 1933, aged sixty-five, left £71,000 (equivalent in 2005, £12.7 million); and Walpole, who died, aged fifty-seven, in 1941 left £29,500 (equivalent in 2005, £3.3 million).

The claims on his wider legacy were mainly unseemly. By October 1924, less than two months after Conrad's death, Ford Madox Ford rushed into print a hastily written memoir titled *Joseph Conrad: A Personal Remembrance*. It is typically Fordian – unbalanced, insouciant as to facts, and extravagantly creative. Despite its manifest intentions, it does little credit to the star of the piece (Ford himself), making wild assertions of his influence on and part in Conrad's genius. Seeing an opportunity to vent a long-suppressed animosity, Jessie Conrad eagerly seized it in a very public and acerbic protest published in the letters to the editor of the *Times Literary Supplement*, which had favourably reviewed the book: 'The author of "A Personal

Remembrance" claims to have been Joseph Conrad's literary adviser, also his literary godfather! That claim is, like nearly everything else in that detestable book, quite untrue.'

She herself wasted no time in rushing into print, and before the year closed *Joseph Conrad: Personal Recollections* appeared in a privately printed, signed limited edition, imitating T. J. Wise's Conrad pamphlets and obviously designed to cash in. It was followed by her *Joseph Conrad as I Knew Him* (1926), *Joseph Conrad's Letters to his Wife* (1927), and *Joseph Conrad and his Circle* (1935). The last provoked a protest by Edward Garnett, who told its author that it was 'the most detestable book ever written by a wife about her husband'. Cunninghame Graham, who likewise judged it 'pretty awful' and 'in the worst taste', went even further: 'Poor Conrad, – Jessie & Borys, are two crosses he has escaped.' Richard Curle also issued a privately printed pamphlet, *Joseph Conrad's Last Day*, later revised for his memoir, *The Last Twelve Years of Joseph Conrad* (1928). Jessie Conrad quickly put up for auction, through Hodgson & Sons, Conrad's library and what little remained in her hands of her husband's manuscripts and typescripts, along with inscribed first editions (some, in fact, belonging to John). Tagged on to the sale were a few pamphlet proofs belonging to Curle, whose own sale of signed first editions in 1927 at New York's American Art Association was a grander, more profitable affair.

The years immediately following Conrad's death saw the publication of several scraps of his writing, homage to his genius and a savvy attempt to make money out of the considerable Conrad boom before its nearly inevitable deflation, signs of which might be read in the reception of *The Rover*. Curle was first off the mark, publishing 'Legends', found on Conrad's desk at his death. The broken-off fragment published in the *Daily Mail* with a facsimile of the last page was intended to suggest the moment at which Conrad left the world. Curle also shoved out the unfinished novel *Suspense* in 1925; in the United States, it even fell victim to a publicity stunt, a competition being held to complete it. (Its prose flaccid and its plot meandering, it vies with *The Arrow of Gold* for the title of the worst novel ever written by a major writer.) In 1928, the extant fragment of *The Sisters* appeared, handsomely bound, with a preface by Ford, who claimed that he had also been asked to complete it, a task he wisely declined.

In the years that followed several blows struck Jessie Conrad. Her mother, who never recovered from her youngest son's death in South Africa, died aged seventy-eight, in October 1925. Humiliation and distress followed quickly, thanks to Borys, who, never fully recovered from shellshock, saw his mental health become increasingly precarious after his father had died. With Conrad's displeasure no longer a threat, he had, in Richard Curle's words, 'lost his head completely with regards to money and had become extremely extravagant'. In August 1926 he was declared bankrupt, with debts amounting to some £5,000, and in early 1927, badgered by creditors, he attempted to receive moneys for manuscripts he did not own. Arrested on a charge of attempting to defraud Dorothy Lucy Bevan, the wife of a friend, Desmond Bevan, he pleaded guilty. (His victim was ill-chosen: Bevan's father was on the board of Barclay's Bank, and the Bevans themselves moved in high society.)

The trial at the Old Bailey saw Wise take the stand in his defence. Curle also testified, stating that Borys had returned from the war 'morose and silent and obviously a changed man mentally'. Passing sentence, the judge rejected the defence's call for clemency, on the grounds that Conrad's name had been dishonoured and that his widow was shamed by her son's behaviour: 'I can not take into account the dishonour to your father's name. That is not a mitigating circumstance. If I did I should consider it an aggravating circumstance that the name of a man who has adorned our English literature should be dishonoured by his son. You have perpetrated a heartless fraud and swindled your best friend.' Borys got a year, served in Wormwood Scrubs Prison, and 'on conviction of the Civil Power' was stripped of his lieutenancy.

His marriage, opposed by his mother from the first, ended in separation in 1933, after a three-year estrangement. Before its official end, Borys was reduced to writing begging letters to old family friends. In January 1932, he was attempting to cadge from the Irish playwright Conal O'Riordan, and in February wrote to Hugh Walpole pleading for £3 to see him through the month. In the late 1930s, he was working as caretaker and engineer at Aldworth, the estate of the Maharaja of Baroda on the Surrey–Sussex borders, and fantasising about re-entering the armed forces. In the end, though somewhat frail as the result of his injuries in the war, he managed to find a measure of domestic happiness and psychological calm in the company of Margaret Rishworth, a determined and vigorous woman who helped found the Joseph Conrad Society (UK) in the early 1970s, of which Borys Conrad served as first president. He later wrote a short pamphlet on the family's homes in Kent, and his memoir *My Father Joseph Conrad* came out in 1970. Joan Conrad, his legal wife, died in London in 1981, three years after his own death, in November 1978, at the age of eighty.

In early 1928, John Conrad, under the name 'John Korzeniowski', married Mary Geraldine Grindrod, who had been in Jessie's employ. His mother thought the match beneath him. He practised as an architect, living mainly in Kent. His two sons, Richard (born in 1929) and Peter (born in 1933) predeceased him, dying in separate motor accidents in the 1960s. He continued actively to administer his father's estate, systematically renewing his father's copyrights in the United States for their second twenty-eight-year terms, as works fell out of copyright. His affectionate memoir of his father, *Joseph Conrad: Times Remembered*, appeared in 1981, and he died the next year, in October, at the age of seventy-six.

Miss Hallowes, a virtual member of the Conrad family, asked the executors via Eric Pinker for the Corona typewriter on which she had typed Conrad's work and correspondence. (She did not receive it.) She retreats into genteel obscurity, dying in Bournemouth, aged eighty, in October 1950, the same year as Jean Aubry.

Shortly after Conrad's death, his widow left Oswalds, establishing herself in Canterbury, in Ethelbert Road near the town centre and then in Westbere House, finally settling at Torrens in the nearby village of Harbledown. She lived occasionally with her sister Eleanor and her only child, Nina (born in 1918), who brightened the house. Fancying herself a countess by virtue of Conrad's *szlachta* descent, Jessie had her sister embroider coronets on her handkerchiefs, and maintained friendly contact with some of the notable men and women whom she had come to know, Walter Tittle and the

Rothensteins in particular, although others once friendly, like Hugh Walpole, dropped off.

She enjoyed being a grandmother, but her relations with Borys, whom she had visited in prison, slowly deteriorated, and for long periods contact was minimal. In 1933, she had not seen him for a year and half and did not know where he was living; his estranged wife made excuses that prevented her seeing her grandson, Philip. Her struggles to control her weight – she complains of a 'strict diet' – proved fruitless, and in the middle of the night she would indulge in cakes and chocolates to sate a rapacious sweet tooth. She eventually weighed 20 stone (280 pounds) and was diabetic. Jessie's mobility was restricted as she aged and as her weight increased; she none the less remained partial to excursions in her chauffeured Cadillac, and enjoyed going to the Curzon for brief stays or for lunch or tea. The pain in her legs did not abate, but she refused to have her kneecap replaced by an ape's, as Sir Robert Jones had counselled. A great sense of humour and reserves of pluck seem to have carried her through, although the declaration, made at sixty, that she was 'a lonely woman' also suggests sadness. In addition to the strained relations with Borys, another blow came when her sister Ethel, to whom she had been close, died in May 1931.

Living at Compayne Gardens in West Hampstead, Jessie died at Guy's Hospital, near London Bridge, on 6 December 1936, aged sixty-three. She was buried next to Conrad. Apart from one legacy, she left her personal belongings and an estate of £531 (£92,500) net to her sons. (Given that she benefited from Conrad's royalties, the small amount left suggests a very comfortable style of life during the twelve years following her husband's death, although some of her money no doubt went on bailing out Borys and helping her sister Ethel, whose finances, after her husband had left her, were precarious.) The stage and screen actor Percy Walsh served as her executor. Her well-attended memorial service at St Pancras Church in Euston Road brought together her sons, former Kentish neighbours and servants, and friends from several walks of life. The Polish Ambassador sent a representative.

The Pinker family continued to flourish until the late 1930s – publicly, at least. The firm founded by J. B. Pinker in 1896 suffered from mismanagement from almost the moment Eric had taken it over on his father's death. Ralph Pinker claimed during bankruptcy proceedings in 1941 that 'It appears that from the start of my brother's management of the business he consistently drew out of the business more than it was earning'. (He himself had done the same, maintaining a country house as well as a flat in town although, in the view of those dealing with the bankruptcy proceedings, the firm had been 'insolvent for years'.) In early 1926, Œnone married Captain Cyril J. Gowland of the Royal Corps of Signals, by whom she had two children in the late 1920s. She died in 1979. In March 1927, Eric divorced his Danish-born wife Margit (a widow with two small boys when he married her in April 1921) to marry the American actress Adrienne Morrison, the former wife of the actor Richard Bennett and the mother of the movie actress Joan Bennett. He emigrated to the United States in 1930, and the partnership with his brother was formally dissolved. He and his second wife ran a successful literary and theatrical agency in New York City until his alcoholism and gambling undid it. In March 1939, when he was arrested for grand larceny by order of District Attorney Thomas E. Dewey (later the 1948 presidential campaign's near-winner). Appearing in a police line-up, 'jaunty in sack suit and bowler', he was denied bail for fear he might flee the country, and was remanded to the Tombs. Pleading guilty to the charge of attempting to purloin his clients' moneys, he was sentenced to two and a half to five years in prison, to be served in the New York State penitentiary of Sing Sing. He died in obscurity in New York City in October 1973.

Ralph continued to work as a literary agent throughout the 1930s. He and his wife, whom he had married in 1928 and by whom he had a daughter in 1929, travelled in society circles, dining, for instance, with Emir Saud, Crown Prince of Saudi Arabia. In March 1941, he was declared bankrupt, and he and his wife separated. In February 1943, he was tried and found guilty at the Old Bailey for fraudulently converting royalties not paid in full to his clients and received a year's sentence, served, like Borys Conrad, in Wormwood Scrubs. He died in December 1959.

By then, Conrad's reputation had recovered from the decline that had set in not long after his death. How much the efforts of his executors in pushing out scraps, his editor and first biographer in his hagio-graphical approach and inaccuracy, and his wife in her lopsided memoirs may have contributed to that decline is a moot point. At the time Conrad became a writer's writer, influencing William Faulkner and F. Scott Fitzgerald (who performed a drunken dance in Conrad's honour on the lawn of F. N. Doubleday's estate when Conrad was *in situ*). And fashions, as Wilde's Lady Bracknell knowingly observes, *can* be altered. Essays in the 1940s by F. R. Leavis in England and Morton Dauwen Zabel in the United States, both highly influential critics, triggered a revaluation, stimulating the rediscovery of Conrad by a new generation of readers. The vogue, if it can be called that some sixty years later, has survived the various critical cross-currents bedevilling, and enlivening, literary criticism. And Conrad's work, uncommonly influential on novelists, has enriched the fiction of Graham Greene and William Golding, to say nothing of writers as diverse as Gabriel García Marquez, V. S. Naipaul, John le Carré, and J. M. Coetzee, to name but a few.

A century and a half after Conrad's birth in Berdichev – once Polish, once Russian, and currently Ukrainian – his protean personality and unquestionable literary achievement intrigues and beckons. Could he do so, he might, bemused and not a little flattered, repeat the question of the novelist Marguerite Yourcenar after being elected, the first woman ever so honoured, to a seat in the august French Academy: 'What? *Immortality?*' For Conrad, something of a gambler by nature, it was always a case of that or nothing.

As he glimpsed in his later years when illness and depression beset him, such victories are close run, won against appalling odds, and often requiring a stroke of luck. Although incontestably a great writer, having contributed to shaping the way his own and the generations after him 'see', he is, perhaps, in the scheme of things, not quite a 'great' novelist, missing – just – the glacial perfection, of a Stendhal or Flaubert, and in this perhaps more closely resembling the achieve-ment of a Tolstoy or Dostoevsky. His style, in the main so sinuously seductive in cadences new to the language and crafted from a polylinguistic heritage, can fall into mere brittle mannerism (that 'performance on the Conrad' mentioned above), or at times flap about as his grasp on grammatical niceties and idiom relaxes. Structurally, even his very finest work tends to teeter precipitously at its close, not out of creative exhaustion but because collapse and ruin are real threats, and because, too, as *Lord Jim* bravely acknowledges, 'There is never time to say our last word – the last word of our love, of our desire, faith, remorse, submission, revolt.' Those words, so carefully chosen, even poised, still resonate, and endings, as Conrad's fiction perhaps too readily testifies, are simply impossible, and even unnatural. Art, like Nature, insists upon continuance.

Resolutely refusing to pronounce that 'last word', Conrad speaks for an awareness of fragmentation so quintessentially modern that his voice, a century and a half after his birth, remains powerful and authoritative. His skills were insistently devoted to exposing 'the horror' (the phrase deserves to bear his trademark) that lies behind the brightly polished or the crude and makeshift façade of so many things. Unlike Keats, who lamented as his life drew to its close that he 'always made an awkward bow', Conrad could at times bow too well, playing the punctilious English gentleman in bowler and monocle. But even as he did so his essential loneliness and sense of the horror of existence was finding a means of expression in highly wrought prose and in fiction of such coruscating insight that it stubbornly refuses to surrender to analytic scalpels, however sharp. On the one hand so remote, so determinedly 'one of them' – an anguished, self-riven man awkwardly straddling the late-Victorian and early-Modern periods – Conrad is also, in a characteristically contradictory and complex fashion, undeniably 'one of us'.

Appendices

Map 1   The Austro-Hungarian and Russian Empires in the mid-
nineteenth century

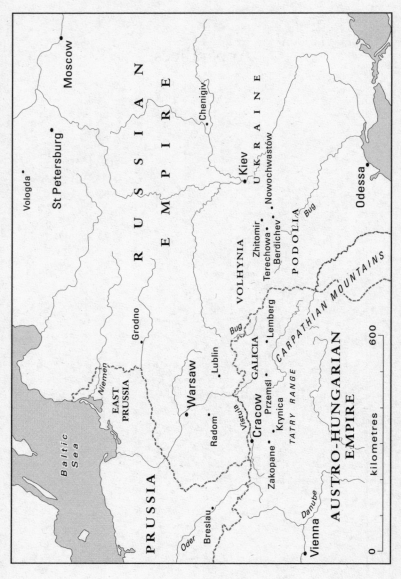

Map 2   The Caribbean in the late nineteenth century

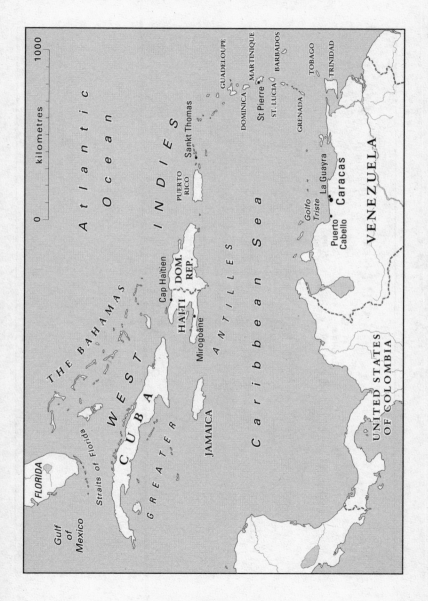

Map 3   Conrad's Eastern world

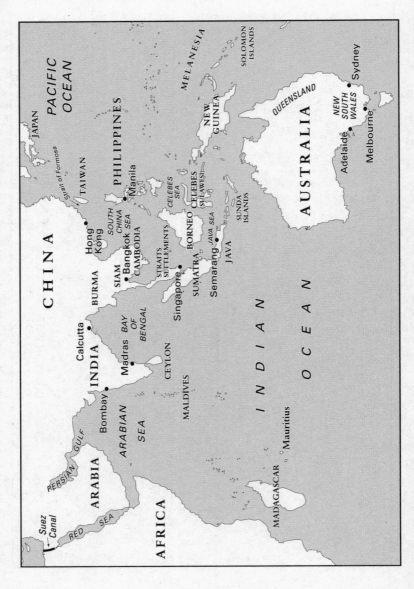

Map 4   Bessborough Gardens and vicinity in the 1890s

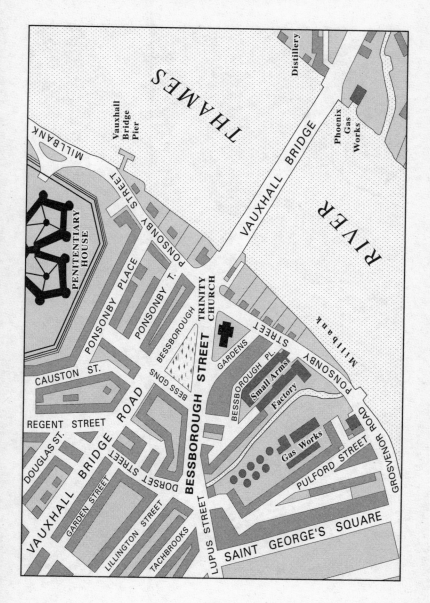

THAMES

Distillery

MILLBANK

Vauxhall
Bridge
Pier

VAUXHALL BRIDGE

Phoenix
Gas
Works

PONSONBY STREET

RIVER

PENITENTIARY HOUSE

PONSONBY PLACE

PONSONBY T.

Millbank

TRINITY CHURCH

BESSBOROUGH

BESS GDNS

GARDENS

PONSONBY STREET

CAUSTON ST.

BESSBOROUGH PL.

Small Arms

Factory

REGENT STREET

BESSBOROUGH STREET

VAUXHALL BRIDGE ROAD

DORSET STREET

Gas Works

PULFORD STREET

GROSVENOR ROAD

DOUGLAS ST.

GARDEN STREET

LILLINGTON STREET

TACHBROOKS

LUPUS STREET

SAINT GEORGE'S SQUARE

Map 5 Gillingham Street and vicinity in the 1890s

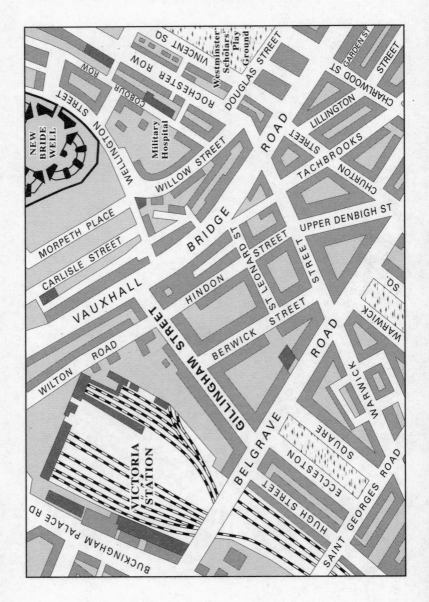

Map 6   Stanford-le-Hope in the 1890s

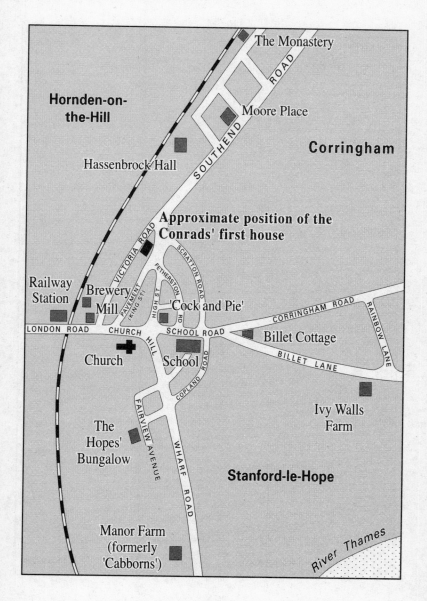

The Monastery

Hornden-on-the-Hill

SOUTHEND ROAD

Moore Place

Corringham

Hassenbrock Hall

Approximate position of the Conrads' first house

VICTORIA ROAD

SCRATTON ROAD

FETHERSTON

Railway Station

Brewery Mill

PAVEMENT (KING ST)

HIGH ST

'Cock and Pie'

CORRINGHAM ROAD

RD

RAINBOW LANE

LONDON ROAD

CHURCH

SCHOOL ROAD

Billet Cottage

BILLET LANE

Church

CHURCH HILL

School

COPLAND ROAD

Ivy Walls Farm

The Hopes' Bungalow

FAIRVIEW AVENUE

Stanford-le-Hope

WHARF ROAD

Manor Farm (formerly 'Cabborns')

River Thames

Map 7   Conrad's London and environs

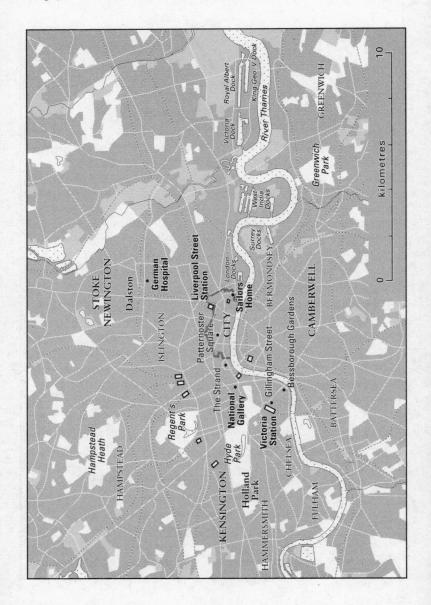

Map 8   Conrad's South-east England

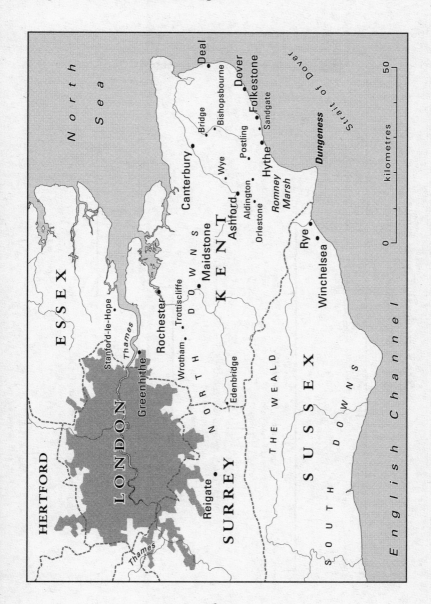

Family trees

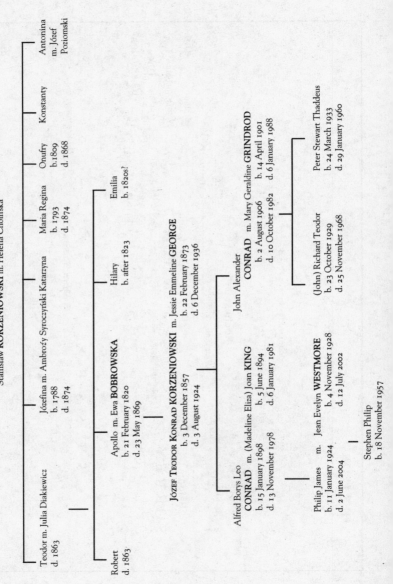

The Korzeniowski/Conrad Family

Stanisław **KORZENIOWSKI** m. Helena Choińska

Teodor m. Julia Diakiewicz
d. 1863

Robert
d. 1863

Józefina m. Ambroży Syroczyński Katarzyna
b. 1788
d. 1874

Apollo m. Ewa **BOBROWSKA**
b. 21 February 1820
d. 23 May 1869

Maria Regina
b. 1793
d. 1874

Hilary
b. after 1823

Emilia
b. 182os?

Onufry
b.1809
d. 1868

Konstanty

Antonina
m. Józef
Poziomski

JÓZEF TEODOR KONRAD KORZENIOWSKI m. Jessie Emmeline **GEORGE**
b. 3 December 1857
d. 3 August 1924
b. 22 February 1873
d. 6 December 1936

Alfred Borys Leo
CONRAD m. (Madeline Eliza) Joan **KING**
b. 15 January 1898
d. 13 November 1978
b. 5 June 1894
d. 6 January 1981

John Alexander
CONRAD m. Mary Geraldine **GRINDROD**
b. 2 August 1906
d. 10 October 1982
b. 14 April 1901
d. 6 January 1988

Philip James m. Jean Evelyn **WESTMORE**
b. 11 January 1924
d. 2 June 2004
b. 4 November 1928
d. 12 July 2002

(John) Richard Teodor
b. 23 October 1929
d. 25 November 1968

Peter Stewart Thaddeus
b. 24 March 1933
d. 29 January 1960

Stephen Philip
b. 18 November 1957

The Bobrowski Family

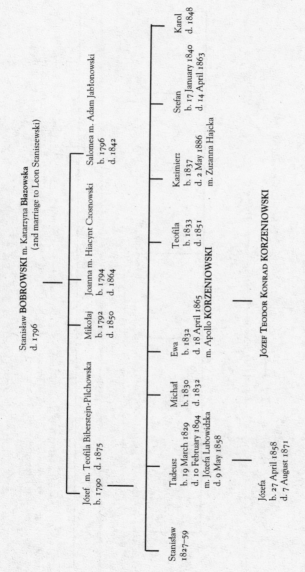

Stanisław **BOBROWSKI** m. Katarzyna **Błazowska**
(2nd marriage to Leon Staniszewski)

Józef m. Teofila Biberstejn-Piłchowska
b. 1790   d. 1875

Mikołaj
b. 1792
d. 1850

Joanna m. Hiacynt Czosnowski
b. 1794
d. 1864

Salomea m. Adam Jabłonowski
b. 1796
d. 1842

Tadeusz
b. 19 March 1829
d. 10 February 1894
m. Józefa Lubowidzka
d. 9 May 1858

Michał
b. 1830
d. 1832

Ewa
b. 1832
d. 18 April 1865
m. Apollo **KORZENIOWSKI**

Teofila
b. 1833
d. 1851

Kazimierz
b. 1837
d. 2 May 1886
m. Zuzanna Hajcka

Stefan
b. 17 January 1840
d. 14 April 1863

Karol
d. 1848

Stanisław
1827–59

Józefa
b. 27 April 1858
d. 7 August 1871

Józef Teodor Konrad KORZENIOWSKI

The Nash-Sex Family

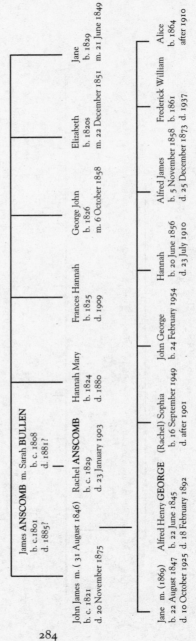

John NASH and Mary SEX (not married)
b. c. 1770?

Robert LYNCH m. Hannah ROWLING

John NASH SEX (m. 11 Sept 1820) Hannah LYNCH
b. October? 1792   b. c. 1798
d. 6 February 1831   d. 1879

James ANSCOMB m. Sarah BULLEN
b. c. 1801   b. c. 1808
d. 1885?   d. 1881?

Hannah Mary	Frances Hannah	George John	Elizabeth	Jane
b. 1824	b. 1825	b. 1826	b. 1820s	b. 1829
d. 1880	d. 1909	m. 6 October 1858	m. 22 December 1851	m. 21 June 1849

Rachel ANSCOMB
b. c. 1829
d. 23 January 1903

John James m. (31 August 1846)
b. c. 1821
d. 20 November 1875

John George	Hannah	Alfred James	Frederick William	Alice
b. 24 February 1954	b. 20 June 1856	b. 5 November 1858	b. 1861	b. 1864
	d. 23 July 1910	d. 25 December 1873	d. 1937	after 1910

(Rachel) Sophia
b. 16 September 1949
d. after 1901

Alfred Henry GEORGE
b. 22 June 1845
d. 10 October 1925

Jane m. (1869)
b. 22 August 1847
d. 18 February 1892

284

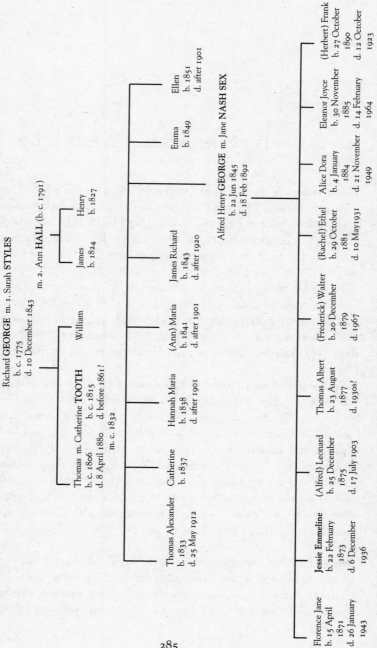

The George Family

Richard GEORGE m. 1: Sarah STYLES
b. c. 1775
d. 10 December 1843   m. 2. Ann HALL (b. c. 1791)

James
b. 1824

Henry
b. 1827

Thomas m. Catherine TOOTH
b. 1806   b. c. 1815
d. 8 April 1880   d. before 1861?
m. c. 1832

William

Catherine
b. 1837

Hannah Maria
b. 1838
d. after 1901

(Ann) Maria
b. 1841
d. after 1901

James Richard
b. 1843
d. after 1920

Emma
b. 1849

Ellen
b. 1851
d. after 1901

Thomas Alexander
b. 1833
d. 25 May 1912

Alfred Henry GEORGE m. Jane NASH SEX
b. 22 Jun 1845
d. 18 Feb 1892

Florence Jane
b. 15 April
1871
d. 26 January
1943

Jessie Emmeline
b. 22 February
1873
d. 6 December
1936

(Alfred) Leonard
b. 25 December
1875
d. 17 July 1903

Thomas Albert
b. 23 August
1877
d. 1930s?

(Frederick) Walter
b. 20 December
1879
d. 1967

(Rachel) Ethel
b. 29 October
1881
d. 10 May1931

Alice Dora
b. 4 January
1884
d. 21 November
1949

Eleanor Joyce
b. 30 November
1885
d. 14 February
1964

(Herbert) Frank
b. 27 October
1890
d. 12 October
1923

285

Conrad's circle: A select Who's Who

Jane Anderson (née Foster Anderson, 1893–1950s?; Mrs Deems Taylor; Señora, or Marquesa de, Cienfuegos), an Atlanta-born writer, came to know Conrad in 1916 through Lord Northcliffe, shortly after arriving in England to cover the war. She quickly attached herself to the Conrads, later entertaining Borys in Paris. In 1934, she married Eduardo Alvarez de Cienfuegos, a professional gambler, who claimed to be the Marqués de Cienfuegos. A correspondent during the Spanish Civil War, she became a supporter of Franco and Hitler, broadcasting for the Third Reich. Arrested in Vienna and charged with treason by the American authorities in 1947, 'Lady Haw-Haw', as she was derisively nicknamed, disappeared, possibly returning to Spain.

Jean-Frédéric-Émile Aubry (1882–1950), a French music critic and writer on literature under the pen-names G. Jean-Aubry, Gérard Jean-Aubry, and Georges Jean-Aubry mixed in musical and literary circles in Paris and London, counting among his acquaintance Paul Valéry and Maurice Ravel. His poems were set to music by Albert Roussel and Manuel de Falla. He replaced André Gide as the director of Conrad's French translations, producing several translations himself as well as writing the first biography in the bridging chapters of *Joseph Conrad: Life & Letters* (1927). His friendship with Conrad, which dates from 1918, rapidly became close.

Roger David Casement (1864–1916; knighted 1911), born near Dublin, lived and worked in Africa for nearly twenty years, where Conrad first met him in 1890. An activist for Congo reform, Casement attempted to engage Conrad in his cause, visiting him in 1903.

Casement was with the British Foreign Service 1892–1903, and later served as consul in Brazil, raising concerns about the exploitation of natives in the Putamayo. An active Irish nationalist, he was accused of collusion with Germany in 1916, the year of the Easter Rising, was tried for treason and hanged at Pentonville Prison in August.

Hugh Charles Clifford (1866–1941; knighted 1909) of the Cliffords of Ugbrooke, was educated at Woburn Park, a Catholic school, before going into the colonial administration, first in Malaya, the scene of many of his sketches and short stories, and later in Borneo, the Gold Coast, Nigeria, Ceylon, and the Straits Settlements. Collaborator on a Malay dictionary, he also translated the Malay colonial penal code. His visits to Conrad, who reviewed his *Studies in Brown Humanity* (1898), were infrequent, the friendship being mainly epistolary. In 1930, Clifford suffered a mental breakdown from which he never recovered.

Sidney Colvin (1845–1927; knighted 1911), art historian, man of letters, and memoirist, was Slade Professor of Fine Arts at Cambridge, and later Keeper of Prints and Drawings at the British Museum (1884–1912). A close friend of Robert Louis Stevenson, he produced editions of the writer as well as writing recollections of this friendship. Conrad and Colvin, who first met in 1905, enjoyed a long friendship, as did Jessie Conrad and Colvin's wife, Frances (née Fetherstonhaugh, 1842–1924).

Stephen Crane (1871–1900), born in Newark, New Jersey, studied briefly at Syracuse University before achieving a meteoric rise to fame with *The Red Badge of Courage* (1895). A writer of short stories and novels, he also covered the Greco-Turkish and Spanish-American Wars as a correspondent. Meeting Conrad through S. S. Pawling of Heinemann's in 1897, Crane soon became a close friend, later living near the Conrads in Sussex with his companion Cora (née Howarth Stewart, 1863–1910; alias Taylor; later Mrs Hammond McNeil), a former and future brothel-keeper and sometime writer of fiction.

Richard Henry Parnell Curle (1883–1968), born in Melrose, Scotland, established himself as a journalist and writer in London after leaving Wellington College (1901). From 1905, he worked in publishing, and was introduced to Conrad through Edward Garnett's Mont Blanc circle. Curle, who wrote the first critical study of Conrad (1914), also wrote on Browning, W. H. Hudson, Meredith, Hardy, and Dostoevsky. A keen traveller, his other writings include *Into the East: Notes on Burma and Malaya* (1923), with a preface by Conrad, and *Caravansary and Conversation* (1937). Acting as one of Conrad's executors, he edited *Suspense* (1925), *Last Essays* (1926), and a volume of Conrad's letters to him. His *The Last Twelve Years of Joseph Conrad* (1928) provides an intimate portrait of the writer.

F(rancis) Warrington Dawson (1878–1962) of Charleston, South Carolina, lived in Paris and Versailles with his mother. A prolific essayist and journalist, he attempted to interest Conrad in his fiction. In 1909, while on an African safari with Theodore Roosevelt, he met the Sandersons, and on arriving in England to cover Edward VII's funeral brought an introduction to Conrad from them. A Conrad enthusiast, Dawson variously attempted to use the connection to promote his writings, while Conrad, ever the gentleman, maintained a correct and cordial relationship with his keen, even gushing, admirer.

(George) Norman Douglas (1868–1952), a polymath born in Austria, after schooling in Britain and at Karlsruhe, wrote scholarly papers on natural history and was briefly in the British Foreign Service, resigning to settle in Naples. Moving to Capri after his divorce (1904), he wrote on the island's geography and history. He met Conrad there in 1905, the more established writer encouraging the younger and providing an introduction to the *English Review*. Living in London from 1907, Douglas was arrested in late 1916 for indecent assault on a boy, and fled the country. The Conrads provided a home for his younger son, Robert ('Robin') Sholto, who, like Borys Conrad, attended St Gregory's School in Luton and trained in the HMS *Worcester*.

John Galsworthy (1867–1933), after Harrow and New College, Oxford, studied for the Bar, but on turning to writing was encouraged by Conrad whom he had met on the *Torrens* in 1893 on a tour of the South Pacific. Of a well-to-do family, he generously assisted Conrad financially throughout his early career, Conrad naming his second son in his honour. Making his early reputation as a playwright, Galsworthy, a champion of numerous social causes, won widespread popularity with his *Forsyte Saga*. In 1932, he was awarded the Nobel Prize for Literature. His wife Ada (née Ada Nemesis Pearson, 1864–1956) also had literary interests, and Conrad wrote a preface to her translations of Maupassant.

Edward William Garnett (1868–1937), a publisher's reader for T. Fisher Unwin and later for Heinemann and Duckworth, was from a bookish family, his father, Richard (1835–1906), a man of letters, being Assistant Keeper of Printed Books at the British Museum, and his grandfather, the Revd Richard (1789–1850), a philologist. A behind-the-scenes force in literary Modernism, Garnett, who wrote plays and essays, mentored Conrad during his early career. Married to the translator of Turgenev, Dostoevsky, and Chekhov, Constance Garnett (née Black, 1861–1946), Garnett maintained a relationship with Ellen ('Nellie') Heath (1873–1962), a painter. The Garnetts mixed with writers and socialists, opening their home to Russian refugees and anarchists.

(Reginald) Perceval Gibbon (1878–1926), son of a Congregationalist minister born in Trelech, Carmarthenshire (Wales) spent his youth in Hackney. After education in Germany, he became a merchant seaman. Turning to journalism and then to fiction and poetry as a client of J. B. Pinker, he became friendly with Conrad through Garnett's Mont Blanc luncheons. Settled in Kent with his wife 'Maisie' (née May Daniels, 1883–?), Gibbon was close to Conrad before the war during which he was first a correspondent and then in the Royal Marines. Loyal to Gibbon throughout his marital troubles (which ended in divorce in 1922), alcoholism, and his 1919 bankruptcy, Conrad enjoyed only an epistolary friendship with Gibbon after he moved to Guernsey.

R(obert) B(ontine) Cunninghame Graham (1852–1936), a socialist and writer (and according to some scholars the rightful King of Scotland), worked and travelled widely in South America and in Morocco. Member of Parliament for North-West Lanarkshire (1885–92), he stood unsuccessfully for West Stirling in the 1918 election. He produced several volumes of tales, sketches, and essays based on his travels, and wrote on the Spanish Conquest. 'Don Roberto's' lasting friendship with Conrad began in 1897, when he wrote a letter praising 'An Outpost of Progress'.

L(ilian) M(ary) Hallowes (1870–1950), Conrad's secretary, was born in Penrith in the Lake District, the daughter of a postal employee. She presumably trained as a typist. She first worked for Conrad on a temporary basis in 1904 on *Nostromo*, and returned to his employ in 1908 and again in 1911. From 1917 onwards, she was virtually a member of the Conrad family, staying for long periods, as Conrad switched over to dictation. She also read proofs, typed his correspondence, and in 1921 joined the Conrads in Corsica for work on *Suspense*.

G(eorge) F(ountaine) W(eare) Hope (né Hopps, 1854–1930), the son of a solicitor, trained in the famous training-ship the *Conway* and served briefly in the *Duke of Sutherland* before turning his hand to various business ventures. He met Conrad in 1880 in a London shipping office. The friendship was one of the closest and most enduring of Conrad's early life in England, and the newly married Conrads moved to Stanford-le-Hope, Essex, to live near Fountaine Hope and his wife (Frances) Ellen (née Mayer, 1854–1931).

(Joseph Leopold) Ford Hermann Hueffer (1873–1939; as of 1919 Ford Madox Ford), son of the music critic Francis Hueffer (né Franz Hüffer, 1845–89) and related to the Rossetti circle through his painter grandfather Ford Madox Brown (1812–93), was educated in Folkestone and at University College School, London. A 'budding writer' when he and Conrad met through Edward Garnett in 1898, Hueffer proved an influence and inspiration. His erratic personality brought the friendship with Conrad past breaking point in 1909, when they were involved in the *English Review*. The two men were never again close. Their collaborations include *The Inheritors* (1901), *Romance* (1903), and *The Nature of the Crime* (1909). Highly prolific, Ford's reputation rests on his masterpiece, *The Good Soldier* (1915), and *Parade's End* (1924–28). Living in America and Paris after the war, he died in Deauville in June 1939.

Arthur Pierson Marwood (1868–1916), born in Stokesley (Yorkshire), the son of a baronet, after leaving Clifton College read mathematics at Trinity College, Cambridge, as his cousin Charles Dodgson ('Lewis Carroll') had at Oxford. Chronically ill, he led the life of a gentleman-farmer in Kent, coming to know Conrad through Ford Hueffer, who drew on him for *The Good Soldier* and *Parade's End*. Conrad, who found him a useful sounding-board for his fiction-in-progress, valued his advice and enjoyed his company.

Eric S(eabrooke) Pinker (1891–1973), after leaving Westminster School (1908), entered his father's literary agency, becoming Conrad's agent on his father's death. On divorcing his Danish-born wife, Margit (née Dietrichson, 1894—?), a widow with two young children whom he had married in 1921, he married the American actress Adrienne Morrison (1883–1940) in 1927. He emigrated to the United States in 1930, and established a literary and theatrical agency with his wife in New York. In 1939, he was arrested on charges of grand larceny for defrauding a client, pleaded guilty, and was sentenced to a term of two and a half to five years in Sing Sing Prison. He died in New York City in October 1973.

J(ames) B(rand) Pinker (1863–1922), London-born of a stonemason father, became a journalist, going out to work on a newspaper in Constantinople, where, in 1881, he married Mary Elizabeth Seabrooke (1862–1945), daughter of a prosperous Essex brewer. Establishing a literary agency in offices off the Strand in 1896, he came to manage a glittering pantheon of writers including Conrad (as of 1900), Arnold Bennett, Stephen Crane, John Galsworthy, Ford Hueffer, Henry James, James Joyce, D. H. Lawrence, and H. G. Wells. Generous to a fault to his client, Pinker fell out with Conrad in 1910, but the relationship survived, becoming closer as the two men aged. They visited one another's homes, collaborated on *Gaspar the Strong Man*, a film scenario of Conrad's story 'Gaspar Ruiz' (1920), and holidayed in Corsica together (1921).

Marguerite-Blanche-Marie Poradowska (née Gachet de la Fournière, 1848–1937), Belgian-born novelist, divided her time between Paris and Brussels, where Conrad met her just before the death of her husband, Conrad's distant cousin, Aleksandr Poradowski (1835–90). His friendship with the older and attractive bluestocking has fuelled speculation about a romance. Poradowska's novels of Ruthenian life, *Yaga* (1887), *Demoiselle Micia* (1888–89), and *Marylka* (1895), were serialised in the prestigious *Revue des Deux Mondes*. She tried to pull strings to find Conrad employment in the Congo, but as he assimilated to English life, the friendship grew distant. She helped place two of his sisters-in-law in a French convent school in Slough in 1901, and translated Conrad's 'An Outpost of Progress' for *Les Nouvelles illustrées* (1903). Interested in music, she was also well connected in Paris's literary circles, serving on the Prix Femina jury from 1904 to 1924.

J(ózef) H(ieronim) Retinger (1888–1960), born in Cracow, studied in Paris, and became a political activist for Polish independence unofficially as well as for the Polish Bureau in London. Meeting Conrad through Arnold Bennett in 1912, Retinger attempted to interest the writer in his political views and activities, and he and his wife Otolia (née Zubrzycka, 1889–1984) accompanied the Conrads to Poland in July 1914. Conrad presented a Note to the Foreign Office on his behalf in 1916, but the friendship faded as Retinger's marriage collapsed, and his political intriguing – the pundit Malcolm Muggeridge later called him 'the Talleyrand of Notting Hill' – saw him become *persona non grata* in France and England during the war.

Stephen Sydney Reynolds (1881–1919), born in Devizes, Wiltshire, read chemistry at Manchester University before spending time in Paris. He met Conrad and Hueffer through Edward Garnett in 1907, and was briefly connected with the *English Review*. His interest in the working classes, evidenced in his *A Poor Man's House* (1908) and *Alongshore* (1910), had a romantic aspect, and, on relocating to Sidmouth (Devon) to live near a married fisherman, 'Bob' Wooley (1865–1947), he worked as Inspector of Fisheries and Adviser on Inshore Fisheries. Dubbed the 'fisherman-author' and 'the Conrad of the shallows', Reynolds died in the great influenza pandemic following the War.

William Rothenstein (1872–1945; knighted 1931), born in Yorkshire of German parents, trained in art in Paris after leaving Bradford Grammar School and London's Slade School of Art, becoming a noted portraitist, graphic artist, and painter. He contributed to the *Yellow Book* and the *Savoy* early in his career, was an official artist during the war, and Principal of the Royal College of Art (1920–35). Rothenstein, who became friendly with Conrad through Cunninghame Graham, did a watercolour portrait of Conrad in 1903 (National Portrait Gallery), and acted as a trustee of his Royal Literary Fund grant in 1905.

E(dward) L(ancelot) ('Ted') Sanderson (1867–1939), after leaving Elstree, his father's preparatory school in Hertfordshire, read Classics at King's College, Cambridge, where he was also a distinguished athlete. Travelling with John Galsworthy to Australia in 1893, he became friendly with Conrad during the *Torrens*'s homeward voyage. Ill health kept Sanderson in Africa after the Boer War in which he served as captain in the Yorkshire Regiment, and he and his Scottish wife (née Helen Mary Watson, 1874–1967) settled first in Johannesburg, then in Nairobi. On home leave in 1910, he was offered the headmastership of Elstree School, a post he held from 1911 until 1935.

Józef (Joseph) Adolph Spiridion (1849–1932) was a watchmaker and jeweller in Cardiff in the business begun by his father Władysław Spiridion (né Kliszczewski, 1819–91), a master gold- and silversmith. The elder Spiridion, who arrived in England in 1837, became naturalised in 1855. Although born in Hampshire of a Welsh mother (Rachel Grant, 1818–93), speaking little or no Polish, and married to a Welshwoman (Maria Llewellyn, 1847–?), the younger Spiridion was so stern a Polish patriot that his friendship with Conrad proved short-lived. A staunch supporter of the Conservative Party, Spiridion worked on the behalf of Hardinge Gifford (later Lord Halsbury) in the Cardiff Boroughs, and was befriended by him.

Arthur William Symons (1865–1945) was born in Milford Haven, Wales, the son of a Cornish Wesleyan minister. A central figure in the aesthetic movements of the 1890s, he championed Baudelaire and Blake. In 1896, he took Conrad's 'The Idiots' for the *Savoy*. A Kentish neighbour of Conrad's, he occasionally visited the novelist. He survived a complete nervous collapse in 1908, re-started his career, and in addition to poetry and criticism, also wrote on music, dance, painting, and the drama, translating Hugo von Hofmannsthal's *Elektra*.

Count Zygmunt Szembek (1844–1907) descended from a Polish *szlachta* family. His grandfather and his father (who studied with Chopin) had fought for the Napoleonic cause. Married in 1876, he was the father of two daughters and two sons. Living off money from family estates, he moved to Capri for his health but also to escape Polish moral strictures, the island then being famous for its homosexual society. Interested in art and literature, he played the piano as a keen amateur. Conrad drew on him for the title-character of 'Il Conde'.

Agnes Tobin (1864–1939), the daughter of a wealthy San Francisco attorney (an Irish immigrant to the United States by way of Chile and Hawaii), was a poet, translator of Petrarch and Racine, and bluestocking. A close friend of the essayist Alice Meynell, she moved in Catholic circles when in England and also knew W. B. Yeats and Edmund Gosse, meeting Conrad through Arthur Symons. She provided Conrad with his valuable connection to the American collector of manuscripts and paintings, John Quinn.

T(homas) F(isher) Unwin (1848–1935) headed the successful publishing firm he founded in 1882. Conrad's first publisher, he brought out *Almayer's Folly*, *An Outcast of the Islands*, and *Tales of Unrest*. An ardent Liberal party supporter, Unwin was also active in publishing organisations and literary affairs. His famous irascibility soon caused a breach with Conrad, and the writer moved to Heinemann's and then to Blackwood's. Arrangements for a collected edition of Conrad saw Unwin win a contract to publish three titles, and he brought out *The Arrow of Gold*, *The Rover*, and the posthumous *Tales of Hearsay*.

Hugh Seymour Walpole (1884–1941; knighted 1937), born in New Zealand, the son of a bishop, was educated at the King's School, Canterbury, and Emmanuel College, Cambridge, and worked briefly as a schoolmaster before taking up writing. Befriended by the elderly Henry James, he had wide literary connections, counting Arnold Bennett and Virginia Woolf as friends. Prosperous and ever seeking an 'ideal friend', he travelled much, seeing the Conrads at Oswalds between lecturing tours in the United States and Canada, and becoming one of Jessie Conrad's confidants. Walpole's many novels, in particular the *Rogue Herries* series, were highly popular in their day.

H(erbert) G(eorge) Wells (1866–1946), a novelist and a writer of scientific romances and science fiction, and a social activist and essayist, was of humble origins, winning a life-changing scholarship to London's Normal School of Science. After writing a textbook on biology, he turned to journalism and then to fiction. Wells's review of Conrad's *An Outcast of the Islands* opened communications between the two men, who were also neighbours in Kent. Temperamentally at odds and with very different politics and artistic methods, they essayed an uneasy friendship from about 1898 to 1904. Conrad dedicated *The Secret Agent* to Wells, who caricatured Conrad in *Tono-Bungay* (1909) and *Boon* (1915).

A guide to pronunciation

Exploring Conrad's world involves contact with the several languages he knew well, had a smattering of, and merely came into contact with, as well as class registers in English. This list provides approximate pronunciations (particularly for Polish where, barring use of the international phonetic alphabet, the sound system is difficult to render) for proper names, place-names, and some miscellaneous words in Dutch, French, German, Malay, and Polish. A few names and place-names in English that native speakers from outside the United Kingdom may find challenging, such as Fetherstonhaugh and Trottiscliffe, also appear here. Included are not only names that appear in the main text but also those found in the Notes and in 'Conrad's circle: A select Who's Who'.

People
Biberstejn-Pilchowska: BEE-ber-shtine peel-HOV-skah
Ewa Bobrowska: EH-vah baw-BROV-skah
Teofila Bobrowska: tay-o-FEE-lah baw-BROV-skah
Thadeusz Bobrowski: tah-DEH-oosh baw-BROV-skee
Stefan Buszczyński: steh-FAHN boosh-CHIN-skee
Cervoni: (Italian) CHER-vo-knee; (French) ser-VOE-knee
Wiktor Chodźko: VIK-tor HODGE-kaw
Witold Chwalewik: VEE-told hvah-LE-vik
Coadou-Brinter: COE-a-doo branh-TAY
Delestang: DEUH-less-stawng
Duteil: DYOO-tay
Fetherstonhaugh: FAN-shaw
Fountaine: fon-TANE

A guide to pronunciation

Hueffer: HOOF-fer
Józef Teodor: YU-zeff teh-AW-dore
Kayaerts: KAI-yerts
Ker: CAH
Kinkead: kin-KADE
Władłysaw Kliszczewski: vwah-DIS-swaff kleesh-CHEV-skee
Knopf: ka-NOFF
Ewa Korzeniowska: EH-vah kaw-zhe-NYOV-skah
Korzeniowski: kaw-zhe-NYOV-skee
Valéry Larbaud: vah-LAY-ree larh-BO
Ottoline Morrell: OTT-lin MORAL
Nałęcz: NAH-wench
Ignace Paderewski: igg-NA-tsih pah-deh-REV-skee
Bronisław Piłsudski: braw-NEE-swaff pew-SOOD-skee
Poradowska: po-rah-DOV-skah
Adam Pulman: AH-dahm PULL-manh
Raczynski: rah-CHIN-skee
Józef Retinger: YU-zeff RHET-ting-er
Rothenstein: ROE-then-stine
Walery Rzewuski: vah-LER-ih zheh-VOO-skee
Spohr: SHPORE
Stanisław: sta-NEE-swaff
Antoni Syroczyński: anh-TOH-nee sih-roh-CHIN-skee
Kazimierz Waliszewski: kah-ZEE-miezh vah-lee-SHEV-skee
Winawer: vee-NAH-ver
Zagórski: za-GOOR-skee
Aniela Zagórska: an-NYEL-lah za-GOOR-skah

Place-names
Champel-les-Bains: sham-PELL lay BAN
Côte des Bruyères: COAT day brew-yehr
Côte de Granit Rose: COAT deuh grah-knee rohz
Gillingham: JILL-ing-uhm
Grangemouth: GRANGE-muth
Greenhithe: GREN-ith
Greenwich: GREN-itch
Harwich: HARE-idge

Kazimierówka: kah-zhee-MYER-oof-kah
Willa Konstantynówka: VEE-lah kon-stanh-TIN-oof-kah
Krynica: kree-NEE-tsah
Léguer: LAY-gyeah
Léopoldville: LAY-oh-pold-veel
Łuczyniec: woo-CHIN-yets
Mirogoâne: mee-rah-GWAHN
Nowochwastów: noh-vaw-HVASS-tooff
Patusan: PAH-too-sanh
Przemyśl: PSHEH-mish-ul
Raszyn: RAH-shin
Rakowice: rah-kaw-VEE-tse
St-Malo: sanh MAH-low
St-Quentin: sanh CAN-tanh
Szpitalna: spee-TAHL-nah
Terechowa: te-reh-HOV-ah
Topolnica: taw-pol-NEE-tsah
Trottiscliffe: TRAWZ-lee
Vauxhall: VOK-sull
Wawel: VAH-vell
Wrotham: ROOT-em
Württemburg: VIRT-tem-boorgh
Zakopane: za-kaw-PAH-neh
Zubrzycka: zoob-JITS-kah

Characters
Antonia Avellanos: ANH-tone-ya AH-ve-yan-os
Susan Bacadou: SOO-zann ba-KAH-dooh
Brierly: BREER-lee
Martin Decoud: MAR-tan DEUH-cooh
Ferraud: FEH-roh
Heyst: HAY-st
Karain: kah-RINE
Stein: sh-TINE
Whalley: WALL-ee
Peter Willems: PAY-ter VILL-ems

Miscellaneous

Delestang et Fils: DEUH-less-stawng ay fees

Escamillo: es-KAH-mee-yo

kalęda: kaw-LEN-dah

Moering: MEUH-ring

Mont-Blanc: MOHN blanh

Mont-Pelée: MOHN PEUH-lay

Saint-Antoine: SANHT-(t)ANH-twanh

szlachcic: SHLAH-tseets

szlachta: SHLAH-tah

Vondel: FON-dulh

Notes

Works listed in the Bibliography are referred to by author and date, apart from unsigned newspaper articles where the newspaper title and date are given with the full title being found in the Bibliography.

The notes give a source for direct quotations but do not provide a source for every fact, which would make the documentation of this volume extraordinarily ungainly. Details have been provided when it has been thought the reader might wish to follow up information, or where information is likely to prove difficult to find or is in archival sources. Conrad's letters should be consulted for specifics.

The given name of Conrad's correspondents appears on first citation in a note to a chapter; thereafter only the surname is given. Where an archival or private source is indicated for a Conrad letter, that letter has not yet appeared in *Letters* (the case for letters dating to 1923 and 1924, in press) or the letter is missing from the appropriate volume. In the latter instance, such letters will appear in *Volume 9: Uncollected Letters, 1892–1923* (in press).

New Style dates are given for Tadeusz Bobrowski's correspondence; readers requiring Old Style dates should see Najder, ed. (1964). The translations from the Polish in Najder, ed. (1964) and Najder, ed. (1983) have occasionally been modified in the interests of stylistic felicity, and thus wording of a quotation is not always exactly as it appears in those two sources, and the same is true of letters in French in *Letters*, where an alternative translation to that published has occasionally been provided. Likewise, citations from Conrad's letters have been modified, so as to avoid [*sic*]; hence, accents and italics are provided where missing and spelling corrected. (See 'A note on sources', pp.339–40, for further discussion of this point.)

On sources for quotations from Conrad's fiction and non-fiction, see the head-note to the Bibliography.

Abbreviations

Berg	Henry W. and Albert A. Berg Collection of English and American Literature, New York Public Library, Astor, Lennox, and Tilden Foundations
Columbia	Rare Book and Manuscript Library, Columbia University, New York
Duke	Rare Book, Manuscript, and Special Collections Library, Duke University, Durham, North Carolina
Ellis Island Archives	American Immigration History Center, Ellis Island (online)
Harvard	Houghton Library, Harvard University, Cambridge, Massachusetts
HRC Texas	Harry Ransom Humanities Research Center, University of Texas at Austin
IGI	International Genealogical Index, Church of Latter-Day Saints
Letters	*The Collected Letters of Joseph Conrad*
Lilly	Lilly Library, Indiana University, Bloomington
Marine Society	Marine Society and Sea Cadets, London
Morgan	Morgan Library and Museum, New York
National Archives	National Archives, London
Princeton	Firestone Library, Princeton University, Princeton, New Jersey
Yale	Beinecke Rare Book and Manuscript Library, Yale University, New Haven, Connecticut

EPIGRAPH

vi   'It is when . . . grasp': *Lord Jim* (Ch. 16), p. 180.

PREFACE

x   'His father . . . princess': Letter from Muriel Dobree to Mrs J. C. L. Pugh, 24 February 1949, cited in Pugh (1960): 54.

x   a reviewer: *The Nation*, 24 February 1912: 857.

x   'as a boy . . . Vienna': Curle (1928a), p. 44.

xii   'Conrad . . . recluse': Roberts (1925): 95.

xii   'a bit . . . author': John Conrad (1981), p. 83.

xii   '*homo duplex*': To Kazimierz Waliszewski, 5 December 1903, *Letters* 3: 89.

CHAPTER ONE: 'POLE-CATHOLIC AND GENTLEMAN' (1857–1878)

1   'Balzac . . . Berdichev': Chekhov (1900; trans. 1969), Act 2, p. 40.

1   'one-character . . . Absurd': Jarrell (1969), p. 136.

1   wedding ceremony: Robb (1994; rpt. 2000), p. 403.

1   'Could . . . interest': 'A Familiar Preface' to *A Personal Record*, p. xx.

1   'as . . . polka' . . . unfortunate incident: Balzac (1847; 1927), pp. 70–71 (translation mine).

2   'a Polish . . . tar' (footnote): To Karol Zagórski, 22 May 1890, *Letters* 1: 52.

2   two centuries: Najder (1998): 45.

3   'Had . . . mankind': To Lewis Browne, 15 May 1918, *Letters* 6: 216.

3   baptismal certificate: Najder, ed. (1983), p. 31.

3   someone . . . Korzeniew: See Rymut (1990).

4   'a laughing-stock . . . progress': Zamoyski (1987), p. 217.

4   'Slavo-Tartar . . . barbarism': To George T. Keating, 14 December 1922, *Letters* 7: 615.

5   'The dog . . . silence': *A Personal Record*, p. 34.

6   joining . . . Polish hopes: For a useful and brief summary of Napoleon's treatment of Polish national aspirations, see Fedosova (1998). Accessed: March 2007.

6   quasi-religious . . . clergy (footnote): Leslie (1963), p. 107.

7   sold his lands: To Lewis Browne, 15 May 1918, *Letters* 6: 217.

7   disapproved . . . 1847: *A Personal Record*, pp. 28–29.

7   wedding eventually taking place: Najder (1983), p. 31.

7   secondary school . . . in . . . Zhitomir: Korzeniowski's school leaving certificate in Zhitomir's District Archives is dated 29 October [= 10 November] 1840 (Personal communication: Zdzisław Najder). This means, however, that he was twenty – a rather late age to finish secondary schooling.

7   1840 to 1846: Najder, ed. (1983), p. 24.

7   one observer: Tadeusz Bobrowski in his *Memoirs*, cited *ibid.*, p. 16.

7   detractors and apologists: See Bross 1995; Bross 1996; and Najder (1983).

8   Surviving photographs: Apollo Korzeniowski (Yale).

8   'Baby son . . . Her': Najder, ed. (1983), p. 33.

8   'peacock . . . sky': Filip, ed. and Michael, trans. (1944), pp. 47ff.

9   Borrowing . . . *kolęda*: Skutnik 1975; Personal communication: Andrzej Busza.

10   all but one of Victor Hugo's plays: Korzeniowski to Stefan Buszczyński, [19–29 October 1868], Najder, ed. (1983), p. 122. The only Hugo play Korzeniowski did not translate was *Cromwell*.

10 Zhitomir . . . flourished: See Berka (1983).

10 extract permission: Ewa Korzeniowska to Apollo Korzeniowski, 4 June 1861, Najder, ed. (1983), p. 42.

10 opening his letters: See *ibid.*, pp. 38–41.

10 several hundred 'suspects': Ewa Korzeniowska to Mr and Mrs Antoni Pietkiewicz, 19 November 1861, *ibid.*, p. 59.

10 half-past midnight: *Ibid.*

11 full mourning: Photograph of Ewa Korzeniowska (Yale).

11 mourning-frock . . . black . . . martyrdom: Ewa Korzeniowska to Apollo Korzeniowski, 2 July 1861, *ibid.*, p. 51; Busza (2003): 9.

11 'ever-ready . . . patriotism': Korzeniowski, 'Poland and Muscovy' (1864), in Najder, ed. (1983), p. 75.

11 'in the courtyard . . . begin': To Wincenty Lutosławski, 9 June 1897, *Letters* 1: 358.

11 Ewa's mother hurried: Najder, ed. (1964), p. 184; Najder, ed. (1983), p. 58.

11 According to his wife: Letter to Władysław Górski, 6 January 1862, MS 8711/IV, Jagiellonian Library, Cracow (Personal communication: Zdzisław Najder).

12 carelessly laid charges: See Najder, ed. (1983), pp. 62–63.

12 'under . . . escort': Korzeniowski, 'Poland and Muscovy,' *ibid.*, p. 82.

12 dosed with calomel: See McLendon (1991).

12 architectural historians: See Brumfield (1991) and Sazonov (1993).

12 population . . . 17,000: Statistics cited in Borisov in Moore, ed. (1992), p. 43.

12 'Vologda . . . half': Korzeniowski to Gabriela and Jan Zagórski, 27 June 1862, Najder, ed. (1983), pp. 66–67.

13 'Take an hour-glass . . . things': Korzeniowski to Gabriela and Jan Zagórski, 14 October 1862, *ibid.*, pp. 70–71.

13 'held . . . society': Longin Panteleev, cited in Borisov, in Moore, ed. (1992), p. 47.

13 'Polish clothing . . . health': *Memoirs* (1900; rpt. 1979: 2: 441), cited in Borisov, in Moore, ed. (1992), p. 46.

13 A photograph of the time: Morf (1930), facing p. 58; see illustrations.

13 'We . . . Warsaw': Najder, ed. (1983), p. 70.

14 a trumped-up duel: For a full account, see Busza in Simmons and Stape, eds. (2000).

14 'not only . . . good, ugly . . . *cheri*': *A Personal Record*, p. 65.

14 'To my . . . Konrad': Photograph (Yale).

15 'persisted . . . treatment': Najder, ed. (1964), p. 184.

15 'Despair . . . everything': Korzeniowski to Kasimierz Kaszewski, 28 February 1865, Najder, ed. (1983), p. 92.

15 18 April 1865: Given in Old Style as 6 April 1865, Najder, ed. (1964), p. 185.

15 age of thirty-three: Death certificate in Najder, ed. (1983), pp. 128–29.

15 read . . . poetry aloud: Dąbrowski (1917), *ibid.*, p. 199.

15 'I . . . cloister': Korzeniowski to Gabriela and Jan Zagórski, 18 January 1866, *ibid.*, p. 102.

16 to Kiev . . . treatment: Korzeniowski to Kaszewski, 31 December 1866, cited in Najder (1983), p. 502, n. 63.

16 unreliable account: Tekla Wojakowska's recollections in Czosnowski, in Najder, ed. (1983), p. 136.

16 'travel abroad . . . years': To Lewis Browne, 15 May 1918, *Letters* 6: 216:

16 'a filthy place . . . Jews': Gustav Mahler to Alma Mahler, [2 April 1903], *Letters*

to his Wife (2004), p. 118.

16   resenting . . . 'Polishness': Korzeniowski to Buszczyński, 17 March 1868, Najder, ed. (1983), p. 112.

16   'the Galicians . . . nothing': Korzeniowski to Buszczyński, [12 October 1868], *ibid.*, p. 121.

17   'an obscure . . . deserted': Korzeniowski to Kaszewski, [24 June 1868], *ibid.*, p. 118.

17   'I am . . . things . . . I am . . . trouble': Korzeniowski to Buszczyński, 13 October 1868; to Kaszewski, 14 October 1868, cited in Najder (1983), p. 26.

17   his later claims: 'The "Knopf Document,"' ed. Stape, in Moore, Simmons, and Stape, eds. (2000), p. 61. For a discussion of the issue, see Najder (1983) and Busza (1966).

17   'six . . . German': *A Personal Record*, p. 121.

17   'I would . . . sleep': 'Poland Revisited' (1915), *Notes on Life and Letters*, ed. Stape (2004), p. 134.

17   portrait . . . death mask: Teofila Bobrowska to Kaszewski, 12 June 1869, Najder, ed. (1983), pp. 130–31.

17   'vanquished man': 'Author's Note' (1919) to *A Personal Record*, p. viii.

17   Last rites: To Lewis Browne, 15 May 1918, *Letters* 6: 217.

18   songs . . . hymns: Stefan Buszczyński, *Kraj*, 27 May 1869, cited in Busza (2003): 7.

18   'The suffering . . . suffering': Buszczyński, 'From A Little Known Poet' (1870), Najder, ed. (1983), p. 24.

18   'A man . . . loved head?': *Nostromo*, p. 379. (Dent reads 'heaven' as does the first edition, but this is either a misprint or an error on Conrad's part.)

18   water cure: On water cures of the period, and specifically, on Conrad's treatment in Switzerland in the 1890s, see Bock (2002), pp. 26–40.

18   Kingdom of Württemberg: 'Bobrowski Document,' Najder, ed. (1964), p. 188.

19   Latin: Morf (1977), p. 73. Morf's earlier version (1930) is less detailed on the texts studied.

19   Regina Korzeniowska: Najder, ed. (1983), p. 101, n. 1.

19   hours . . . drawing maps: 'Geography and Some Explorers' (1924), *Last Essays*, p. 15.

19   putting his finger . . . central Africa: The books are James S. Jameson's *Story of the Rear Column of the Emin Pasha Relief Expedition* (1890) and E. J. Glave's *In Savage Africa, or Six Years of Adventure in Congo-Land* (1892). Fletcher (2001), p. 63; Personal communication: Owen Knowles.

19   Faculty of Medicine: Jagiellonian University Archives, cited in Najder (1983), p. 31n.

20   'unforgettable Englishman': *A Personal Record*, p. 40.

20   tried to keep up: See Adam Pulman to Stefan Buszczyński, 10 March 1879, Najder, ed. (1983), pp. 146–47.

20   legal guardian: See the Act of Nomination of 2 August 1870, *ibid.*, p. 133.

20   'an uncompromising . . . patriotism': 'Author's Note' (1917), *Nostromo*, pp. xiii–xiv.

20   Austrian nationality: 'Bobrowski Document,' Najder, ed. (1964), pp. 192–93.

21   dream . . . Pola: *A Personal Record*, p. 121.

21   'to fight . . . enemy': Clifford (1927), p. 11; Clifford (1904): 844. This story about the flight to Turkey is repeated in a review of *A Personal Record*, suggesting that Clifford was its author or had related the anecdote to an acquaintance: 'Mr Conrad's Recollections,' *Birmingham Daily Post*, 2 February 1912: 4.

21 'not ... difficult': Bobrowski to Conrad, 20 September 1869, Najder, ed. (1964), p. 35.

21 Easter holiday: Adam Pulman to Conrad, 14 March [1874], Najder, ed. (1983), pp. 145–46.

21 Paris-born Chodźko: Personal communication: Claudine Lesage.

22 photograph taken: By Walery Rzewuski, ulica Podwale 27B, Cracow (Yale).

22 Conrad's grandmother ... heart: Bobrowski to Conrad, 20 September 1869, Najder, ed. (1964), p. 39.

22 'one September day ... still': To Harriet Mary Capes, 21 July 1914, *Letters* 5: 400–01.

22 3 rue Arcole ... 1851: *Annuaire almanach du commerce* (1874) and 1850 and 1851.

22 'the puppy ... eyes': To John Galsworthy, 8 May 1905, *Letters* 3: 240.

23 'Since the age of 17 ... boy': Jotting on a used envelope, 26 May 1923 (private collection; courtesy of Owen Knowles).

23 'a great composer': To John Galsworthy, 18 June 1910, *Letters* 4: 338; for the repertoire, see *Le Petit Marseille*, 15 October–17 December 1874. The writings in which the operatic allusions referred to occur are *Almayer's Folly*, *Nostromo*, *A Personal Record*, and *The Arrow of Gold*.

23 'who ... (ough!)' (footnote): *The Mirror of the Sea*, p. 23.

23 storm-tossed Majorca: *Ibid.*, p. 153.

23 Bahamas ... 'stagnation and poverty': To F. N. Doubleday, 13 March 1923, Jean-Aubry (1927), 2: 297.

24 'the quaintest ... fruit': Hearn (1890), pp. 35, 36, 45–46.

24 'short, few, and fleeting ... interesting': 'Author's Note' (1917), *Nostromo*, p. xlii.

24 'Monsieur Georges': Bobrowski to Stefan Buszczyński, 24 March 1879, Najder, ed. (1964), p. 178.

25 'reading boy': 'Poland Revisited' (1915), p. 133.

25 'a black ... ravine': *The Mirror of the Sea*, p. 154.

25 a cyclone ... the region: *Sankt Thomas Tidende*, 30 September 1875, cited in Van Marle, ed. Moore (2005): 82.

25 Conrad stayed briefly: To Jean-Aubry, 1 September 1923, *Lettres françaises* (1930), p. 188, testifies to a short sojourn in Le Havre, Conrad recalling a hotel in the main square.

25 'Do you need ... role': Bobrowski to Conrad, 27 September 1876, O. S., Najder, ed. (1964), p. 38.

25 'And ... begin life': To Galsworthy, 8 May 1905, *Letters* 3: 240.

26 accounts of financial outlays: Bobrowski to Conrad, 27 September 1876 O. S. and 26 October 1876, Najder, ed. (1964), pp. 36–45; 'Bobrowski Document,' *ibid.*, pp. 194–95.

26 'disguised ... death': *The Arrow of Gold*, p. 291.

27 'dreary coast' ... Caracas: To Richard Curle, 22 July 1923, Curle, (1928b), p. 120.

27 strong earthquake: *Sankt Thomas Tidende*, 21 September 1976, cited in Van Marle, ed. Moore (2005): 82.

27 'plain Mr Jones: 'Author's Note' (1919), *Victory*, p. xxxvii.

27 'Class ... hateful thing': To Elbridge L. Adams, 20 November 1922, *Letters* 7: 595.

28 'de Korzeniowski': Cited in Van Marle, ed. Moore (2005): 36.

28 'more . . . nephew': To Edward Garnett, 20 January 1900, *Letters* 2: 246.

28 grandmother had died . . . Tadeusz paints: 'Notes,' *A Personal Record*, p. 159 n. 34. Only the year of her death has been established (Personal communication: Zdzisław Najder). See Bobrowski's *Memoirs*, cited in Najder, ed. (1983), p. 5.

28 A photograph of her: Duke (Najder 1983, after p. 266).

29 '*irrealité*': Pierre Le Franc, 'Notice. Le Miroir de la mer' in *Conrad: Œuvres*, ed. Monod (1985), 2: 1433.

29 'stood . . . bridge': To Edward Candler, 3 April 1922, *Letters* 2: 246.

30 romantic fantasy: See Allen (1965). Her speculations were disproved by Van Marle (1976b).

30 Horvath . . . Carlos: Najder (1983), p. 50.

30 tragic affair: See Lesage (1992) and Lesage (2003).

30 Bobrowski fretted: Bobrowski to Conrad, 8 August 1877, *ibid.*, pp. 47–49.

31 CONRAD . . . ARRIVEZ: Bobrowski to Buszczyński, 24 March 1879, *ibid.*, p. 176. (The year cited is correct: this is a retrospective account.)

31 breached French Merchant Service regulations: *Ibid.*

31 casual . . . employment: *Ibid.*, p. 178.

32 American naval vessel: *Ibid*, p. 177.

32 'Would . . . navy': Arthur Rimbaud to US Consul in Bremen, 14 May 1877 in Rimbaud, trans. Harding (2004), p. 266.

32 political appeaser: See Najder (1983), *passim*.

32 'not a bad boy . . . excitable': Bobrowski to Buszczyński, 24 March 1879, Najder, ed. (1964), p. 177.

33 'most . . . man': To Garnett, 20 January 1900, *Letters* 2: 246.

33 'I attribute . . . possess': To Kazimierz Waliszewski, 5 December 1903, *Letters* 3: 89.

33 motto: Bobrowski to Conrad, 9 November 1891, Najder, ed. (1964), p. 155.

CHAPTER TWO: 'TELL ME THE SEA:' APPRENTICE, MATE, AND MASTER (1878–1890)

34 'Anciens . . . la mer': 'Old, beloved exiles, / Tell me the sea,' 'L'Esprit,' 'Comédie de la soif,' Rimbaud (2004), pp. 118–19.

34 Malta . . . Azov: Hans van Marle's research in *Lloyd's List, Shipping and Mercantile Gazette, Le Sémaphore de Marseille*, April–June 1898, cited in Najder (1983).

35 'No line . . . contributes': Gautier (1856), p. 74 (translation mine).

35 'as we . . . San Stephano': To Joseph de Smet, 23 January 1911, *Letters* 4: 409.

35 Russian troops . . . fever: *The Times*, 25 March 1878: 6.

35 'thick with the memories . . . life': 'Poland Revisited' (1915), *Notes on Life and Letters*, p. 137.

35 'the historic anchorage . . . time': To Admiral Sir William Goodenough, 25 September 1920, *Letters* 7: 181.

36 'up till now . . . do': Bobrowski to Conrad, 8 July 1878, Najder, ed. (1964), p. 56.

36 'East Coast . . . card': To R. B. Cunninghame Graham, 4 February 1898, *Letters* 2: 35.

36 son of a French tailor: Hope, 'Friend of Conrad' in Moore, Simmons, Stape, eds. (2000), p. 35.

36 'The Great Circumnavigator': Clifford (1927), p. 11.

36 public library . . . accommodation: Stebbings [c. 1886], pp. 59, 111–12; Anon. (1866), p. 50.

36   'though mainly prompted . . . officer': To Kazimierz Waliszewski, 5 December 1903, *Letters* 3: 89.

37   'a traveller . . . lonely': 'Poland Revisited' (1915), p. 121.

37   15 per cent: Najder (1983), p. 82.

37   Sutherland: 'Poland Revisited' (1915), pp. 121–23.

37   'Dickensian . . . wonder-city': *Ibid.*, p. 122.

37   One recollection: Hope, 'Friend of Conrad,' pp. 12–13.

37   less comfortable: Bobrowski to Buszczyński, 30 May 1879, Najder, ed. (1964), p. 179.

37   did not get on well: Hope, 'Friend of Conrad,' p. 35.

37   Kerguelen's Land . . . *Salammbô*: To J. G. Huneker, 16 April 1909, *Letters* 4: 218.

38   nightwatchman: *The Mirror of the Sea*, p. 122.

38   'night-prowlers . . . ghosts': *Ibid.*, pp. 122–23.

38   'Sun-kum-on's . . . bad': *Ibid.*, p. 122.

38   'White Australia' . . . Britain: To Alfred Harmsworth, Lord Northcliffe, [c. 21 February 1922], *Letters* 7: 422.

38   trading possibilities: See Bobrowski to Stefan Buszczyński, 30 May 1879, Najder, ed. (1964), p. 180.

38   'incorrigible . . . Don Quixote': *A Personal Record*, p. 44.

39   Sailors' Home: For Conrad's periods of residence at the London Sailors' Home, see Kennerley (forthcoming).

39   Certificate of Discharge: Yale.

39   'three . . . service': See the facsimile of this testimonial in Jean-Aubry (1927), 1: facing 38.

39   *Jeddah* affair: For press reports, see Moore, comp., in Simmons and Stape, eds. (2000).

40   Stuart's belongings: '"Well Done!"', *Notes on Life and Letters*, pp. 146–48, 436–37n.

40   'An artisan . . . pink': Booth, B348, pp. 42–43.

41   left for other lodgings: Krieger married on 4 September 1881 (Copy of an Entry of Marriage July–Sept 1881 Pancras 1b/137). The certificate gives his age as thirty.

41   William and Dolores Ward . . . 'machinists': Registrar General 1881 Census RG 11/0282 (101), p. 52; Stape, 'Conradiana in the 1901 Census and Other Sources of Record' (forthcoming); see also Kennerley (forthcoming).

41   recently married: Hope married on 20 October 1880 (Copy of an Entry of Marriage Oct–Dec 1880 Wandsworth 1d/989).

41   son of a county solicitor: See Registrar General 1861 Census RG9/1587 (87), p. 13 under Edwin Chorley Hopps. Hope and his brothers later changed their surname (see Stape, 'Conradiana', forthcoming).

41   'solitary and nocturnal walks . . . days': *The Secret Agent*, ed. Reid and Harkness (1990), p. 7.

42   bout of measles . . . 'very prevalent' . . . 'very numerous': Admissions Register of the Dreadnought Sailors' Hospital Record No. 125129 under the name 'Conrad Korzenwin.' The register notes his entry on 2 August 1881 and his discharge on 11 August (National Maritime Museum; courtesy of Alston Kennerley). On the disease's prevalence in London, see *The Times*, 14 July 1881: 11, and 16 August 1881: 10.

43   'it is the lonely . . . obedience': *Lord Jim* (Ch. 21), p. 222.

43 'Admiral': Bobrowski to Conrad, 31 August 1883, Najder, ed. (1964), p. 93.

44 a liver ailment: Bobrowski to Conrad, 14 August 1885, *ibid.*, p. 99.

45 first mate's examination: See Van Marle (1976a).

45 In 1891 (footnote): Kelly's (1895), pp. 1567, 1573. On the firm's Stuttgart connection, see Franke (2006).

46 *John P. Best . . . Antwerp:* Van Marle, ed. Moore 2005: 55–56; *The Mirror of the Sea*, p. 107; see Curle (1914), p. 17.

46 Madame Modjeska: *The Hull Express*, 21–25 April 1888.

46 Władysław Spiridion: See Registrar General 1881 Census RG11/5276 (25), p. 6; RG11/5284 (153), p. 74; IGI; and Stape, 'Conradiana' (forthcoming). Born in 1819, Spiridion, who arrived in England in 1837, became a naturalised Briton in 1855. (His Petition for Naturalization [HO1/63/2028, National Archives] gives 1840 for his arrival in England, but his extensive account of his early years places his arrival in England on 4 August 1837: see Kliszczewski). In addition to Józef (on whom see 'Conrad's Circle: A select Who's Who') he had a daughter, Wanda Karolina, born in Fareham (Hampshire) in 1852.

46 to pay back a loan: See Jean-Aubry (1927), 1: 78.

47 speculative business venture: Najder (1983), pp. 89–90.

47 Dundee . . . Sailors' Home: To Kliszczewski, 6 January 1886, *Letters* 1: 21.

47 plans for a career in trade: Bobrowski to Conrad, 5 April 1886, Najder, ed. (1964), p. 101.

47 master's examination: See Van Marle (1976a) for details. Conrad's certificate in the name of Conrad Korzeniowski is at the National Maritime Museum, Greenwich (C.08361).

47 'I had . . . caprice': *A Personal Record*, p. 120.

48 British nationality: Application: July, Knowles (1990), p. 11. 'Certificate of Naturalization to an Alien,' issued 19 August 1886, HO 144/177/A 44314 Certificate A4800; 'Oath of Allegiance,' signed 31 August 1886, registered by the Home Office (National Archives).

48 'When speaking . . . Britain': To Spiridion, 13 October 1885, *Letters* 1: 12.

48 'I am more British . . . it': Bone (1955), p. 160.

48 a month's wages: Bojarski and Stevens (1970–71): 199.

48 Hope . . . recalls: 'Friend of Conrad,' (2000), p. 39.

48 Conrad arrived in Amsterdam: For details, see Moore in Moore, ed. (1992).

49 'many days . . . unrest': *Lord Jim* (Ch. 2), p. 11.

49 'lounge . . . existence': *Ibid.*, p. 13.

50 'the Railway . . . other': Kipling, 'The Man who would be King' (1888; rpt. 1899), p. 44.

50 The Dutch suspected: See Campo (2000).

50 'didn't . . . Malays': 'Author's Note' (1919), *A Personal Record*, p. iv. See also Holden (2000).

50 'Malays . . . existence ': *A Personal Record*, p. 9.

51 'exact autobiography': 'Author's Note' (1920), *The Shadow-Line*; see also to John Quinn, 24 December 1915, *Letters* 5: 543.

52 'sympathetic doctor': See Shidara (2005).

52 'Fever . . . Cholera': William Willis to Conrad, February 1888, in Stape and Knowles, eds. (1996), p. 2.

52 the *Otago* . . . Simpson & Son: Parsons (1982), pp. 10, 24.

52 Jucker & Sigg & Company: '100 Years of Berli Jucker,' *The Nation*

(Bangkok), 26 November 1982, Supplement: 7.

52 'stole . . . Siam': To Bertrand Russell, [22–23] October 1922, *Letters* 7: 542.

52 'tried to kill me . . . house': *Ibid.*

52 'Bangkok Trilogy': On this, see Shidara (1998).

53 highly itinerant Wards: To Amelia Ward, 24 May 1924 (Private collection);
Stape, 'Conradiana' (forthcoming).

53 'Asses': To Captain David Bone, 28 September 1920, *Letters* 7: 183. (Sydney's
dailies establish that Conrad mistakenly transposes the maritime troubles to
Adelaide.)

54 'The whole . . . harmonious': Darwin (1839; rpt. 1852), Ch. 21, p. 483.

54 'From one citizen . . . Mauritius': Twain (1897), Ch. 62.

54 The local papers announced: *Le Journal de Maurice*, 1 October 1888, p. [3], 22
November 1888, p. [3]; *Commercial Gazette and Anglo-Indian Advertiser*, 22
November 1888, p. [3]; *Merchant and Planters Gazette*, 11 December, p. 353.

54 loading of the cargo: Maritime Register, Port-Louis, 22 November 1888
(National Archives of Mauritius).

54 Eugénie Renouf: According to IGI, Laure-Eugénie (1862 or 1864–15 May 1939),
the daughter of Charles Renouf (born *c.* 1838) and Caroline Loumeau (born *c.*
1842), married François-Edmond Loumeau (1846–1932) on 14 January 1889.
The fact that Caroline Loumeau's father, Jean-Pierre Loumeau, was born in
France in 1820 casts doubt, at least with respect to Eugénie Renouf's maternal
side, on the claim that the family was one of the island's 'old' French families.

55 'Their costume . . . parasol': Anon., *A Transport Voyage to Mauritius and Back*
(1851), pp. 114–15.

55 the *Nürnberg*: Entry on *Nürnberg* (updated 1998), *Palmer's List of Merchant
Vessels*.

55 'People groaned . . . head': 'Amy Foster,' p. 114.

56 warm testimonial: See Henry Simpson & Sons to Conrad, 2 April 1888, in Stape
and Knowles, eds. (1996), p. 5.

56 'more disreputable . . . Road': Booth, B362, pp. 12–13.

57 Sarah Bernhardt . . . *La Tosca*: 'Opéra Comique Theatre,' *The Times*, 19 July
1889: 4.

58 'had . . . "crystallized" ': 'Author's Note' (1919), *A Personal Record*, p. v.

58 Large demonstrations: See McCarthy, ed. (1988).

58 to sail to Mexico: To Albert Thys, 4 November 1889, *Letters* 1: 25.

58 'Autumn of Terror': *Casebook: Jack the Ripper* (Accessed: September 2004.)

58 'Attila . . . dress': Taylor, *New Statesman*, 25 October 1963: 576.

58 'an impression . . . French': 'Heart of Darkness,' p. 56.

58 Colonel Albert Thys: Cover, *L'Illustration Européenne: Journal internationale de la
famille*, 18 août 1889, Musée comunal du Général Thys, Dalhem, *Les Musées en
Wallonie*; Stockmans; Denoël (1992).

58 'the vilest . . . exploration': 'Geography and Some Explorers' (1924), *Last Essays*,
p. 17.

CHAPTER THREE: CRISIS: FINDING A HOME (1890–1895)

60 fifty-five-year-old: *Acte de décès* of Marie-Alexandre-Étienne-Constantin-
Joseph Poradowski, dated 9 February 1890, Commune d'Ixelles (courtesy of
Anne Arnold-Fontaine). It indicates that they were resident at 48 rue Veydt.

60 philologist and historian: *Biographie nationale de Belgique* 7: 406–11. Her full name

appears in her Acte de décès, dated 15 June 1937, Commune Saint-Benin-d'Azy, Nièvre (Burgundy).

60   in Van Gogh's words (footnote): Vincent van Gogh to Paul Gauguin, c. 17 June 1890 (Letter 643). Brooks (Accessed: January 2007).

61   Friedrichstrasse Bahnhof: See *A Personal Record*, p. 19.

61   reminiscence of the visit: Perłowski in Najder, ed. (1983), pp. 155–57.

62   Freiesleben: Sherry (1971), pp. 16–22.

62   'there is no . . . worries': Kingsley (1897; rpt. 1965), pp. 681, 684–85.

62   'the little . . . course': 'Heart of Darkness,' p. 105.

62   'the dark . . . cruelty': Psalm 74. For the widespread use of this phrase in colonialist discourse, see Stape (2004).

62   *Ville de Maceio*: *The Ships List*. (Accessed: June 2006).

63   'Dismal . . . future': To Marguerite Poradowska, 15 May 1890, *Letters* 1: 51.

63   partial solar eclipse: *International Eclipse Tables, 1700–2100*. (Accessed: June 2007).

63   'most intelligent . . . very friendly': 'The Congo Diary,' Knowles and Hampson eds. (2007) p. 99.

64   'Mosquitos . . . seedy': *Ibid.*, p. 109.

64   fraught history (footnote): See Ureel. (Accessed: September 2004).

65   intense dissatisfaction: See Bobrowski to Conrad, 22 July 1890, Najder, ed. (1964), p. 130.

65   variously interpreted: See Najder (1983), p. 133.

65   Captain Léon Rom: See Firchow (2000), pp. 112, 128–31, 230n.

65   an attack of dysentery . . . training: To Poradowska, 26 September 1890, *Letters* 1: 62–63.

65   Klein: Sherry (1971), pp. 77–78.

65   'Palm . . . assembly': Ward (1890): 140.

66   'Everything . . . repugnant': To Poradowska, 26 September 1890, *Letters* 1: 62 (translation mine).

66   River Kassai: To Maria Tyszkowa, 24 September 1890, *Letters* 1: 58.

66   'Idiotic employment': 'The Congo Diary,' ed. Knowles and Hampson (2007), p. 99.

66   'to select . . . station': To Poradowska, 26 September 1890, *Letters* 1: 63 (translation mine).

67   in London . . . not yet settled: See *Letters* 1: 67–71.

67   Antwerp . . . Hope . . . Scotland: To Poradowska, [8 February 1891] and 17 February 1891, *Letters* 1: 70, 71.

67   stomach . . . rheumatism: To Poradowska, 12 March 1891, *Letters* 1: 73.

67   Census Day: Registrar General 1891 Census RG12/203 (117) p. 4; see also Van Marle (1992).

67   Poles, not separately listed: German Hospital, Dalston: Monthly Report of In and Out Patients: GMR 6/1; German Hospital Reports 1891 to 1894: GHA 15/11, St Bartholomew's Hospital Archives and Museum, London (information courtesy of Allan H. Simmons).

67   fathered a son: Personal communication: Laurence Davies.

68   Gustav Ludwig: Registrar General 1881 Census RG11/0367 (75), p. 14.

68   'fairly respectable . . . drunk': Booth, B362, pp. 6–7.

68   'the hot . . . neighbourhood': To E. L. Sanderson, 24 August 1895, *Letters* 1: 239.

68   hydropathic therapy: Bobrowski to Conrad, 12 April 1891, Najder, ed. (1964), pp. 139–40.

68 La Roseraie: Kirschner (1988); Kirschner in Moore, ed. (1992), pp. 223–54; Bock (2002), pp. 26–40. The last of these offers an extended discussion of Conrad's possible condition and therapies.

69 'for a doctor . . . patient': Maupassant to Henry Cazalis, [août 1891], *Correspondance*, ed. Suffel (1973), Letter No. 705 (translation mine).

69 seventh chapter: *Almayer's Folly*, ed. Eddleman and Higdon (1994), pp. 162–63.

69 fashionable Passy: *Letters* 1: 84, n. 3.

69 on the River Niger: Bobrowski to Conrad, 27 June 1891, Najder, ed. (1964), p. 143.

69 translating: De Ternant (1928).

69 bookkeeping . . . straw plait: To J. B. Pinker, 14 January 1908, *Letters* 4: 21.

69 yawl, the *Nellie*: Lloyd's *Yacht Register*, *1889–1893* establishes that Hope owned the yawl from 1888–89 until 1893, quite precisely limiting the time period of these excursions; see also Stape and Knowles (2006).

70 *Torrens* arrived in Adelaide: *Letters* 1: 105, n. 1.

70 record sixty-five days: See Bruseliuz (Accessed: July 2006).

70 'terribly busy . . . torpor': To Poradowska, 6 April 1892, *Letters* 1: 109.

70 losing . . . diver: Stape and Van Marle (1995): 23.

70 Pulman had died: *A Personal Record*, p. 45; L'viv Historical Archives, cited in Omelan (2004).

70 *Madame Bovary*: To Poradowska, 6 April 1892, *Letters* 1: 109.

70 on the lookout for a captaincy: Bobrowski to Conrad, 18 September 1892, Najder, ed. (1964), p. 164.

71 William Henry Jacques: See *A Personal Record*, pp. 16–18.

71 'for health': See 'The "Torrens": A Personal Tribute,' *Last Essays*, p. 27.

71 'Reminders . . . climate': To Poradowska, 3 February 1893, *Letters* 1: 125.

71 'He was engaged . . . pirate': John Galsworthy to William Archer, 29 September 1906, Stape and Knowles, eds. (1996), p. 53.

72 'most steadfast . . . friends': 'Knopf Document,' ed. Stape, in Moore, Simmons, and Stape, eds. (2000), p. 68.

72 'very young brother': *Lord Jim* (Ch. 21), p. 223.

72 lodgers at 17 Gillingham Street (footnote): Registrar General 1891 Census RG12/72 (152), pp. 16–17.

72 via Berlin and Warsaw: To R. B. Cunninghame Graham, 8 February 1899, *Letters* 2: 158.

72 He fell ill: To Poradowska, 14 September 1893, *Letters* 1: 128.

73 offices of the Shipmasters' Society: See *A Personal Record*, pp. 6–7.

73 pilgrim trade . . . leaky: Personal communication: Stephen Donovan.

73 caught up with Galsworthy: See *Castles in Spain* [1927], pp. 81–82; *The Times*, July–December 1893.

73 Snyder, an American: *Le Journal de Rouen*, 7 décembre 1893: 1; *The Times*, 6 December 1893: 10.

73 dynamite attack: *Le Journal de Rouen*, 10 décembre 1893: 1.

73 bomb-carrying anarchist: To Poradowska, [7 January 1894], *Letters* 1: 142.

74 in litigation: To Poradowska, 18 December 1893, *Letters* 1: 134.

74 attended the opera: *Le Journal de Rouen*, December 1893–January 1894.

74 Paramor . . . Cole: *A Personal Record*, pp. 10, 12, 4. See also Gill (1978) and Gill (1998). Cole's first name, unmentioned by Conrad, is established by the reference to his father's being a retired colonel; see *The New Annual Army List*,

1893, verified by the 1901 Census, which lists Richard Cole as an able-bodied seaman.

74 prospects . . . unappealing: To Poradowska, 20 January 1894, *Letters* 1: 145.

74 'my great passion . . . words': *The Mirror of the Sea*, Dedication and 'Author's Note' (1919), p. x.

75 Bobrowski's death: To Poradowska, 18 February 1894, *Letters* 1: 148.

75 *Tristan und Isolde* . . . Chopin: To Christopher Sandeman, 5 June 1917 (Private collection); Lekime (1894). Poradowska's articles on Chopin appeared in *Revue politique et littéraire* (1899) and *Revue hebdomadaire* (1902).

75 Sanderson at Elstree: Registrar General 1881 Census RG11/1360 (12), p. 18. On the family, see Eddison [1979].

75 'Books . . . places': *A Personal Record*, p. 3.

76 There are two versions: Hamlin Garland, cited in Ray, ed. (1990), p. 41; *Journals of Arnold Bennett*, ed. Newman Flower (1932–33), 2: 1 (16 June 1911).

76 Pseudonym Library: See Bassett (2004): 146.

76 suggested . . . 'rudder': To Poradowska, [18? August 1894], *Letters* 1: 169.

77 'Hold on to this': Chesson 1919 in Ray, ed. (1990), p. 83.

77 'effusively': To Poradowska, 10 October 1894, *Letters* 1: 179.

77 'as inviting . . . reassuring': Garnett (1928), p. xi.

78 National Liberal Club: *Ibid.*, pp. vi–ix.

78 Ellen Hope: Letter from Frances Ellen Hope to James T. Babb, 7 March 1928 (Yale).

78 George family legend: Personal communication: Gill Woods, May 2006. Source cited as Nina Hayward, the only daughter of Jessie's Conrad's sister, Eleanor Grenham (née George).

78 employment as a typist (footnote): To E. B. Redmayne, 23 February 1896, Stape and Van Marle (1995): 32; to Karol Zagórski, 10 March 1896, *Letters* 1: 265.

78 'two-finger typist' (footnote): Personal communication: Nina Hayward, June 2006.

79 known facts: Van Marle (1992); Stape, 'Conradiana' (forthcoming).

79 bricklayer . . . plasterer: Copy of an Entry of Marriage: 31 August 1846: John James Nash Sex and Rachel Anscomb; Copy of Entry of Birth: Jane Nash Sex 1847 St George Hanover Square.

79 customary . . . double name: Personal communication: Nina Hayward, January 2007.

79 painter and glazier: Registrar General 1861 Census RG9/358 (119), p. 1.

79 Having returned home . . . health: Personal communication: Nina Hayward, May 2006.

79 'acute . . . syncope': Copy of an Entry of Death: Alfred Henry George, 18 February 1892; registered Jan–March 1892 Camberwell 1d/776.

80 Henry James . . . Ottoline Morrell: Henry James's comment, cited in Ray, ed. (1990), p. 27.

80 not a Roman Catholic . . . deathbed: Alfred Henry George and Jane Nash Sex married 'according to the Rites and Ceremonies of the Established Church' (Copy of an Entry of Marriage, 5 December 1869). With the evidence then available Han van Marle (1992) stated that one of Jessie Conrad's brothers was a priest; in fact, Leonard had only studied for the priesthood (Copy of an Entry of Death: Alfred Leonard George, 17 July 1903, registered on 20 July; Registration of Death: July–Sept 1903 Lewisham 1d/570). Deathbed conversion

of Jane Nash Sex: Personal communication: Nina Hayward, June 2006.

80   Constance Garnett: For details, see Garnett (1991).

80   her translation . . . *On the Eve*: Ibid., pp. 129, 142–43.

80   'you don't know . . . respect': To Garnett, 20 October 1911, *Letters* 4: 488.

81   'Father in Letters': To Edward Garnett, 16 October 1896, *Letters* 1: 307.

81   'the literary . . . London': Ford, Introduction to *The Sisters* (1928), p. 4.

81   'snug bachelor quarters': Garnett (1928), p. ix.

81   trip to Newfoundland: To Poradowska, [23? February 1895], *Letters* 1: 201.

82   Danish . . . French translation: Ehrsam (1969), pp. 335–36.

82   'powerful' . . . 'story-tellers': *Saturday Review*, 15 June 1895: 797; rpt. Sherry, ed. (1973), p. 53; *The Times*, 28 June 1895: 12.

82   'The book . . . power': *Academy*, 15 June 1895: 52; *Scotsman*, 29 April 1895: 3; *Bookman*, September 1895: 176; rpt. Sherry, ed. (1973), pp. 54, 48, 58.

82   'Mr. Conrad . . . place' . . . letter: Unsigned review *Daily Chronicle*, 11 May 1895: 3; rpt. Sherry, ed. (1973), p. 50. (Henry Norman to Conrad, 16 May 1895, Stape and Knowles, eds. (1996), p. 17, establishes the reviewer's identity; Conrad's letter to Norman, mentioned therein, does not survive.)

83   . . . 650 copies: 'The Texts: An Essay,' *Almayer's Folly*, ed. Eddleman and Higdon (1994), p. 172.

83   Paul . . . literary interests: On his poetry, see the catalogue of the Bibliothèque de Nancy.

83   promised to see Poradowska: To Poradowska, 20 May 1895 and 25 May 1895, *Letters* 1: 220–22.

83   by 4 June: Émilie Briquel, Diary entry of 26 May, cited in Najder (1983), p. 179; *Letters* 1: 224, n. 1.

84   'many worries': To Poradowska, 11 June 1895, *Letters* 1: 229.

84   Edmond Lalitte: Najder (1983), p. 190. He was born on 19 May 1866: Lunéville (IGI); medical studies: Bibliothèque municipale de Nancy.

84   'destroyed' his letters: Najder (1983), p. 181.

85   Arthur Burroughs: Hamer (1967); Registrar General 1881 Census RG11/258 (33), p. 59; 1901 Census RG13/214 (75), p. 39 (which gives Arthur Burroughs's age as thirty-one).

85   Krieger had three children . . . four: Registrar General 1891 Census, cited in Stape, 'Conradiana' (forthcoming).

86   alternate title: To Alfred A. Knopf, 5 September 1913, *Letters* 5: 280.

86   'Stephen . . . priest': Ford, Introduction to *The Sisters* (1928), p. 8.

87   trip to Paris: To E. B. Redmayne, 16 December 1895, Stape and Van Marle: (1995) p. 31.

CHAPTER FOUR: HUSBAND AND WRITER (1896–1898)

89   'I am very *motherly*': Jessie Conrad to Walter Tittle, 1 December 1930 (HRC Texas).

89   'reposeful mattress': Morrell, cited in Ray, ed. (1990), p. 28.

90   'we shall be surprised . . . future': *Manchester Guardian*, 19 May 1896: 5; rpt. Sherry, ed. (1973), p. 77.

90   'If it be possible . . . done': T. P. [O'Connor], *Weekly Sun*, 10 May 1896: 1.

90   'there is plenty . . . satisfied': To Katherine Sanderson, 6 April 1896, *Letters* 1: 271.

90   'scared . . . lodgings': To John Quinn, 18 July 1913, *Letters* 5: 256.

90 married Jessie George: Copy of an Entry of Marriage Jan–March 1896 St George Hanover Square 1a/720 (facsimile of certificate in Sherry (1972), p. 71).

90 'sunny': To Agnes Sanderson, 18 April 1908, *Letters* 4: 77.

90 'little café in Victoria' . . . Overton's: Jessie Conrad (1935), p. 19.

91 'I am glad . . . qualifications': To Katherine Sanderson, 6 April 1896, *Letters* 1: 270.

91 'somewhat unwell . . . days': To Edward Garnett, 9 April 1896, *Letters* 1: 272.

91 'all kitchen . . . upstairs': *Ibid.*

92 9 April: To T. F. Unwin, 9 April 1896 (Private collection).

92 'The coast . . . clouds': To Edward L. Sanderson, 14 April 1896, *Letters* 1: 274.

92 'Is the thing . . . supportable': To Edward Garnett, [13 April 1896], *Letters* 1: 273.

92 raved in his native language: Jessie Conrad (1935), p. 26.

93 'great fun . . . critics': Najder (1983), p. 195.

93 'Just a line . . . on!': Garnett to Conrad, 17 June 1896, Stape and Knowles, eds. (1996), p. 25.

94 request . . . *Cornhill Magazine*: Charles L. Graves to Conrad, 3 June 1896, *ibid.*, p. 24.

94 'It . . . grey mist': To Garnett, 5 August 1896, *Letters* 1: 296.

94 The *Cornhill* took it: *Cornhill Magazine* to Conrad, 19 August 1896, Stape and Knowles, eds. (1996), p. 25; to Garnett, [6 June 1895], *Letters* 1: 285.

95 'A respectable . . . worked': To T. Fisher Unwin, 18 October 1896, *Letters* 1: 308–09.

95 'rather lugubrious': *Return to Yesterday* (1931), p. 52.

95 The Bungalow: See Whitaker (1978) and Pugh (1960).

95 Rorke, who died (footnote): John Rorke Copy of Death Notice, Master's Office, Kimberley, dated 4 March 1908 (date of death 14 November 1895); Helen Sarah Rorke (née Hopps) Death Notice, DN 3343 registered 22 April 1886 (date of death 27 January 1886). (Information courtesy of Pam Barnes.)

95 'Damned . . . hutch': Jessie Conrad (1935), p. 44.

96 'difficult . . . temperament': Unwin (1976), p. 69.

97 wobbly financial state: Henley, *Selected Letters*, ed. Atkinson (2000), p. xv.

97 'the wilds of Essex': To Garnett, 26 March [1897], *Letters* 1: 347.

97 'I . . . endlessly': To Karol Zagórski and Aniela Zagórska, 20 December 1896, *Letters* 1: 324

97 in their luggage: To Garnett, 19 December 1896, *Letters* 1: 323.

97 a fortnight's stay: To E. B. Redmayne, 19 December 1896, Stape and Van Marle (1995): 37.

97 skirted disaster: Chwalewik in Najder, ed. (1983), pp. 174–76.

97 'always . . . Christmas': To Józef Spiridion, 5 April 1897, *Letters* 1: 350.

97 'last . . . scoundrel': Entry 7 April 1775: *Boswell*, ed. Chapman (1970), p. 615.

97 'clung . . . Polonism': Retinger (1941), p. 117.

97 Spiridion . . . late father: Stape, 'Conradiana' (forthcoming). Registration of Death: 'Waldislaw S. Kliszezowski' [*sic*] Jan–March 1891 Cardiff 11a/234.

98 first translation . . . into Polish: Piechota (2005).

98 'My gorge rises . . . novels in English: Najder, ed. (1983), p. 187.

98 'torture chamber': Jessie Conrad (1935), p. 50.

98 nightmares and . . . neuralgia: To Garnett, [10 January 1897], *Letters* 1: 330.

98 Ivy Walls Farm . . . Ellen Hope: See Morrowsmith (1999); Whitaker (1978); Pugh (1960).

101 'hundreds . . . crockery': 'Stephen Crane' (1923), *Last Essays*, p. 105.

101 'an alley cat': Entry of 2 August 1922, Garland, *Diaries*, ed. Pizer (1968), p. 121.

101 'marriage' ceremony: See Gilkes (1960).

101 'interested in the man . . . know': To Garnett, 26 November [1897], *Letters* 1: 413.

102 'He is . . . likes me': To Sanderson, 26 December 1897, *Letters* 1: 434.

102 Heinemann and F. N. Doubleday: Doubleday (1972), p. 121.

102 'The future . . . write': To Sanderson, 26 December 1897, *Letters* 1: 434–35.

102 published . . . 1897: Several standard bibliographical and reference sources give the Heinemann publication date as 2 December. *The Times* of 30 November lists the book among 'Publications To-day', but advertises it the next day as 'Published to-day' (*The Times*, 1 December 1897: 8).

102 'a writer of genius': *Spectator*, 25 December 1897: 940; rpt. Sherry, ed. (1973), p. 93.

102 'On board . . . world': Constance Garnett to Conrad, 30 December 1897, Stape and Knowles, eds. (1996), p. 29.

102 'that . . . miraculous': E. V. Lucas to Conrad, 10 January 1898, *ibid.*

102 'there . . . Fear': W. H. Chesson to Conrad, 13 January 1898, *ibid.*, p. 30.

103 Unwin . . . Pawling's intentions: To T. Fisher Unwin, 7 January 1898, *Letters* 2: 9–10.

103 'My books! . . . water': To Minnie Brooke, 3 January 1898, *Letters* 2: 3.

103 'a woman . . . setting': Grant Allen in the *Spectator*, cited in 'Marie Corelli,' *Wikipedia*.

103 'an infant of male persuasion' . . . midday: To R. B. Cunninghame Graham, 14–15 January 1898, *Letters* 2: 17.

103 midday . . . 'little . . . book': 'Supplementary Notes' in Moore, Simmons, and Stape, eds. (2000), p. 69.

104 'exactly . . . Borys': *Letters* 5: 194, n. 4.

104 Jessie choosing 'Alfred': To Aniela Zagórska, 21 January 1898, *Letters* 2: 23–24.

104 'magnificent . . . monkey': *Ibid.*, 2: 23.

104 'doesn't . . . pig?': To Cora Crane, 27 June 1898, *Letters* 2: 74.

104 'nervous disturbance' . . . gout: To John Galsworthy, [24 January 1898]; to R. B. Cunninghame Graham, 31 January 1898, *Letters* 2: 26, 29.

104 'strong iron cage': To Cora Crane, 25 January 1897, *Letters* 2: 28.

104 '"The Rescue" . . . pages': To Graham, 31 January 1898, *Letters* 2: 31.

105 'And now . . . alone': To Aniela Zagórska, 6 February 1898, *Letters* 2: 37.

105 'nerve trouble . . . hell': To Graham, 16 February 1898, *Letters* 2: 39.

105 invited several people . . . Frederic: To Jane Cobden Unwin, 22 February 1898; to Graham, 5 March 1898, *Letters* 2: 40–41, 44.

105 'as no other . . . progress': *Saturday Review*, 12 February 1898: 211; rpt. Sherry, ed. (1973), pp. 99, 100.

105 'on the theme . . . island': Garnett, Introduction (1928), p. xvi.

105 stay in Brittany: To Stephen Crane, 5 March 1898, *Letters* 2: 43.

105 'some gossip . . . illnesses': To Hamlin Garland, 25 July 1922, Knowles and Stape (2006): 66.

106 'overloaded . . . mountains of words': *The Times*, 16 August 1898: 4.

106 'beastly nervous trouble': To Edward Garnett, 29 March 1898, *Letters* 2: 49.

106 'the despotism . . . wretched health': To Helen Watson, 2 April 1898, *Letters* 2: 52.

106 'We live . . . is': To Aniela Zagórska, *Letters* 2: 56. In the original: *'Que la vie est cruelle et bête!'*

107 'Spring! . . . mankind': To Graham, [14 April 1898], *Letters* 2: 57.

107 McClure offered: To Graham, 5 March 1898, *Letters* 2: 44.

107 'In the course . . . despair': To Garnett, 29 March [1898], *Letters* 2: 49.

107 more short stories: To Garnett, [7 June 1898], *Letters* 2: 66.

107 late 1890s . . . circulation: Finkelstein (2002), p. 166.

107 a return to the sea: To Graham, [2 or 9 July 1898], *Letters* 2: 75.

108 'I am suicidal': To Garnett, 3 August 1898, *Letters* 2: 83.

108 'to do . . . heap of work': To Helen Sanderson, 31 August 1898, *Letters* 2: 91.

108 'Some day . . . yours': To H. G. Wells, 6 September 1898, *Letters* 2: 93.

108 'already . . . distinction': *The Times*, 25 June 1894, p. 3.

108 'a real calamity . . . him': Muriel Dobree, letter of 2 March 1949, cited in Pugh (1960): 55.

108 'Five bedrooms . . . below': To William Rothenstein, [24?] June [1906], *Letters* 3: 337.

108 land title (footnote): 'Postling Court Lodge, 1785,' Brabourne Manuscripts (Ref. U274/T17), Centre for Kentish Studies, Maidstone. Registrar General. 1841 Census HO 107/479/5 on Broadley.

110 'through the sleeping city': Neil Munro (1931) in Ray, ed. (1990), p. 94.

110 'I've destroyed . . . now': To Garnett, [12 October 1898], *Letters* 2: 103.

110 'unutterable rubbish': To Ford Hueffer, [20 October 1898], *Letters* 2: 111.

111 'The affair . . . me': To W. H. Henley, 18 October 1898, *Letters* 2: 107.

111 talking up Hueffer: To Ford, [30 January 1899], *Letters* 2: 154.

111 'bad dream': Olive Garnett Diary, cited in Edel (1972), p. 47.

111 'you began . . . nonsensical': Ford Madox Ford to H. G. Wells, 1 August 1920, Ludwig, ed. (1965), p. 120.

111 'I feel . . . changed': To Garnett, [7 November 1898], *Letters* 2: 116.

111 'a narrative . . . Central Africa': To William Blackwood, 31 December 1898, *Letters* 2: 139.

CHAPTER FIVE: 'THE FATAL PARTNERSHIP': COLLABORATOR AND FRIEND (1899–1904)

113 'I've been . . . B[lack]wood': To Stephen Crane, 13 January 1899, *Letters* 2: 151.

113 'It is . . . marvellous manner': William Blackwood to Conrad, 10 February 1899, Blackburn, ed. (1958), p. 49.

114 'agitation . . . botheration': To Edward Garnett, [31 March 1899], *Letters* 2: 176.

114 'my memory . . . craziness': To John Galsworthy, 17 April 1899, *Letters* 2: 178.

114 'long short story . . .': To Neil Munro, 10 July 1899, *Letters* 2: 187.

114 'I am writing . . . gods': To Garnett, 16 September 1899, *Letters* 2: 198.

115 'Very little . . . endless': In a copy of *The Inheritors*, cited in Zelie (1925), pp. 18–19.

115 'appalling . . . abominable': To David S. Meldrum, 3 December 1899; to Galsworthy, [12 or 19 December 1899], *Letters* 2: 224, 225.

115 'in a nude . . . struggle': *Southend Standard*, 7 December 1899: 7, and 21 December 1899: 7.

115 'murder': To Garnett, 2 December 1899, *Letters* 2: 224.

116 'very solitary': To William Blackwood, 26 December 1899, *Letters* 2: 231.

117 'lucidity . . . easiness': To H. G. Wells, 6 January 1900, *Letters* 2: 239.

117 'unsuccessful . . . astray': *The Times*, 3 September 1901: 9.

117 Marseilles . . . letter . . . Zagórska (footnote): Jessie Conrad (1935), p. 103;

Poradowska to Conrad, 26 avril 1907, Stape and Knowles, eds. (1996), pp. 62–63; to Pinker, 5 February and 10 February 1920, *Letters* 7: 20–22.

118 'wistfully . . . sky': 'Stephen Crane: A Note without Dates' (1919), *Notes on Life and Letters*, p. 45.

118 'I sent wife and child . . . London': To Galsworthy, [20 July 1900], *Letters* 2: 284.

119 talked up . . . 'nightmarish . . . terrible': Jessie Conrad (1935), p. 71.

119 'raw beef . . . water': Jessie Conrad to Cora Crane, 25 August 1900 (Columbia).

119 neuralgia . . . 'cold . . . bowels': To Helen Sanderson, 9 September 1900; to Ford, [mid-September? 1900], *Letters* 2: 293.

120 'that little parvenu . . . books': Lawrence to S. S. Koteliansky, 3 July 1917, *The Letters of D. H. Lawrence* (1984), 3: 692.

120 mere 5 6 : Passenger's manifest: *Aquitania*, Arr. New York, 3 February 1922 (Ellis Island Archives).

120 'the front rank . . . the English language': *The Speaker*, 24 November 1900: 215, cited in Sherry, ed. (1973), p. 120; *New York Times*, 1 December 1900: 8.

120 'graphic . . . formlessness': *Pall Mall Gazette*, 5 December 1900: 4; rpt. Sherry, ed. (1973), pp. 124, 123. (Knowles [1985] establishes the reviewer's identity.)

120 'absolutely enthusiastic': To Meldrum, [27 November 1900], *Letters* 2: 307.

120 'I have to see . . . Garnett': To Galsworthy, [8 December 1900?], *Letters* 2: 309.

120 'the last year . . . Jim': To Blackwood, 30 December 1900, *Letters* 2: 313.

121 'This is the age . . . agent': Heinemann in *Athenaeum*, November 1893, cited in Hepburn (1968), p. 1.

122 *Typhoon* . . . too expensive: George R. Halkett to J. B. Pinker, 21 January 1901 (Berg): see *Letters* 2: 321, n. 1

122 'No doubt . . . first': To J. B. Pinker, 23 January 1901, *Letters* 2: 321.

122 'extremely bad' . . . 'too horrible': To Galsworthy, [10 March? 1901]; to Cora Crane, 24 March 1901; to Galsworthy, 24 March 1901, *Letters* 2: 325–26.

123 'Conrad talks . . . together': Ford Hueffer to John Galsworthy, Ludwig, ed. (1965), p. 15, where it is wrongly dated [March 1901]; as the Hueffers did not arrive in Winchelsea until 10 April (Moser [1974]: 523 citing Mizener [1972], p. 61).

123 'a fine drawing . . . feather': 'Author's Note' (1919), *Typhoon and Other Stories*, p. ix.

124 'shekels' . . . pocket: To Hueffer, [28 June? 1901], *Letters* 2: 335.

124 'A work . . . of the times': Cited in *The Times*, 30 July 1901: 12.

124 'The Fatal partnership': To Garnett, 4 August 1901, *Letters* 2: 351.

124 'Hueffer's story . . . forced': David Meldrum to William Blackwood, 5 August 1901; Blackwood to Conrad, 15 August 1901, Blackburn, ed. (1958), pp. 131, 132.

125 'disastrous year . . . there': To Meldrum, 7 January 1902, *Letters* 2: 367–68.

125 'Really . . . know——': To Pinker, 6 January 1902, *Letters* 2: 365.

125 'about Ships . . . two': To Meldrum, 7 January 1902, *Letters* 2: 368.

126 William Martindale: See Moser (1974): 527; *The Times*, 6 February 1902: 7.

126 'Troubles . . . Whalley': To William Blackwood, 5 June 1902, *Letters* 2: 423.

127 'I am *modern* . . . mouth': To Pinker, 31 May 1902, *Letters* 2: 418.

127 'all my art . . . publishers': To Garnett, 10 June 1902, *Letters* 2: 424.

127 The Royal Literary Fund: See Smith (1990), pp. 2–3.

128 'Cause . . . appreciation' . . . receipt: Application, Royal Literary Fund, signed and dated by Gosse on 17 June 1902; Minutes of 9 July 1902 Meeting at 7 Adelphi Terrace; Receipt signed and dated 11 July 1902, Royal Literary Fund Papers: Case No. 2629 (British Library M1077/107 and M1077/129).

128 'the very finest . . . fortune': Henry James to Edmund Gosse, 26 June 1902, Stape and Knowles, eds. (1996), pp. 36–37.

128 'Quite broken . . . spirited': To Galsworthy, 22 August 1902, *Letters* 2: 439.

128 'Constantly . . . postponed': William L. Alden, *New York Times Book Review*, 13 December 1902: 10; see also Knowles and Stape (forthcoming).

128 'the high-water . . . talent': *Academy and Literature*, 6 December 1902: 606; rpt. Sherry, ed. (1973), p. 132.

129 'most unconvincing . . . rhetoric': *Speaker*, 31 January 1903: 442; *Times Literary Supplement*, 12 December 1902: 372; rpt. Sherry, ed. (1973), pp. 142, 136. On Thomas, see *Times Literary Supplement Centenary Archive* <www.tls.psmedia.com>.

129 'the strongest . . . comparison': George Gissing to Clara Collet, 24 December 1902, cited in Sherry, ed. (1973), p. 140.

129 James . . . toys . . . 'all the talk about him': Olive Garnett: Diary entry of 5 January [1903], cited in Moser (1974): 525.

129 'disliked . . . legend': To Garnett, 22 December 1902, *Letters* 2: 468.

129 'very proper . . . appreciation': S. S. Pawling to Conrad, 3 January 1903, Stape and Knowles, eds. (1996), p. 41.

130 'Of "Typhoon" . . . ass': George Gissing to Conrad, 9 May 1903, *ibid.*, pp. 41–42.

130 Arthur Quiller-Couch: *Bookman* (June 1903): 108–09; rpt. Sherry, ed. (1973), pp. 155–57.

130 Hugh Clifford . . . Thomas Hardy: Ray (1996): 82–84.

131 'Conrad did not . . . confidence': Clifford (1927), p. 8.

131 'The end . . . me': To Ford, [early November 1903], *Letters* 3: 74.

132 'old time regard': To Barrie, 14 November 1903, *Letters* 3: 77.

132 'Always so nervous . . . me!': Ray, ed. (1990), p. 158.

132 'over-sensitised . . . baseness': *Ibid.*, p. 111.

133 'a Grand Seigneur . . . met': T. S. Eliot in conversation with Stravinsky, cited in Stravinsky (1972), p. 71.

133 'I *feel* . . . wreck': To H. G. Wells, 30 November 1903, *Letters* 3: 86.

133 Johnson Club: Johnson Club (1914), pp. 123–24; Various hands (1899), pp. v, xi, xvi.

133 'of no mind . . . emotion': To John Quinn, 24 May 1916, *Letters* 5: 598.

133 'I would help . . . game': To R. B. Cunninghame Graham, 26 December 1903, *Letters* 3: 102.

133 'never talked politics': To Quinn, 24 May 1916, *Letters* 5: 597.

133 'an awful year of it': To Ernest Dawson, 21 December 1903, *Letters* 3: 98.

133 'chilly . . . down': To Harriet Mary Capes, 26 December 1903, *Letters* 3: 98.

134 Galsworthy's study: See Galsworthy (1924), p. 6.

134 'I can dictate . . . hours': To Wells, 7 February 1904, *Letters* 3: 112.

134 Galsworthy wept: Galsworthy to Conrad, 30 September 1906, Stape and Knowles, eds. (1996), p. 54.

135 Lilian M. Hallowes: See Miller (2006a).

135 'tall . . . arm-chair': Borys Conrad (1970), p. 14.

135 the suggestion . . . his mistress: The claim is made by Armstrong, *The Hallowes Genealogy* (Accessed: March 2004).

135 'Half . . . insanity': To Meldrum, 5 April 1904, *Letters* 3: 129.

136 'The sands . . . dead': To Garnett, 6 July 1904; to Ford, 29 July 1904, *Letters* 3: 151, 152.

136 Pinker . . . Wells . . . Gosse: J. B. Pinker to Wells, 18 July 1904, Stape and Knowles, eds. (1996), pp. 43–44; to Gosse, 19 [or 18] August 1904, *Letters* 3: 153–54.

136 Balfour: Edmund Gosse to Henry Newbolt, 26 June 1904 (Private collection; see Knowles forthcoming).

137 'a pathetic . . . unnecessarily': William Rothenstein to Henry Newbolt, 24 May 1905 (Private collection; see Knowles forthcoming).

137 a 36-hour assault: To Ford, 5 September 1904, *Letters* 3: 164.

137 'Finished! . . . water': To Galsworthy, 1 September 1904, *Letters* 3: 158.

137 coolly asked . . . £100: To Pinker, [26 August 1904], *Letters* 3: 156–57.

137 'We really must . . . paper': Harper & Brothers to Conrad, 1 September 1904, Stape and Knowles, eds. (1996), p. 45.

137 'my sojourn . . . absence': 'Author's Note' (1917) to *Nostromo*, p. x.

137 'Personally . . . for': To William Rothenstein, 3 September 1904, *Letters* 3: 163.

138 'The finishing . . . death': To Elsie Hueffer, 19 September 1904, *Letters* 3: 167.

138 mentioning to Graham: Letter to Graham, 7 October 1904, *Letters* 3: 169.

138 'After all . . . trade': To Garnett, 18 March 1921, *Letters* 7: 262.

138 'a bad sendoff': To Pinker, 31 October 1904, *Letters* 3: 178.

138 '*Nostromo* . . . survive it': *TLS*, 21 October 1904: 320; rpt. Sherry, ed. (1973), p. 165. (For the reviewer's identity see, *The Times Literary Supplement Centenary Arhive* <www.tls.psmedia.com>.)

138 'It would . . . demands': *Spectator*, 19 November 1904: 800–01; rpt. Sherry, ed. (1973), p. 179.

139 'the least lucky . . . ignored': To Violet Paget, 12 November 1909 (Private collection).

139 'the slovenliness . . . marks': To Pinker, 19 October 1904, *Letters* 3: 171.

139 'broken-down crocks': To Alice Rothenstein, [4? November 1904], *Letters* 3: 179.

140 'accursed': To Ford, 22 November 1904, *Letters* 3: 183.

140 'Work is the law': 'Tradition' (1918), *Notes on Life and Letters*, p. 153.

141 'extravagance': To Pinker, 4 January 1905, *Letters* 3: 199.

CHAPTER SIX: THE ANALYST OF ILLUSIONS (1905–1909)

142 'a good . . . novel': To J. B. Pinker, 4 January 1905, *Letters* 3: 200.

143 writing 60,000 words . . . weeks: To John Galsworthy, 21 January 1905, *Letters* 3: 208.

143 via Giardini di Augusto: Cerio (n.d.), p. 101.

143 'nearly died of cold': To Edmund Candler, 9 January 1924 (Morgan).

144 'impossible . . . thunder': To Pinker, 23 February 1905, *Letters* 3: 219.

144 'I've done nothing . . . all': To Henry-D. Davray, 12 March 1905, *Letters* 3: 221 (translation mine).

144 'to receive . . . Mother Earth': Mackenzie (1927; rpt. 1964), p. 51.

144 '*petite famille*': To Ford, 9 May 1905, *Letters* 3: 241.

145 'motley . . . piazza': Draper (1929), cited in Holloway (1976), p. 157.

145 friendly . . . Cerio: See Fiorentino (2005).

145 Szembek: See Carabine (2005).

145 'very charming . . . happen': 'Author's Note' (1920) to *A Set of Six*, p. vii.

145 'The scandals . . . flavoured': To Ford, 9 May 1905, *Letters* 3: 241.

146 '*un circolo di degenerati*': *La propaganda* (Naples), 15 October 1902: 1.

147 to enquire of Newbolt: Edmund Gosse to Henry Newbolt, 12 July 1904 (Private collection; see Knowles forthcoming).

147 'the appearance . . . himself': To Edmund Gosse, 16 May 1905, *Letters* 3: 247.

147 'I, in my state . . . day': To Gosse, 11 April 1905, *Letters* 3: 227.

147 'whiff of tainted air': To Pinker, [c. 6 April 1905], *Letters* 3: 226.

148 'get something . . . life': To H. G. Wells, 25 April 1905, *Letters* 3: 234.

148 'condemnation . . . rhapsody': *Weekly Review*, 3 September 1921: 217.

148 'this climate . . . impossible': To Galsworthy, 8 May 1905, *Letters* 3: 239.

148 'I *am* . . . last:' To Pinker, 12 May 1905, *Letters* 3: 243.

148 'of extracts . . . it': *Ibid.*

149 Poradowska . . . Folkestone: Jessie Conrad (1935), p. 103.

149 marked by ill-temper: William Rothenstein to Henry Newbolt, 24 May 1905 (Private collection; see Knowles forthcoming).

149 'hysterical': William Rothenstein to Henry Newbolt, [19 May 1905] and 5 June 1905 (Private collection; see Knowles forthcoming).

149 'especially well just now': Galsworthy to Edward Garnett, 5 July 1905, Garnett, ed. (1934), p. 94.

149 'an exceptionally intelligent . . . ages': 'The Censor of Plays' (1910), *Notes on Life and Letters*, p. 65.

149 'a sort . . . concerned': To Allan Wade, 9 April 1922, *Letters* 7: 451.

150 'awful': To Christopher Sandeman, 27 March 1917 (Private collection).

150 'the exigencies . . . production': H. A. Gwynne to Conrad, 26 October 1905, Stape and Knowles, eds. (1996), p. 51.

150 'nervous . . . sort': To Ada Galsworthy, 31 October 1905, *Letters* 3: 293.

151 Borys . . . complications: William Rothenstein to Henry Newbolt, 3 December 1905 (Private collection; see Knowles forthcoming).

151 Its acceptance . . . for £126: To John Galsworthy, 11 January 1906, *Letters* 3: 308.

151 'constant . . . calamities': To David Meldrum, 5 January 1906, *Letters* 3: 307.

151 'luxury . . . life': To William Rothenstein, 7 February 1906, *Letters* 3: 315.

152 'always . . . manage': Jessie Conrad to Dolly and Harold Moor, 17 September 1924, Carabine and Stape, eds. (2005): 129.

152 'They were born . . . private': 'Author's Note,' *Chance*, p. viii; 'First News,' *Notes on Life and Letters*, p. 140; *The Secret Agent* (Ch. 2), p. 17.

153 Edward Garnett's father: *The Times*, 18 April 1906: 7.

153 'wide, tree-lined': Gindin (1987), p. 248.

153 setting up a luncheon: See Galsworthy to Pinker, 27 May 1906 (HRC Texas); to Pinker, [26 May 1906] but dated [2? June 1906] in *Letters* 3: 334 (on the re-dating, see Stape and Knowles [2006]: 50, n. 1).

153 'by a merciful . . . things': To Galsworthy, 7 July 1906, *Letters* 3: 340.

153 'detached house . . . railings': Gindin (1987), p. 248.

153 'of an amiable . . . disposition': To Jane Wells, 4 August 1906, *Letters* 3: 346.

153 'the wilderness of bricks': To Rothenstein, 21 August 1906, *Letters* 3: 351.

153 'strawberries . . . fruit' (footnote): To Percival Gibbon, [4 or 11 July 1909], *Letters* 4: 253.

154 chorus of praise: See Stape and Knowles, eds. (1996), pp. 54–59.

155 'really appreciative': To Pinker, [mid-October 1906], *Letters* 3: 367.

155 exiled him to the ocean: See to H.-D. Davray, 8 November 1906, *Letters* 3: 372.

155 temperature . . . 'cold . . . brilliant': *Le Petit Méridional* (Montpellier), 18–31 décembre 1906; to R. B. Cunninghame Graham, 31 December 1906, *Letters* 3: 392.

155 'inexpressible . . . colour': To Ford, 8 January 1906, *Letters* 3: 403.

156 'I'm . . . absorbs me': To Davray, 8 January 1906, *Letters* 3: 402 (translation mine).

157 'not . . . shed' . . . told Pinker: *Titus Andronicus*, III. i. 263; to Pinker, 25 May 1907, *Letters* 3: 441.

157 paper birds . . . reading: Borys Conrad (1970), p. 57.

157 'a fresh start . . . live in': To Pinker, 30 July 1906, *Letters* 3: 460.

157 'this damnable outing': *Ibid.*, 459.

158 'old Farmhouse . . . Luton': To Rothenstein, 21 August 1906, *Letters* 3: 467.

158 'a heavenly . . . garden': Diary entry, cited in Gilkes (1960), p. 345.

158 'an honourable failure': To Galsworthy, 6 January 1908, *Letters* 4: 9.

158 'a disappointing . . . slightness' . . . 'simplicity . . . read': Sherry, ed. (1973), pp. 190, 194.

158 'distinctly good': To Wells, [12 October? 1907], *Letters* 3: 500.

158 'sordid . . . squalor': 'Author's Note' (1919), *The Secret Agent*, p. 3.

159 'stately . . . derision': To Galsworthy, 24 October 1907, *Letters* 3: 502.

159 letter to *The Times*: *The Times*, 29 October 1907: 15.

159 'I'm a Pinkerite': Stephen Reynolds to Edward Garnett, 24 July 1907; Reynolds to Pinker, 28 August 1907, Wright, ed. (1923), pp. 93, 97.

159 'proper big welcome': Jessie Conrad to Cora McNeil, 22 October 1907, Knowles and Stape (2006): 67. On 'Mrs Barrett,' see Gilkes (1960), pp. 345–46.

160 'a fair-haired school-boy . . . cap': Jessie Conrad to Cora McNeil, 19 November 1907, Knowles and Stape (2006): 68.

160 'good lunch . . . invalid': Cora Crane, Diary entry of 20 November 1907, cited *ibid.*

160 'the very essence . . . Russian': To Galsworthy, 6 January 1908; to Pinker, 7 January 1908; *Letters* 4: 8–9, 14.

160 'a kind notion . . . good': Stephen Reynolds to J. B. Pinker, 17 December 1907, Wright, ed. (1923), p. 101.

161 Bridge's Fleur-de-Lis Taproom: See Fred Arnold, Ray, ed. (1990), p. 220. Arnold refers to the 'Fleur-de-Lys, Canterbury'; however, neither of two possible locales was so spelled: a hotel at 34 Canterbury High Street, and the Fleur-de-Lis Taproom operating in Bridge's White Horse Inn (Kelly's 1913 *Directory for Kent, Surrey and Sussex*, pp. 1075, 1138). In Bridge High Street, the White Horse was within easy walking distance of Oswalds (Private communication: Keith Carabine), Conrad's home from 1919 to 1924, and seems to be the location at issue. Kelly's Directory also places the White Horse in 'Canterbury' rather than in the small village of Bridge, at the town's outskirts.

161 'the greatest . . . ever known: Norman Douglas, Ray, ed. (1990), p. 121.

161 'last loose shillings': To Galsworthy, 14 January 1908, *Letters* 4: 19.

162 applied . . . for relief: Application, Royal Literary Fund, signed and dated by Gosse on 27 March 1908 (see facsimile in Knowles and Moore [2000], p. 144); Minutes of 8 April 1908 Meeting at 7 Adelphi Terrace; Receipt signed and dated 10 April 1908, Royal Literary Fund Papers: Case No. 2629, British Library, M1077/107 and M1077/129.

162 'life . . . head above water': Galsworthy to Llewelyn Roberts, Secretary of the Royal Literary Fund, 29 March 1908, Stape and Knowles, eds. (1996), pp. 64–65.

162 'an attack . . . dyspepsia': To Pinker, [28? July 1908], *Letters* 4: 97.

162 'I have been ill . . . here': To Ford, [31 July or 7 August? 1908], *Letters* 4: 98.

162 'a man . . . language': To Garnett, 21 August 1908, *Letters* 4: 107.

162 'A writer who ceases . . . homeless person': *Daily News*, 10 August 1908: 3; rpt. Sherry, ed. (1973), pp. 210, 211.

162 'My brain . . . far': To Albert E. Tebb, 4 November 1908 (courtesy of Thomas Czyz).

162 'characteristically English': *Times Literary Supplement*, 13 August 1908: 261.

164 'I felt . . . surrender': 'Poland Revisited' (1915), *Notes on Life and Letters*, p. 119.

164 'a sort of freak . . . English': To Edward Garnett, [4 October 1907], *Letters* 3: 488.

164 'Nothing is more foreign . . . thought': 'Author's Note,' *A Personal Record*, p. vii.

165 'that damned Luton . . . place': To Pinker, 18 September [1908], *Letters* 4: 125.

165 'a supplement . . . women': *The Times*, 1 April 1909: 6.

165 'to make Polish life . . . serfs': To Pinker, [7] October 1908, *Letters* 4: 138.

166 'I can't . . . point': To Elsie Hueffer, 12 December 1908, *Letters* 4: 161.

166 fire . . . in his study: To Pinker, 21 December 1908 (Berg).

166 'little hole': To Ada Galsworthy, 17 January 1909, *Letters* 4: 187.

166 'a little cottage . . . impossible': To Davray, 10 March 1909; to R. D. Mackintosh, [26? March 1909]; to John Galsworthy, 7 September 1909, *Letters* 4: 202, 209, 271.

167 'gone to pieces': To Stephen Reynolds, 30 January 1909, *Letters* 4: 191.

167 'awful piffle': Ford Hueffer to Elsie Hueffer, cited in Saunders (1996): 1: 65.

167 'mania . . . people': To R. D. Mackintosh, 11 April 1909; to Norman Douglas, [14 March 1909], *Letters* 4: 214–15, 205.

168 'horrible . . . revelations': To Galsworthy, 30 April 1909, *Letters* 4: 224.

168 'sounding board': John Conrad (1981), p. 72.

168 'detested . . . bovine': Borys Conrad to Richard Curle, n.d., cited in Anon., *Richard Curle* (1995), p. 54.

168 'I am too English . . . prints': To Pinker, [22 December 1909], *Letters* 4: 307.

169 'that horrible Jew': To Galsworthy, [17 July 1909], *Letters* 4: 255.

169 '*Ragged condition*': To Hueffer, 31 July 1909, *Letters* 4: 263.

169 'serious illness': *English Review*, July 1909: 824.

169 '*impossible*': To Pinker, [4 August 1909], *Letters* 4: 265.

169 'that infernal . . . raving': To Stephen Reynolds, 27 November 1909, *Letters* 4: 293.

169 'for hours on end': Borys Conrad to Richard Curle, cited in Anon., *Richard Curle* (1995), p. 54.

170 long letter: See Carlos M. Marris to Conrad, 18 July 1909, Stape and Knowles, eds. (1996), pp. 66–68.

170 'soft-eyed black-bearded': To Sir Hugh Clifford, 19 May 1910, *Letters* 4: 331.

170 'more of the stories they like': To Pinker, [11 October 1909], *Letters* 4: 278.

170 '*Quite* . . . story': To Pinker, [c. 18 December 1909], *Letters* 4: 300.

170 'fling . . . fire': To Gibbon, 19 December [1909]; to Galsworthy, 22 December 1909, *Letters* 4: 302, 305.

171 'nearly . . . mind': To Galsworthy, *Letters* 4: 305.

171 'Pinker's scalp': To Gibbon, [29 December 1909], *Letters* 4: 312.

CHAPTER SEVEN: BREAKDOWN AND RECOVERY (1910–1914)

172 'did not speak English': To J. B. Pinker, 23 May 1910, *Letters* 4: 334.

172 'complete breakdown . . . months': Jessie Conrad to Pinker, 3 February 1910 (Berg).

173 debt . . . £2,700: See Stape, 'Finances' in Knowles and Moore (2000), pp. 114–16.

174 'Jackolo . . . gravity': To John Galsworthy, 17 May 1910, *Letters* 4: 328.

174 'Gout . . . present': Jessie Conrad to Alice and William Rothenstein, 6 February 1910 (Harvard; courtesy of Keith Carabine).

174 'spoke . . . Pinker': See Jessie Conrad (1935), p. 143.

174 'mixed . . . characters': Jessie Conrad to David Meldrum, 6 February 1910, Blackburn, ed. (1958), p. 192.

175 'I am . . . world': To Galsworthy, 17 May 1910, *Letters* 4: 329.

175 'picturesque and roomy': To William Rothenstein, 20 May 1910, *Letters* 4: 332.

175 'an engaging . . . personality': To E. L. Sanderson, 27 June 1910, *Letters* 4: 345.

176 'Very safe bunkum that': To Galsworthy, [31 May 1910], *Letters* 4: 336.

176 'fiendish': To Galsworthy, [13 July 1910], *Letters* 4: 347.

176 Cadillac . . . 'pony and trap . . .' ditches: John Conrad (1981), p. 46; Borys Conrad (1974), p. [6].

176 'never took a map . . . bit': Borys Conrad, cited in *The Times*, 7 October 1968: 8.

176 'Dear Sir': To Pinker, 23 May 1910, *Letters* 4: 334.

176 cautious intermediary: See Galsworthy to Pinker, [19 July 1910], Stape and Knowles (2006): 54.

177 Jessie Conrad's version . . . Borys's: See Jessie Conrad (1935), pp. 153, 158–59; Borys Conrad (1970), pp. 68–69.

177 petition . . . Asquith: *The Times*, 15 June 1910: 7.

177 'take all possible . . . style': *The Times*, 20 July 1910: 10.

177 'As you have thought . . . pace': To Pinker, 20 August 1910, *Letters* 4: 361.

178 'in a sense . . . side': To E. L. Sanderson, 7 June 1911, *Letters* 4: 449.

178 resigned it: From HM Assistant Paymaster General to Conrad, 6 June 1917, Stape and Knowles, eds. (1996), p. 123.

178 Hugh Clifford . . . Gordon Bennett: See Clifford (1927), p. 15.

178 Jessie's leg . . . 'flat and sceptical': To Galsworthy, 25 September 1910, *Letters* 4: 367.

179 polishing 'A Smile of Fortune': See Reid (2006).

179 'vigorous agitation': *The Times*, 23 November 1910: 8.

179 'I can't . . . somehow': To Pinker, 10 December 1910, *Letters* 4: 395.

179 'miserable mental state': To Harriet Mary Capes, 22 December 1910, *Letters* 4: 395.

179 'silly story': To Garnett, 12 January 1911, *Letters* 4: 407.

179 'I am . . . *Chance*': To Ford, 29 March 1911, *Letters* 4: 433.

179 'no two . . . world': To Galsworthy, [15 February 1911], *Letters* 4: 414.

180 the story earned £60: To Pinker, 2 March 1911, *Letters* 4: 418.

180 'Slow Dam' slow': To Galsworthy, 15 March 1911, *Letters* 4: 429.

180 'I did not write . . . gale': To Ford, 29 March 1911, *Letters* 4: 434.

180 signed a contract: See Nash (1941), pp. 171–73.

180 'I can't . . . subject': To Thomas, [early Summer? 1911], *Letters* 4: 444.

181 'No . . . girls': To Garnett, 5 November 1912, *Letters* 5: 128.

181 'a good cry': To Galsworthy, 23 September 1911, *Letters* 4: 479.

181 André Gide . . . Valéry Larbaud . . . Agnes Tobin: See Steel (2000).

182 'like a nightmare': To Galsworthy, [18 August 1911], *Letters* 4: 473.

183 'Never . . . forget': To Douglas, [16 or 23 October 1911], *Letters* 4: 487.

183 'I suppose . . . salt': To Garnett, 20 October 1911, *Letters* 4: 488.

183 'entitled . . . us': *Pall Mall Gazette*, 11 October 1911: 5, and *Morning Post*, 12 October 1911: 3; rpt. Sherry, ed. (1973), pp. 227, 231.

183 'It positively pains me . . . do': To Pinker, [20 November 1911], *Letters* 4: 507.

183 'The last . . . Horrors!': To Garnett, 28 December 1911, *Letters* 4: 530.

184 'I hesitate . . . Elba': To Pinker, 23 [=24] January 1912, *Letters* 5: 10.

184 'working lamp . . . black': To John Quinn, 27 March 1912, *Letters* 5: 43.

185 'stupefied for a fortnight': To André Gide, 14 April 1912, *Letters* 5: 53.

185 Pinker . . . at white heat: See Telegram from Conrad to Pinker, 23 April 1912, received in London at 4.18 p.m. (Berg); Maxwell (1924); Megroz (1922).

185 'very . . . kind': 'Some Reflexions on the Loss of the *Titanic*' (revised title) in *Notes on Life and Letters*, p. 171.

185 'Trade . . . linen': 'Some Aspects of the Admirable Inquiry into the Loss of the *Titanic*' (revised title), *Notes on Life and Letters*, p. 191.

186 the novella was simmering: To Pinker, [19 May 1912], *Letters* 5: 67.

186 'long short story': To Garnett, 27 May 1912, *Letters* 5: 71.

186 'somewhat less nervous . . . vitality': Arthur Symons to Rhoda Symons, 1 June [1912], Stape and Knowles, eds. (1996), p. 82.

186 'a worthy . . . antiquity: To Sir Sidney Colvin, 13 August 1912, *Letters* 5: 96.

186 prize day: *The Times*, 27 July 1912: 8.

186 'I don't know . . . crow': To Pinker, [19 August 1912], *Letters* 5: 101.

186 'formally': To Pinker, [3 September 1912], *Letters* 5: 105.

186 an interview: *New York Times Magazine*, 17 November 1912: 4; rpt. in Ray, ed. (1990), pp. 21–26.

187 meeting . . . (1909): *The Times*, 22 February 1921: 9; Passenger manifest, *Berlin*, Dep. Gibraltar 18 October 1909 Arr. New York 26 October (Ellis Island Archives).

187 'quite the best . . . insight': Edward Garnett to Richard Curle, 10 October 1912 (Lilly), cited in Anon (1995), p. 13.

187 'All . . . comparison': To Garnett, 16 October 1912, *Letters* 5: 117.

187 'a big sort . . . chap': Garnett to Conrad, [c. 15 October 1912], Stape and Knowles, eds. (1996), p. 86.

187 'rather . . . hurt': Richard Curle to Hugh Walpole, 7 December 1921 (HRC Texas).

188 'Rousing . . . day': To Arnold Bennett, 17 November 1912, *Letters* 5: 135.

188 'Talleyrand . . . tactless': Malcolm Muggeridge, cited in Biskupski (1998): 62, 39.

188 'objective . . . reticent': Retinger (1941), p. 116.

188 'The very . . . girl': To Colvin, [late 1912?], *Letters* 5: 141–42.

188 'The more one is anxious . . . inkstand': To Pinker, [17 November 1912], *Letters* 5: 136.

189 'the vapid depths . . . stuff': To Norman Douglas, 16 December 1912, *Letters* 5: 148.

189 'indispensable . . . life': Display advertisement for the *English Review*, *The Times*, 3 November 1913: 13.

189 Gide . . . Brighton . . . toys: *Correspondance André Gide/Jacques Copeau*, ed. Jean Claude (1987), 1: 694; John Conrad (1981), p. 35.

189 his son recalls: John Conrad, BBC Third Programme 1947 (HRC Texas).

189 'face . . . size': To Pinker, 20 February 1913, *Letters* 5: 181.

189 bread pellets . . . calf's head: John Conrad (1981), p. 190; Personal communication: Nina Hayward, May 2006.

190 decision not to serialise: J. M. Dent to Conrad, 13 February 1913 (Berg), cited in *Letters* 5: 177, n. 2.

190 'I don't shake . . . sleeve' replied: To Messrs Methuen & Co., 21 March 1913, *Letters* 5: 195; Methuen & Co. to Conrad, 2 April 1913 (Yale).

190 'a killing job simply': To Pinker, [26 May 1913], *Letters* 5: 225.

190 'biggest . . . work': To Pinker, [1 June 1913], *Letters* 5: 229.

190 annual . . . trip: Doubleday had been in England in 1906, 1907, 1908, 1909, 1911, and 1912 (see Ellis Island Archives).

191 'very . . . ungentlemanly': John Galsworthy to Pinker, 2 November 1914, Stape and Knowles (2006): 60.

191 Fresh Air Art Society: See *The Times*, 23 June 1913: 11; 29 November 1913: 11.

192 openly racist views: On his racism, see Kushner (Accessed: December 2006).

192 'life at sea . . . hypersensitivity': Cited in Ray, ed. (1990), pp. 27, 28.

192 'The emotion . . . affairs': Russell (1967–69), 1: 281; see also Knowles 1990b.

192 'all . . . egotism': To Bertrand Russell, 13 September 1913, *Letters* 5: 282.

193 'horrible . . . epidemic': To Pinker, 29 December 1913, *Letters* 5: 322.

193 Powell . . . men: Several websites available in 2006 'out' Powell: see <www.365gay.com/lifestylechannel/intime/months/09-September/September. htm>, <www.andrejkoymasky.com>, <www.youthfirsttexas.org/ famous_gay_ people.html>.

194 'delightfully ladylike': To R. B. Cunninghame Graham, 23 January 1914, *Letters* 5: 336.

194 'qualms . . . it went on': Bertrand Russell to Conrad, 22 January 1914, Stape and Knowles, eds. (1996), p. 95.

194 'a bore . . . early novels': W. H. Hudson to Lady Margaret Brooke, [February 1914], *ibid.*, p. 96.

194 'prolonged . . . doing': 'The New Novel,' *Times Literary Supplement*, 19 March and 2 April 1914; rpt. Sherry, ed. (1973), pp. 267, 265.

194 'infinitely . . . time': Henry James to Edith Wharton, 27 February 1914, *ibid.*, p. 97.

195 'It had . . . reception': To F. N. Doubleday, 29 January 1914, *Letters* 5: 339.

195 delivery by 1 May: Conrad's due dates vary: He reported the novel due by mid-April to William Rothenstein, 17 February 1914; the 1 May date is mentioned to Bertrand Russell, 17 February 1914, and to Eric S. Pinker, [9 April 1914], *Letters* 5: 354, 355, 371.

195 'the devil . . . editor': To Russell, 4 February 1914, *Letters* 5: 345.

195 sale price was $6,000: Garland (1932), p. 533.

195 'a once noble . . . undertaker': William Allen White, *Emporia Gazette* (Kansas) on Frank A. Munsey's death in December 1925.

195 'early books . . . "frost"': Garland (1932), p. 533.

195 'The Island Story' . . . 'a long . . . dreary machine': To Warrington Dawson, 17 February 1914; to William Rothenstein, 17 February 1914, *Letters* 5: 351, 354.

195 'I am not blind . . . earth': To Garnett, 23 February [1914], *Letters* 5: 358.

196 first-class certificate: Cadet report: Alfred Borys Conrad. Date of entry in HMS *Worcester* 22 September 1911; date of leaving 23 April 1914; awarded first class in scholastics and seamanship (Marine Society, London, courtesy of Richard Niland).

196 Robey: See Borys Conrad (1970), p. 88.

196 'mixed feelings' . . . 'much rather': To Galsworthy, 25 July 1914, *Letters* 5: 407.

196 Galsworthy wondered: Galsworthy to Pinker, 28 July 1914 (HRC Texas).

197 Retinger . . . *The Rescue*: Galsworthy to Pinker, 23 October 1914, cited in Stape and Knowles (2006): 59.

197 'We . . . plight': Conrad to Pinker, 15 September 1914, *Letters* 5: 412.

198 shooting-gallery: Borys Conrad (1970), pp. 99–100.

198 government order: See Frederic C. Penfield to F. N. Doubleday, 9 December 1914 (Yale), and 'Poland Revisited,' *Notes on Life and Letters*, p.136 .

198 Edmund Candler: On the meeting and friendship, see Corkhill (2005).

198 by April in Egypt: Eric S. Pinker: National Archives Medal Card WO/372/16 (Image No. 2187).

CHAPTER EIGHT: THE ENGLISHMAN (1915–1919)

199 'The shadow . . . loins': To Eugene F. Saxton, 17 August 1915, *Letters* 5: 500.

199 'sort of sick-apathy': To Ada and John Galsworthy, 15 November 1914, *Letters* 5: 424.

199 'actual war experiences': Eugene F. Saxton to J. B. Pinker, 22 January 1915 (Berg).

200 'First Command' . . . October': To J. B. Pinker, 3 February 1915, *Letters* 5: 441.

200 'false realism': *Daily Telegraph*, 3 March 1915: 4.

200 'not so much art . . . efforts:' To John Galsworthy, [March? 1915], *Letters* 5: 455.

201 'not quite half': To Pinker, [7 April 1915] (MS Berg).

201 'ugly . . . adventure': To John Quinn, 18 April 1915, *Letters* 5: 468.

201 'Wretched . . . sinister': To Galsworthy, 10 April 1915], *Letters* 5: 467.

201 'strongest . . . rooted': To Quinn, 18 April 1915, *Letters* 5: 468.

201 'There's no doubt . . . book': *The Times*, 29 March 1915: 5.

201 'Russian names' were to appear: To Ignace Paderewski, [27 March 1915], *Letters* 5: 460.

201 'Under . . . review': *The Times*, 1 June 1915: 6.

202 'indubitably . . . conviction': Note to the First Edition, *Victory* (1915), p. viii.

202 Garnett . . . cold steel: *The Times*, 13 November 1962: 14.

202 'for *Safe keeping*': To Pinker, [10 June 1915], *Letters* 5: 481.

203 Cunninghame Graham . . . torpedoed: Watts and Davies (1979), p. 242.

203 'fresh complexion . . . attire': John Conrad (1981), p. 104.

203 'deplorable': To Warrington Dawson, 11 August 1915, *Letters* 5: 498.

204 'war atmosphere . . . sight': To F. N. Doubleday, 17 September 1915, *Letters* 5: 509.

204 'listening . . . patrol airship?': To Eugene F. Saxton, 17 August 1915, *Letters* 5: 500.

204 'Yes mon cher! . . . pieces': To Ford, [30 August 1915], *Letters* 5: 503.

204 commission as second lieutenant: To Iris Wedgwood, 22 September 1915 (Private collection).

204 'Portal . . . earth': To Ford, 19 October 1915, *Letters* 5: 519.

204 Hadji . . . moped: To Galsworthy, 23 September 1915, *Letters* 5: 513.

205 'an alarming . . . gout': Jessie Conrad to J. B. Pinker, 13 October 1915, cited in *Letters* 5: 520, n. 2.

205 'Frank' . . . Egypt: Private communication: Nina Hayward, June 2006.

205 'to be running . . . itself': To Pinker, 23 December 1915, *Letters* 5: 542.

205 'this . . . slaughter': To E. L. Sanderson, 24 December 1915, *Letters* 5: 545.

205 'All . . . front' (footnote): To Pinker, [c. 21 November 1916], *Letters* 5: 678; Private communication: Nina Hayward, June 2006.

205 'It is extraordinary . . . language': *A Personal Record*, p. 71.

206 'It is very interesting here': To Pinker, [6 January 1916], *Letters* 5: 551.

206 'incoherent' joy: To Ford, 19 October 1915, *Letters* 5: 519.

206 'absolutely boyish': To William Rothenstein, 9 May 1916, *Letters* 5: 586.

206 *'cette guerre . . . engagée'*: To Graham, 28 October 1915, *Letters* 5: 526.

206 helped his mother-in-law: To Pinker, [c. 21 November 1916], *Letters* 5: 678.

206 'We . . . intimate': To Pinker, [3 or 10 May 1916], *Letters* 5: 584.

207 'too filthy . . . of': John Quinn to Conrad, 29 June 1916 (Berg), cited in *Letters* 5: 620, n. 3.

207 'a stab . . . back': To Quinn, 15 July 1916, *Letters* 5: 620.

207 inquiry . . . in 2002 (footnote): The committee, struck at Goldsmith College, University of London, pronounced in March 2002.

207 Clifford's . . . brother . . . Curle's wife: Wedgwood: Clifford: Commonwealth War Graves Commission; Wedgwood: see Conrad to Iris Wedgwood, 8 July 1916 (Private collection); Cameron: 'Fallen Officers,' *The Times*, 21 December 1915: 5; Curle: Woodhouse, *The Guardian*, 4 October 2006.

208 'curious impression': To Pinker, 4 July 1916, *Letters* 5: 615.

208 'small house . . . rooms': Jane Anderson Taylor to Deems Taylor, 19 April 1916, cited in Halverson and Watt (1991): 63.

208 'fishy': Rebecca West to Ian Watt, 19 May 1959, cited *ibid.*, 75.

208 Buffalo Bill Cody: Pegolotti (2003), p. 29.

208 'very beautiful . . . manner': Cited in Halverson and Watt (1991): 74.

208 'dear Chestnut filly': To Jessie Conrad, 29 September 1916, *Letters* 5: 666.

209 'quite yum-yum': To Richard Curle, 20 August 1916, *Letters* 5: 637.

209 'a nervous breakdown': Pegolotti (2003), p. 44.

209 'clenched . . . rolled into one': Payne (1961), p. 218.

209 reading the novel: Lord Northcliffe to Conrad, 7 August 1916, Stape and Knowles, eds. (1996), p. 108.

209 old friend of Hugh Clifford: Hugh Clifford to Conrad, 31 May 1921, *Ibid.*, p. 179.

209 'great void' . . . South Africa: To Curle, 20 August 1916, *Letters* 5: 637; Anon (1995), p. 7.

210 'very strung-up . . . whirl': To Jessie Conrad, [15 September 1916], *Letters* 5: 662.

210 Jessie's . . . version: *Blue Peter*, 11 (1931): 252–55.

211 'almost tempestuous': To Pinker, [27 November 1916], *Letters* 5: 679.

211 He received 'V. Poor' (footnote): Cadet report: Robert Sholto Douglas. Date of entry in HMS *Worcester* 21 September 1916; date of leaving December 1918 (Marine Society, London; information courtesy of Richard Niland). (Conrad's name and address appear on the record as guardian, a position he later relinquished to a Mrs Uniake.)

211 left in January: Passenger manifest: *La Touraine*, ex. Bordeaux, Arr. New York, 25 January 1917 (Ellis Island Archives).

211 advice of Conrad: Mullin. (Accessed August 2005).

211 revise an article: Pegolotti (2003), p. 44, citing the diary of Jane Anderson's father.

212 'It's very Young . . . life': To Pinker, [17? December 1916], *Letters* 5: 691–92.

212 'rather deliriously . . . façade': Hueffer to Conrad, 19 December 1916, Stape and Knowles, eds. (1996), p. 117.

212 *'un homme à . . . femmes'*: To Quinn, [late January 1917], *Letters* 6: 21.

212 'really fine officer': To Pinker, [16 January 1917], *Letters* 6: 9.

212 *'des idées de gentilhomme'*: To Graham, 17 January 1917, *Letters* 6: 10.

212 'this business . . . language': Perceval Gibbon to Conrad, 27 February 1917, Stape and Knowles, eds. (1996), p. 120.

212 three articles: See to Pinker, [early January 1917], *Letters* 6: 7.

212 Lieutenant Conrad: See to Pinker, 2nd letter of [16 January 1917], *Letters* 6: 9.

213 'without much grip on': To F. N. Doubleday, 20 January 1917, *Letters* 6: 14.

213 'curiously . . . obvious': To Pinker, [*c.* 12 February 1917], *Letters* 6: 28.

213 'I creep . . . crawls': To Pinker, [24 January 1917]; [early February 1917], *Letters* 6: 16, 24.

213 'no interest whatever': To Hugh R. Dent, 19 March 1917, *Letters* 6: 46.

213 'tone of elation': To Wedgwood, 22 March 1917, *Letters* 6: 51.

213 'very respectful': To Pinker, 26 March 1917, *Letters* 6: 53.

213 'never-ending sorrow': To Iris Wedgwood, 22 March 1917, *Letters* 6: 51.

213 'who . . . nightmare?': To Richard Curle, 27 March 1915 [= 1917], *Letters* 6: 55.

214 'I saw her . . . cried': To Sir Sidney Colvin, [21 April 1917], *Letters* 6: 74.

214 'warlike caper': To Pinker, [11? April 1917], *Letters* 6: 69.

214 'not noisy . . . fine': To W. T. H. Howe, 20 April 1917, *Letters* 6: 72.

214 'O! . . . brains': To Pinker, [2 May 1917], *Letters* 6: 83.

214 '5 words . . . twenty-four': To Pinker, [19 June 1917], *Letters* 6: 103.

214 'dislike . . . mentality': J. H. Retinger to Ian Watt, 15 May 1957, cited in Halverson and Watt (1991): 85.

214 'qualified . . . Russian': To Garnett, [late April 1917], *Letters* 6: 78.

215 Civil List pension: To Paymaster General, 2 June 1917, *Letters* 6: 96; HM Assistant Paymaster General to Conrad, 6 June 1917, Stape and Knowles, eds. (1996), p. 123.

215 'Certainly I carried . . . pleasant': To Dolly Moor, 31 January 1924, Carabine and Stape (2005): 128.

215 'even harder . . . before': To Edith Wharton, 1 October 1917, *Letters* 6: 128.

215 Ashford Grammar School: John Conrad's version is muddled (1981, pp. 110–11). He entered Ashford Grammar School not in 1915, as he says, but in the autumn of 1917 (To Pinker, 15 August 1917, *Letters* 6: 115–16) and went to Ripley Court only in January 1918 (To Pinker, [10 or 11 January 1918] and [13 January 1918], *Letters* 6: 172–73).

216 'I am attending . . . it': To Pinker, 27 September 1917, *Letters* 6: 126.

216 'We shall be giving . . . not': *Nostromo* (Pt 1, Ch. 6), p. 77.

216 'I am chilly . . . aside': To Ada and John Galsworthy, 31 December 1917, *Letters* 6: 163.

217 Dolly . . . Battle of Cambrai: See Carabine and Stape (2005); Stape and Carabine (2006).

217 air-raid warnings: Borys Conrad (1970), p. 128.

217 'delightful . . . vitality': Henry James to A. C. Benson, 5 June 1909, *The Letters of Henry James*, ed. Edel (1984), cited in 4: 522; James to Hugh Walpole, 19 May 1912, cited in Henry James, *Dearly Beloved Friends*, ed. Gunter and Jobe (2001), p. 178.

217 'even better . . . Corsair': Walpole: Diary entry of 23 January 1918 (HRC Texas).

217 '*un repas* . . . plates': To Hugh Walpole, 30 January 1918, *Letters* 6: 178.

218 'As melancholy . . . ever': Walpole: Diary entry of 8 February 1918 (HRC Texas).

218 'a moody . . . away': To Cecil Roberts, 19 February 1918, *Letters* 6: 188.

218 Ripley Court Survey: John Conrad (1981), p. 111; to Pinker, [13 January 1918], *Letters* 6: 173.

218 'there . . . quiet': John Conrad (1947; transcript HRC Texas).

218 'the dear . . . collar': To John Galsworthy, [25 February 1918], *Letters* 6: 189.

218 *'de bon coeur'*: To Lord Northcliffe, 7 March 1918, *Letters* 6: 192.

218 'eminently distinguished': To Pinker, 14 March 1918, *Letters* 6: 193.

218 'feverish . . . clay': *Ibid.*, 194; to Walpole, 30 January 1918, *Letters* 6: 195.

218 'horrible time': To Pinker, 8 April 1918, *Letters* 6: 199.

219 'in the thick of things': To Garnett, 27 March 1918, *Letters* 6: 198.

219 Military Cross: *London Gazette*, Supplement of 26 September 1917: 9978; to Pinker, [13 September 1917], *Letters* 6: 121.

219 'very bad': To Borys Conrad, 27 April 1918, *Letters* 6: 204.

219 'the best . . . time': *The Times*, 27 April 1918: 9.

219 'a military . . . temperament': To Colvin, 28 April 1918, *Letters* 6: 206.

219 'I have no earthly . . . caste': Edward Garnett to Conrad, 13 May 1918, Stape and Knowles, eds. (1996), p. 129.

219 'The beastly thing . . . Stretches': To Pinker, [3 May 1918], *Letters* 6: 209.

219 'It's probably rubbish': To Helen Sanderson, 20 April 1918, *Letters* 6: 202.

219 'racial . . . Christian': To Lewis Browne, 15 May 1918, *Letters* 6: 215–16.

219 'he sent . . . subject': *Ibid.*, 6: 216.

220 'purely Polish . . . Italian': *New York Times Book Review*, 9 May 1926: 25; see Preface.

220 The allegation . . . England (footnote): Fothergill (2006), pp. 133–65.

220 'lapdog': Personal communication: the late Hans van Marle.

220 'simply superb . . . fine': Walpole: Diary entry of 2 June 1918 (HRC Texas).

221 'beastly seedy': To Walpole, 12 August 1918, *Letters* 6: 252.

221 'doing . . . anything': To Pinker, [17 August 1918], *Letters* 6: 254.

221 'charming person': To Colvin, 9 September 1918, *Letters* 6: 265.

221 'to go to Capel House . . . "malheurs"': J. H. Retinger to Jessie Conrad, 7 August 1918 and 9 August 1918 (HRC Texas).

222 'moral claim': To Thomas J. Wise, 2 October 1918, *Letters* 6: 276.

222 chlorine gas . . . shellshock: To Pinker, [23 October 1918]; to Pinker, [20 November 1918], *Letters* 6: 292, 307.

222 'soberly thankful': To Colvin, 11 November 1918, *Letters* 6: 301.

222 'Great . . . world': To Walpole, 11 November 1918, *Letters* 6: 302.

222 Nellie Lyons . . . dead: Registration of Death, Jan–March 1919 Elham 2a/1992; to Pinker, 21 January, *Letters* 6: 348.

223 'moody fits': Jessie Conrad (1935), p. 212.

223 'Shellshock . . . men': *The Times*, 9 June 1921: 7.

223 'detestable. . . purposes': To Garnett, 22 December 1918, *Letters* 6: 335.

223 Cunninghame Graham . . . politically active: See R. B. Cunninghame Graham to Conrad, 24 December 1918, Stape and Knowles, eds. (1996), p. 136; Watts and Davies (1979), pp. 243–46.

223 Doubleday honeymoon: See <www.FamilySearch.org>.

223 'care a damn': To Pinker, 26 February 1919, *Letters* 6: 373.

224 'American influence . . . be': To Sir Hugh Clifford, 25 January 1919, *Letters* 6: 349.

224 Oswalds: Personal communication: Wolfgang Kierck, June 2004; Borys Conrad (1974), pp. [11–13].

225 'with great and increasing . . . end': *Daily Telegraph* review, cited in *The Times*, 29 March 1919: 12.

225 King and Queen: *The Times*, 2 April 1919: 15.

225 Maugham's . . . Rostand: *The Times*, 24 March 1919: 16.

225 'very . . . unwell': To Pinker, 30 April 1919, *Letters* 6: 411.

225 'charming house . . . odious': To Captain Anthony Halsey, 5 May 1919; to Garnett, 7 July 1919, *Letters* 6: 415, 444.

225 attracting numerous visitors: Borys Conrad (1974), p. [8].

225 'savage . . . pessimistic': To Colvin, [14 or 21? May 1919], *Letters* 6: 421.

226 'Jane . . . distracted': To Pinker, 27 May 1919, *Letters* 6: 429.

226 'double and treble . . . lightly': *Morning Post*, 6 August 1919: 3; *New Statesman*, 16 August: 498; rpt. Sherry, ed. (1973), pp. 314–16, 322.

226 'very poor . . . none': To Colvin, 7 August 1919, *Letters* 6: 459.

226 'failing powers': To Pinker, 14 August 1919, *Letters* 6: 465.

227 *Publishers Weekly* . . . copies: Cited in Marages (Accessed: January 2007).

227 '*Arrow of Lead*': E. M. Forster to Robert Trevelyan, 23 February 1920, *Selected Letters of E. M. Forster*, ed. Lago and Furbank (1983–85): 1: 314.

227 Borys . . . pension: Borys Conrad (1970), p. 153.

227 'with a few sticks . . . carpets': To Curle, 15 October 1919, *Letters* 6: 505.

227 'well advanced': To Pinker, 7 October 1919, *Letters* 6: 502.

227 Burys Court: See <www.buryscourtschool.co.uk/html/history.htm>.

228 'I have . . . kind': To J. M. Dent, 25 October 1919, *Letters* 6: 509.

228 'between "Rebecca" & "Doris"': Cunninghame Graham to Conrad, 25 October 1919, Stape and Knowles, eds. (1996), p. 143.

228 '43' club: See Najder (1983), pp. 464–65.

228 'Cocaine . . . criminals': Shore (Accessed: September 2005).

228 father's sex life: Personal communication: the late Hans van Marle.

228 'I feel my approaching . . . return': To Walpole, 19 September 1919, *Letters* 6: 490.

228 'a woman . . . *The Arrow*': To G. Jean-Aubry, 14 October 1919, *Letters* 6: 503; see Gide to Conrad, 4 November and 21 November 1919, Stape and Knowles, eds. (1996), pp. 145–49.

229 'Personally . . . production': To Pinker, 11 November 1919, *Letters* 6: 519–20.

229 'keep a list . . . bye': To Curle, 12 November 1919, *Letters* 6: 521.

230 daughter-in-law: Borys Conrad (1970), p. 143.

230 'Life . . . here': To Pinker, [2 or 3 December 1919], *Letters* 6: 539.

230 'rather heavy . . . impossible': To Pinker, 10 December 1919; to Curle, 12 December 1919, *Letters* 6: 541.

230 'air of faded gentility': John Conrad (1981), p. 127.

230 'a beastly complaint . . . more': To Garnett, 1 January 1920, *Letters* 7: 3.

CHAPTER NINE: 'SMILING PUBLIC MAN' (1920–1924)

231 'where . . . Conrad!': Huneker (1922), p. 172.

231 'tidying up': 'Author's Note' (1920), *Notes on Life and Letters*, p. 3.

232 'managed . . . cab-drive': To John Galsworthy, 28 March 1920, *Letters* 7: 63.

232 'more knife-work': To Eric S. Pinker, [27 April 1920], *Letters* 7: 87.

232 'a four-inch . . . bone': To Pinker, 2 [= 3] May 1920, *Letters* 7: 89.

232 'I have grown . . . wits': To Lady Colvin, 13 May 1920, *Letters* 7: 95.

233 'why should I . . . book': To Pinker, [15 May 1920], *Letters* 7: 96.

233 'depths of the dumps': To Hugh Walpole, 14 June 1920, *Letters* 7: 111.

233 'the greatest novel . . . absorption': *Punch*, 14 July 1920: 39, and *Sketch*, 21 July 1920: 428; rpt. Sherry, ed. (1973), pp. 336, 342.

233 'long and elaborate . . . him': *Times Literary Supplement*, 1 July 1920: 419; rpt. Sherry, ed. (1973), p. 335.

234 John Powell: 'Concerts &c.,' *The Times*, 21 May 1920: 14; to Warrington Dawson, 9 July 1920, *Letters* 7: 131.

234 'uneasy' . . . *Mirror of the Sea*: See Hoenselaars and Moore (1995).

235 'I was grateful . . . this': To Lady Millais, 20 January 1921, *Letters* 7: 247.

236 'I have done nothing . . . long': To Edward Garnett, 16 December 1920, *Letters* 7: 220.

236 'the conquest of Corsica': To Walpole, 26 December 1920, *Letters* 7: 226.

236 'two or three months': To Aniela Zagórska, 19 January 1921, *Letters* 7: 247.

236 Mary . . . Œnone: The presence of Mrs Pinker and Œnone is attested by passports issued to 'Mary E.' and 'Mary O.' Pinker for travel to France on 26 January 1921 (National Archives FO 610/162/Sheet No. 4027). Conrad's passport was issued on 22 January (FO 610/162/Sheet No. 4003B), replacing a previous passport issued on 23 July 1914 (FO 610/123). See also Jessie Conrad (1935), p. 223.

237 'Throw care . . . dispatch': To J. B. Pinker, 30 January 1921, *Letters* 7: 255.

237 'Cold. Wet . . . wilder': To Eric S. Pinker, 5 February 1921, *Letters* 7: 256.

237 '*charmants*': To G. Jean-Aubry, 23 February 1921, *Letters* 7: 258.

238 true relaxation: On the excursion, see Jessie Conrad (1935), pp. 230–35.

240 'close sitting': To J. B. Pinker, 30 September 1921, *Letters* 7: 344.

240 'Those things . . . vision!': To William Rothenstein, 17 November 1921, *Letters* 7: 372.

240 'Seedy . . . pain': To R. B. Cunninghame Graham, 6 December 1921, *Letters* 7: 390.

241 'within . . . limits': To Pinker, 19 December 1921, *Letters* 7: 397.

241 'Not good friends': Jessie Conrad to Hugh Walpole, 8 February 1922 (HRC Texas).

241 their last meeting: See Jessie Conrad (1935), p. 238.

241 *Aquitania* . . . Biltmore Hotel: Passenger manifest: *Aquitania*, Dep. Southampton 28 January 1922, Arr. 3 February (Ellis Island Archives); *New York Times*, 10 February 1922: 13.

241 'sense of irreparable loss': Telegram to Eric S. Pinker, 10 February 1922, *Letters* 7: 416.

241 'a bundle . . . indecision': Jessie Conrad to Walpole, 10 February 1922 (HRC Texas).

241 'kindliness of heart': *The Times*, 10 February 1922 (late edition): 9.

242 'Usual atmosphere . . . evening': Walpole: Diary entries of 4 and 5 February 1922 (HRC Texas).

242 'I love him . . . back': Hugh Walpole to Jessie Conrad, 18 May 1922; Lady Colvin to Hugh Walpole, [18 May 1922] (HRC Texas).

243 'I have my dear fellow . . . years': To Eric S. Pinker, 30 May 1922, *Letters* 7: 474.

243 'The story . . . one': To Pinker, 13 July 1922, *Letters* 7: 489.

243 'I am feeling . . . it': To Richard Curle, 24 July 1922, *Letters* 7: 497.

243 'The foolish . . . money': Jessie Conrad to Warrington Dawson, 18 May 1926 (Duke; courtesy of Zdzisław Najder).

243 'I was very fond . . . parent': Conal O'Riordan to Charles Lahr, 20 January 1932

(University of London, Senate House Library, Lahr Papers MS 985/1/21; courtesy of Richard Niland).

243 'smiling public man': Yeats, 'Among School Children' (1928).

243 'very successful': To Pinker, 26 July 1922, *Letters* 7: 501.

244 'His body . . . accents': Ray, ed. (1990), p. 40; see also Knowles and Stape (2006).

244 signed his will: See 'Conrad's Last Will and Testament,' ed. Hans van Marle in Moore, Simmons, and Stape, eds. (2000), pp. 245–51.

244 'a great . . . time': To John Galsworthy, 7 August 1922, *Letters* 7: 505–06.

244 'Something unique . . . world': To Garnett, 22 August 1922, *Letters* 7: 513.

244 excursion to North Wales: See John Conrad, (1981), pp. 192–94.

245 Tadaichi Hidaka: See Okuda (1998).

245 Japanese readership: See Shidara (1996).

245 signed a contract: See Lilian M. Hallowes, 'Note Book of Joseph Conrad,' ed. Simmons and Stape, in Moore, Simmons, and Stape, eds. (2000), pp. 226–27.

245 '*the* evening of her life': To Agnes Sanderson, 7 November 1922, *Letters* 7: 572.

245 'rather silly' . . . To J. Harry Benrimo, 6 November 1922, *Letters* 7: 566.

246 'noisy parrot-house . . . volumes . . . talk': To Frank Swinnerton, 11 November 1922, *Letters* 7: 582. For the reviews and the cartoon (*Stage*, 9 November 1922), see Hand (2001): 18–68.

246 'A woman . . . importance': Capes, ed. (1915), p. 40.

246 'the damned thing': To Pinker, 19 November 1922, *Letters* 7: 591.

247 'excessive publicity': To F. N. Doubleday, 8 December 1922, *Letters* 7: 610.

247 'regulation . . . gout': To Pinker, 25 December 1922, *Letters* 7: 627.

247 'salary of £85': To Curle, 2 January 1923, Curle 107.

247 introductions: Garnett to Conrad, 7 March 1923, Stape and Knowles, eds. (1996), p. 202; to Garnett, 10 March 1923, Garnett, ed. (1928), p. 321.

247 just before . . . New York: Passenger manifest: *Celtic*, Dep. Liverpool 10 March 1923. Arr. New York 19 March (Ellis Island Archives).

247 Criticised at the time: See, for example, 'Stephen Crane: A Study in American Letters,' *The Times*, 29 August 1924: 15.

248 fabricated 'evidence': See Wertheim and Sorrentino (1990) and Sorrentino (2003).

248 'I have tried . . . master': Garnett to Conrad, 19 March 1923, Stape and Knowles, eds. (1996), p. 207.

248 'mostly twaddle' and 'hack-work': To Pinker, 22 March 1923 and 23 March 1923 (Berg).

248 sold . . . for £4,000: To Pinker, 23 March 1923 (Berg).

248 interviewed: To Doubleday, 2 April 1923 (Princeton).

248 it held no appeal: To Karola Zagórska, [late March 1923], Najder, ed. (1983), p. 253.

248 'without enthusiasm': To Sir Robert Jones, 19 April 1923, Jean-Aubry, ed. (1927), 2: 305.

248 Curle would accompany him: To Curle, 12 March 1923, Curle (1928b), p. 110.

248 five-minute . . . Æolian Hall: To Pinker, 9 April 1923 (Berg); to Doubleday, 9 April 1923 (Princeton).

248 Ravel . . . in London: *The Times*, 16 April 1923: 15.

249 two 'mobs': To Jessie Conrad, 4 May 1923, Jessie Conrad (1927), No. 75.

249 'Take your hat off . . . bandaged': Morley (1923), pp. 6, 4.

249 editor . . . 'enormous nosegays': 'Poles to Welcome Conrad,' *New York Times*, 1 May 1923: 10; Jessie Conrad (1927), No. 75.

249 'I will not attempt . . . experience': Jessie Conrad (1927), No. 75.

250 'Got very angry . . . detests': Walpole: Diary entry of 19 July 1920 (HRC Texas).

250 'very delicate . . . health': Florence Doubleday (1937), p. 67.

250 'like an aspen leaf': *Ibid.*, p. 81.

250 'audible snuffling': To Jessie Conrad, 11 May 1923, Jessie Conrad (1927), No. 91.

251 'stony . . . overorganized': Cited in Garland (1934), p. 80.

251 Press interest: 'Conrad Visits Boston,' *New York Times*, 21 May 1923: 15.

251 curtailed because of illness: *The Times*, 1 June 1923: 14.

251 'with . . . generosity': To Elbridge L. Adams, 31 May 1923, Jean-Aubry ed. (1927), 2: 315.

251 'I am leaving . . . ideals': '*Majestic* Took 800 in her First Cabin. Joseph Conrad, Novelist of the Sea, Sails on Big Liner with Praise for America,' *New York Times*, 3 June 1923: S5.

251 learning from his wife: See Jessie Conrad to Walter Tittle, 27 June 1923 (HRC Texas).

251 the marriage: Copy of an Entry of Marriage: Borys Conrad and Madeline Joan King, 2 September 1922, St Giles Registry Office.

252 'Marrying . . . inconsiderate': To Pinker, 11 June 1923 (Berg).

252 Joan King . . . on the scene: Personal communication: Zdzisław Najder.

252 'Apart from the secrecy . . . nowhere': Jessie Conrad to Warrington Dawson, 18 May 1926 (Duke; courtesy of Zdzisław Najder). See also Jessie Conrad (1935), pp. 242–58.

252 her background: Copy of an Entry of Marriage (as above); Registrar General 1901 Census RG13/1634 (82), p. 28. Her mother, Ada L. A. King, who witnessed the marriage, appears in the 1901 Census as 32-year-old widow, born in Hoxton. The marriage of James Edward King and Ada Lauretta A. Taylor was registered Jan–March 1893 Camberwell 1d/905; the death of James Edward King, aged 37, was registered July–Sept 1897 West Ham 4a/112. Joan Conrad's registration of death gives her birth date as 5 June 1894 (Apr–June 1981 Camden 14/1646).

252 'with clenched teeth': To Sir Sidney Colvin, 4 August 1923 (Yale).

252 impromptu arrival: To Curle, 17 July 1923 (Lilly).

253 stay at Oswalds . . . depot: To Jean-Aubry, 5 August 1923, Jean-Aubry, ed. (1930), p. 185; to Doubleday, 13 August 1923 (Princeton).

253 made his excuses: To André Gide, 16 October 1923, Jean-Aubry, ed. (1930), p. 190.

253 'a pronounced . . . heart' . . . Jessie's knee: To Pinker, 8 November 1923; 26 November 1923 (Berg).

253 'shaky': Jessie Conrad to Edward Garnett, 4 December 1923 (HRC Texas).

254 death of her brother: Personal communication: Nina Hayward, May 2006; *Eastern Province Herald* (Port Elizabeth, South Africa), 5 and 6 October 1923.

254 'crocky . . . sorry': To Walpole, 19 November 1923 (HRC Texas).

254 'nothing to complain of . . . coup': To Sydney Cockerell, 21 November 1923 (HRC Texas); to Doubleday, 20 November 1923, Jean-Aubry, ed. (1927), 2: 324.

254 'enthusiastic': To Pinker, 4 December 1923 (Berg); Garnett to Conrad, 2 December 1923, Stape and Knowles, eds. (1996), pp. 225–26; to Garnett, 4 December 1923 (Yale; printed in part in Jean-Aubry, ed. [1927], 2: 325).

254 'The Rover . . . another': Desmond MacCarthy, Portraits (1931), cited in Sherry, ed. (1973), p. 361.

255 the festivities: See to F. N. and Florence Doubleday, 7 January 1924, Jean-Aubry ed. (1927), 2: 331.

255 health had somewhat improved: To Pinker, 16 December 1923 (Berg).

255 'I have been captious . . . well': To Arnold Bennett, 2 January 1924, Jean-Aubry, ed. (1927), 2: 331.

255 'in the rush . . . war-path': Garland (1934), p. 80.

255 'semi-asthmatic condition:' To F. N. and Florence Doubleday, 7 January 1924, Jean-Aubry, ed. (1927), 2: 331.

255 handsome 1912 Daimler . . . £200: To Doubleday, 28 January 1924 (Princeton).

255 'curious . . . reserve': Jessie Conrad to Walpole, 25 September 1923 (HRC Texas).

256 'neurasthenic symptoms': To Doubleday, 7 February 1924 (Princeton).

256 'talked . . . of old times': To Pinker, 4 February 1924 (Berg).

256 'sweep . . . Great Britain': To Pinker, 1 May 1924 (Berg).

256 A 5,000-word introduction . . . £250: To Pinker, 12 February 1924 (Berg).

257 'incapable . . . subject!': To Galsworthy, 22 February 1924, Jean-Aubry, ed. (1927), 2: 339.

257 'a better grip': To Pinker, 10 March 1924 (Berg).

257 arranged through Muirhead Bone: Bone to Walpole, 7 February 1924 (HRC Texas).

257 'played out . . . ill': Epstein (1940), p. 91.

257 'marvellously effective': To Curle, 25 March 1924, Curle, ed. (1928b), p. 144.

257 'Semitic-appearance . . . lips': Walpole: Diary entry of 5 September 1924 (HRC Texas). Bone (1955) to Walpole (7 February 1924, HRC Texas) mentions a possible six castings; to Adams (see 26 March 1924, Jean-Aubry, ed. (1927), 2: 341) mentions five. One is in London's National Portrait Gallery, another in the Museum of Canterbury and one was sold at auction by Sotheby's, London, in December 2006.

257 Alice Gachet: The Times, 4 November 1960: 15.

257 'better . . . improving': To Adams, 26 March 1924, Jean-Aubry, ed. (1927), 2: 341.

258 sat for . . . Alice Kinkead: L. M. Hallowes to Jean-Aubry, 1 April 1924 (Yale; courtesy of Gene M. Moore). The portrait is reproduced in The Studio, 88 (September 1924): 157; see also Jones (forthcoming).

258 'constant': To Jean-Aubry, 27 April 1924 (Yale).

258 'hard toil . . . men': To Ramsay MacDonald, 27 May 1924 (Berg).

258 'a fit . . . as it were': To Curle, 2 July [1924], Curle (1928b), p. 148.

259 Grace Willard: To Jessie Conrad, [2 July 1924], Jessie Conrad (1927), No. 29; Passenger manifest: The France, Dep. Plymouth 20 July, Arr. New York 25 July 1924 (Ellis Island Archives).

259 'chirpy': To Curle, 2 July [1924], Curle (1928b), p. 148.

259 'Sailors . . . Legend': To Curle, 8 July [1924], Ibid., p. 149.

259 'done any work that counts': To Sir Robert Jones, 10 July 1924, Jean-Aubry, ed. (1927), 2: 346.

259 'damnable . . . bills': To Pinker, 8 July 1924 (Berg).

260 'very well . . . spirits': Curle (1924), p. 12. For details of Conrad's death, see this, reprinted in altered form in Curle (1928a); Jessie Conrad to Dolly and Harold

Moor, 17 September 1924, Carabine and Stape (2005): 129–30; and John
Conrad (1981), pp. 213–16.

260 'about six . . . treatment': Curle (1924), p. 22.

260 Jessie found comfort: Jessie Conrad to Tadaichi Hidaka, 15 November 1924,
Okuda (1998): 76.

261 'Your . . . dead': John Conrad (1981), p. 215.

AFTER

262 'Sleepe . . . please': Edmund Spenser, *The Faerie Queene*, Book IX, stanza 40: 8–9.

262 'all-pervading . . . void': John Conrad (1981), p. 215.

262 John Conrad designed (footnote): Jessie Conrad to Mrs Melish, 31 December
1925 (Berg; courtesy of Keith Carabine).

262 During the night it rained: *Kent Herald*, 6 August 1924: 2.

263 *Weekly Scotsman . . . Romance*: *Weekly Scotsman*, 9 August 1924: 6; *Daily Sketch*,
4 August 1924: 7; Cruikshank (1924): 4; *Cork Weekly Examiner*, 9 August 1924: 4.

263 'rather mediocre . . . things': Walpole: Diary entry of 8 August 1924 (HRC
Texas).

263 'the shifting glamour . . . beauty': *The Times*, 4 August 1914: 10.

263 close friends: Telegram from Jessie Conrad to William Rothenstein, 4 August
1924 (Harvard; courtesy of Keith Carabine); to Thomas J. Wise, 4 August 1924
(British Library, Ashley 2953).

263 Nellie Lyons's brother: John Conrad (1981), p. 215. His first name comes from
the Registrar General 1891 Census RG12/709 (8), p. 10; his profession was given
as carpenter in the 1901 Census RG13/792 (90), p. 18; details of arrangements:
Kent Herald, 13 August 1924: 6.

263 her mother and her sister: Personal communication: Nina Hayward, June 2006.

263 service . . . at 1:15: *The Times*, 7 August 1924: 8.

264 'great . . . man': *The Times*, 12 August 1924: 15.

264 The wreaths: *Kent Herald*, 13 August 1924: 6.

264 'all Paris . . . sheer genius': R. B. Cunninghame Graham to Edward Garnett, 13
August 1924, Stape and Knowles, eds. (1996), p. 249.

265 worth £2 million: Boyce, *DNB* online (2005).

265 'miles . . . crowds': *The Times*, 18 August 1922: 13.

265 last will and testament: Van Marle, ed., in Moore, Simmons, and Stape, eds.
(2000), pp. 245–51.

265 estate . . . Walpole: Conrad: *The Times*, 17 November 1924: 17; Pinker: *The
Times*, 28 March 1922: 15; Galsworthy: *The Times*, 8 April 1933: 8; Walpole: *The
Times*, 4 August 1941: 6.

265 'The author . . . untrue': Jessie Conrad to the editor of the *Times Literary
Supplement*, 4 December 1924: 826; rpt. Stape and Knowles, eds. (1996), pp.
250–51.

266 'the most detestable book . . . husband': Garnett to Jessie Conrad, 11 July 1935,
Stape and Knowles, eds. (1996), p. 256.

266 'pretty awful . . . escaped': Cunninghame Graham to Richard Curle, 8 August
1935 (Lilly).

266 'Legends' . . . last page: *Daily Mail*, 15 August 1924: 8.

267 Her mother . . . died: Copy of an Entry of Death: Jane Nash George on 10
October 1925, Cranbrook, of carcinoma of the pancreas and asthenia; registered
11 October 1925 (Oct–Dec 1925 Cranbrook 2d/1152).

267 'lost his head . . . extravagant': *The Times*, 23 July 1927: 9.

267 August 1926 . . . declared bankrupt: BT221/2270, National Archives.

267 'morose . . . mentally': *New York Times*, 23 July 1927: 2.

267 'I can not take . . . friend': *Ibid.*

267 'on . . . Civil Power': *London Gazette*, 7 October 1927: 6314.

267 begging letters: See Conal O'Riordan to Charles Lahr, 20 January 1932 (University of London, Senate House Library, Lahr Papers MS 985/1/21; courtesy Richard Niland); Borys Conrad to Hugh Walpole, 12 February 1932 and 22 October 1939 (HRC Texas).

268 frail . . . Margaret Rishworth: Personal communications: the late Hans van Marle, C. T. Watts, and Mario Curreli; Personal knowledge.

268 asked . . . Corona typewriter: L. M. Hallowes to Eric S. Pinker, 1 September 1924 (Berg), cited in Miller (2006a): 94.

269 In 1933 . . . grandson Philip: Jessie Conrad to Alice Rothenstein, 10 July 1933 (Harvard; courtesy of Keith Carabine).

269 'strict diet' . . . sweet tooth . . . kneecap: Jessie Conrad to Walter Tittle, 1 December 1930 (HRC Texas); Personal communication: Nina Hayward, June 2006.

269 'a lonely woman': Jessie Conrad to Alice Rothenstein, 10 July 1933 (Harvard).

269 Ethel . . . 1931: Personal communication: Nina Hayward, June 2006.

269 personal belongings . . . estate: Last Will and Testament, 21 October 1936; Probate granted HM High Court of Justice, 18 June 1937.

269 memorial service: *Kentish Observer and Canterbury Chronicle*, 10 December 1936: 5.

269 alcoholism and gambling: Aldous Huxley to Eugene F. Saxton, 8 June 1937 (Woodson Research Center, Fondren Library, Rice University; courtesy of James Sexton); Cass (1971), p. 90.

270 'It appears . . . earning' . . . 'insolvent for years': Statement of J. R. Seabrooke–Pinker of 18 April 1941 and related documents, BT226/S170, National Archives; *London Gazette*, 11 March 1941: 1484.

270 Œnone married: Announcement: *The Times*, 3 November 1925: 19; registered under 'Mary O. Pinker' Registrar General Apr–June 1926 Chelsea 1a/894.

270 Eric divorced . . . dissolved: See Stape, 'Conradiana,' forthcoming; *London Gazette*, 28 November 1930: 7619.

270 'jaunty . . . bowler': *Time*, 27 March 1939: 15.

270 had a daughter: Siri Elizabeth Seabrooke-Pinker: birth registered July–Sept 1929 Marylebone 1a/587; announced: *The Times*, 17 June 1929: 1.

270 March 1941 . . . declared bankrupt: *The Times*, 11 March 1941: 1484; *ibid.*, 12 March 1941: 9.

270 separated: Yvonne Seabrooke-Pinker's engagement was announced (*The Times*, 28 April 1942: 6), but she appears in London phone books until 1947 under the name 'Seabrooke-Pinker'.

270 year's sentence: *The Times*, 17 February 1943: 2.

271 Yourcenar: *Quoi? L'éternité* (1988).

272 'There is never time . . . revolt': *Lord Jim* (Ch. 21), p. 225.

272 'always . . . bow': John Keats to Charles Armitage Brown, 30 November 1820, *The Letters of John Keats*, ed. Foreman (1935), p. 527.

Select bibliography: Conrad

Novels and novellas
Almayer's Folly (1895)
An Outcast of the Islands (1896)
The Nigger of the 'Narcissus' (1897)
Lord Jim (1900)
Nostromo (1904)
The Secret Agent (1907)
Under Western Eyes (1911)
Chance (1914)
Victory (1915)
The Shadow-Line (1917)
The Arrow of Gold (1919)
The Rescue (1920)
The Rover (1923)

Posthumous fiction
Suspense, ed. Richard Curle (1925)
The Sisters (1928)

Collections of short fiction
Tales of Unrest (1898) 'Karain, A Memory', 'The Idiots', 'An Outpost of Progress', 'The Return', 'The Lagoon'
Youth, A Narrative; and Two Other Stories (1902) 'Youth', 'Heart of Darkness', 'The End of the Tether'
Typhoon and Other Stories (1903) 'Typhoon', 'Amy Foster', 'Falk', 'To-morrow'
A Set of Six (1908) 'Gaspar Ruiz', 'The Informer', 'The Brute', 'An

Anarchist', 'The Duel', 'Il Conde'

'Twixt Land and Sea (1912) 'Smile of Fortune', 'The Secret Sharer', 'Freya of the Seven Isles'

Within the Tides (1915) 'The Planter of Malata', 'The Partner', 'The Inn of Two Witches', 'Because of the Dollars'

Tales of Hearsay (1925) 'The Black Mate', 'The Warrior's Soul', 'Prince Roman', 'The Tale'

Collections of non-fiction

The Mirror of the Sea (1906)

A Personal Record (1912)

Notes on Life and Letters (1921)

Notes on My Books (1921)

Last Essays (1926), ed. Richard Curle

Dramatisations

One Day More (1905)

Laughing Anne (1920)

The Secret Agent (1922)

Collaborations with Ford Hueffer

The Inheritors (1901)

Romance (1903)

The Nature of a Crime (1909)

Translation

The Book of Job by Bruno Winawer (1921; published 1931)

Bibliography

A note on texts

For Conrad's published fiction and non-fiction, references, except where works are available in the Cambridge Edition of the Works of Joseph Conrad (see Primary sources) are to 'Dent's Collected Edition', 1946–55. This 'edition' (technically, an issue) reprints Doubleday's collected edition of 1920–21. This was made available in England under the title 'Dent's Uniform Edition' (1924), and in the United States was reprinted with various names and bindings throughout the 1920s. It was most recently selectively reprinted in the Oxford World's Classics series in the 1980s and 1990s; the World's Classics texts published since 2000 have been reset. The widespread availability of Dent's Collected Edition, not its reliability, has recommended its citation. Conrad's texts have circulated in unreliable forms from their first publication, and will do so until completion of the Cambridge Edition, which began publication in 1990.

A note on sources

As mentioned in the Preface, the facts of Conrad's life have been established through painstaking research in archival sources extending back several decades and involving an international scholarly community. Conrad's Polish experience is presented in the documents collected and translated in Najder, ed., (1964) and Najder, ed., (1983). Precise dates are available for Conrad's maritime experience in Najder (1983; revised in its French and Polish versions and in English in 2007) and in Knowles 1990a. Allen 1965 remains useful, if not always meticulous, on Conrad's maritime career.

The Collected Letters of Joseph Conrad, a collaborative effort of several decades, is essential for all other facets of Conrad's life. Minor adjustments have been made to quotations from this edition so as not to burden the general reader with pedantry. Thus, for instance, although 'one september' [*sic*] is the editors' correct transcription of Conrad's hand in a letter of 21 July 1914 'one September' appears here. Similarly, omitted apostrophes and missing italics are silently supplied, and his *currente calamo* errors corrected; however, his capitals, which may appear odd, have been allowed to stand as he often, particularly in the earlier part of his career, used the continental convention of addressing a correspondent as 'You' rather than 'you'.

Online sources are cited with essential information for retrieval, with due acknowledgement of authorship (where indicated) and with date of access. Given the varying reliability of factual information available on the Internet, several such sources, not all listed below, have been accessed to verify information.

Primary sources

The Collected Letters of Joseph Conrad. 9 vols. Ed. Laurence Davies and Frederick R. Karl. Vol. 6 with Owen Knowles, Vol. 7 with J. H. Stape, and Vol. 8 with Gene M. Moore. Cambridge: Cambridge University Press, 1983–2007.

'The Congo Diary.' In *Heart of Darkness and The Congo Diary*. Ed. Owen Knowles and Robert Hampson. Harmondsworth: Penguin, 2007. Pp. 97–109.

Joseph Conrad: Letters to William Blackwood and David S. Meldrum. Ed. William Blackburn. Durham, NC: Duke University Press; Cambridge: Cambridge University Press, 1958.

'Supplementary notes' [July–August 1913]. In 'The "Knopf Document": Transcriptions and Commentary,' ed. J. H. Stape. In *Conrad between the Lines: Documents in a Life*. Ed. Gene M. Moore, Allan H. Simmons, and J. H. Stape. Amsterdam: Editions Rodopi, 2000. Pp. 57–86.

Almayer's Folly (1895). Ed. Eugene Floyd Eddleman and David Leon Higdon. Cambridge: Cambridge University Press, 1994.

Lettres françaises. Ed. G. Jean-Aubry. Paris: Gallimard, 1930.

Notes on Life and Letters (1921). Ed. J. H. Stape. Cambridge: Cambridge University Press, 2004

The Secret Agent (1907). Ed. Bruce Harkness and S. W. Reid. Cambridge: Cambridge University Press, 1990.

Secondary sources
Archival materials

Certificates of Competency: Master, Second Mate, First Mate and Applications for Examination, National Maritime Museum, Greenwich.

German Hospital, Dalston: Monthly Report of In and Out Patients: GMR 6/1; German Hospital Reports 1891–94: GHA 15/11, St Bartholomew's Hospital Archives and Museum, London.

Great Britain, National Archives: Registrar General Census 1841, 1851, 1861, 1871, 1881, 1891, 1901.

The Marine Society and Sea Cadets, London. *The Incorporated Thames Nautical Training College H.M.S. Worcester Register 8 (1910–17)*. Cadet reports in HMS *Worcester*: Alfred Borys Conrad and Robert Sholto Douglas, folios 69, 483.

The Royal Literary Fund, Case No. 2629 and Minutes of 9 July 1902 and 8 April 1908. The British Library, Manuscripts Department, M.1077/107 and M.1077/129.

Books, articles, signed contributions to newspapers

Academie royale des Sciences, des Lettres, et des Beaux-arts de Belgique. *Biographie nationale de Belgique*. 44 vols. Brussels: Academie royale, 1866–1986.

Alden, William L. Review of *Lord Jim. New York Times*, 1 December 1900: 8.

Alden, William L. Review of *Youth, A Narrative; and Two Other Stories. New York Times Book Review*, 13 December 1902: 10.

Allen, Jerry. *The Sea Years of Joseph Conrad*. New York: Doubleday, 1965.

Annuaire almanach du commerce, de l'industrie, de la magistrature et de l'administration. 2ème partie. Paris: F. Didot frères et fils, 1850–74.

Anon. *The Handbook of Lowestoft and its Neighbourhood*. Lowestoft: J. Chapman, 1866.

Anon. *A Transport Voyage to Mauritius and Back*. London: John Murray, 1851.

Anon. *Agnes Tobin: Letters, Translations, Poems, with Some Account of her Life*. San Francisco: Printed for John Howell at the Grabhorn Press 1958.

Anon. *Richard Curle: The Pre-eminent Conradian*. York: Stone Trough Books, 1995.

Atkinson, Damian, ed. *The Selected Letters of W. H. Henley*. London: Ashgate, 2000.

Balzac, Honoré de. *Lettre sur Kiew: Fragment inédit* (1847). Les Cahiers balzaciens, No. 7. Paris: Editions Lapina, 1927.

Bassett, Troy J. 'T. Fisher Unwin's Pseudonym Library: Literary Marketing and Authorial Identity.' *English Literature in Transition*, 47.2 (2004): 142–60.

Baxter, Katherine Isobel. 'Conrad's Application to the British Museum: An Unpublished Letter.' *The Conradian*, 31.2 (2006): 83–88.

Bennett, Arnold. *The Journals of Arnold Bennett, 1896–1928*. 3 vols. Ed. Newman Flower. London: Cassell, 1932–33.

Berka, F. P. 'Zhitomir and the Ukrainian Background in the Early Childhood of Joseph Conrad.' *The Conradian*, 8.2 (1983): 4–11.

Biskupski, M. B. 'Spy, Patriot or Internationalist: The Early Career of Józef Retinger, Polish Patriarch of European Union.' *Polish Review*, 43.1 (1998): 23–67.

Blackburn, William, ed. *Joseph Conrad: Letters to William Blackwood and David S. Meldrum*. Durham, North Carolina: Duke University Press, 1958.

Bock, Martin. *Joseph Conrad and Psychological Medicine*. Lubbock: Texas Tech University Press, 2002.

Bojarski, Edmund A. and Harold Ray Stevens. 'Joseph Conrad and the *Falconhurst*.' *Journal of Modern Literature*, 1.2 (1970–71): 197–208.

Bone David. *Landfall at Sunset: The Life of a Contented Sailor*. London: Duckworth, 1955.

Borisov, Viktor. 'Vologda – Konrad Korzeniowski's City.' In Moore, ed. (1992). Pp. 39–48.

Boswell, James. *Life of Johnson*. Ed. R. W. Chapman corrected by J. D. Fleeman. London: Oxford University Press, 1970.

Branny, Grażyna. 'Bruno Winawer's *The Book of Job*: Conrad's Only

Translation.' *The Conradian*, 27.1 (2002): 1–23.

Bross, Addison. 'Apollo Korzeniowski's Mythic Vision.' *The Conradian*, 20.1–2 (1995): 77–102.

Bross, Addison. 'The January Rising and its Aftermath: The Missing Theme in Conrad's Political Consciousness.' In *Conrad and Poland*. Ed. Alex S. Kurczaba. Boulder: Eastern European Monographs – Lublin: Maria Curie-Składowska University, 1996. Pp. 61–87.

Brumfield, William Craft. *The Origins of Modernism in Russian Architecture*. Berkeley: University of California Press, 1991.

Busza, Andrzej. 'Conrad's Polish Literary Background and Some Illustrations of the Influence of Polish Literature on his Work.' *Antemurale*, 10 (1966): 109–225.

Busza, Andrzej. "Usque ad Finem': *Under Western Eyes, Lord Jim,* and Conrad's Red Uncle.' In *'Lord Jim': Centennial Essays*. Ed. Allan H. Simmons and J. H. Stape. Amsterdam: Rodopi, 2000. Pp. 64–71.

Busza, Andrzej. 'Conrad and Polish History.' *CON-texts*, 4/5 (2003): 7–23.

Campo, J. N. F. M. à. 'A Profound Debt to the Eastern Seas: Documentary History and Literary Representation of Berau's Maritime Trade in Conrad's Malay Novels.' *International Journal of Maritime History*, 12.2 (2000): 85–125.

Candler, Edmund Candler. *Youth and the East: An Unconventional Autobiography*. 2nd edn. Edinburgh: Blackwell, 1932.

Capes, H. M., ed. *Wisdom and Beauty from Conrad*. London: Andrew Melrose 1915.

Carabine, Keith. 'A very charming old gentleman: Conrad, Count Szembek, and "Il Conde."' *Conradiana*, 37.1–2 (2005): 53–73.

Carabine, Keith and J. H. Stape, eds. 'Family Letters: Conrad to a Sister-in-law and Jessie Conrad on Conrad's Death.' *The Conradian*, 30.1 (2005): 127–31.

Cass, Canfield. *Up and Down and Around*. New York: Harper & Row, 1971.

Cerio, Edwin. *Capri: Prima visione dell'isola*. Naples: La Voce di Napoli Press, n. d.

Chekhov, Anton. *The Three Sisters*. Trans. Randall Jarrell. London: Macmillan, 1969.

Clifford, Hugh. 'The Genius of Mr. Joseph Conrad.' *North American Review*, 178 (June 1904): 842–52.

Clifford, Hugh. *A Talk on Joseph Conrad and his Work*. The English Association – Ceylon Branch. Colombo: H. W. Cave, 1927.

Conrad, Borys. *My Father Joseph Conrad*. New York: Coward-McCann, 1970.

Conrad, Borys. *Joseph Conrad's Homes in Kent*. London: Joseph Conrad Society (UK), 1974.

Conrad, Jessie. Letter to the Editor. *Times Literary Supplement*, 4 December 1924: 826.

Conrad, Jessie. *Joseph Conrad as I Knew Him*. London: Heinemann, 1926.

Conrad, Jessie, ed. *Joseph Conrad's Letters to His Wife*. London: Privately printed, 1927.

Conrad, Jessie. 'Joseph Conrad's War Service'. *Blue Peter*, 11 (1931): 252–55.

Conrad, Jessie. *Joseph Conrad and his Circle*. London: Jarrolds, 1935.

Conrad, John. 'Joseph Conrad', BBC Third Programme. Talks Department, BBC: Broadcast Sunday, 16 November 1947 (Transcript HRC Texas).

Conrad, John. *Joseph Conrad: Times Remembered*. Cambridge: Cambridge University Press, 1981.

Corkhill, Rachael. 'Conrad and Edmund Candler: A Neglected Correspondence.' *Conradiana*, 37.1–2 (2005): 11–22.

Courtney, W. L. Review of *Within the Tides*. *Daily Telegraph*, 3 March 1915: 4.

Cox, James Stevens. 'Memories of Richard Curle.' In *Richard Curle: The Pre-eminent Conradian*. York: Stone Trough Books, 1995. Pp. 70–72.

Cruikshank, R. J. 'Joseph Conrad: A Picture of the Man.' *Daily News*, 4 August 1924: 4

Curle, Richard. *Joseph Conrad: A Study*. London: Kegan Paul; New York: Doubleday, 1914.

Curle, Richard. *Joseph Conrad's Last Day*. London: Privately printed, 1924.

Curle, Richard. *The Personality of Joseph Conrad*. London: Privately printed, [1925].

Curle, Richard. 'Objection and Reproof.' *New York Times Book Review*, 9 May 1926: 25.

Curle, Richard. *The Last Twelve Years of Joseph Conrad.* London: Sampson Low, Marston, 1928a.

Curle, Richard, ed. *Letters: Joseph Conrad to Richard Curle.* New York: Crosby Gaige, 1928b.

Czosnowski, Stefan. 'Conradiana' (1929). In Najder, ed. (1983). Pp. 134–37.

Dąbrowski, Marian. 'An Interview with J. Conrad' (1917). In Najder, ed. (1983b). Pp. 196–201.

Darwin, Charles. *Journal of Researches into the Natural History and Geology of the Countries visited during the Voyage of H.M.S. Beagle.* 1839; rpt. London: Murray, 1852.

Delcommune, Alexandre. *Vingt années de vie africaine: récits de voyages, d'aventures et d'exploration au Congo Belge, 1874–1893.* Brussels: Larcier, 1922.

Denoël, Thierry, comp. 'Thys, Albert.' *Le Nouveau Dictionnaire des Belges.* Brussels: Édition Le Cri, 1992.

De Ternant, Andrew. 'An Unknown Episode in Conrad's Life.' *New Statesman and Nation*, 28 July 1928: 511.

Dostoevsky, Feodor. *Journal d'un écrivain 1873, 1876, 1877.* Trans. J. W. Bienstock and John-Antoine Nau. Paris: Charpentier, 1904.

Doubleday, Florence. *Episodes in the Life of a Publisher's Wife.* New York: Privately printed, 1937.

Doubleday, F. N. *Memoirs of a Publisher.* New York: Doubleday, 1972.

Doubleday, Page, & Co. *Joseph Conrad: A Sketch with a Bibliography.* Garden City, New York: Doubleday, Page, 1924.

Ducas, Sylvie. 'La Prix Femina: La consécration littéraire au féminin.' *Recherches féministes*, 16.1 (2003): 43–95.

Eddison, John. *A History of Elstree School and Three Generations of the Sanderson Family.* Privately printed, [1979].

Eddleman, Eugene Floyd and Leon Higdon, 'The Texts: An Essay.' In *Almayer's Folly.* The Cambridge Edition of the Works of Joseph Conrad. Cambridge: Cambridge University Press, 1994. Pp. 159–98.

Edel, Leon. *Henry James: The Master, 1901–1916.* Philadelphia: Lippincott, 1972.

Ehrsam, Theodore G. *A Bibliography of Joseph Conrad*. Metuchen, New Jersey: Scarecrow Press, 1969.

Epstein, Jacob. *Let There Be Sculpture: An Autobiography*. London: Michael Joseph, 1940.

Evans, Nicholas J. 'Indirect Passage from Europe: Transmigration via the UK, 1836–1914.' *Journal for Maritime Research*, June 2001.

Filip, T. M., ed., and M. A. Michael, trans. *A Polish Anthology/Moja ojczyzna-polszczyzna. Wybór poezji polskiej*. London: Duckworth, 1944.

Finkelstein, David. *The House of Blackwood: Author–Publisher Relations in the Victorian Era*. University Park: Pennsylvania State University Press, 2002.

Finneran, Richard J., ed. *W. B. Yeats: The Poems – A New Edition*. Dublin: Gill & Macmillan, 1984.

Fiorentino, Carmelina. 'Norman Douglas e i Cerio: Note da un amicizia.' *Norman Douglas: Drittes Symposium, Bregenz und Thüringen, 22–23. 10. 2004*. Ed. Wilhelm Meusburger and Helmut Swozilek. Graz: W. Neugebauer Verlag, 2005.

Firchow, Peter Edgerly. *Envisioning Africa: Racism and Imperialism in Conrad's 'Heart of Darkness.'* Lexington: University Press of Kentucky, 2000.

Fletcher, Chris. 'Kurtz, Marlow, Jameson, and the Rearguard: A Few Further Observations.' *The Conradian*, 26.1 (2001): 60–64.

Ford, Ford Madox. *Return to Yesterday*. London: Victor Gollancz, 1931.

Forster, E. M. *The Selected Letters of E. M. Forster*. 2 vols. Ed. Mary Lago and P. N. Furbank. London: Collins, 1983–85.

Fothergill, Anthony. *Secret Sharers: Joseph Conrad's Cultural Reception in Germany*. Cultural History and Literary Imagination, vol. 4. Bern: Peter Lang, 2006.

Franke, Hans. *Geschichte und Schicksal der Juden in Heilbronn*. Heilbronn: Stadtarchiv, 2006.

Galsworthy, John. Introduction. *Laughing Anne & Other Plays*. London: John Castle, 1924.

Galsworthy, John. *Castles in Spain and Other Screeds*. London: Heinemann, 1927.

Garland Hamlin. *My Friendly Contemporaries: A Literary Log*. New

York: Macmillan, 1932.

Garland Hamlin. *Afternoon Neighbors: Further Excerpts from a Literary Diary*. New York: Macmillan, 1934.

Garland Hamlin. *Diaries*. Ed. Donald Pizer. San Marino, California: Huntington Library, 1968.

Garnett, Edward. Introduction. *Letters from Conrad: 1896 to 1924*. Ed. Edward Garnett. London: Nonesuch, 1928. Pp. v–xxxiii.

Garnett, Edward, ed. *Letters from John Galsworthy: 1900–1932*. London: Jonathan Cape, 1934.

Garnett, Richard. *Constance Garnett: A Heroic Life*. London: Sinclair-Stevenson, 1991.

Gautier, Théophile. *Constantinople*. 3rd edn. Paris: Michel Lévy frères, 1856.

Gide, André. *Paul Claudel et André Gide: Correspondance: 1899–1926*. Ed. Robert Mallet. Paris: Gallimard, 1949.

Gide, André. *Correspondance André Gide/Jacques Copeau*. 2 vols. Ed. Jean Claude. Paris : Gallimard, 1987.

Gilkes, Lilian. *Cora Crane: A Biography of Mrs. Stephen Crane*. Bloomington: Indiana University Press, 1960.

Gill, David. 'Joseph Conrad and the S.S. *Adowa*.' *Notes and Queries*, 25.4 (1978): 323–24.

Gill, David. 'Joseph Conrad, William Paramor, and the Guano Island: Links to *A Personal Record* and *Lord Jim*.' *The Conradian*, 23.2 (1998): 17–26.

Gindin, James. *John Galsworthy's Life and Art*. London: Macmillan, 1987.

Golbéry, Roger. *Mon oncle, Paul Gachet*. Paris: Éditions du Valhermeil, 1990.

Great Britain Hydrographic Office. *China Sea. Gulf of Siam. Koh-ta-Kut to Cape Liant*.

Halverson, John and Ian Watt. 'Notes on Jane Anderson: 1955–1990.' *Conradiana*, 23 (1991): 59–87.

Hamer, Douglas. 'Conrad: Two Biographical Episodes.' *Review of English Studies*, 18 (1967): 54–56.

Hand, Richard J. 'Conrad and the Reviewers: *The Secret Agent* on Stage.' *The Conradian*, 26.2 (2001): 1–67.

Handbook of the Bombay Presidency. 2nd edn. London: 1881.

Hart-Davis, Rupert. *Hugh Walpole: A Portrait of a Man, an Epoch, and a Society*. London: Hart-Davis, 1952.

Hearn, Lafcadio. *Two Years in the French West Indies*. New York: Harper & Brothers, 1890.

Henley, W. E. *The Selected Letters of W. E. Henley*. Ed. Damian Atkinson. Aldershot: Ashgate, 2000.

Hepburn, James. *The Author's Empty Purse and the Rise of the Literary Agent*. London: Oxford University Press, 1968.

Hochschild, Adam. *King Leopold's Ghost: A Story of Greed, Terror, and Heroism in Colonial Africa*. Boston: Houghton Mifflin, 1998.

Hodgson & Co., *A Catalogue of Books, Manuscripts and Corrected Typescripts from the Library of the late Joseph Conrad*. London: Privately printed by Riddle, Smith, & Duffus, 1925.

Hoenselaars, Ton and Gene M. Moore. 'Joseph Conrad and T. E. Lawrence.' *Journal of the T. E. Lawrence Society*, 5.1 (1995): 25–44.

Holden, Philip. *Modern Subjects/Colonial Texts: Hugh Clifford and the Discipline of English Literature in the Straits Settlements and Malaya, 1895–1907*. Greensboro, North Carolina: ELT Press, 2000.

Holloway, Mark. *Norman Douglas: A Biography*. London: Secker & Warburg, 1976.

Hope, G. F. W. 'Friend to Conrad'. In *Conrad between the Lines: Documents in a Life*. Ed. Gene M. Moore, Allan H. Simmons, and J. H. Stape. Amsterdam: Editions Rodopi, 2000. Pp. 1–56.

Huneker, James. *Letters of James Gibbons Huneker*. Ed. Josephine Huneker. New York: Charles Scribner's Sons, 1922.

James, Henry. *The Letters of Henry James*. 2 vols. Ed. Percy Lubbock. New York: Scribner's, 1920.

James, Henry. *The Letters of Henry James*. 4 vols. Ed. Leon Edel. Cambridge, Massachusetts: Belknap Press of Harvard University, 1974–84.

James, Henry. *Dearly Beloved Friends: Henry James's Letters to Younger Men*. Ed. Susan E. Gunter and Steven H. Jobe. Ann Arbor: University of Michigan Press, 2001.

Jarrell, Randall. 'About *The Three Sisters*: Notes.' In Anton Chekhov, *The Three Sisters*. Trans. Randall Jarrell. London: Macmillan, 1969. Pp. 101–60.

Jean-Aubry, G. 'Joseph Conrad and Music.' *The Chesterian* (London), 6. 42 (November 1924): 37–43.

Jean-Aubry, G., ed. *Joseph Conrad: Life & Letters.* 2 vols. London: Heinemann, 1927.

Jefferson, George. *Edward Garnett, A Life in Literature.* London: Cape, 1982.

Johnson Club. *Annals of the Club, 1764–1914.* London: Printed for the Club, 1914.

Jones, Susan. 'Alice Kinkead and the Conrads.' *The Conradian* (forthcoming).

Keats, John. *The Letters of John Keats.* Ed. Maurice Buxton Foreman. 2nd rev. edn. London: Oxford University Press, 1935.

Kelly's. *The Post Office London Directory for 1895.* London: Kelly's Directories, 1895.

Kelly's. *Directory for Kent, Surrey and Sussex for 1913.* London: Kelly's Directories, 1913.

Kennerley, Alston. 'Conrad at the London Sailors' Home.' *The Conradian* (forthcoming).

Kingsley, Mary H. *Travels in West Africa.* (1897). Rpt. as *Travels in West Africa: Congo français, Corisco and Cameroons.* London: Frank Cass, 1965.

Kipling, Rudyard. 'The Man Who Would Be King' (1888). In *The Phantom 'Rickshaw and Other Stories.* The Writings in Prose and Verse of Rudyard Kipling. New York: Scribner's, 1899. Vol. 5: 39–97.

Kirschner, Paul. '"Making you see Geneva": The Sense of Place in *Under Western Eyes.*' *L'Époque Conradienne,* 1988: 101–27.

Kirschner, Paul. 'Topodialogic Narrative in *Under Western Eyes* and the Rasumoffs of "La Petite Russie".' In Moore, ed., 1992. Pp. 223–54.

Kliszczewski, Władysław. 'An Account of my Early Life.' Unpublished typescript (1911). Collection: J. H. Stape.

Knowles, Owen. 'Arnold Benett as an "Anonymous" Reviewer of Conrad's Early Fiction.' *The Conradian,* 10.1 (May 1985): 26–36.

Knowles, Owen. *A Conrad Chronology.* New York: G.K. Hall, 1990a.

Knowles, Owen. 'Joseph Conrad and Bertrand Russell: New Light on their Relationship.' *Journal of Modern Literature,* 17 (1990b): 139–52.

Knowles, Owen. 'Conrad's Life.' In *The Cambridge Companion to Joseph Conrad*. Ed. J. H. Stape. Cambridge: Cambridge University Press, 1996. Pp. 1–24.

Knowles, Owen. ' "Saving Conrad from himself ": The Administration of the Royal Bounty Award, Unpublished Letters, 1904–1906.' *The Conradian* (forthcoming).

Knowles, Owen and Gene M. Moore. *Oxford Reader's Companion to Conrad*. Oxford: Oxford University Press, 2000.

Knowles, Owen and J. H. Stape. 'Conrad and Hamlin Garland: A Correspondence Recovered.' *The Conradian*, 31.2 (2006): 67–82.

Knowles, Owen and J. H. Stape. 'Conrad's Early Reception in America: The Case of W. L. Alden.' *The Conradian* (forthcoming).

Korzeniowski, Apollo. 'Poland and Muscovy' (1864). Trans. Halina Carroll-Najder. In Najder, ed., 1983. Pp. 75–88.

Lawrence, D. H. *The Letters of D. H. Lawrence. Volume 3: October 1916–June 1921*. Ed. James T. Boulton and Andrew Robertson. Cambridge: Cambridge University Press, 1984.

Lekime, Nelson. 'La Première de *Tristan et Iseult*.' *L'Art musical* (Paris), 29 mars 1894 : 98–99.

Lesage, Claudine. *La Maison de Thérèse: Joseph Conrad, Les années françaises, 1874–1878: Enquête littéraire*. Amiens: Sterne, 1992.

Lesage, Claudine. *Joseph Conrad et le continent*. Paris: Michel Houdiard Éditeur, 2003.

Leslie, R. F. *Reform and Insurrection in Russian Poland, 1856–65*. London: Athlone Press, 1963.

Lloyd's Register of British and Foreign Shipping. *Lloyd's Yacht Register, 1889* and *Lloyd's Yacht Register, 1892*. London: Lloyd's, 1889, 1892.

Ludwig, Richard M., ed. *Letters of Ford Madox Ford*. Princeton: Princeton University Press, 1965.

M. G. H. 'Joseph Conrad: Great Novelist and Master Mariner.' *The Daily Sketch*, 4 August 1924: 7.

McCarthy, Terry, ed. *The Great Dock Strike, 1889*. London: Weidenfeld & Nicolson with the Transport and General Workers' Union, 1988.

Macdonald, Peter D. *British Literary Culture and Publishing Practice, 1880–1914*. Cambridge: Cambridge University Press, 1997.

Mackenzie, Compton. *Vestal Fire* (1927). London: Chatto & Windus, 1964.

McLendon, M. J. 'Conrad and Calomel: An Explanation of Conrad's Mercurial Nature.' *Conradiana*, 23.2 (1991): 151–56.

Mahler, Gustav. *Letters to his Wife*. Ed. Henry-Louis de La Grange and Guenther Weiss. London: Faber & Faber, 2004.

Marx, Karl and Fredrick Engels. *Marx/Engels Collected Works*. 50 vols. Moscow: Progress, 1975–2004.

Maupassant, Guy de. *Correspondance*. Ed. Jacques Suffel. Évreux: Le Cercle du bibliophile, 1973.

Maxwell, Perriton. 'A First Meeting with Joseph Conrad.' *New York and Herald Tribune Magazine*, 24 August 1924: 1.

Megroz, R. L. 'Talks with Famous Writers VI: Mr. Joseph Conrad.' *Teacher's World*, 15 November 1922: 367–68.

Mérédac, Savinien. 'Joseph Conrad et nous.' *Essor* (Port-Louis), 15 February 1931.

Meyers, Jeffrey. *Joseph Conrad: A Life*. New York: Charles Scribner's Sons, 1991.

Michael, Marion C. and Steven J. Daniell, 'Conrad in the British Museum Reading Room.' *Conradiana*, 36.3 (2004): 245–52.

Miller, David. 'Amanuensis: A Biographical Sketch of Lilian Hallowes, "Mr Conrad's Secretary."' *The Conradian*, 31.1 (2006a): 86–103.

Miller, David. 'The Unenchanted Garden: Conrad, Children, and Childhood.' *The Conradian*, 31.2 (2006b): 30–50.

Mizener, Arthur. *The Saddest Story: A Biography of Ford Madox Ford*. New York: World Publishing, 1972.

Monod, Sylvère, ed. *Conrad: Œuvres*. Edition de la Pléiade. 5 vols. Paris: Gallimard, 1982–92.

Moore, Gene M. 'Conrad in Amsterdam.' In Moore, ed., 1992. Pp. 95–123.

Moore, Gene M., ed. *Conrad's Cities: Essays for Hans van Marle*. Amsterdam and Atlanta: Rodopi, 1992.

Moore, Gene M., comp., 'Newspaper Accounts of the *Jeddah* Affair.' *'Lord Jim': Centennial Essays*. Ed. Allan H. Simmons and J. H. Stape. Amsterdam: Rodopi, 2000; rpt 2004. Pp. 104–39.

Moore, Gene M., Allan H. Simmons, and J. H. Stape, eds. *Conrad between the Lines: Documents in a Life*. Amsterdam: Rodopi, 2000.

Morf, Gustav. *The Polish Shades and Ghosts of Joseph Conrad*. London: Sampson Low, Marston, 1930.

Morf, Gustav. *The Polish Heritage of Joseph Conrad*. London: Faber & Faber, 1977.

Morley, Christopher. *Conrad and the Reporters*. New York: Doubleday, Page, 1923.

Morrowsmith, Alex. 'Stanford's Literary Claim to Fame.' *This Is Essex*, 15 July 1999.

Moser, Thomas C. 'From Olive Garnett's Diary: Impressions of Ford Madox Ford and his Friends, 1890–1906.' *Texas Studies in Literature and Language*, 16.3 (1974): 511–33.

Najder, Zdzisław, ed. *Conrad's Polish Background: Letters to and from Polish Friends*. Trans. Halina Carroll-Najder. Oxford: Oxford University Press, 1964.

Najder, Zdzisław. *Joseph Conrad: A Chronicle*. Trans. Halina Carroll-Najder. New Brunswick, New Jersey: Rutgers University Press, 1983.

Najder, Zdzisław, ed. *Conrad under Familial Eyes*. Trans. Halina Carroll-Najder. Cambridge: Cambridge University Press, 1983.

Najder, Zdzisław. 'Conrad and Ukraine: A Note.' *The Conradian*, 23.2 (1998): 45–54.

Nash, Eveleigh. *I Liked the Life I Lived*. London: John Murray, 1941.

Neveux, Pol. *Guy de Maupassant: Étude*. Paris: Conard, 1908.

The New Annual Army List, 1893. London: John Murray, 1893.

[O'Connor], T. P. 'A Book of the Week,' *Weekly Sun*, 10 May 1896: 1.

Okuda, Yoko. 'East Meets West: Tadaichi Hidaka's Visit to Conrad.' *The Conradian*, 23.2 (1998): 73–87.

Omelan, Lilia. ' "How short his years and how clear his vision!": Adam Pulman: Conrad's Unforgettable Tutor.' *Conradiana*, 36.1–2 (2004): 131–41.

Parsons, Ronald. *The Black Diamond Line of Colliers (Henry Simpson & Sons, Port Adelaide)*. 1972; revised edn. Murray Bridge: privately Printed, 1982.

Paszkowski, Lech. 'Joseph Conrad in Australian Ports.' *Poles in Australia and Oceania, 1790–1940*. Sydney: Australian National University, 1987. Translation of *Polacy w Australii i Oceanii, 1790–1940* (1962).

Payne, Stanley G. *Falange: A History of Spanish Fascism*. Stanford, California: Stanford University Press, 1961.

Pegolotti, James A. *Deems Taylor: A Biography*. Boston, Northeastern University Press, 2003.

Perłowski, Jan. 'On Conrad and Kipling.' In Najder, ed., 1983, pp. 150–70.

Peters, John G., ed. *Conrad in the Public Eye: Biography/ Criticism/ Publicity*. Amsterdam: Rodopi, 2007.

Piechota, Marcin. 'The First Conrad Translation: *An Outcast of the Islands* in Polish.' *The Conradian*, 30.1 (2005): 89–96.

Pugh, Mrs J. C. L. 'Some Sidelights on Joseph Conrad.' *Thurrock Historical Society Journal*, 5 (Autumn 1960): 52–56.

Randall, Dale B. J. *Joseph Conrad and Warrington Dawson: The Record of a Friendship*. Durham, North Carolina: Duke University Press, 1968.

Ray, Martin. 'Hardy and Conrad.' *Thomas Hardy Journal*, 12.2 (May 1996): 82–84.

Ray, Martin, ed. *Joseph Conrad: Interviews and Recollections*. Basingstoke: Macmillan, 1990.

Reid, S. W. 'The Unpublished Typescript Version of "A Smile of Fortune."' *The Conradian*, 31.2 (2006): 92–102.

Retinger, J. H. *Conrad and his Contemporaries: Souvenirs*. London: Minerva, 1941.

Rimbaud, Arthur. *Selected Poems and Letters*. Trans. Jeremy Harding and John Sturrock. Harmondsworth: Penguin Books, 2004.

Rivoallan, Anatole. 'Joseph Conrad and Brittany' (1949). Trans. Alan Heywood Kenny. *The Conradian*, 8.2 (1983): 14–18

Robb, Graham. *Balzac: A Biography*. 1994; rpt. London: Picador, 2000.

Roberts, Cecil. 'Joseph Conrad: A Reminiscence.' *The Bookman* (London), November 1925: 96–99.

Russell, Bertrand. *The Autobiography of Bertrand Russell*. 3 vols. London: Allen & Unwin, 1967–69.

Rymut, Kazimierz. *Slownik nazwisk wspolczesnie w Polsce uzywanych* [Dictionary of Surnames Currently Used in Poland]. 10 vols. Ed. Kazimierz Rymut. Cracow: Instytut Jezyka Polskiego PAN, 1990.

Saunders, Max. *Ford Madox Ford: A Dual Life.* 2 vols. Oxford: Oxford University Press, 1996.

Sazonov, Aleksandr. *Takoi gorod v Rossii odin* [The Only Such Town in Russia]. Vologda: Poligratist, 1993.

Scoble, Christopher. *Fisherman's Friend: A Life of Stephen Reynolds.* Tiverton: Halsgrove, 2000.

Sherry, Norman. *Conrad's Eastern World.* Cambridge: Cambridge University Press, 1966.

Sherry, Norman. *Conrad's Western World.* Cambridge: Cambridge University Press, 1971.

Sherry, Norman. *Conrad.* Literary Lives. London: Thames & Hudson, 1972.

Sherry, Norman, ed. *Conrad: The Critical Heritage.* London: Routledge & Kegan Paul, 1973.

Shidara, Yasuko. 'Japanese Translations of Conrad's Works, 1914–1995.' *Tokyo Conrad Group Newsletter*, 2 (1996): 4–7.

Shidara, Yasuko. 'Conrad and Bangkok.' In *Journey, Myths, and the Age of Travel: Joseph Conrad's Era.* Ed. Karin Hansson. Karlskrona: University of Karlskrona/Ronneby, 1998. Pp. 76–96.

Shidara, Yasuko. '*The Shadow-Line*'s "Sympathetic Doctor": Dr William Willis in Bangkok, 1888.' *The Conradian*, 30.1 (2005): 97–110.

Simmons, Allan H., ed. *The Nigger of the 'Narcissus'* Centennial edn. London: Dent-Everyman, 1997.

Skutnik, Tadeusz. 'Conrad w poezji polskiej' [Conrad in Polish Poetry]. *Glos Wybrzeza*, 21 December 1975.

Smith, Janet Adam. *The Royal Literary Fund, 1790–1990.* London: Royal Literary Fund, 1990.

Sorrentino, Paul. 'The Legacy of Thomas Beer in the Study of Stephen Crane and American Literary History.' *American Literary Realism*, 35 (2003): 187–211.

Speaight, Robert. *William Rothenstein: The Portrait of an Artist in his Time.* London: Eyre & Spottiswoode, 1962.

Stape, J. H. 'The "Knopf Document": Transcription and Commentary.' In *Conrad between the Lines: Documents in a Life.* Ed. Gene M. Moore, Allan H. Simmons, and J. H. Stape. Amsterdam: Rodopi, 2000. Pp. 57–86.

Stape, J. H. 'The Topography of "The Secret Sharer."' *The Conradian*,

26.1 (2001): 1–16.

Stape, J. H. '"The Dark Places of the Earth": Text and Context in "Heart of Darkness."' *The Conradian*, 29.1 (2004): 148–66.

Stape, J. H. and Keith Carabine. 'Further Light on Conrad's Sister-in-Law Dolly Moor.' *The Conradian*, 31.1 (2006a): 128–29.

Stape, J. H. and Owen Knowles. '"In-between Man": Conrad–Galsworthy–Pinker.' *The Conradian*, 31.2 (2006b): 51–65.

Stape, J. H. 'Conradiana in the 1901 Census and Other Sources of Record.' *The Conradian* (forthcoming).

Stape, J. H. 'Jessie George: A Family History.' *The Conradian* (forthcoming).

Stape, J. H., ed. 'The Kliszczewski Document.' *The Conradian* (forthcoming).

Stape, J. H. and Hans van Marle. '"Pleasant Memories" and "Precious Friendships": Conrad's *Torrens* Connection and Unpublished Letters from the 1890s.' *Conradiana*, 27 (1995): 21–44.

Stape, J. H. and Owen Knowles, eds. *A Portrait in Letters: Correspondence to and about Conrad.* Amsterdam: Rodopi, 1996.

Stebbings, Arthur. *Guide-book to Lowestoft and its Vicinity.* Lowestoft: Stebbings, [c. 1886].

Steel, David. 'Gide à Cambridge, 1918.' *Bulletin des Amis d'André Gide*, 125 (janvier 2000): 11–74.

Stravinsky, Igor. *Themes and Conclusions.* London: Faber & Faber, 1972.

Taylor, A. J. P. 'Pirate King.' Review of Neal Ascherson, *The King Incorporated: Leopold the Second and the Congo. New Statesman*, 25 October 1963: 576.

Thomas, Helen. 'Mr. Ralph Hodgson.' *The Times*, 13 November 1962: 14.

Twain, Mark. *Following the Equator. A Journey around the World.* New York: Harper's, 1897.

Unwin, Philip. *The Printing Unwins: A Short History of Unwin Brothers, The Gresham Press, 1826–1976.* London: Allen & Unwin, 1976.

Van Marle, Hans. 'Plucked and Passed on Tower Hill: Conrad's Examination Ordeals.' *Conradiana*, 8 (1976a): 99–109.

Van Marle, Hans. 'Young Ulysses Ashore: On the Trail of Konrad

Korzeniowski in Marseilles.' *L'Époque Conradienne*, 2 (1976b): 22–34.

Van Marle, Hans. 'Conrad's 'Rooms in Bessborough Gardens': After the Unveiling of a Commemorative Plaque.' *The Conradian*, 10.1 (May 1985): 37–46.

Van Marle, Hans. 'An Ambassador of Conrad's Future: The *James Mason* in Marseilles, 1874.' *L'Époque Conradienne*, 14 (1988): 63–67.

Van Marle, Hans. 'Lawful and Lawless: Young Korzeniowski's Adventures in the Caribbean.' *L'Époque Conradienne*, 17 (1991): 91–113.

Van Marle, Hans. 'Conradiana in the 1891 Census.' *The Conradian*, 17.1 (1992): 73–77.

Van Marle, Hans. *The Hans van Marle Files: Letters and Papers about Conrad*. Ed. Gene M. Moore. Amsterdam: Rodopi, 2005.

Various hands. *The Johnson Club Papers*. London: T. Fisher Unwin, 1899.

Ward, Herbert. 'Life among the Congo Savages.' *Scribner's Magazine*, 7.2 (February 1890): 135–57.

Watts, Cedric and Laurence Davies. *Cunninghame Graham: A Critical Biography*. Cambridge: Cambridge University Press, 1979.

Wertheim, Stanley and Paul Sorrentino. 'Thomas Beer: The Clay Feet of Stephen Crane Biography.' *American Literary Realism*, 22 (Spring 1990): 2–16.

Wesolowski, Capt. Zdzisław P. *The Order of the Virtuti Militari and its Cavaliers, 1792–1992*. Miami: Hallmark Press, 1992.

Whale, George. *The Forty Years of the Johnson Club, 1884–1924*. London: Privately printed, 1925.

Whitaker, James. *Joseph Conrad at Stanford-le-Hope*. Stanford-le-Hope: Bream Press, 1978.

Woodhouse, Tom. 'Adam Curle, Quaker and Pioneer of Peace Studies in Britain.' *Guardian*, 4 October 2006 <www.guardian.co.uk>.

Woolf, Virginia. *The Essays of Virginia Woolf*. 4 vols. Ed. Andrew McNellie. London: Hogarth Press, 1986–94.

Wright, Harold, ed. *Letters of Stephen Reynolds*. London: Hogarth Press, 1923.

Yourcenar, Marguerite. *Quoi? L'éternité*. Paris: Gallimard, 1988.

Zamoyski, Adam. *The Polish Way: A Thousand-Year History of the Poles and Their Culture*. London: John Murray, 1987.

Zelie, John Sheridan. *A Burial in Kent*. New York: William Edwin Rudge, 1925.

Newspapers

Series

The Commercial Gazette and Anglo-Indian Advertiser (Port-Louis), 30 September–22 November 1888.

The Hull Express, 21–25 April 1885.

Le Journal de Maurice (Port-Louis), 1 October–22 November 1888.

Le Journal de Rouen, 4 December 1893–11 January 1894.

Marseille-Théâtre: Journal artistique et littéraire, 25 December 1875–4 June 1876.

The Merchant & Planters Gazette (Port-Louis), 11 October–11 December 1888.

Le Petit Marseille, 13 October–17 December 1874, January–June 1876.

Le Petit Mériodional (Montpellier), 9 February–15 April 1906, 18 December 1906–15 May 1907.

Articles (unsigned)

'An Academic Committee of English Letters.' *The Times*, 20 July 1910: 10.

'An Elusive Personality.' *The Nation*, 24 February 1912: 857–58.

'Bail denied Pinker on Theft Charge.' *New York Times*, 15 March 1939: 28.

'Beauty in Horror. Mr. Rothenstein's War Pictures.' *The Times*, 27 April 1918: 9.

'A Busy Theatrical Week.' *The Times*, 24 March 1919: 16

'Capri-Sodoma.' *La propaganda* (Naples), 15 October 1902: 1.

'Canterbury Cricket Week.' *Kent Herald* (Canterbury), 6 August 1924: 2.

'The Censorship of Plays.' *The Times*, 29 October 1907: 15.

'Concerts &c.' *The Times*, 21 May 1920: 14.

'Conrad Dead. Polish Seaman who Learned English on Collier. The

Skipper-Novelist.' *Weekly Scotsman* (Edinburgh), 9 August 1924: 6.

'Conrad Visits Boston.' *New York Times*, 21 May 1923: 15.

'Conrad's Great Theme. Dean of Canterbury's Tribute.' *The Times*, 12 August 1924: 15.

'Contents of the Magazines.' *The Times*, 1 April 1909: 6.

'Court Circular.' *The Times*, 2 April 1919: 15.

'Court News.' *The Times*, 18 April 1906: 7.

'Death of Mr. Huneker. America's Foremost Critic.' *The Times*, 22 February 1921: 9.

'Death of Mr. J. B. Pinker.' *The Times*, 10 February 1922: 9.

'Death of Mrs. Jessie Conrad. Widow of Famous Author.' *Kentish Observer and Canterbury Chronicle*, 10 December 1936: 5.

Display advertisement: *English Review*, cited in *The Times*, 3 November 1913: 13.

'Dynamite Scare at Hampstead.' *The Times*, 6 December 1893: 10.

'Fallen Officers.' *The Times*, 21 December 1915: 5.

'Famous Authors Write Enthusiastically of *The Way of The Red Cross*.' *The Times*, 29 March 1915: 5.

'The Fresh Air Art Society.' *The Times*, 29 November 1913: 11.

'Funeral. Mr. Joseph Conrad,' *The Times*, 8 August 1914: 15.

'Funeral of Lord Northcliffe.' *The Times*, 18 August 1922: 13.

'Funeral of Mr. Joseph Conrad.' *Kent Herald* (Canterbury), 13 August 1924: 6.

'James B. Pinker Dies Here.' *New York Times*, 10 February 1922: 13.

'Joseph Conrad. A Philosopher of the Sea.' *The Times*, 4 August 1914: 10.

'June Magazines.' *The Times*, 1 June 1915: 6.

'Literary Agent Held on Author's Charge.' *New York Times*, 14 March 1939: 22.

'Literary Agent Indicted.' *New York Times*, 17 March 1939: 23.

'The Lord Chamberlain and Mr Philpotts's Play.' *The Times*, 14 February 1912: 10.

'*Majestic* Took 800 in her First Cabin. Joseph Conrad, Novelist of the Sea, Sails on Big Liner with Praise for America.' *New York Times*, 3 June 1923: S5.

'The Mishap to "York Castle."' *Eastern Province Herald* (Port Elizabeth), 6 October 1923: n.p.

'Mme. Alice Gachet de la Fournière: Producer and Theatrical Coach.' *The Times*, 4 November 1960: 15.

'Mr Conrad's Recollections.' *Birmingham Daily Post*, 2 February 1912: 4.

'Mr. Joseph Conrad Ill.' *The Times*, 1 June 1923: 14.

'Mr. Moiseiwitsch's Recital.' *The Times*, 9 March 1914: 10.

'New Year's Honours.' *The Times*, 1 January 1918: 10.

'News in Brief. Prize Day in the *Worcester*.' *The Times*, 27 July 1912: 8.

'Obituary. William Martindale.' *The Times*, 6 February 1902: 7.

'Odds and Ends of the Week. Joseph Conrad.' *Cork Weekly Examiner*, 9 August 1924: 4.

'100 Years of Berli Jucker.' *The Nation* (Bangkok), 26 November 1982, Supplement: 7.

'Opéra Comique Theatre.' *The Times*, 19 July 1889: 4.

'Oppenheim Agent Guilty.' *New York Times*, 3 May 1939: 21.

'Pinker Sentenced to 2½ to 5 years.' *New York Times*, 8 June 1939: 31.

'Poles to Welcome Conrad.' *New York Times*, 1 May 1923: 10.

'Publications To-Day.' *The Times*, 30 November 1897: 7.

'Ravel as Conductor. Queen's Hall Symphony Concert.' *The Times*, 16 April 1923: 15.

'Recent Novels.' *The Times*, 16 August 1898: 4.

'Recent Novels.' *The Times*, 3 September 1901: 9.

[Review of *Notes on Life and Letters*]. *Weekly Review*, 3 September 1921: 217.

[Review of *A Set of Six*]. *Times Literary Supplement*, 13 August 1908: 261.

'The Russians at San Stefano.' *The Times*, 25 March 1878: 6.

'Sleuth to Sleuth.' *Time* (New York), 27 March 1939: 15.

'A Stanford Mystery. Naked Body Found with a Large Bruise on the Forehead.' *Southend Standard* (Southend-on-Sea, Essex), 7 December 1899: 7.

'The Stanford Mystery. An Open Verdict Returned.' *Southend Standard* (Southend-on-Sea, Essex), 21 December 1899: 7.

'Stephen Crane: A Study in American Letters.' *The Times*, 29 August 1924: 15.

'Suffragist Disturbances.' *The Times*, 23 November 1910: 8.

'Thefts of $100,000 are Laid to Pinker.' *New York Times*, 18 March 1939: 15.

'*The Times* Column of New Books and New Editions.' *The Times*, 28 June 1895: 12.

'*The Times* Column of New Books and New Editions.' *The Times*, 30 July 1901: 12.

'*The Times* Diary: Conrad by his Son.' *The Times*, 7 October 1968: 8.

'To-day's Engagements.' *The Times*, 23 June 1913: 11.

'The Weather,' *The Times*, 14 July 1881: 11.

'The Weather,' *The Times*, 16 August 1881: 10.

'Wills and Bequests.' *The Times*, 28 March 1922: 15.

'Wills and Bequests.' *The Times*, 17 November 1924: 17.

'Wills and Bequests.' *The Times*, 8 April 1933: 8.

'Wills and Bequests.' *The Times*, 4 August 1941: 6.

'The Woman Suffrage Bill.' *The Times*, 15 June 1910: 7.

'"York Castle" in a Hurricane.' *Eastern Province Herald* (Port Elizabeth), 5 October 1923: 8

Online sources

Armstrong, Gilbert Keith. *The Hallowes Genealogy*. <www.ourworld. compuserve.com/homepages/gkarmstrong> Accessed: March 2004.

Boyce D. George. 'Harmsworth, Alfred Charles William, Viscount Northcliffe (1865–1922).' *Oxford Dictionary of National Biography*. Oxford: Oxford University Press, 2004 <www.oxforddnb.com/ view/article/33717> Accessed: August 2006.

Brooks, David. 'The Complete Letters'. *The Vincent Van Gogh Gallery*. Accessed: January 2007.

Bruseliuz, Lars. *The Maritime History Virtual Archives*. <www.bruseliuz. info/Nautica/Nautica. html.> Accessed: September 2004.

Burys Court School.<www.buryscourtschool.co.uk/html/history. htm> Accessed: December 2005.

Casebook: Jack the Ripper. <www.casebook.org.> Accessed: September 2004.

Church of Jesus Christ of Latter-Day Saints. International Genealogical Index. <www.familysearch.org> Accessed: August 2004.

Commonwealth War Graves Commission. <www.cwgc.org> Accessed: December 2006.

Donovan, Stephen. *Conrad First: An On-line Database of Conrad Serials.* <www.conradfirst.com> Accessed: December 2006.

Economic History Services. 'How Much Is That?' ed. Samuel H. Williamson. <www.eh.net> Accessed: January 2007.

Ellis Island Archives. Statue of Liberty – Ellis Island Foundation, Inc. <www.ellisisland.org.> Accessed: January 2005.

Fedosova, Elena I. 'Polish Projects of Napoleon Bonaparte.' *Napoleonic Scholarship: The Journal of the International Napoleonic Society*, 1.2 (1998). <napoleon-series.org/ins/scholarship98/c_polish.html> Accessed: January 2007.

Historical Directories. <www.historicaldirectories.org> Accessed: January 2007.

HMS *Worcester* – History. <www.hms-worcester.co.uk.> Accessed: May 2005.

International Eclipse Tables, 1700–2100. <eclipse.astronomie.info/sofi/inter.htm> Accessed: September 2004.

Joseph Conrad Society (UK). <www.josephconradsociety.org> Accessed: November 2004 – January 2007.

Kushner, David Z. 'John Powell: His Racial and Cultural Ideologies.' <www.hichumanities.org/AHproceedings> Accessed: December 2006.

London School of Economics and Political Science. *Charles Booth Online Archive: Inquiry into the Life and Labour of the People in London, 1886–1903.* < www.booth.lse.ac.uk> Accessed: December 2004.

Marages, Kate. *Twentieth-Century Bestsellers: 'The Arrow of Gold.'* <www3.isrl.uiuc.edu/ ~unsworth/courses/bestsellers/search.cgi?title=The+Arrow+of+Gold> Accessed: January 2007.

Mullin, Katherine. 'Douglas, (George) Norman (1868–1952).' *Oxford Dictionary of National Biography.* Oxford: Oxford University Press, 2004. <www.oxforddnb.com/view/article/ 32874> Accessed: August 2005.

'Musée comunal du Général Thys, Dalhem.' *Les Musées en Wallonie.* <www.lesmuseesenwallonie.be> Accessed: September 2004.

Officer, Lawrence H. 'Five Ways to Compute the Value of a UK Pound.' <www.measuringworth.com> Accessed: January 2007.

Palmer, Michael P. *Palmer List of Merchant Vessels*. 2000. <www.geocities.com/mppraetorius> Accessed: September 2004.

Port Cities London. Training Ships on the River Thames. <www.portcities.org.uk.> Accessed: May 2005.

Shore, Heather. ' "Kings, Gangsters, and Greenhorns": Kate Meyrick and the Gendering of Club Land in Inter-war London.' <www.cheshire.mmu.ac.uk> Accessed: September 2005.

Stockmans, Charles. *Congo Belge et Ruanda-Urundi: Septante-sept ans d'histoire postale en Afrique centrale, 1885–1962*. <www.users.skynet. be/chst> Accessed: September 2004.

Swiggum, S. and M. Kohli. *The Ships List*. <www.shipslist.com.> Accessed: August 2005.

Times Literary Supplement Centenary Archive. <www.tls.psmedia. com> Accessed: January 2007.

Ureel, Urbain. *Congo River Shipping at the End of the 19th and Beginning of the 20th Century*. <users.pandora.be/urbiehome/ Congoship.html> Accessed: January 2007.

Wilson, John Marius. 'Dover.' *Imperial Gazetteer of England and Wales* (1870–72). <www.visionofbritain.org> Accessed: January 2007.

Index

Biberstejn-Pilchowska: *see also* Bobrowska, Teofila, Teofila (maternal grandmother), 7

Bizet, Georges, 41; *Carmen*, 30, 73, 74, 118

Black Forest (Germany), 18

Black Sea, 34, 46

Blackwood (publisher), 99–100, 107, 110, 111, 112, 113, 120, 123, 126

Blackwood, George, 126

Blackwood, William, 100, 105, 120–1

Blackwood's Magazine, 83, 105, 107, 113, 114, 115, 127, 138, 149

Bobrowska, Ewa (mother), marriage, 7–8; separated from husband, 10–11; in exile, 12–13; ill-health and death, 14–15

Bobrowska, Teofila (maternal grandmother), 14, 15, 16, 18–19, 20, 22, 28

Bobrowski, Józef (maternal grandfather), 7

Bobrowski, Kazimierz (uncle), 14, 61

Bobrowski, Mikołaj (great-uncle), 4–5

Bobrowski, Stanisław (maternal great-grandfather), 3

Bobrowski, Stefan (uncle), 14

Bobrowski, Tadeusz (uncle), 85; and petition to the Tsar, 10; comment on Conrad's father, 13; and death of Conrad's mother, 15; arranges for Conrad to go to sea, 20–1; as Conrad's guardian and financier, 22, 26, 36, 42, 45; reproaches Conrad's for loss of family mementoes, 25; frets over Conrad's education, 30–1; rushes to Marseilles, 32; character of, 32–3; fondness for nephew, 32–3; holiday in Europe with Conrad, 43–4; visited by Conrad, 59; financial assistance to Conrad, 69; death of, 72, 75; visited by nephew, 60–1, 72

Boer War, 115, 116, 122, 148

Boma, 63

Bombay (Mumbai), 44, 178

Bone, David, 248

Bone, John, 249

Bone, Muirhead, 248, 249, 250, 255, 257

Bookman, 82, 130, 235

Booth, Charles, *Inquiry into the Life and Labour of the People in London*, 40–1, 56, 68

Borbón y Borbón, Don Alfonso de, 29

Bordeaux, 62, 67

Borneo, 50, 77, 94, 103

Bosporus, 34, 35 and note

Brassey, Lord, 186

Brede Place (Sussex), 113, 114, 116, 117

Bremen, 32, 55

Bridlington (Yorkshire), 210

Briquel, Émilie, 83–4, 87, 88, 89

Briquel, Paul, 83, 84

British Merchant Marine, 32, 33, 37, 66–7, 218, 225

Brittany, 89, 93, 105, 123

Broadstairs (Kent), 208

Brooke, Sir James, 194

Brown, Ford Madox, 109, 124

Brownrigg, Captain Sir Douglas, 209, 210

Bruce, Gordon, 208

Brussels, 58, 60–1, 68, 75, 81, 85, 255

Brussels Conference Relative to the Africa Slave Trade (1890), 62

Buchan, John, 138

Buls, Charles, 68

Bulungan (Borneo), 50

Burroughs, Arthur, 85

Buszczyński, Stefan, 18

Caesarini, Nino, 146

Caine, Hall, 103

Calcutta, 44, 47, 70

Cambridge University, 71, 72, 192, 195, 206, 217, 258

Cameron, Sir Maurice, 207, 237

Candler, Edmund, 198, 255

Canterbury (Kent), 110, 232, 234, 235, 239, 241, 255, 263–4

Cape of Good Hope, 37, 71

Cape Town, 70, 71

Capel House (Kent), 175, 176, 180, 181, 186–7, 192, 196, 201, 203, 205, 206, 210, 212, 213, 214, 218, 220, 221, 224

Capes, Harriet M., *Wisdom and Beauty from Joseph Conrad*, 246

Capri, 138, 140, 142–7, 151, 177, 211

Caracas, 27

Cardiff, 36, 46, 48, 97, 98; Sailors' and Fishermen's Home, 36

Caribbean, 27, 111: *see also* French Antilles

Carlist War (Third), 29–30, 200

Carlsbad, 68

Carpathians, 19, 21